DATE DUE

Information Sources in
Sport and Leisure

Guides to Information Sources

A series under the General Editorship of
D. J. Foskett, MA, FLA
and
M. W. Hill, MA, BSc, MRIC

This series was known previously as 'Butterworths Guides to Information Sources'.

Other titles available include:

Information Sources in Patents
  edited by C.P. Auger
Information Sources for the Press and Broadcast Media
  edited by Selwyn Eagle
Information Sources in the Medical Sciences (Fourth edition)
  edited by L.T. Morton and S. Godbolt
Information Sources in Information Technology
  edited by David Haynes
Information Sources in Grey Literature (Second edition)
  by C.P. Auger
Information Sources in Pharmaceuticals
  edited by W.R. Pickering
Information Sources in Metallic Materials
  edited by M.N. Patten
Information Sources in the Earth Sciences (Second edition)
  edited by David N. Wood, Joan E. Hardy and Anthony P. Harvey
Information Sources in Cartography
  edited by C.R. Perkins and R.B. Barry
Information Sources in Polymers and Plastics
  edited by R.T. Adkins
Information Sources in Science and Technology (Second edition)
  edited by C.C. Parker and R.V. Turley
Information Sources in Physics (Second edition)
  edited by Dennis Shaw
Information Sources in Economics (Second edition)
  edited by John Fletcher
Information Sources in the Life Sciences (Third edition)
  edited by H.V. Wyatt
Information Sources in Engineering (Second edition)
  edited by L.J. Anthony

Information Sources in
Sport and Leisure

Editor
Michele Shoebridge

BOWKER
SAUR

London • Melbourne • Munich • New York

British Library Cataloguing in Publication Data
Information sources in sport and leisure.
  I. Shoebridge, Michele
  016.796

  ISBN 0 86291 901 1

Library of Congress Cataloging-in-Publication Data
Shoebridge, Michele.
    Information sources in sport and liesure / Michele
  Shoebridge, editor.
  xxxp. xxcm. — (Guides to information sources)
    Includes index.
    ISBN 0-86291-901-0
    1. Sports — Bibliography. 2. Leisure — Bibliography.
  3. Recreation — Bibliography. I. Title. II. Series: Guides to
  information sources (London, England)
  Z7511.S48 1991
  [GV704]
  016.796—dc20
                                              91-21637
                                                  CIP

Bowker-Saur is part of the Professional Publishing Division of Reed International Books, Borough Green, Sevenoaks, Kent TN15 8PH

Cover design by Calverts Press
Printed on acid-free paper
Typeset by SunSetters
Printed and bound in Great Britain by Antony Rowe Ltd, Chippenham, Wiltshire

Series editors' foreword

As is obvious, any human being, faced with solving a problem or with understanding a task, reacts by thinking, by applying judgement and by seeking information. The first two involve using information from the most readily available source, namely one's memory, though searching this and retrieving what is wanted may be conducted below the level of consciousness. If this source does not provide all that is needed then the information searcher may turn to all or any of three external sources: observation (which can consist simply of 'going and looking' or can involve understanding sophisticated research); other people, who may be close colleagues or distant experts; and stores of recorded information, for example a local filing system or an electronic databank held on a computer network or even a book or journal in a national library.

The order (observation; other people; recorded information), is not significant though it is often a common sequence. Certainly it is not intended to impute an order of importance. Which of the three or what combination of them one uses depends on a number of factors including the nature of the problem and one's personal circumstances. Suffice to say that all three have their place and all three are used by every literate person.

Nowadays the amount of information in any field, even if one can exclude that which has been superseded, is so large that no human being or small group of people can hope to know it all. Thus, company information systems, for example, get bigger and bigger even when there are efficient means of discarding unwanted and out-of-date information. Managing these systems is a complex and full time task.

Many factors contribute to the huge information growth and overload. Throughout the world, large amounts of research continue to be undertaken and their results published for others to use or follow up. New data pours out of the financial markets. Governments keep passing new legislation. The law courts keep generating new rulings. Each organization and everyone in it of any significance, it seems, is in the business of generating new information. Most of it is recorded and much of it is published.

Although there is a growing tendency to record information in electronic media and to leave it there for distribution via electronic networks of one sort or another, the traditional media are still in use. Even tablets of stone are still used in appropriate circumstances but, of course, it is paper that predominates. The electronic age has not yet led to any reduction in the amount of printed material being published.

The range of types of published or publicly available information sources is considerable. It includes collections of letters, monographs, reports, pamphlets, newspapers and other periodicals, patent specifications, standards, trade literature including both manufacturers' product specifications and service companies' descriptions of their services, user manuals, laws, bye-laws, regulations and all the great wealth of leaflets poured out by official, semi-official and private organizations to guide the information in other than verbal form; maps; graphs; music scores photographs; moving pictures; sound recordings; videos. Nor, although their main content is not published information, should one forget as sources of information collections of artefacts.

In an attempt to make some of the more frequently needed information more easily accessible, these sources of primary information are supplemented with the well-known range of tertiary publications, and text books, data books, reviews and encyclopaedias.

To find the information source one needs, another range of publications has come into being. To find experts or organizations or products there are directories, masses of them, so many that directories of directories are published. To find a required publication there are library catalogues, publishers' list indexes and abstracting services, again a great many of them.

For librarians and information specialists in the industrialized countries, access to abstracting services is now normally achieved online, i.e from a computer terminal over the telephone lines to a remote computer-base database host. Since 1960 the use of libraries by information and even document seekers has changed considerably and can be expected to change further as the British Library study *Information 2000* indicates. More and more primary information is being stored electronically and more and more copies of printed documents are supplied via telephone or data networks. Sets of newspapers or other major publications can be acquired on optical discs for use in-house. Scientists in different universities, perhaps working on a common project, are sharing their results via the medium of electronic bulletin boards. The use of electronic messaging systems for disseminating information is now commonplace. Thus the combination of computer technology with telecommunications engineering is offering new ways of accessing and communicating information. Nevertheless, the old ways continue to be important and will remain so for many years yet.

The huge wealth of sources of information, the great range of resources, of means of identifying them and of accessing what is wanted increase the need for well aimed guides. Not all sources are of equal value even when only those well focused on the required topic are considered. The way new journals proliferate whenever a new major topic is established, many it seems just trying to 'climb on the bandwagon' and as a consequence substantially duplicating each other, illustrates this. Even in an established field the tendency of scientists, for example, to have a definite 'pecking order' for selecting journals in which to publish their research is well known. Some journals submit offered articles to referees; some others publish anything they can get. Similar considerations apply to other publications. The degree of reliance that can be placed on reports in different newspapers is an illustration. Nor is accuracy the only measure of quality. Another the depth to which an account of a given topic goes.

The aim of this series *Guides to Information Sources* is to give within each broad subject field (chemistry, architecture, politics, cartography etc.) an account of the types of external information source that exist and of the more important individual sources set in the context of the subject itself. Means of accessing the information are also given though only at the level of the publication, journal article or database. individual chapters are written by experts, each of whom specializes in the field he/she is describing, and give a view based on experience of finding and using the most appropriate sources. The volumes are intended to be readable by other experts and information seekers working outside their normal field. They are intended to help librarians concerned with problems of relevance and quality in stock selection.

Since not only the sources but also the needs and interests of users vary from one subject to another, each editor is given a free hand produce the guide which is appropriate for his/her subject. We, the series editors, believe that this volume does just that.

Douglas Foskett
Michael Hill

About the contributors

Stuart Biddle

Dr. Stuart Biddle is Associate Director of the Physical Education Association Research Centre and Lecturer in the School of Education, University of Exeter. He holds BEd, MSc and PhD degrees. His research interests are in psychology of sport, exercise and health, areas in which he has published extensively. In 1991, his book, co-authored with Nanette Mutrie, *Psychology of physical activity and exercise*, was published by Springer-Verlag. Dr. Biddle is Secretary of the British Association of Sports Sciences and a member of the Managing Council of the European Federation of Sports Psychology.

Richard W. Cox

Dr. Richard Cox is presently Physical Recreation Officer at the University of Manchester Institute of Science and Technology. He is a graduate in History, Physical Education and Information Studies and holds BEd, MA, MSc and PhD degrees. In 1982, he founded the British Society of Sports History and was inaugural co-editor of the *British Journal of Sports History* (now the *International Journal of the History of Sport*). He has recently completed a 14-year project to document the literature on the history of sport in the UK, the first part of which was published by Manchester University Press in 1991.

Nerida Clarke

Nerida Clarke, originally a teacher librarian, has worked in a number of educational and special libraries including medical libraries in Australia, New Zealand and England. She has a BA, is a Graduate Diploma of Arts and is an AALIA (Associate of the Australian Library and Information Association). Currently she is Manager of the National Sport Information Centre, Australia's most comprehensive collection of sporting information which offers services to specialist clientele and the general public. She is Regional Vice President (Oceania) of the International Association for Sports Information and is currently undertaking a Master's degree in Information Science looking at the information-seeking behaviour of coaches.

Jackie Cutts

Jackie Cutts has an Honours degree in Leisure Studies from Leeds Polytechnic, and is a leisure researcher with Leisure Management GT. Jackie has also worked as a researcher with a local authority.

Gretchen Ghent

Gretchen Ghent is a graduate of Ohio State University and the School of Library, Information and Archival Studies, The University of British Columbia. She is a former Pan American Games swimmer. Currently she is Head of the Sciences/Professions Area, the University of Calgary Library, Alberta, Canada and is working on a bibliography of publications surrounding the XV Olympic Winter Games, Calgary, 1988 which will be published electronically as part of the SPORT database (Gloucester, Ontario) and in print form. She is one of the founding Steering Committee members of the fledgling organization, North American Sport Library Network.

Gwynne Griffiths

Gwynne Griffiths is a Principal Researcher, Consultant and Associate in Leisure Management GT, with a background in commercial leisure, banking and public authorities. A former Course Director for the Diploma of Management Studies (Recreation), he holds a Master's degree in management from Cranfield College.

Lisbeth Hodgkinson

Lisbeth Hodgkinson is Site/Tutor Librarian at Bedford College of Higher Education. She has a BA and MA, is an Associate of the Library Association.

John Horne

John Horne obtained degrees from Bristol Polytechnic (CNAA) and the University of Essex. Since 1980 he has been responsible for the coordination and development of sociology courses on the degree in Sport and Recreation Studies at Staffordshire Polytechnic, where he is Senior Lecturer in Sociology. He has published several articles on sport and leisure and is author of *Work and unemployment*, Longman, 1988, and co-editor (with David Jary and Alan Tomlinson) of *Sport, leisure and social relations*, Routledge, 1987.

Margaret Leighfield

Margaret Leighfield is an information scientist and has worked in various libraries. She is now Consultant Editor for *Leisure, Recreation*

& *Tourism Abstracts*, Editor of *European Leisure and Recreation Association Newsletter*, and is Associate Editor of the *World Travel and Tourism Review*.

Bill Martin

Bill Martin is Joint Principal of Leisure Consultants, an independent research firm, which he established in 1972 to provide a specialist source of research on sport, leisure and tourism. He was formerly a merchant bank director, responsible for investment research and management.

Sandra Mason

Sandra Mason graduated from Cambridge University in Economics with Statistics in 1960. She worked as an economist in the City of London and was a Senior Research Officer at the London Business School. Since 1972, she has been Joint Principal of Leisure Consultants, a research firm specializing in sport, leisure and tourism.

Betty Millman

Betty Millman obtained her MLS degree from the university of Western Ontario in 1979. For many years she was the database Manager and Consultant at SIRLS (Specialized Information retrieval and Library Services) and editor of *Sport and Leisure: A Journal of Social Science Abstracts*. Betty now works in one of the campus libraries at the University of Waterloo.

Mary Nevill

Dr. Mary Nevill graduated from Loughborough University of Technology with a BSc in Geography and Physical Education and Sports Science and her doctorate is in exercise physiology. She has been a lecturer in the Department of Sport and Exercise Science at Birmingham University and in the department of Sport and Human Sciences at Crewe and Alsager College of Higher Education. She is currently a lecturer in Sport Science in the Department of Physical Education and Sports Science at Loughborough University. Her research interests lie in the causes of fatigue in high-intensity exercise.

Dan Tunstall Pedoe

Dr. Dan Tunstall Pedoe is senior lecturer, consultant cardiologist and physician at St. Bartholomew's Hospital and Homerton Hospital, London. He is Medical Director of the London Sports Medicine Institute, Chairman of the British Association of Sport and Medicine and, Medical Director of the London Marathon.

Albert Remans

Albert Remans studied Social Sciences at the Catholic University of Leuven before specializing in Sociology of Leisure Time and Sports. After gaining experience as a researcher at the Sociologic Research Institute (Leuven) he became Director of the 'Sport for All' Clearing House which is a sports information centre under the aegis of the Council of Europe. Since 1988, he has been Secretary-General of the International Association for Sports Information (IASI).

Michele Shoebridge

Michele Shoebridge is currently Systems Librarian at the University of Birmingham, but was Librarian at the Sports Documentation Centre for nine years where she was responsible for editing the Centre's current- awareness journal and developing an in-house database. Whilst at the Centre she played a leading role in developing sports information in the UK by co-founding and later chairing the UK Sport and Recreation Information Group. Publications include a major bibliography on women in sport and a number of other bibliographies and catalogues. Michele was also an active member of the International Association for Sports Information and has visited a number of sports information centres abroad. She has a BA in History, MA and is an Associate of the Library Association.

George Torkildsen

Dr. George Torkildsen is a Leisure and Recreation Planning and Management Consultant, and Principal of Leisure Management: GT. He was a Fulbright Scholar studying and researching in America and a Churchill Fellow in Scandinavia. He qualified as a teacher, has a Diploma in Physical Education from Loughborough College, took his Master's degree at the University of Wisconsin and Doctorate at the Polytechnic of Central London. He is the author of *Leisure and recreation management*.

Kathryn Walter

Kathryn Walter has been Librarian at the National Sports Medicine Institute since 1986. She previously worked in Guy's Hospital medical library. She holds a BSc in Biochemistry and a Diploma in Information Science.

Linda A. Wheeler

Linda Wheeler has BA and MA degrees and an MLS from McGill University in Canada. She has been with the Sport Information Resource Centre (SIRC) since the early 1980s and is currently a reference librarian at the Centre as well as the Promotion and

Marketing Co-ordinator for SIRC products and services. She edited the multi-volume *Sport bibliography* series and is active in the development of other SIRC publications.

Margaret Whitehead

Margaret Whitehead is currently Course Director, Initial Teacher Training (Secondary) at Bedford College of Higher Education, and formerly Head of Physical Education at Homerton College Cambridge. She qualified as a physical education teacher and then studied at London University Institute of Education for an Advanced Diploma in Philosophy of Education and a PhD looking into Existentialism and Phenomenology with particular reference to embodiment.

Wayne Wilson

Dr. Wayne Wilson is Director, Research & Library Services at the Amateur Athletic Foundation of Los Angeles. Before joining the Foundation he worked for several years in academic libraries in the USA and was Director of the Library at Chapman College in Orange, CA. His degrees include a doctorate in Sport Studies and a Master's in Library Science. He is a founder member of the North American Sport Library Network.

Contents

Introduction

M. SHOEBRIDGE

Sport and leisure, the title chosen for this volume, form an important element in the lives of people throughout the world. However, the very terms raise problems of definition, since sport and leisure are open to many different interpretations and there is considerable overlap between the two. This makes it difficult to define what is a sporting activity and what is a leisure activity. In a number of the chapters sport and leisure are both discussed alongside each other, but the distinction between them is recognized by the inclusion of a separate chapter on leisure.

Like many subjects, sport and leisure operate at different levels. At a research level, sports science, as taught in higher education, includes biomechanics, exercise physiology, psychology, sociology, etc. In the UK, sport is now being introduced into the school curriculum at both 'A' and GCSE level and sport and leisure studies are represented in BTEC courses. On a more general level, there is considerable interest in sporting events and the facts and feats associated with sport.

Unfortunately the development of the literature has not always kept pace with the development of the subject. Poor dissemination of information has also caused problems and attempts have been made to rectify this. The International Council for Health, Physical Education and Recreation (ICHPER) recognized the need to control the literature of this emerging subject area when it commissioned Dr. Jan Broekhoff to write a report on the subject in 1980. Entitled *Ways and means of organizing a system for the standardized collection of documentation in physical education and sport*, it was published by Unesco (ED-80/WS/68). In the same year the first *International Leisure Information Network Conference* was held in Brussels (1980), which looked at various aspects of information provision for leisure and two Aslib conferences were held in the UK in the 1970s and early 1980s which took the theme of information sources for leisure, recreation and tourism.

The International Association for Sports Information (IASI), established in 1960, has had a limited impact on the control and dissemination of the literature at an international level, although it has become more active over the last few years. In the UK the Sport and Recreation Information Group (SPRIG) has done much to co-ordinate the work of sports information professionals and to improve awareness of sports information since its inception in 1984. A similar group, the North American Sport Library Network, has recently been set up in North America.

Certain areas of the literature have developed more quickly than others. Sports science is one area that has developed rapidly, so much so that library classification schemes have difficulty reflecting its complexities. In other areas, e.g. ethnic groups and leisure, there is little published research and information is much more difficult to trace.

Information on both sport and leisure became available electronically from the 1970s with the arrival of the SPORT database, provided by the Sport Information Resource Centre (SIRC) in Canada, and LRTA, the leisure database compiled by CAB International. In addition the SPORT database on CD-ROM, SPORT DISCUS, was one of the earliest CD-ROMs to be made available by SiverPlatter.

Not all the trends in sport and leisure can be reflected in one volume and some subjects which have developed recently have not been covered in any depth. Such areas include sports fiction, the geography of sport, and children in sport. In addition the popular area of sports biography has not been covered in any depth.

One aim of this book has been to give some indication of the quality and level of the various services and sources cited. The first chapter gives a general overview of all the major sources which may be useful both to users undertaking research, and those simply wanting to find out more about a specific subject. It also provides a context for the chapters which follow. Chapters 2 and 3 are also fairly general, covering the important areas of statistics and government publications. The former chapter presents an international perspective on a whole range of statistics, whilst the chapter on government highlights how changes in legislation in the UK have affected the development of sport and leisure.

Part II begins with a chapter on sports science. This relatively new discipline is concerned with the application of scientific research to sport performance, driven partly by the need to understand how the athletic body works and partly to improve records. Sports science in this volume encompasses exercise physiology, biochemistry, biomechanics and sports psychology. The next chapter covers sports medicine, a subject closely allied to sports science. Sports medicine has developed significantly over the last decade and now incorporates such subjects as nutrition, drugs, physiotherapy, sports therapy, chiropractice and natural medicine.

Part II also includes individual chapters on sports history and sports sociology, subjects often included under the general heading of 'sports science'. Sports history draws on a wide range of sources and has a longer tradition than sports sociology which is still in its relative infancy. Both have developed at a faster rate in North America. Unfortunately there is still very little information available in some branches of sports sociology. Ethnic groups have already been mentioned and in the UK the literature in this area is limited to a small number of studies commissioned by organizations like The Sports Council. The final chapter in this section covers the important area of individual sports, and this section aims to identify resources that appeal to an audience wider than those carrying out research. It also covers material published by the Sports Governing Bodies in the UK.

Part III covers subjects of general interest to those studying sport and leisure. The Olympic Games become larger each time the event is staged, and Chapter 9 reflects on all aspects of the Games. Chapter 10 provides an international perspective of leisure sources, excluding tourism. Physical education, a long-established part of school life in many countries, but under scrutiny both for its content and as a core curriculum subject in the UK and North America is covered in Chapter 11. Physical fitness is the subject of Chapter 12. Again both research literature and the more popular material are represented. Coaching is covered in the last chapter of Part III. This particular area has grown considerably during the last decade, reflecting the increasing importance nations now place on winning medals.

Part IV highlights the growing interest in the international aspects of sport, again a trend which has led to a demand for information with which the literature has not always kept pace. This section attempts to provide answers to some of the questions that are regularly posed about sport in individual countries. The chapter on Europe describes the Council of Europe and its publications and highlights the information sources of selected European countries. Recent political changes have been taken into account, but these changes will inevitably continue to re-shape sport over the next few years. The arrival of the Single European market in 1993 may also change the nature of sport in Europe. Chapter 15 attempts to bring together the vast array of North American sports information centres and major sources — a very difficult task given the amount of material. Finally Chapter 16 concentrates on Australia, which, over the last ten years, has developed a very efficient sports information system and produces a number of significant publications.

Part I

CHAPTER ONE

General overview of sources

M. SHOEBRIDGE

Tracing material on sport and leisure is not always an easy task. Established tools like the national bibliographies cover the mainstream sport-related literature, have good coverage of biographies, and include some less obvious material like individual histories and handbooks of sports clubs and societies, but are nowhere near complete. There are a small number of dedicated introductory texts to the literature. The most recent, by R. Prytherch entitled *Sports and fitness, an information guide* (Aldershot: Gower, 1988) provides a limited review of the available literature, listed under the following headings: basic information; publishing; journals; audio-visual and online; abstracts and indexes; special needs and organizations. It does, however, provide useful examples of the sources quoted. A more detailed guide which concentrates on the North American literature is R.J. Higgs, *Sports: a reference guide* (Conn.: Greenwood Press, 1982). It takes a subject approach rather than concentrating on the type of sources that can be used to find material.

Another North American series is the Gale *Sports, games and pastimes information guide series*. Volumes published so far include those on golf, motorsports and women. More than just a bibliography of books, this series covers films, Halls of Fame, etc.

The Department of the Environment Library has published an introductory guide in their 'Information Series' (No. 27): C. Lambert, *Sport and recreation: sources of information on sport and recreation* (2nd edn) (London: Department of the Environment & Department of Transport, 1987). It is divided into eight sections which cover: central government and official organizations like The Sports Council; local authorities; independent specialist and numerous governing bodies; research and consultancy bodies, current research projects; higher educational institutions; specialist libraries & information centres, booksellers and publishers; directories, periodicals, statistics, etc. It has a general index but is in need of updating now.

Turning to more mainstream sources, the *British national bibliography (BNB)* follows a classmark arrangement, with subject and author indexes. Sport-related literature appears in different sections – classmark 796, 'Sports and games', contains the majority of sport material, whilst physical education can be found under education and sports medicine in the medical section. *BNB* is published weekly by the British Library. It is also available online via BLAISELINE and on CD-ROM. Another service covering British material is *Whitaker's British books in print* which covers British books and English-language titles published overseas but available in the UK. It is available in printed, microfiche and CD-ROM format as well as online via BLAISELINE and DIALOG.

A similar publication, but covering the North American literature is *Books in Print,* published by Bowker, and available in print, microfiche, CD-ROM and online. The online service, available on BRS and DIALOG, is useful for the North American literature. *Cumulative Book Index,* an H.W. Wilson publication, represents a world list of books published in the English language for a given year, albeit with a North American bias.

Publishers' catalogues and fliers are another useful source, provided they list the date of publication for the books included. There has been a general increase in publications with a sport and leisure theme. In North America, Human Kinetics have been active in publishing in the sports science area, particularly conference proceedings. They also have a leisure outlet, Leisure Press. In the United Kingdom, E. & F.N. Spon have emerged as the leading publisher, and like Human Kinetics have been responsible for publishing a number of conference proceedings. The latest, published in 1990, is *Science and golf: the proceedings of the First World Scientific Congress of Golf,* edited by A. Cochran.

Video producers also publish catalogues. More information can be found in the *British National Film and Video Catalogue (BNFV),* published quarterly with annual cumulations. A more specialist document published by the National Coaching Foundation and Sheffield Sports Information Service, is *Action replay: audio visual resources in sport and recreation.* It includes over 900 videos, but makes no attempt at evaluation. SportsPages bookshop in London stocks a large range of both printed and audio-visual material relevant to both the researcher, planner or anyone with a casual interest in sport and leisure material.

SportsPages is located at Caxton Walk, 94–96 Charing Cross Road, London WC2 0JG.

A considerable amount of information can be extracted from journals, and from the bulletins of various societies. The latter are especially good for tracing the more ephemeral publications. These include the bulletins of the Sport and Recreation Information Group (SPRIG), the Leisure Studies Association (LSA) and the British Association of Sports Sciences (BASS) and at an international level the International Society for the History of Physical Education and Sport (ISHPES) and the North American Society for the Sociology of Sport (NASSS). The accessions lists of organizations like the Scottish Sports Council and The Countryside Commission often list material not found elsewhere.

For biographies, a useful publication is the *Bibliography of biography*, a list of biographical works published throughout the world. Entries are provided by the British Library and the Library of Congress in the USA. Books are arranged in two alphabetical sequences: a name sequence where the names are subjects and an author/title sequence. The latest edition, published by the British Library covers the literature of 1988. A microfiche edition published in 1984 covers 1970-1984. For those specifically interested in women the *Dictionary of women's biography* edited by J. Uglow (London: Macmillan, 1982), although rather dated, has a section on physical achievements which includes competitive sport.

Dissertation Abstracts International (DAI) lists North American dissertations in two series: A – 'Humanities and social sciences' and B – 'Sciences and engineering'. A third series, C, lists the dissertation output of a limited number of European universities. *DAI* will be covered in more detail later in this chapter. The English equivalent is *Aslib index to theses with abstracts*, published by Aslib and Expert Information. The University of Oregon has published *Microform Publications: health, physical education and recreation* since 1949. A supplement is issued twice a year. A publication directly related to sport and physical education is *PERDAS 1950-1980: a list of theses, dissertations and projects on physical education, recreation, dance, athletics and sport, presented at UK universities* and compiled by J.S. Keighley (Lancaster: LISE, 1981). It lists material according to author but, unfortunately, it has a rather poor subject index and is in need of updating.

Official documents can often be a neglected source of information. Chapter 3 describes government publications in more detail. In the UK, the HMSO catalogues list the output of government departments whilst *Hansard* reflects debate in Parliament and can be very useful for topical information. *Hansard* is published on CD-ROM by Chadwyck-Healey.

Some useful texts are *Guide to libraries and information units in Government Departments and other organizations* (29th edn) edited by P. Dale (London: British Library, Science Reference and Information Service, 1990) and S. Richard's *Directory of British official publications* (London: Mansell, 1984). Basic introductory texts to North American official publications include J.A. Downey, *US Federal official publications: the international dimension* (London: Pergamon, 1978) and *United States Government publications* (London: British Library, 1990). I. Thomson's *Documentation of the European communities: a guide* (London: Mansell, 1989) provides a very good introductory text. Official EEC and Council of Europe documents are covered in more depth in Chapter 14.

Current research in Britain is a national register of current research in universities, polytechnics and colleges. It is published in four main sections: 'Physical sciences' and 'Biological sciences' which both appear in two parts annually; 'Social sciences' and 'Humanities' are single volumes, the latter published biennially. Relevant research appears in each of the sections under a variety of headings ranging from physical education and leisure in social sciences, to sport and sport pitches in biological sciences. Sources that list specific sport and leisure research are badly out of date. The Sports Council has published two editions of *Sports research in the UK*. The last edition was edited by A. Dye and P.N. Grimshaw (London: The Sports Council, 1983). The Leisure Studies Association published *International handbook of leisure studies and research*, edited by S. Parker (London: LSA, 1985). Some of the smaller subject areas have also attempted to highlight research, e.g. *Comparative physical education and sport directors*, edited by R.C. Wilcox (Hampstead, Long Island: Hofstra University, 1986). The European Sports Research Projects Database and associated printed research guides are covered in Chapter 14.

There are a large number of conferences, seminars, etc. held on sports and leisure topics each year. If it is sometimes difficult to identify the venue, it is often more difficult to establish if the proceedings have been published. *Index to Conference Proceedings* is a monthly list of all types of conference proceedings arranged alphabetically according to subject. Relevant subject headings include sports, sports equipment, and sports medicine. The index is published by the British Library, Document Supply Centre, and is also available online. Other sources that index conference proceedings include The Sports Documentation Centre's *Sports Documentation Monthly Bulletin* and The Sports Council's *SCAN*.

Bibliographies are an obvious way of tracing publications. However, one of their disadvantages is that they date very quickly. This is not such a problem with historical subjects, but can be when more contemporary topics are being covered. There are a large number of bibliographies in the sport and leisure area, ranging from the general to the sport specific. One of the largest of the general bibliographies has originated from the Sport Information Resource Centre (SIRC) in Canada. Published in 13 volumes, the *Sport bibliography* is a comprehensive printed index of material for the years 1974-1980 inclusive, with some incomplete coverage prior to 1974. SIRC also publish *Sport and recreation for the disabled: a bibliography 1984-1989* which reflects the holdings of 23 organizations and resource centres across Canada. It is updated regularly and the last edition was published in 1990. SIRC is now offering specialist bibliographies taken from the SPORT database. Subjects range from ethics to spectator violence and employee fitness.

There are a large number of smaller, one-off bibliographies which cover particular types of material or specific subjects. They can range in size from long annotated bibliographies to computer listings or home-produced bibliographies. The following highlight some of the different types: V. Scannell's *Sporting literature: an anthology* (Oxford: OUP, 1987) and H.M. Zucker and L.J. Babich's *Sports films: a complete reference* (Jefferson, N.C.: McFarlane, 1987). Specific subject bibliographies include: P. Bale's *A bibliography of research papers on physique, somatotyping and body composition related to sports performance* (2nd edn) (Eastbourne: Brighton Polytechnic, Chelsea School of Human Movement 1985), and F.R. Forbes' *Dance: an annotated bibliography 1965-1972* (New York: Garland, 1986).

Examples of major bibliographies that have been updated are E. W. Padwick (compiler) *A bibliography of cricket* (2nd edn) (London: Library Association, 1984) and P.J. Fentem, N.B. Turnbull and E.J. Bassey, *Benefits of exercise, the evidence* (Manchester, Manchester University Press, 1990). The latter updates a bibliography on the same subject, *Exercise and health: a bibliography of references collected during a literature search for evidence that exercise is of benefit to health*, sponsored by The Sports Council in 1979 and published by Nottingham University Medical School. Finally, examples of bibliographies produced by enthusiasts include a series covering bicycle literature published privately by D.J. Luebbers in the 1970s and J. Hay's *Bibliography of biomechanics literature* (1987) which was originally published by the compiler, but the 5th edition has been published by the University of Iowa.

Finding basic information about sport and leisure

Such is the importance of sport in society that most of the general reference books and general encyclopaedias are useful sources of information on sport. *Whitaker's almanack* (London: Whitaker, 1990) has a general section on sport which covers UK records and results, plus sections on The Sports Council, courses and events. For a more international picture readers should consult the *World almanac and book of facts 1990* (N.Y.: World Almanac, 1990). It presents a retrospective list of records for events like the Olympic Games and for U.S. national events. The *New encyclopaedia Britannica* is issued in three sections: 'Propaedia', 'Micropaedia' and 'Macropaedia' (Chicago, London: Encyclopaedia Britannica Inc., 1986). The 'Macropaedia' has a major entry on sport entitled 'Major team and individual sports', plus a section on 'History of sports and games'. Both sections have bibliographies. Other encyclopaedias have sections on sports and list a considerable amount of information under individual sports.

There are a large number of sport-specific encyclopaedias, but many of them are out of print and in need of updating. The latest title is edited by J.R. White, *Sports rules encyclopedia* (2nd edn, Champaign, Ill.: Leisure Press, 1990). The book has a definite North American bias, having been written with the cooperation of the American sports-governing bodies. It covers 51 sports, some of which are minority sports outside of North America.

Of the more general titles, the *Oxford companion to sports and games* (Oxford: OUP, 1975) provides a brief entry for over 200 sports and games covering techniques, equipment, events and personalities. A similar publication, but with a slightly wider coverage, is the *Macmillan dictionary of sports and games* (London: Macmillan, 1980). Despite being more up to date, it is more difficult to use because of an odd layout and a lack of detailed cross-referencing. The section on encyclopaedias and dictionaries in Chapter 6 provides a historical perspective.

Official rules of sports and games, published annually by Heinemann provides useful information on each sport, whilst *Sports laws: the authoritative, up-to-date, illustrated guide to the regulations, history and subject of all major sports* compiled by the Diagram Group (London: Dent, 1984) offers comprehensive coverage but is older. The Guinness series provides a number of titles related to sport, the latest of which is the *Guinness encyclopaedia of sports records and results*, compiled by P. Mathews and I. Morrison (Guinness Superlatives, 1987). *Olympic Games: the records*, edited by S. Greenberg (London: Guinness, 1987) provides information specific to the Games.

Dictionaries

Examples of this type of publication include: *The language of sport*, by

T. Considine (London: Angus and Robertson, 1982), a brief dictionary of terms related to nine major sports; the *Dictionary of sporting champions*, edited by I. Morrison (Manchester: World International Publishing, c.1987); and the *Biographical dictionary of American sports* (1987-1989), edited by D.L. Porter, and published in four volumes by the Greenwood Press.

Guides and histories

Examples of guides are: *Sport and leisure: guide to the trade* (Harpers Sport and Leisure, annual); and *Sport: a guide to historical sources in the United Kingdom*, compiled by R. Cox (London: The Sports Council, 1983), which lists all British historical collections. General histories are covered in more detail in Chapter 6. Two which have been published in specific areas recently are A.R. Ashe's *A hard road to glory: a history of the African-American athlete* (New York: Warner Books, 1988) published in three volumes covering the years 1619-1986 and *American women in sport eighteen eighty-seven to nineteen eighty-seven: a 100 year chronology*, compiled by R.M. Sparhawk *et al.* (N.J.: Scarecrow, 1989).

Directories and yearbooks

Current British directories (11th edn) (Beckenham: CBD Research, 1988), lists a number of sporting directories, mainly related to individual sports. There has been a proliferation of directories in the UK leisure area, e.g. *Leisure studies yearbook 1989-90* (London: Longman, 1989).

There are a number of directories of organizations and associations which are useful in tracing sporting bodies. Unfortunately there are problems with the currency of the information provided and the scope, which often excludes the smaller and more obscure bodies. There is a general on-line service, *Encyclopaedia of associations* produced by Gale Research and hosted by DIALOG, which also appears in printed form. Other printed sources include *Directory of British associations and associations in Ireland 1989/1990* (Beckenham: CBD Research, 1990) which lists relevant organizations under the headings sport and the individual sports. *The Yearbook of international organizations 1989/90*, published by Saur, has a wider brief. Appendix II lists international organizations. The Sports Council's annual *Address Book* is also very useful.

Statistics

Statistics are covered in more detail in Chapters 2 and 15 (the latter concentrates on North America). Specific statistics for sport or leisure are not easy to find and use has to be made of the general secondary sources that are available. In the UK these include *Social trends* (CSO, annual) and *General household survey* (OPCS, annual). In North America *Statistics Canada* (Statistics Canada) and *Statistical abstract of the United States* (Washington: USGPO) are the general sources. A useful publication for the UK is the *Digest of sports statistics for the UK* (2nd edn), written and edited by the Centre for Leisure Research (London: The Sports Council, 1986). It provides a brief résumé of the development of each sport covered and statistics about participation, membership of clubs, etc. A third edition is in preparation. The Sports Council also provides statistical data through its five-year plans and annual reports. Some individual sports produce their own statistics and readers should refer to Chapter 8 on individual sports for more details of these. SPRIG has published a useful guide to statistical and market research type material, *Market research sources in sport in the UK* (London: SPRIG, 1990).

Major libraries and information centres

Few libraries specialize in providing sports and leisure information. It is generally acknowledged that the biggest is the Sport Information Resource Centre (SIRC) located at the Canadian Sport and Fitness Administration Centre, Gloucester, Ottawa, Canada. SIRC has a fairly comprehensive library of books, periodicals, reports, dissertations and audio-visual material, but does not attempt to collect everything that is published on sport. The Centre buys mainly for its client group, which consists of the National Sports Associations and the employees and programmes of the Government Ministry – Fitness and Amateur Sport. The main emphasis of the collection is on top-level and international sport, the Olympic Games, disabled, doping and sport sciences.

An effort is made to collect all bibliographies and conference proceedings, and the Centre receives over 2000 current journal titles. Prime users receive a detailed monthly SDI provided through the CAN/OLÉ online system. A document delivery service is provided, both in Canada and outside, although the actual delivery can be very slow, depending on the request.

Historically, SIRC has made a significant contribution to sports information by providing the SPORT database and, more recently, its CD-ROM equivalent, SPORT DISCUS. These will be reviewed under separate sections later in this chapter. The hard copy of the SPORT database, the *Sport bibliography*, appeared in 13 volumes, and although no longer published, it has also been an important resource in many libraries. The SPORT database is now updated by *SportSearch*, a monthly current-awareness journal and the Centre targets specific groups with a series of low-priced bibliographies, *SportBiblio*, culled from the SPORT database.

Another significant North American library which had an international reputation, was the SIRLS library at the University of Waterloo, Canada. It consisted of a small specialist microfiche collection dedicated to the sociological aspects of sport and leisure which was mainly used by the students at the university, although outside visitors were welcomed. SIRLS provided a database from the 1960s and published an abstracting journal *Sport and Leisure* until 1990. The collection and database has recently been bought by SIRC.

Chapter 14 on European sources will cover the major European libraries but mention must be made of the information service at the Bundesinstitut für Sportwissenschaft (BISp) (Federal Institute of Sports Science) in Cologne, Germany. BISp has a substantial collection of over 24 000 monographs and 450 periodical titles. The main thrust of the collection is in the sport sciences, but it also has considerable holdings in sports practice. BISp produces SPOLIT, a bibliographic database, SPOFOR, a research projects database and SPOMED which contains the medical data on top German athletes. It also publishes an indexing journal *Sportdokumentation* (Sport scientific literature), *Sportwissenschäftliche Forschungsprojekte* (Research projects) and *Neuerbundliste* (list of new acquisitions).

With holdings of over 250 000 monographs and subscriptions to over 1400 periodicals the Zentralbibliothek der Sportwissenschaften of the Deutsche Sporthochschule is a bigger library than BISp and is also located in Cologne. It has a good collection of audio-visual material and press cuttings and offers access to a number of online databases.

The major sports library in what was formerly the German Democratic Republic was located at the Zentralbibliothek für Körperkultur und Sport an der Deutschen Hochschule für Körperkultur, Leipzig, and had been in existence since the 1950s. The unification of Germany has resulted in much closer cooperation between the Library and Information Service in Leipzig, and BISp in Cologne.

Special libraries

The Sports Documentation Centre, at the University of Birmingham in the UK, has also been in existence since the early 1970s and has an international reputation. The collection concentrates on the sport sciences, physical education and leisure. The main clientele is the student population, but visitors from outside are welcomed, as are written and telephone enquiries. The Centre produces the indexing journal – *Sports Documentation Monthly Bulletin*.

The various Sports Councils all provide a very useful information service. The English, Scottish, Welsh and Northern Ireland Sports Councils all have Information Centres with a Regional Coordinating Officer coordinating the work of the Regional Information Officers of the seven regions of the English Sports Council.

The English Sports Council's Headquarters in London has a large reference-only collection and subscribes to over 350 British and foreign journals, many of which are magazines from the Governing Sports Bodies not easily found elsewhere. The subject coverage includes built and national facilities for sport, individual sports, leisure, sport for specific groups, recreation management, sports administration, sponsorship and international sport. The Centre has a number of in-house databases mainly concerned with facilities throughout the UK. These can be searched via staff at the Centre. A bibliographic database is being developed. It is also a provider on the Prestel system.

The Sports Council publications include a number of bibliographies, a current-awareness journal – *SCAN*, a calendar of major sporting events, and a useful list of all the governing bodies. The Centre welcomes personal, written and telephone enquiries, answering on average over 40 000 enquiries per year. The Council also provides a Press Release service, which is useful for those interested in sport policy in England.

The Scottish Sports Council has a very good Information Centre in Edinburgh, and provides documentation on a range of topics. Particularly useful for those wishing to keep up with the latest publications is the bi-monthly *Accessions list* which lists annual reports, handbooks, directories, etc. The Sports Council for Wales has a smaller collection and publishes a monthly accessions bulletin.

The Sports Council also takes a lead in a number of information-related initiatives, both in the UK and abroad. They have been involved, in conjunction with the British Library, in a proposal for a Sport Information Plan for the UK, and have published *Classification/thesaurus for sport and physical education (and allied topics).* This document is currently in its third edition and is used by a number of libraries. The Head of the Information Centre represents the UK at the Council of Europe on matters related to sports information. The 'sports information group' has the remit to support projects initiated by the Committee for the Development of Sport. Much of the finished research is published in the Clearing House's *Sports Information Bulletin.* They also have some commitment to continuing the European Sports Research Projects Database, although it is not clear if any printed copy will be forthcoming.

A UK organization involved in sport at a national and international level is the Central Council of Physical Recreation. The Council does not have an extensive Library but can provide information on sponsorship, the press and media, taxation, local authorities, and national and international sports administration.

The National Sports Medicine Institute (formerly the London Sports Medicine Institute) has a small library of books, reports and leaflets, and subscribes to over 70 journals in the area of sports medicine. It has an in-house database and also offers online searching of external databases. NSMI publishes *Sports Medicine Bulletin*, and a series of specialist bibliographies, *Sport physiotherapy*, *Sports nutrition*, and *Ergogenic aids in sport*. See Chapter 5 for more information.

The National Coaching Foundation, located at Leeds Polytechnic, also has a small collection of books and journals concerned with subjects of interest to coaches. It provides a useful information service for coaches, publishing *Coaching Update*, and *Sporting Update* which concentrates on individual sports. The main client group is coaches but enquiries from non coaches are welcome. Chapter 13 on Coaching gives more information on the NCF.

The National Advice Centre for Outdoor Education, located at Doncaster Institute for Higher Education, High Melton, Doncaster, provides a specialist service on outdoor education. Other useful information services for outdoor education located in London include the Expedition Advisory Centre at the Royal Geographical Society, Kensington Gore.

The Physical Education Association has traditionally provided a Library and Information service to its membership. However economic problems have forced the Library, formerly housed at Whitelands College, South London, to be dispersed with most of the stock being transferred to other libraries. A few basic books and core journals remain at the Association's headquarters, and the archives have been deposited at the University of Liverpool.

The National Resource Centre for Dance, located at the University of Surrey, offers various services to its members which include a resource centre and a current-awareness journal *Dance Current Awareness Bulletin*. The Centre will provide a limited service to the wider public.

Many universities, polytechnics and colleges of higher education run courses in sports science, leisure studies or provide teacher-training courses. In theory, they should all have good collections to support these courses, although some are better than others. The Sports Documentation Centre at the University of Birmingham has already been described, but there are two other libraries worth mentioning at the University – the National Centre for Athletics Literature and the Local Government and Development Library which specializes in management and policy studies for British local government. Other good collections can be found at Loughborough University, Brighton Polytechnic, Trent Polytechnic and Bedford College of Higher

Education. Charlotte Mason College and Liverpool Polytechnic both have strengths in outdoor education. The Queen's University of Belfast has a good sports collection and the Science Library publishes the *APIS Bulletin* (Architecture & Planning Information Service) which is of peripheral interest to sports planners, etc.

Public libraries

The public libraries provide a considerable amount of information on sport, in particular individual sports, biographies and 'how-to-do-it' books. Unfortunately, economics dictate that they are often out of date. Greenwich Public Library houses the metropolitan special collection on recreation and has a good coverage of all sports and official books for most sports organizations. The Sheffield Sports Information Service located within the Sheffield Public Library Service provides a specialist service to public library authorities throughout the country and has some special collections. The Local Studies Departments of many public libraries house a considerable amount of sport-related material.

Government libraries

The Department of the Environment and the Department of Transport have a joint library and publish an *Annual list of publications* (which also appears monthly) and, until 1990, published *Library Bulletin*, an abstracting journal which listed the current literature on a range of social and environmental planning topics which include sport and recreation. The library's publication *Sport and recreation: sources of information on sport and recreation* (1987) has already been mentioned.

The Countryside Commission has a very good library in Cheltenham and publishes a *Research register* and two current-awareness bulletins, *Selected periodical articles*, which abstracts periodicals received in the library, and an *Accessions list*, arranged in subject order, of which the section on countryside recreation is the most relevant.

The subject coverage of the National Children's Play and Recreation Unit is play provision, theories, activities, education, playground design and child development. It has a collection of over 4000 books, reports, videos etc. and subscribes to over 80 journals. The Centre issues abstracts of recent acquisitions on a regular basis and offers a public information service.

Readers should refer to the *Directory of information sources in the United Kingdom* (6th edn) compiled by E.M. Codlin (London: Aslib, 1990) for full details of a wide range of library and information services, since there are obviously a number of other resources which are of relevance to researchers in this area. A similar publication, *Directory of libraries and information centers*, covers over 18 000

North American resource centres. Published in two volumes by Gale Research, it is updated regularly.

Abstracting and indexing journals

There are a considerable number of abstracting and indexing services, ranging from in-house indexes to commercial publications. Some of the major titles are printed versions of online databases. Of the more general services *SportSearch* (formerly *Sport and Recreation Index*) from SIRC, is a listing of articles, conference papers and book chapters, arranged in subject order with a general subject index. Conforming closely to the style of the *Sport bibliography* it updates the SPORT database in printed form. It is published monthly and covers a good range of English- and French-language journals, which are listed along with the publishers' addresses. It is particularly useful for material on individual sports, and for tracing forthcoming conferences through the comprehensive conferences calendar.

Another general interest title is *Completed Research in Health, Physical Education, Recreation and Dance, including international sources*. Published annually by the American Alliance for Health, Physical Education, Recreation, and Dance (AAHPERD), it lists research completed during the year prior to publication. It is particularly useful for identifying Master's and Doctoral theses in American higher education institutions. Most entries are accompanied by abstracts and there is a very general subject index. Of less use is the list of published research, mainly articles. Another Alliance publication is *Abstracts of Research Papers*, again published annually and listing abstracts of papers presented at the Research Consortium session of the AAHPERD Convention. Since it does not contain a subject index it is not always easy to trace material.

Another broadly-based printed source is *Sportdokumentation*, published by the Bundesinstitut für Sportwissenschaft in Germany. This has an international coverage, with an obvious emphasis on the German literature. Subjects range from anthropology to individual sports, with considerable emphasis on sports medicine. The other German-language indexing journal, published in the former GDR, is *Indexed list of titles* (formerly *Körperkultur und Sport Überblicksinformation*). Other countries publish current-awareness journals, e.g. *Sportenta* (Finland), *Litt om Litt* (Norway), *Mensuel Signaletique* (France). These are all covered in greater detail in Chapter 14 on European sources.

Although not commercially marketed in the UK, *SCAN*, the English Sports Council's current-awareness service is produced in-house and distributed on a fairly *ad hoc* basis. It abstracts articles from a wide range of journals including a number relating to local government that are not covered in the other indexing journals cited here. It also lists handbooks, yearbooks, new publications and forthcoming conferences.

Sports Documentation Monthly Bulletin (formerly *Sports Information Bulletin*) is a monthly current-awareness journal which indexes articles and conference papers, some with abstracts. Published by the Sports Documentation Centre, at the University of Birmingham, UK, it has a very wide subject coverage and is particularly strong in foreign-language material as the Centre subscribes to a large number of overseas journals. The *Bulletin* has an author and subject index which is cumulated annually.

Some of the current-awareness services deal with more specific subject areas. The major abstracting source covering the whole range of leisure subjects is *Leisure, Recreation and Tourism Abstracts (LRTA)*. Published quarterly by CAB, and in conjunction with the World Leisure and Recreation Association, it provides 2500 abstracts each year from worldwide literature. Foreign language material is accompanied by an English abstract. It has a detailed subject index. Two foreign-language services also devoted to leisure are *REDOC* from the Netherlands and *Loreto* (Loisir, Récréation, Tourisme) published in Belgium. These are described in more detail in Chapter 10.

Relevant to sport as well as leisure is *Sport and Leisure: a Journal of Social Science Abstracts* (formerly *Sociology of Leisure and Sport Abstracts*), the hard-copy version of the SPORT AND LEISURE database. It was published by the University of Waterloo Press until 1990 and gave full abstracts for journal articles, books and book chapters, theses and other grey literature with an emphasis on sociological aspects. Publication ceased at the end of 1990.

There are a large number of publications serving the more scientific area of sports science. A UK publication of central importance to doctors and clinicians is the *Sports Medicine Bulletin*, published monthly by the National Sports Medicine Institute, with additional input from the British Library, Medical Information Service. Limited to articles, it concentrates on sports medicine and applied physiology. The *Bulletin* has an author index and detailed subject index. Another British Library publication, and of specific interest to physiotherapists is *Physiotherapy Index*. Generated from the British Library's CATS database, it scans a wide range of journals. Articles are arranged in broad subject headings, with an author and subject index.

A North American publication, *Sports medicine research today* includes some of the items from *Biological Abstracts* and updates the bibliography, *Collected papers on sports medicine research 1982-1987*. It monitors over 9000 titles but is not the most useful service because it is arranged by document type rather than by subject. A subject index helps, but does not make searching that much easier.

Physical Fitness/Sports Medicine is a quarterly index, published by the President's Council on Physical Fitness, consisting of citations retrieved from the National Library of Medicine's MEDLINE database. Subject coverage concentrates on exercise physiology, sports injuries, physical conditioning and medical aspects of exercise. It follows the layout of *Index Medicus*, but without a subject index is more difficult to search. *Excerpta Medica* can also provide useful references. Further details of all the abstracting services for medicine can be found in Chapter 5.

Of specific interest to those researching in sports psychology is *Psychological Abstracts*, published by the American Psychology Association. Published monthly, it scans over 1000 journals each year, providing non-evaluative summaries. The relevant headings to look under are 'sports' and 'recreation' because they include 'see also' references.

Coaching Update, published quarterly by the National Coaching Foundation, includes articles from coaching and Governing Body magazines aimed specifically at the coach. For further information on other abstracting journals relevant to coaching see Chapter 13.

Physical education in the UK does not have its own current-awareness service but there is a U.S. publication called *Physical Education Index*. It is not solely confined to literature about physical education, but has a good coverage of sports-related subjects. It indexes over 200 journals arranged in subject order with no author or subject indexes. An index produced in the UK which scans over 250 journals a year is *British Education Index*.

More specific, but of some interest to physical educationalists, is *Dance Current Awareness Bulletin*, published three times a year by the National Resource Centre for Dance, based at the University of Surrey. It is a conventional indexing journal but also contains details of forthcoming conferences, events and new publications.

Both the *Social Science Citation Index* and *Science Citation Index* contain information on relevant topics. *Sociological Abstracts* is also useful for sociologists.

Mention has already been made of *Dissertation Abstracts International*, an important service published monthly, which abstracts doctoral dissertations submitted by 550 participating institutions in North America, and to a lesser extent, Europe. It is published in three sections: A – 'Humanities', B – 'Sciences and engineering', C – 'Worldwide' (published quarterly, it covers non-North American material). Each section has an author and keyword index. The latter reflects terms taken from the title of the thesis. Consult 'A' for physical education, business, sociology of sport, and 'B' for physiology, biomedical and psychological subjects. The printed format is rather difficult to use, but the compact disc format enables the data to be extracted more easily. The UK equivalent is *Index to Theses, with Abstracts*, published by Aslib and Expert Information Ltd.

Newspapers are an important source of topical information that are sometimes neglected. *British Humanities Index*, published quarterly by Bowker-Saur, indexes a large number of journals, all of which are listed at the beginning of each issue. These include *The Guardian*, the *New Statesman and Society* and *The Spectator*. Relevant articles are listed in a subject arrangement with 'see references'. Another useful index is *The Times Index*. This covers all *The Times* newspapers and periodicals and has a detailed subject index. Unfortunately there are no services which cover the tabloid newspapers.

Finally, there are a large number of current-awareness services which are of more peripheral interest to anyone undertaking sports and leisure research. These include:

- *APIS Bulletin*, published by the Queens University Belfast, Architecture and Planning Information Service, provides a fortnightly service aimed at architects and planners and includes some articles on sports and recreational facilities.
- *Urban Abstracts*, the printed version of the ACOMPLINE database covers leisure and recreation from an urban and local government perspective.
- *Current Contents* (social and behavioural sciences) reproduces the tables of contents of over 1340 journals and is worth consulting. The most relevant words in the index are sports, sporting and leisure. It is also useful for book reviews and for the addresses of a wide range of publishers. The section on online services should be consulted for information on printed services that appear online or on CD-ROM.

Journals

The journals required by researchers in sport and leisure range from the academic journal to the more light-weight popular magazines. For the purposes of this chapter 'journals' and 'periodicals' will be interchangeable terms and will define any publication that appears at intervals of a year or less.

There has been a substantial increase in the journal literature over the last decade in response to new subject areas and the emergence of the leisure market. The main impetus for publishing has come from North America but new international journals have also appeared, as well as some new titles from UK publishers.

Like many other disciplines, the bibliographic control of the journal literature presents problems for the researchers. The academic journals are easier to trace because they tend to form the core periodical collection for most libraries and are also covered by the abstracting and indexing services. It is the more transient material that is harder to trace; the journals and newsletters of the Governing Bodies of sport and of various associations. These tend not to be covered by *Ulrich's international periodical directory* (London, New York: Bowker, annual) published in three volumes which now includes irregular serials and annuals, or in *Serials in the British Library* (Boston Spa: British Library, annual), which is available in CD-ROM format as Boston Spa Serials.

The Sport and Recreation Information Group (SPRIG) attempted to improve the bibliographic control of the literature by publishing the *Union catalogue of sport periodicals* (edited by M. Shoebridge) in 1988. It covers a large range of journals along with the holdings of over 40 higher education institutions throughout the UK. A new and expanded edition is currently in preparation.

Publications like *SportSearch* list all the journals indexed, along with addresses and this approach is useful; whilst some information centres publish lists of their journal holdings, e.g. SIRC, the Sports Documentation Centre, and the National Sport Information Centre in Australia.

Some of the academic journals used by researchers are very well established, have detailed indices, contents pages, diagrams and tables whilst others are of a more transient nature and have shorter articles. The following overview of current journals should be supplemented by the evaluation of the subject specific journals in the individual chapters, since it is impossible to list all the relevant journals. Few countries can sustain a general sports periodical and the only title that has attracted continuing success is *Sports Illustrated* (1954–) one of the most popular and requested journals. Although not an academic journal, it does contain information of interest to all levels of research into sport and leisure.

A large number of associations have an active publications programme. Into this category falls the oldest sport-related journal, *Research Quarterly for Exercise and Sport* (USA) published since 1930 by the American Alliance for Health, Physical Education, Recreation, and Dance (AAHPERD). The American College of Sports Medicine (ACSM) has published *Medicine and Science in Sports and Exercise* since 1969, whilst the *American Journal of Sports Medicine* is the official journal of the American Orthopedic Society for Sports Medicine (AOSSM). Two journals on sport psychology are published by Human Kinetics. They are the *Journal of Sport and Exercise Psychology* and the *Sport Psychologist*. The latter has a more practical emphasis and is the official journal of the International Society of Sport Psychology (ISSP). The *International Journal of Sport Psychology* is also an official journal of the ISSP. The latter is more practical based, as is the *Journal of Applied Sport Psychology*, the official journal of the Association for the Advancement of Applied Sport Psychology (AAASP). Human Kinetics also publish the *International Journal of Sport Biomechanics* for the International Society of Biomechanics (ISB).

The following is a list of major journals:

Sport sciences

Canadian Journal of Sport Sciences (Canada) 1976–

Exercise and Sport Sciences Reviews (USA) 1973–

Human Movement Science (Netherlands) 1975–

International Journal of Sport Biomechanics (USA) 1985–

International Journal of Sport Psychology (Italy) 1970–

Journal of Applied Sport Psychology (USA) 1989–

Journal of Human Movement Studies (UK) 1975–

Journal of Motor Behavior (USA) 1969–

Journal of Sport and Exercise Psychology (USA) (1979–)

Journal of Sports Sciences (UK) 1983–

Pediatric Exercise Science (USA) 1989–

Perceptual and Motor Skills (USA) 1949–

Research Quarterly for Exercise and Sport (USA) 1930–

Sport Psychologist (USA) 1987–

Sports medicine

Advances in Sports Medicine and Fitness (USA) 1987–

American Journal of Sports Medicine (USA) 1972–

Annals of Sports Medicine (USA) 1982–

Australian Journal of Science and Medicine in Sport (Australia) 1982–

British Journal of Sports Medicine (UK) 1964–

Clinical Sports Medicine (UK) 1989– (ceased)

Clinics in Sports Medicine (USA) 1983–

Deutsche Zeitschrift für Sportmedizin (Germany) 1949–

International Journal of Sport Nutrition (USA) 1991–

International Journal of Sports Medicine (Germany) 1980–

International Journal of Sports Cardiology (Italy) 1986–

Journal of Sports Medicine and Physical Fitness (Italy) 1961–

Journal of Sports Traumatology and Related Research (Italy) 1980–

Medicina dello Sport (Italy) 1947–

Medicine and Science in Sports
and Exercise (USA) 1969–

Medicine du Sport (France) 1925–

Medizin und Sport (Germany)
1961–

New Zealand Journal of Sports
Medicine (New Zealand) 1973–

Physician and Sportsmedicine
(USA) 1973–

Physiotherapy in Sport (UK)
1976–

Scandinavian Journal of Medicine
& Science in Sports (Denmark)
1991–

Schweizerische Zeitschrift für
Sportmedizin (Switzerland)
1964–

Sport Health (Australia) 1983–

Sports Medicine (New Zealand)
1984–

Sports Medicine and Soft Tissue
Trauma (UK) 1989–

Sports Therapy (UK) 1990–

Sports history

Canadian Journal of History of
Sport (Canada) 1970–

International Journal of the
History of Sport (UK) 1984–

Journal of Sport History (USA)
1974–

Sports sociology

International Review for the
Sociology of Sport (Germany)
1966–

Journal of Sport and Social Issues
(USA) 1976–

Journal of Sport Behavior (USA)
1978–

Sociology of Sport Journal (USA)
1984–

Leisure

ACADEMIC JOURNALS

Journal of Leisure Research
(USA) 1969–

Journal of Sport Management
(USA) 1987–

Leisure Studies (UK) 1982–

Leisure Sciences (USA) 1977–

Loisir et Société/Society and
Leisure (Canada) 1978–

Therapeutic Recreation Journal
(USA) 1967–

PROFESSIONAL JOURNALS

Australian Parks and Recreation
(Australia) 1964–

Groundsman (UK) 1947–

Journal of Leisurability (USA)
1974–

Leisure Management (UK) 1981–

Leisure Manager (UK) 1936–

Recreation (UK) 1931–

Parks and Recreation (USA)
1966–

Sport and Leisure (UK) 1949–

Physical education

ACHPER National Journal
(Australia) 1983–

Adapted Physical Activity
Quarterly (USA) 1984–

Adventure Education and
Outdoor Leadership (UK)
1984–

British Journal of Physical
Education (UK) 1970–

Bulletin of Physical Education
(UK) 1948–

CAHPER Journal (Canada) 1933–

Education Physique et Sport
(France) 1959–

FIEP Bulletin (UK) 1930–

Geneeskunde en Sport
(Netherlands) 1978–

International Journal of Physical
Education (Germany) 1963–

Journal of Comparative Physical
Education and Sport
(Germany) 1983–

Journal of Physical Education,
Recreation, and Dance (USA)
1896–

Journal of Teaching in Physical
Education (USA) 1981–

Leibesübungen-Leiberziehung
(Austria) 1973–

New Zealand Journal of Health,
Physical Education and
Recreation (New Zealand)
1954–

Physical Education Review (UK)
1978–

Physical Educator (USA) 1940–

Quest (USA) 1963–

Sportunterricht (Germany) 1973–

Coaching

Coaching Focus (UK) 1985–

Journal of Applied Research in
Coaching and Athletics (USA)
1986–

Modern Athlete and Coach
(Australia) 1962–

National Strength and
Conditioning Association
Journal (USA) 1978–

Sports Coach (Australia) 1977–

Sports (sports periodical on
research and technology in
sport) (Canada)

Various Governing Body
magazines

Other journals used by researchers

Aethlon: the Journal of Sport
Literature (USA) 1983–

European Journal of Applied
Physiology and Occupational
Physiology (Germany) 1941–

Journal of Applied Physiology,
Respiratory, Environmental,
and Exercise Physiology
(USA) 1948–

Journal of the Philosophy of Sport
(USA) 1974–

Play and Culture (USA) 1988–

Sports Illustrated (USA) 1954–

Sports Place, an international
Journal of Sports Geography
(USA) 1987–

Databases

Databases are a quick and efficient way of searching for material on a specific subject. Users unfamiliar with online databases should, however, approach them with some caution. Searches can be very expensive and the quality of records retrieved often depends on the

TABLE 1.1 Online services relevant to sport and leisure

Database	Hosts	Year of commencement	Scope	CD-ROM	Printed version
ABI-INFORM, UMI Data/Courier	BRS, Datastar, Dialog	1970	Business and management	ABI/INFORM	
ACCOMPLINE/URBALINE London Research Centre Library	ESA/IRS (file 35)	1973	Public administration, local government Emphasis on UK material		*Urban Abstracts*
BIOSIS PREVIEWS Biosciences Information Service	Datastar, Dialog, DIMDI, BRS, CAN-OLE	1969	Good coverage of physiology		*Biological Abstracts*
BRITISH EDUCATIONAL INDEX University of Leeds	Dialog	BEI, 1976 BETI, 1950	Contains *British Education Index* and *British Education Theses*		*British Education Index*; *British Education Theses*
COMPUTER SPORTS WORLD Computer Sports World	Computer Sports World Compuserve Info Service	1970	Animal breeding, U.S. professional sports		
DISSERTATION ABSTRACTS ONLINE University Microforms International	Dialog, BRS	1861	Comprehensive coverage of North American dissertations and some European input	DAO	*Dissertation Abstracts International*, series A, B, and C
EMBASE Elsevier Science Publishers	Datastar, Dialog, DIMDI, Soe, BRS	1974	Good coverage of sports medicine	EMBASE	
ENCYCLOPAEDIA OF ASSOCIATIONS Gale Research	Dialog	Current year associations and organizations	20 000 U.S. associations and organizations	Available on CD-ROM	
ERIC U.S. Department of Education, Office of Educational Research Improvement	BRS, Dialog, Orbit	1966	Education and education-related areas	ERIC	*ERIC*
HERACLES Sport Doc	L'Européenne de données	1973	Good general coverage, emphasis on French language		*Mensuel Signaletique*

JUSTIS Context Legal Systems Ltd English Language Subset	Context Legal Systems	Varies according to file	Full text or citations to European, EEC and UK case law and legislation	JUSTIS	Various
LRTA *CAB International*	Dialog, ESA/IRS CAN-OLE, BRS, DIMDI, JICST University of Tsukuba	1979	Worldwide leisure literature	LRTA	*Leisure, Recreation and Tourism Abstracts*
MEDLINE National Library of Medicine	BRS, Datastar, Dialog, DIMDI, SDC, JICST	1966	Major sources of medical literature including sports medicine	Medline on CD-ROM	*Index Medicus*
NEXIS Mead Data Central	Mead Data Central	Varies according to file	Newspapers, business finance, current affairs		
PROFILE Profile Information	Profile Information	1981	International news, current affairs, business information	Various	
PSYCHINFO American Psychological Association	Dialog, ESA/IRS CAN-OLE, BRS	1967	Major source for sports psychology	PSYCHINFO	*Psychological Abstracts*
SOCIAL SCISEARCH Institute for Scientific Information	Datastar, Dialog BRS, DIMDI	1972	Comprehensive coverage of social science literature	SSCI	*Social Sciences Citation Index*
SPOLIT Bundesinstitut für Sportwissenschaft	DIMDI	1974	Sport sciences, individual sports, emphasis on German language	SPOLIT	*Sportdokumentation*
SPORT Sport Information Resource Centre	Datastar, Dialog, DIMDI SOC, CAN-OLE, BRS	1949	All aspects of sport material is graded	SPORT DISCUS	*Sport bibliography SportSearch*
SPORT AND LEISURE SIRLS	Datapac	1970	Emphasis on sociological aspects of sport and leisure		*Sport and Leisure – a Journal of Social Science Abstracts*

standard of the data input into the database, and the policy concerning indexing standards and thesaurus control. The quantity of records retrieved may also depend on the skill of the searcher in selecting the most appropriate keywords. It seems likely that the advent of databases on CD-ROM will decrease the demand for online searching because users prefer the convenience of searching a database in their own time because of the pressures of being online. The compact discs also have a more user-friendly approach because of their ability to use colour and windows to aid searching, etc. Two useful guides to online databases are *The directory of online databases* published quarterly by Cuadra/Elsevier, New York, and the UK equivalent, *Brit-line*, published by McGraw-Hill, Maidenhead, and updated on a regular basis. Although CD-ROM is a relatively new medium, guides exist and more will no doubt appear on the market. One useful guide compiled by N. Desmarias, is *CD-ROMs in print, 1990: an international guide* (Meckler, 1990). See Table 1.1 for a list of sport- and leisure-related databases.

Commercial databases

A number of commercial and in-house databases specific to sport have already been mentioned. The major international database is the SPORT database produced at SIRC in Canada. It has a good coverage of sports literature from 1949 onwards and is recognized by the International Association for Sports Information as the international sport database. Available on the following hosts: BRS, Dialog, Datastar, DIMDI and CAN-OLE, its subject coverage ranges from sports science, physical fitness, sport for special groups, sociology, training, to individual sports. The database contains over 250 000 bibliographic records, some with brief abstracts. It includes citations for over 22 000 books, articles from more than 2000 current journal titles, and 7000 microforms. Each record is assigned a basic, intermediate or advanced level code. This is particularly useful because a considerable amount of information on the database is not only of a low level, but often emanates from fairly obscure journals or conference proceedings which are not freely available outside North America. In addition, SIRC did not introduce a strict indexing policy until the database had been in existence for some years, which means that searches are not always as precise as they could be. The CD-ROM version – SPORT DISCUS – is available from SilverPlatter, and is updated twice yearly. Because of the ability to take a more leisured approach to a search, the CD-ROM version of the database is often more productive. SIRC publish two search aids, which have to be purchased separately. They are the *SPORT thesaurus* and the *SPORT database user aid*.

SPOLIT, provided by the Deutsche Bundesinstitut für Sportwissenschaft, and available on DIMDI, is the online version of the
printed index, *Sportdokumentation*. The database contains
approximately 40 000 records with an obvious emphasis on German-
language material, and is available on CD-ROM. This latter version is
published by Verlag Ingrid Czwalina.

HERACLES, the French database hosted by l'Européenne de données,
is made available by a cooperative of French institutions involved in
producing sports information led by the Service de Documentation de
l'Institut National du Sport et de l'Éducation Physique. It contains over
45 000 references with abstracts, all in the French language.

There are a number of medical and scientific databases. MEDLINE, the
database of the U.S. National Library of Medicine (NLM), provides the
major source for sports medicine. It is available on Datastar, Dialog,
DIMDI and SDC and is updated monthly. The database is also available
on CD-ROM, extending over a number of discs which are updated
monthly. Although coverage is good and begins in 1966, the emphasis
is on clinical material and some of the smaller, more obscure sports
medicine journals are not indexed.

Another medical database is EMBASE (formerly EXCERPTA MEDICA).
It is hosted by Datastar, DIMDI, Dialog and SDC and has a good
coverage of sports medicine, including drugs and nutrition.

BIOSIS PREVIEWS is particularly useful for covering physiological
data. Its coverage begins in 1969 and it is available on Datastar, Dialog
and DIMDI.

PSYCHINFO, the American Psychological Association's database is
the online version of *Psychological Abstracts*. Available on BRS,
Dialog, DIMDI, SDC and Datastar, its coverage dates from 1967.

Although fewer searches are undertaken on social science databases
there are a number of relevant databases. LRTA, the online version of
Leisure, Recreation and Tourism Abstracts is the major database
providing worldwide access to leisure information. Provided by CAB
International, it is available on Dialog, ESA/IRS, CAN-OLE, BRS and
JICST and Tsukuba-Daiguku. Citations cover monographs, articles,
conference papers and theses, many in languages other than English.
LRTA is a sub-file of CAB ABSTRACTS. The *LRTA user handbook* is a
useful search aid.

Less well used in the UK because it was not mounted on a
commercial host, is the SPORT AND LEISURE database which can be
accessed via Datapac, the Canadian telecommunications system. The
database has recently been bought by SIRC and will be integrated into
the SPORT database.

SOCIAL SCISEARCH, provided by the Institute for Scientific
Information (ISI, Philadelphia), is available on Datastar or Dialog and

on CD-ROM as SSCI. This database is the hard copy version of *Social Science Citation Abstracts*. It contains over 2 million citations of significant articles from social science journals worldwide.

ACOMPLINE, a database covering urban and local government issues, is produced by the London Research Centre Library. ESA-IRS and Pergamon Financial Data Services provide access to ACOMPLINE. Subject coverage ranges from public administration and local government, to leisure and recreation. Records include abstracts. The printed version is *Urban Abstracts*.

CELEX is the official database of European law and is used by Context Legal Systems Ltd to provide a database service, hosted by Dialcom Ltd, using its own retrieval software. The database contains legal information in the form of law reports, indexes, newsletters and encyclopaedias, plus a European Community law file. A CD-ROM version is also available. See Chapter 14 for more information.

In the area of physical education, BRITISH EDUCATION INDEX online has been available since 1988 and covers material published since 1976. Apart from articles it also includes education theses accepted for higher degrees by universities in the UK between 1950 and 1987. ERIC, the American educational database, is available online and on CD-ROM. It has a North American bias, but can yield material on the UK scene, e.g. a search on 'physical education' and 'Great Britain' yielded 17 references, mainly from the *British Journal of Physical Education*. It does not index the lesser-known British physical education journals.

Newspapers offer a wealth of information and are easier to search online. PROFILE, a full-text database which covers international news, current affairs, company information, international business and finance, marketing, advertising and the media, carries the major international papers, magazines like *New Scientist*, *FT Reports* and *Mintel Reports* and the Henley Centre publications. The host is Profile Information. A number of British newspapers are becoming available on CD-ROM. These include *The Guardian*, (Chadwyck-Healey), *The Independent* and *The Independent on Sunday* (Bowker-Saur), *The Sunday Times* which will be known as *THOR*, and *The Northern Echo*.

The New York Times is available online as a NEXIS database. NEXIS has more than 100 newspapers, while the *National Newspaper Index* also indexes *The New York Times*, *The Wall Street Journal*, *The Washington Post* and *The Los Angeles Times*. A number of these are now available on CD-ROM. ABI/INFORM, produced by Data Courier and hosted by Dialog, Orbit, Datastar and BRS, covers articles on business, management, accounting and finance. It has some information relevant to the economics aspects of sport, e.g. a search of the database on CD-ROM, which covers five years of data (1985-1990), yielded 46 references when the keyword soccer was used, 245 under football and

245 under sport itself. Chapter 2 should be consulted for more information on databases in the business area.

Produced by Gale Research, the *Encyclopedia of associations* provides information on over 22 000 U.S. associations and organizations relating to the current year. The information is revised annually. The service is available via Dialog and is also produced on CD-ROM.

COMPUTER SPORTS WORLD is a full-text database which covers animal breeding and racing, and the major professional and collegiate sports in the USA and Canada from 1970 onwards. It is updated continuously to reflect the latest scores, statistics, injuries and reports, etc.

DISSERTATIONS ABSTRACTS ONLINE, produced by UMI, is available via BRS and Dialog. It corresponds to *Dissertation Abstracts International, Comprehensive Dissertation Index* and *Masters Abstracts*. The CD-ROM format is particularly useful. An archive disc covers 1861-1980, and three further discs bring the literature up to date.

Representing a current trend in the dissemination of information, some databases have made the transmission direct from printed form to CD-ROM. One important service for government-related information is UKOP (*Catalogue of United Kingdom official publications*). It amalgamates two *HMSO catalogues* – *Publications* and the *International organizations* – *catalogue* with Chadwyck-Healey's *Catalogue of British official publications not published by HMSO*. The period covered is 1980 onwards. It can be useful for European sport because it includes the documents of international organizations, including the European Community and the Council of Europe. A similar service which also made the transition directly to CD-ROM is *Hansard*, published by Chadwyck-Healey, in conjunction with *Hansard.*

This trend is bound to continue as more printed sources find it economically viable to distribute their product on disc. SPORTING NEWS BASEBALL GUIDE AND REGISTER is typical of the kind of product that is becoming increasingly available. It represents a lengthy review of major league baseball from 1984 to 1990, which includes biographical information about players and managers, results, directories, photographs, etc. It is available for IBM compatibles and the Macintosh by applying to Quanta Press, in St. Paul, Minnesota.

In-house databases

As the proliferation of microcomputers and networks continues, more and more organizations are developing in-house databases. Quite often these databases have emerged as the by-product of the need to produce information bulletins, lists, catalogues, etc. but have become useful products in their own right. Hopefully, as the technology becomes easier, and interest grows, they will be made available through networks like PSS (British Telecom's packet-switching system) and JANET (the joint academic network used by British universities and polytechnics), in the same way as the SIRLS database was made available outside the University of Waterloo via Datapac, the Canadian equivalent of PSS. Alternatives will be to put specific collections on CD-ROM. Readers should note that searches of any of the databases quoted in this section are only possible by applying to the relevant institutions.

The Sports Council in England has a number of in-house databases mainly concerned with facilities for sport and leisure. These are the *facilities* database, the core of which covers sport centres, swimming pools, golf courses, squash courses, ski slopes and ice rinks; *surfaces*; *facility equipment* (not personal equipment); and *events*. These are used to produce lists of sports centres, events calendars, etc. but searches can be requested through the Information Centre staff.

The Sports Council also took over responsibility for the European Sports Research Projects Database some years ago. However, it is not clear if it will ever be made available online. The Information Centre has also been developing a *bibliographic* database for some years, which will reflect the stock of the Information Centre's library and the contents of *SCAN*, their current-awareness service. It is also hoped that the database will become public in the near future.

Both the National Sports Medicine Institute and the Sports Documentation Centre have online versions of their printed indexes which can be searched on request. The National Coaching Foundation has a similar bibliographic database and it has developed an online audio-visual database in cooperation with the Sheffield Sports Library and Information Service. The National Resource Centre for Dance has a substantial database available to those who subscribe to the Centre's service and to outsiders.

Public viewdata systems

One area of online information which has undergone considerable development in the UK in the last few years is that of public information. British Telecom's Prestel was an early provider in this area in the UK, and carries a considerable amount of sports information from organizations like The Sports Council and the National Coaching Foundation. The Sports Council currently provide over 3000 free pages of participation and facilities information. However, a decline in usage has meant that some services are not as extensive as they were. The sports results service is one example of this. The Minitel service in France has proved more popular and carries some sports information.

The services provided by television companies, Oracle and Ceefax, provide a results service, but this only extends to the major competitions, and tends to exclude minority sports.

Local viewdata services are also becoming more usual, one well-developed service being the Berkshire Viewdata Service. This provides community information on local government, education, health and welfare services, events and sport, etc. More local authorities are following this example. Another company providing user access to sports information is Online Leisure. It provides a number of the London boroughs, and Regional Sports Councils in the South East, with comprehensive information about tourist attractions, sports, arts and entertainment, special events and countryside activities. The system can be accessed in offices or at strategic information points. Finally, mention should be made of Campus 2000, a service for education formed by the merger of TTNS (The Times Network System) and Prestel Educational, and hosted by Dialcom. It provides information and communications to schools, colleges and various education support institutions. Access to the system is on a subscription basis and almost two-thirds of the education market subscribe to Campus 2000. It is attempting to appeal to the physical educationalists by providing a database of physical education, which includes sport, leisure activities, dance, gymnastics, athletics, health hygiene and nutrition but has had limited success in this area.

CHAPTER TWO

Statistical sources

W.H. MARTIN AND S. MASON

Introduction

The aim of this chapter is to provide a critical overview of the available sources of statistics on sport and leisure. This is not an easy task. Not only is sport and leisure a wide-ranging area, lacking in agreed definitions, there are also many ways in which the features of sport and leisure can be quantified and a plethora of different people and organizations that compile relevant statistical data.

Before plunging into a search of the available statistics, any student or researcher in this area needs to be very clear about what he or she is seeking. This introductory section looks more closely at the topics covered by the available statistics, and some of the more general secondary sources of data. The principal sources are then discussed in more detail under four main topic areas:

- People and activities
- Time use
- Markets and spending
- Specific sectors and industries

The wide range of topics covered under the heading of sport and leisure, and the differing national approaches to the gathering of statistical data, means that it is not possible to cover all the potential data sources on a comprehensive basis. Instead, the main types of statistical data generally available on particular topics are set out, with illustrations of important publications in each case. The intention is to provide the researcher with pointers for his or her own, more detailed, investigation. Special attention is paid to international sources and to the material available in the UK, France, Germany, the Netherlands and the USA. North American statistics are also covered in Chapter 15.

Area covered

Lack of an agreed definition for sport and leisure means that the first question to be asked when looking at any source of statistical data is, what do the figures cover? This chapter takes a broad view of the area, defining leisure to encompass not just sport and recreation, but also all the other activities that people do, by free choice, in their free time.

Such a broad view is the one taken in most of the general analyses of sport and leisure, for example in major participation surveys like the UK *General household survey* (OPCS, annual) or time budget surveys (e.g. Szalai, 1972). But much leisure data covers a narrower area. The focus is often only on leisure in or outside the home; these categories are generally defined to include some or all of the following activities:

- *Leisure at home:* reading; TV and video viewing; listening to radio, records etc.; DIY and gardening; hobbies and pastimes; relaxing and doing nothing.
- *Leisure at home or away:* casual socializing with family and friends; drinking alcohol; voluntary service.
- *Leisure away from home:* sport and active recreation; formal entertainment; visits and sightseeing; eating out; gambling; holidays and travel.

Sometimes coverage is even more limited, with data relating to one sector within these broad groupings such as sport and recreation, or visits and sightseeing.

The second key question to be asked about data sources is, what aspect of sport and leisure is measured? Is it the numbers and types of *people who take part*, the *time used* on the activities, the *money spent* on the goods and services used, features of the *suppliers* of these goods and services, or the *space or facilities* used as a location for the activities?

Generally speaking, each of these five aspects is covered by a different set of primary sources, for example, participation surveys for the people who take part, expenditure surveys for the money spent. It is mainly the more wide-ranging secondary sources which view the topic on a broader basis.

General secondary sources

Secondary sources, which bring together a variety of data from different origins, are a very valuable starting point for anyone coming new to statistics on sport and leisure. Of particular use are the various compilations of social indicators. These are available at the international level in, for example, *Living conditions in OECD countries* (OECD, 1986), as well as for many individual countries; for example, *Social trends* in the UK (CSO, annual (a)), *Données sociales* in France (INSEE, 1984), *Social indicators* in the USA (Department of Commerce, 1980). All of these reports have sections which cover Leisure and recreation in varying degrees of depth and detail. In *OECD* (1986) it is chapter IV on 'Time and leisure', while, in the 1989 *Social trends*, chapter 10 entitled 'Leisure', has sub-headings as follows: 'Availability of leisure time'. 'Social and cultural activities', 'Holidays', 'Resources'. Tables 2.1(a) and (b) give examples of the type of material included.

TABLE 2.1(a). Extract from UK Social Trends.
Participation[1] in selected social and cultural activities: by sex and age, 1986.

	Males					Females				
	16-19	20-29	30-59	60 or over	All aged 16 or over	16-19	20-29	30-59	60 or over	All aged 16 or over
Percentage in each age group engaging in each activity in the 4 weeks before interview										
Open air outings										
Seaside	4	6	8	4	6	9	9	9	5	8
Country	1	2	3	3	3	2	3	3	3	3
Parks	3	3	4	2	3	4	6	5	2	4
Entertainment, social, and cultural activities										
Going to the cinema	24	16	6	1	8	28	16	7	1	8
Visting historic buildings	6	9	11	7	9	8	11	11	7	10
Going to the theatre/opera/ballet	2	5	5	3	4	4	7	8	4	6
Going to museums/art galleries	3	5	4	3	4	2	5	4	2	4
Amateur music/drama	6	5	4	3	4	7	3	3	2	3
Going to fairs/amusement arcades	4	4	5	2	4	7	6	6	2	5
Going out for a meal[2]	41	56	50	35	47	50	57	51	35	47
Going out for a drink[2]	71	87	68	41	65	72	73	52	18	47
Dancing	19	13	9	5	9	32	18	11	5	12
Home-based activities										
Listening to records/tapes[2]	96	88	71	42	69	96	88	70	35	65
Gardening[2]	19	30	54	56	47	9	28	47	39	39
Needlework/knitting[2]	4	3	3	3	3	28	43	54	46	48
House repairs/DIY[2]	29	52	64	41	54	15	33	34	15	27
Reading books[2]	46	50	53	52	52	68	64	65	62	64
Sample size (=100%) (numbers)	704	1611	4409	2167	8891	674	1841	4755	3048	10318

[1]. Annual averages of particpation of people aged 16 or over.
[2]. The high participation levels are partly attributable to the fact that these items were prompted.
Source: General household survey, 1986.
Reproduced with permission from Central Statistics Office, Annual (a).

TABLE 2.1(b). Extract from UK Social Trends
Television and radio: average viewing and listening per week, by age

	Television (hours:minutes per week)				Radio listening (hours:minutes per week)			
	1984	1985	1986	1987	1984	1985	1986	1987
Age groups								
4-15	16:10	19:59	20:35	19:14	2:46	2:24	2:12	2:07
16-34	18:16	21:36	21:10	20:03	11:42	11:42	11:24	11:18
35-64	23:24	28:04	27:49	27:25	9:59	9:43	9:56	10:16
65 +	29:50	36:35	36:55	37:41	8:01	8:04	8:27	8:44
Reach[1]								
Daily	74%	79%	78%	76%	46%	43%	43%	43%
Weekly	90%	94%	94%	93%	81%	78%	75%	74%

[1]. Percentage of UK population aged 4+ who viewed television for at least three consecutive minutes or listened to radio for at least half s programme over a day (averaged over 7 days) or a week.
Source: Broadcasting Audience Research Board; British Broadcasting Corporation; Audits of Great Britain
Reproduced with permission from Central Statistical Office, Annual (a).

A glance at any of these publications shows the diversity of information sources used to quantify leisure patterns and trends. Data from official surveys and national accounts is mixed in with material from academic studies and individual leisure industries like broadcasting, records, the cinema or football clubs. The results of one-off surveys of participation or consumer attitudes are included, along with regular time series on spending or working hours. Most of the material is culled from other published sources. But, from time to time, data from unpublished surveys are included.

In no way do these compendia of social statistics give a comprehensive view of sport and leisure. This is not the fault of the compilers, but rather a fair reflection of the fragmentary nature of the available statistics and the complexity of the subject area. The publications also illustrate clearly another feature of sport and leisure statistics, namely the need to extract relevant material from more general statistical sources not compiled with leisure in mind. National accounts and statistics on working time are two obvious examples. Subsequent sections return to some of the problems of interpretation that this produces.

Other general sources of statistics that frequently contain some leisure data are the national statistical year books or their equivalent, such as the *Annual abstract of statistics* in the UK (CSO, annual (b)), and the *Statistisch zakboek* in the Netherlands (CBS, annual (a)). These do not always have a specific leisure or recreation section; the U.S. publication (Department of Commerce, annual (a)) is a notable exception, with an excellent section on 'Parks, recreation and travel', which ranges rather more widely than the title suggests. Frequently, however, it is necessary to plough through material on employment and working patterns, consumption expenditures and industrial production to locate the items of interest to the sport and leisure researcher. Differences in national priorities show up both in the nature of the material available and the way in which it is presented.

In addition to these more or less regular official statistical publications, there are many books, reports and journal articles which contain useful summary statistics on sport and leisure. These originate from both the academic and the commercial world. Commercial sources are dealt with in more detail on p.40 under Markets and spending. The academic material (and some commercial reports) can be surveyed using one of the abstracting services, notably the specialist *Leisure, Recreation and Tourism Abstracts (LRTA)* (CAB, quarterly).

LRTA is a wide-ranging international database, available both in the form of a quarterly journal of abstracts (with subject, author and geographical indexes) and as an on-line service via Dialog and a number of other host systems. Unlike some of the market research guides discussed on p.44 *LRTA* has no special emphasis on statistical data. But it can be helpful in searching out one-off studies which are more difficult to locate. An associated French-language abstracting service is provided in the *LORETO* (Loisir, Récréation, Tourisme) review by the Brussels-based Centre de Documentation sur le Loisir, la Récréation et le Tourisme. See Chapter 10 for more information on *LRTA* and *LORETO*.

People and activities

One of the questions most commonly asked about sport and leisure is, who does what in their free time? Which are the most popular forms of sport and leisure, how many people take part in specific activities and how does the profile of participants differ from activity to activity?

The principal sources of these types of statistics are participation surveys. Such surveys come in all shapes and sizes, with widely differing degrees of coverage and reliability.

The most comprehensive, and generally the most reliable, participation data come from national surveys. In some countries, such surveys are made by official or semi-official bodies; they include the *General household survey (GHS)* (OPCS, annual), and the *National countryside recreation survey* (Countryside Commission, 1985) in the UK, and the *National outdoor recreational survey* in the USA (Department of the Interior, 1978).

In the Netherlands, the *Public services survey (Aanvullend voorzieningen onderzoek, AVO)* provides information on a broad range of leisure activities; the results are published by the Dutch Central Statistical Bureau in their *Sociaal-Cultureel Bericht* (CBS, monthly – previously quarterly).

The advantages of major official surveys, like the *GHS* or the *AVO* as data sources are two-fold. First, they are based on large samples, 19 209 adults in the case of the 1987 *GHS* (the latest published report with questions on leisure), 16 151 people aged 6 and over for the 1987 *AVO*. This greatly enhances the reliability of the survey results. Second, they are repeated from time to time, every three years in the case of the *GHS* between 1977 and 1986. It is possible therefore to use the results to make some analysis of the changes in leisure patterns over time.

Fairly regular information on leisure participation is also produced by a variety of commercial market research organizations (see p.44). These investigations are usually based on much smaller samples than the official surveys, normally under 5000 people. A notable exception is the data provided by the British Market Research Bureau in their *Target Group Index* (BMRB, annual) which is currently based on a 24 000 sample; this information, like many other commercial survey reports, is costly to obtain. Otherwise the researcher has to make use of one or more of the many *ad hoc* surveys covering leisure activities, produced at varying times by official bodies, commercial and trade organizations, and academic researchers.

The best guide to the most recent participation surveys in each country is gained from an examination of the general secondary sources already discussed. In addition to those mentioned, there are occasional summary reports from leisure research institutes like the BAT Freizeit-Forschungsinstitut in Germany (H.W. Opaschowski, ed., 1982). Earlier studies in the UK (mostly now of historical interest only), are documented in two useful bibliographies, by Veal (1981) and Brodie (1982). Regular journals, like *Leisure Studies, Loisirs et Société* and the *Journal of Leisure Research* contain the results of a variety of academic studies of participation. These are often of highly specific interest, but many of the surveys are based on relatively small samples.

Apart from the question of sample size, participation surveys present the user with a number of other problems. The coverage and categorization of leisure activities is rarely identical in different surveys. Even more of a problem, the basic question about leisure participation is seldom the same. Sometimes, as in the UK *General household survey*, people are asked 'What have you done in your leisure time in the previous four weeks?' In other cases, the question is a much more general one, for example 'What are your principal leisure interests nowadays?'

The numbers of people identified as taking part in individual leisure activities can be widely different depending on the specific question asked. A classic example relates to the numbers taking part in angling in the UK; the *National angling survey* estimated that 8% of the population had 'been angling in 1979' compared with a 3% figure in the 1980 *GHS*, based on a much narrower definition of participation (Duffield *et al.*, 1983). The lack of commonly agreed definitions, of both the limits of leisure activities and the nature of participation, make many of the surveys that are carried out less useful to the researcher than they might otherwise be.

Time use

Leisure activities are frequently defined in relation to a period of time. As discussed by Parker (1983), 'free time, spare time, uncommitted time, discretionary time, choosing time. All ... describe some aspect of what is meant by leisure'. Yet good statistical data on the time dimension of sport and leisure are surprisingly hard to find.

The problem starts with the measurement of free time itself. Because this is a residual concept (the time free from paid work, eating, sleeping and other essential activities), the amount of free time is seldom measured directly. Instead, the information is obtained either from more general time budget surveys or by means of calculations using indicators of working hours and holidays.

Time budgets

Time budget surveys provide data on how time is used through the day by a sample of people; respondents usually complete a diary or other record of their activities over a continuous period of 24 hours. An example of the output from a time budget enquiry is given in Table 2.2. Since the surveys normally need to cover every day of the week to give a reasonably representative picture of time use, they are costly to carry out. As a result, comprehensive time budget data are only available intermittently and, in some countries, the material may be well out of date.

The most extensive set of international time budget information is that reported in Szalai (1972). This covered a series of national surveys, carried out in the 1960s, which were compared and contrasted by a team of researchers. The material provides a fascinating insight into national differences in behaviour regarding sport and leisure, and the relationship of these activities to other aspects of people's lives at a particular point in time, but is now largely of historic interest.

A more up-to-date, but much less extensive, compilation of time

Table 2.2. Example of time budget survey results. The people's activities and use of time

Summer
Mondays-Fridays

Average time in hours spent in main activities
per day (5.00 a.m. to 2.00 a.m.)
by population and subgroups

(the sub-totals are summations of the rounded-off figures above them)   (A dash indicates <0.05 hours)

		M* F-T	F* F-T	F* Pt-T	*Hsewvs	Retired	A	B	C	Sct.*	Wls*.	Lnd*	S&W*&SW	Mds*&EA	N&NE	NW
	(N) =	560	221	134	295	98	109	507	1170	205	165	339	251	312	305	244
		Employment					Social class			BBC region						
1	Listening	0.1	0.1	0.1	0.1	0.4	0.1	0.1	0.1	0.1	0.1	0.2	0.1	0.1	0.1	0.1
2	Viewing	1.6	1.2	1.9	2.1	3.0	1.3	1.7	1.9	2.0	2.0	1.8	1.7	1.8	2.0	1.9
3	Reading	0.3	0.2	0.2	0.3	0.9	0.4	0.3	0.2	0.3	0.2	0.3	0.2	0.3	0.2	0.3
4	Pastimes, Hobbies, etc.	0.1	0.1	0.1	0.2	0.2	0.3	0.2	0.1	0.2	0.1	0.2	0.2	0.2	0.1	0.2
5	Play/Study	-	-	-	-	-	0.4	0.2	0.2	0.1	0.3	0.2	0.2	0.1	0.2	0.1
6	Knitting/Sewing	-	0.2	0.1	0.2	0.1	0.1	0.1	0.1	0.1	0.1	0.1	0.1	0.1	-	0.1
7	Entertaining	0.1	0.1	0.3	0.3	0.3	0.2	0.2	0.1	0.2	0.1	0.2	0.2	0.1	0.1	0.1
8	Conversation	0.1	0.2	0.3	0.2	0.2	0.2	0.2	0.1	0.2	0.2	0.2	0.2	0.2	0.1	0.2
9	Listening to Music	-	-	-	-	-	-	-	0.1	-	-	0.1	-	-	0.1	-
10	Relaxing	0.5	0.4	0.6	0.8	1.1	0.5	0.5	0.5	0.5	0.6	0.5	0.6	0.5	0.5	0.5
11	Gardening	0.2	0.1	0.1	0.1	0.6	0.2	0.2	0.1	0.1	0.1	0.2	0.2	0.2	0.1	0.1
12	Taking a Nap	-	-	-	-	0.2	-	-	-	-	-	-	-	-	0.1	-
	Total leisure at home	3.1	2.6	3.7	4.3	7.0	3.7	3.7	3.5	3.8	3.8	4.0	3.7	3.6	3.6	3.6
13	Visiting	0.4	0.5	0.5	0.7	0.4	0.3	0.5	0.6	0.6	0.5	0.5	0.5	0.5	0.6	0.6
14	Cinema/Dancing etc.	0.1	0.2	0.1	0.1	0.1	0.2	0.1	0.1	0.1	0.1	0.1	0.1	0.1	0.1	0.1
15	Club	0.2	0.1	0.2	0.1	0.2	0.1	0.1	0.1	0.1	0.1	0.1	0.1	0.1	0.2	0.1
16	Pub	0.2	0.1	-	0.1	-	0.1	0.1	0.1	0.1	0.1	0.1	0.1	0.1	0.2	0.1
17	Church	-	-	-	-	-	-	-	-	-	-	-	-	-	-	-
18	Playing/Classes	-	0.2	-	-	-	0.2	0.2	0.4	0.2	0.4	0.2	0.2	0.3	0.5	0.3
19	Other Indoor	0.2	0.3	0.3	0.2	0.3	0.1	0.3	0.2	0.2	0.4	0.2	0.2	0.2	0.3	0.2
20	Playing Sport	0.1	-	-	-	0.1	0.1	0.1	0.1	0.2	0.1	0.1	0.1	0.2	0.1	0.1
21	Watching Sport	-	-	-	-	-	-	-	-	-	-	-	-	-	-	-
22	Walks	0.1	0.1	0.1	0.1	0.2	0.1	0.1	0.1	0.1	0.1	0.1	0.2	0.1	0.1	0.1
23	Excursion etc.	0.1	0.2	0.2	0.1	0.2	0.4	0.2	0.2	0.1	0.3	0.2	0.3	0.2	0.2	0.2
24	Leisure Travel	0.3	0.3	0.2	0.3	0.4	0.3	0.3	0.3	0.3	0.2	0.2	0.3	0.2	0.4	0.3
	Total leisure not at home	1.6	2.0	1.6	1.7	1.9	1.9	2.0	2.2	2.0	2.3	1.8	2.1	2.0	2.7	2.1
25	At Work	7.0	5.9	2.7	0.1	0.1	2.9	3.0	3.0	3.2	2.5	3.1	2.8	3.4	2.7	3.1
26	At School/College	-	-	-	-	-	0.4	0.6	0.7	0.7	0.8	0.5	0.8	0.7	0.8	0.5
27	Work at home	0.1	-	0.1	-	-	0.2	0.1	-	-	0.1	0.1	0.1	0.1	-	0.1
28	Second Job	-	-	-	-	-	-	-	0.1	-	-	-	0.1	-	0.1	-
29	Work/School Travel	0.8	0.8	0.4	-	-	0.4	0.5	0.4	0.5	0.3	0.5	0.4	0.5	0.4	0.4
	Total work/school	7.9	6.7	3.2	0.1	0.1	3.9	4.2	4.2	4.4	3.7	4.2	4.2	4.7	4.0	4.1
30	Child Care	0.1	0.1	0.2	0.7	0.1	0.2	0.2	0.3	0.2	0.2	0.2	0.2	0.1	0.2	0.2
31	Housework	0.2	1.6	3.4	4.5	1.8	1.5	1.5	1.6	1.6	1.5	1.6	1.6	1.4	1.2	1.9
32	Odd Jobs (in home)	0.5	0.2	0.2	0.3	0.7	0.4	0.4	0.3	0.2	0.4	0.3	0.3	0.4	0.3	0.3
33	Shopping, etc.	0.2	0.4	0.7	0.9	0.7	0.5	0.5	0.4	0.4	0.4	0.5	0.5	0.4	0.4	0.5
34	Domestic Travel	0.1	0.1	0.2	0.3	0.1	0.2	0.1	0.4	0.1	0.1	0.1	0.1	0.1	0.1	0.1
	Total domestic work	1.1	2.4	4.7	6.7	3.4	2.8	2.7	3.0	2.5	2.6	2.7	2.7	2.4	2.2	3.0
35	Getting Up/Going to bed	0.7	0.8	0.8	0.7	0.8	0.8	0.8	0.8	0.8	0.8	0.9	0.8	0.8	0.7	0.7
36	Personal care (at home)	0.3	0.4	0.3	0.3	0.2	0.2	0.3	0.3	0.3	0.3	0.3	0.3	0.3	0.3	0.3
37	Meals/Snacks	1.4	1.4	1.4	1.6	1.9	1.6	1.6	1.4	1.5	1.4	1.5	1.5	1.5	1.4	1.4
38	Other Personal	-	0.1	0.1	0.1	0.1	0.1	0.1	0.1	0.1	-	-	0.1	0.1	-	0.1
	Total personal	2.4	2.7	2.6	2.7	3.0	2.7	2.8	2.6	2.7	2.5	2.7	2.7	2.7	2.4	2.5
39	In Bed	4.8	4.9	5.0	5.4	5.4	5.7	5.6	5.5	5.4	5.8	5.5	5.6	5.6	5.7	5.4
40	No information	0.1	0.1	0.1	0.3	0.5	0.2	0.1	0.2	0.2	0.2	0.2	0.1	0.1	0.2	0.2

*M. F-T = males full time; F. F-T = females full time; F. Pt-T = females part-time; Hse-wvs. = housewives; Sct = Scotland; Wls = Wales'
Ldn. = London; S&W&SW = South and West and Southwest; Mds. & EA = Midlands and east Anglia; N&NE = North and North East; NW = North West.

Source: Reproduced with permission from British Broadcasting Corporation, 1984.

budget figures is contained in the OECD's *Compendium of social indicators* (OECD, 1986). It is indicative of the gaps in such information that data are given for only 10 of the 24 OECD member countries and the survey results included in the 1986 publication relate to as far back as 1971/72.

In quite a number of countries, time budget surveys are carried out from time to time by official or semi-official bodies. They include those by the Social and Cultural Planning Bureau in the Netherlands (reported in SCPB, biennial, as well as by CBS, monthly), the Institut National de la Statistique in France (reported in INSEE, 1984), and the Central Bureau of Statistics in Norway (SSB, 1983). But, in countries like the USA and Germany, there is more emphasis on data derived from academic and/or commercial sources (see for example, Department of Commerce, 1980, H.W. Opaschowski, ed., 1982).

In the UK, the most comprehensive time budget data comes from the British Broadcasting Corporation in three studies carried out at roughly 10-yearly intervals (BBC, 1965, 1978, 1984). More recently, the Henley Centre for Forecasting has produced some survey material on leisure time and its use; this is quoted in summary in the latest *Social trends* (CSO, annual (a)) and more extensively in the Centre's *Leisure futures* reports (Henley Centre, quarterly).

The leisure elements of the first two BBC surveys have been examined by Gershuny and Thomas (1980). These two earlier surveys were particularly useful in that the data were in a form enabling analyses to be made of the total amount and use of leisure time, the rate of participation in different activities and the significance of primary and secondary types of leisure (e.g. reading while listening to the radio). However, a change in survey procedure for the 1984 report means that the distinction between primary and secondary activities is no longer made, with the consequence that the material is now less generally useful as a basis for analysis.

Trends in leisure time

The value of time budget data is that they usually provide an indication of both the amount of leisure time and the way this is divided between different activities, with an analysis of how patterns differ between people of different ages, social groups, etc. More limited information on overall trends in the amount of leisure time can also be gained from data on working hours, holidays and other employment statistics. Given the intermittent availability of time budget surveys, this is often the only way of examining how leisure time has changed over a period of years.

Basic statistics on weekly working hours are widely available in international and national publications such as the International Labour

Office's *Year book of labour statistics* (ILO, annual), Eurostat's reports on their *Labour force sample surveys* (e.g. Eurostat, 1989), and in the UK, the Department of Employment's monthly publication, *Employment Gazette*. Data on paid holidays can be more difficult to obtain since they are often based on special surveys, for example, in the UK, the *New earnings survey* which covers working hours on an annual basis but holidays only every few years (Department of Employment, annual). One-off summaries of international data are produced from time to time, as for example in the European Commission's *Social Europe* (1986). Long-term trends in annual and lifetime working hours in the UK have been documented by the Technical Change Centre (1984).

A number of sources, mainly commercial organizations, use these data on working hours to calculate trends in leisure time measured in different ways. They include the groups producing special leisure reports discussed in the next section, notably Leisure Consultants and the Henley Centre for Forecasting.

Markets and spending

The money dimension of sport and leisure is nowadays in many respects the best documented. As the markets for sport and leisure goods and services have grown, an increasing volume of statistical data on these areas of spending has become available. But once again the problem of definitions raises its ugly head. In addition to the question of the coverage in different sources of particular types of leisure, there is a further aspect, namely whose spending is being measured? Do the data relate to outlays by private consumers alone, by all purchasers including businesses and government bodies or by just one of these institutional categories?

Those researching into spending on sport and leisure have the choice of two main sets of data. There are the official statistics on spending by various economic sectors, published in national accounts, reports on family expenditure surveys and other, mostly regular, series. There is also a variety of commercial research, reports and services covering various aspects of leisure and leisure markets. Each of these data sets warrants more detailed examination.

Official sources and data

Every country produces a set of national accounts of some kind; these are published at least annually, as for example in the CSO *Blue book* in the UK (CSO, annual (c)). The precise format and degree of detail vary

TABLE 2.3. Example of leisure items in national accounts Consumers' expenditure (£million) at current market prices: classified by function

		1978	1979	1980	1981	1982	1983	1984	1985	1986	1987	1988
Transport and communication:												
Cars, motorcycles and other vehicles	CCDT	4 811	6 493	6510	6557	7407	9105	9004	9989	11 604	13 776	17 437
Petrol and oil	CDDY	2610	3554	4646	5695	6331	6913	7450	7972	7327	7721	8038
Vehicle excise duty	CDDZ	590	601	726	840	1022	1184	4289	1482	1566	1612	1672
Other running costs of vehicles	CDEA	2730	3193	3797	4195	4439	4831	4942	5444	6058	6817	7615
Rail travel	CDEB	773	884	1063	1123	1093	1287	1348	1474	1618	1770	1988
Buses and coaches	CDEC	1154	1282	1492	1572	1697	1789	1833	1971	1952	2047	2178
Air travel	CDED	1026	1337	1818	2060	2323	2496	2688	2784	3179	3692	4044
Other travel	CDEE	448	572	727	814	798	939	1041	1185	1333	1572	1776
Postal services	CDEF	224	240	309	379	423	467	485	494	535	553	567
Telecommunications	CDEG	1246	1448	1938	2413	2678	2846	3108	3495	3983	4465	5083
Total	CDEH	15 612	19 604	23 026	25 648	28 211	31 859	33 188	36 290	39 155	44 025	50 398
Recreation, entertainment and education:												
Radio, television and other durable goods	CDEI	1312	1552	1590	1769	2061	2477	2752	2755	3203	3410	3638
Television and video hire charges, license fees and repairs	CDEJ	1183	1351	1578	1692	1951	2034	2113	2327	2441	2578	2775
Sports goods, toys, games and camping equipment	CDEK	888	1124	1273	1339	1454	1638	1801	1944	2274	2564	2760
Other recreational goods	CDEL	1699	2069	2471	2443	2656	2802	3071	3427	3786	4197	4741
Betting and gaming	CDEM	1131	1283	1520	1626	1776	1842	1972	2117	2257	2439	2613
Other recreational entertainment and services	CDEN	1093	1291	1529	1778	1761	1907	2082	2360	2735	3161	3707
Books	CDEO	315	367	458	529	556	620	665	708	810	922	984
Newspapers and Magazines	CDEP	990	1108	1332	1686	1907	1967	2096	2347	2442	2621	2753
Education	CDEQ	783	883	1135	1337	1442	1432	1510	1623	1763	1931	2125
Total	CDER	9394	11 028	12 886	14 199	15 564	16 719	18 062	19 608	21 711	23 823	26 096

Other goods and services:												
Pharmaceutical products and medical equipment	CDES	403	502	615	689	787	930	1123	1213	1258	1311	1417
National health service payments and other medical expenses	CDET	430	509	676	857	1055	1214	1236	1414	1590	1842	2147
Toilet articles; perfumery	CDEU	1006	1209	1387	1567	1803	1979	2250	2663	2882	3136	3577
Hairdressing and beauty care	CDEV	557	668	793	860	910	1022	1129	1310	1439	1580	1744
Jewellery, silverware watches and clocks	CDEW	828	1019	1083	1094	1169	1281	1413	1433	1633	1924	2299
Other goods	CDEX	883	1058	1273	1300	1458	1610	1787	1858	2191	2481	2852
Catering (meals and accommodation)	CDEY	5840	6874	8288	8820	9461	10936	12491	13831	16031	18545	23557
Administrative costs of life assurance and pension schemes	CDEZ	1227	1497	1778	2092	2475	2935	3393	3765	4438	5134	5939
Other services	CDFA	1334	1557	1841	2088	2516	3070	3538	4275	5493	7005	7316
Total	CDFB	12 508	14 893	17 734	19 367	21 634	24 977	28 360	31 762	36 955	42 958	50484
Total household and tourist expenditure in the United Kingdom	CDFC	100 190	118 419	137 015	151 813	166 431	182 540	195 279	213 420	233 746	255 335	283 991
Less expenditure by foreign tourist, etc. in the United Kingdom	CDFD	-2891	-3207	-3436	-3513	-3792	-4661	-5344	-6282	-6456	-7212	-7065
Household expenditure abroad	CDFE	1592	2079	2648	3131	3483	3855	4275	4540	5651	6689	7542
Total household expenditure on goods and services	CDFF	98 891	117 291	136 227	151 431	166 122	181 734	194 210	211 678	232 941	254 812	284468
Final expenditure by private non-profit making bodies	CDFG	1956	2255	2789	3270	3694	4161	4685	5345	6215	6886	7601
National accounts statistical adjustment	CARR	-	-	-	-	-	-	-	-	-	-	1500
Total consumers' expenditure	AIIK	100 847	119 516	139 016	154 701	169 816	185 895	198 895	217 023	239 156	261 698	293 569

Source: Reproduced with permission from Central Statistical Office, annual (c).

from country to country. Similar data are available on a broadly consistent basis in a number of international publications; of greatest use to the
sport and leisure analyst are those prepared by the OECD (annual) and
the Eurostat (annual).

The particular advantages of national accounts data on sport and
leisure spending are three-fold: the coverage of spending is, in principle,
comprehensive; the figures on different markets are adjusted on to a
comparable basis; and they are published very regularly, in some cases
quarterly.

As well as these advantages, there are also two disadvantages. First,
the degree of detail given of different types of leisure spending can be
limited. This is notably true of the international reports which in terms
of consumer spending generally confine themselves to a few broad
headings. For example, in the Eurostat figures, the leisure-related
headings are: 'Recreation and entertainment equipment and
accessories'; 'Entertainment, recreational and cultural services';
'Books, newspapers and magazines'; 'Expenditure in restaurants, cafes
and hotels'; 'Alcoholic beverages'. A further classification of packaged
tours is seldom separately identified in the actual figures.

Second, even in the national reports where more details of consumer
spending are given, leisure spending items are often not brought all
together in one category. Broad leisure groupings are now more
commonly used, generally under a heading like recreation and
entertainment, but major items like catering, alcoholic drink and travel
are usually not included. The distinction made in the *UK national
accounts* is illustrated in Table 2.3. Some types of leisure spending,
notably on do-it-yourself and gardening may be almost impossible to
identify from national accounts data alone; the same is usually true for
spending in specific sectors within recreation and entertainment, like
sports goods and services, which are aggregated with other items.

A much more detailed analysis of consumer spending on leisure is
given in the national family (or household) expenditure surveys that are
produced in most countries; examples are the *Family expenditure survey*
reports (CSO — formerly Department of Employment, annual (d)) produced each year in the UK and *Einkommens- und Verbrauchsstichprobe*
published less frequently by the German Federal Statistics Office (Statistisches Bundesamt, irregular). These surveys usually provide useful
breakdowns of spending patterns by household type and region. But, as
with national accounts, the leisure items may not all be brought together
under one heading. Care is also needed when using the figures for categories where spending may be underreported; alcoholic drink and
gambling are notorious in this regard.

Researchers seeking information on government or industrial
spending on sport and leisure generally face a more difficult task. The

national accounts data may, as in the UK, provide some broad classification of spending under these headings. For further details, it is necessary to look either to sources covering the sector being researched or to more specific analyses of the organizations of interest. For example, in the UK, the Chartered Institute of Public Finance and Accountancy provides detailed surveys of spending on sport and leisure by local government authorities (CIPFA, annual). Their figures cover expenditure and income of individual authorities for the operation of different types of leisure services. Much of the material is based on authorities' estimates for the year ahead rather than actual spending. CIPFA remains the only comprehensive source of statistics in the UK on local government leisure interests; the Institute also provides regular figures on the charges for, and usage of, leisure facilities.

In the Netherlands, there are also regular surveys of outlays on public sector leisure provision (published by CBS, monthly). However detailed analyses of topics like capital investment in leisure sectors are extremely hard to find; one of the few examples is research by the Centre for Construction Market Information which formed the basis for a one-off UK report on this topic (*Interbuild87*, 1987).

Depending on the nature of the sport and leisure enquiry, relevant market figures may be found in a variety of other official statistical sources, such as: publications covering retail sales; censuses of retailers, production and distribution; regular series on manufacturers' output; overseas trade statistics. In the UK, the available material is generally published in the *Business monitor* series and the *Overseas trade statistics*. Guides to what can be found in official statistical publications exist in most major countries; an example is CSO (1989). Harvey (1987) provides a good overview of European data.

Some words of caution are required for the leisure analyst who is new to these more general statistics. In particular, things are not always what they seem and all the explanatory notes should be read with care. Very few of the classifications used are designed with the needs of the leisure researcher in mind; most categories are supply- rather than demand-related in origin. Definitions of individual items can vary, not only from country to country, but also from series to series, for example as between production and overseas trade statistics. Allowance for imports and exports, and stock changes, can make a major difference to the market trend shown by supply-oriented figures; manufacturers' sales figures alone can be extremely misleading, unless of course it is the position of domestic suppliers that is the area of research interest.

Commercial reports and services

Commercial sources of data on sport and leisure include a wide variety of reports and on-line services, generally provided by private sector information companies. These data are usually sold on a full-cost basis to business and government users of statistics. They are mostly expensive to obtain compared with data from official or academic sources, though occasionally reports are issued at low or nil costs for public relations or teaching purposes.

Most of this commercial research is directed towards providing data on market sizes and levels of spending, particularly that by consumers. It is worth noting that many reports also cover other aspects of leisure; in addition to the dimensions of participation and time use discussed earlier, there may be data on, for example, major suppliers and facilities, or advertising outlays.

Most commercial market research reports combine some original survey material or other new statistical data, with the analysis and interpretation of data from the types of sources considered above. There is usually some presentation of recent trends and, increasingly, an element of quantified forecasts.

The forecasting content is one feature that distinguishes much commercial market research from official or academic sources of sport and leisure statistics. Forecast material is particularly important in the data produced by some of the specialist leisure researchers, such as Leisure Consultants' *Leisure forecasts* (Leisure Consultants, annual) and the studies of the Institut für Freizeitwirtschaft on the western part of Germany (IFF, 1987). Other commercial researchers in the UK with a strong emphasis on leisure topics include: the Henley Centre for Forecasting with their quarterly *Leisure futures* report; Mintel, with the quarterly *Leisure intelligence;* and Euromonitor and KeyNote Publications with a variety of one-off studies; the last are listed in the market research guides discussed below. Business Trends Analysts and Marketdata Enterprises provide a number of leisure-related reports in the USA; EMNID-Institut and GFK do likewise in Germany (see H.W. Opaschowski, ed., 1982).

Much leisure-related market research is only available in the form of intermittent or one-off studies from these and other general commercial information suppliers. Trade journals for individual leisure sectors are a useful source of summary information on newly-published market research reports. Information on what is published can also be obtained from one of the many market research guides. These have an increasingly international coverage.

Among the more comprehensive guides, mainly covering English language reports, are the US-based *Findex* (Cambridge Information Group, annual) and *Off-the-Shelf* (bi-monthly), and the UK-based *Marketsearch* (Arlington Management Publications, annual) and *Marketing Surveys Index* (MSI, monthly). There are also other less regular guides, with more limited coverage, by organizations like KeyNote (Gofton, 1987) and Euromonitor (1987, 1988).

Such guides to published market research usually provide a brief description of the contents and coverage of individual reports, together with their cost and how they are to be obtained. A classified subject index is included, and a listing of report publishers. Table 2.4 provides an illustration of the representation in *Marketing Surveys Index*. None of the guides is comprehensive; they are dependent on the publishers who send data for inclusion, but they provide a valuable starting point.

All the guides are available in published form. *Findex* and *Marketsearch* have 'hot line' telephone numbers for the most recent information. *Marketing Surveys Index* is accessible on-line, through PROFILE INFORMATION, which is one of the major on-line hosts in the UK for individual market research reports, and for a variety of official statistics as well; the Henley Centre, Mintel and KeyNote Publications are all included. *Findex* is available on-line through a comparable U.S.-based service, Dialog, which has a wide coverage of other relevant data. Listings for these and other useful on-line statistical sources are given in the *On line business source book* (Foster and Foster, 1989) and in Gofton (1987). Another potential starting point is the *International directory of online databases* published by Cuadra Associates Inc. three times a year although this also includes much material of little relevance to the researcher primarily seeking leisure statistics.

Most market research reports contain some information on the supply aspects of the sport and leisure sectors that they cover. But there are a number of more specialist information providers who focus especially on corporate data, providing accounting and other financial statistics on companies operating in the leisure sector.

In some cases, the data are provided in the form of fairly regular reports; Jordans and Inter-company Comparisons provide this type of publication in the UK, Standard and Poors in the USA. Certain of these, and other organizations like Datastream and Telecom Gold provide on-line access to corporate data. The on-line guides cited above (Gofton, 1987; Foster and Foster, 1989) provide an introduction to what is available.

Specific sectors and industries

Many people looking for statistical data on sport and leisure are interested primarily in only one specific sector or market within this diverse area. For them, there may well be additional statistical sources of use, though the extent of such specific information varies greatly from sector to sector.

The general guides to official statistics and market research reports already mentioned cover some of the data on specific leisure sectors and industries. But there are additional statistics compiled within many industries, as well as from academic research. These and the other most important specific sources come under three broad headings:

● Sport and active recreation
● Culture, including the arts and the media
● Other sectors

Sport and active recreation

Sports researchers are generally well served in terms of data on adults taking part in different activities, but there is a lack of data on children's sport. The involvement of government bodies with sports provision means that most official surveys of leisure participation provide considerable detail on sporting activities. In addition, national sporting organizations and the governing bodies of individual sports are active, though to varying degrees, in the collection of data on participation, sports facilities and other topics. For more information on individual sports see also Chapter 8.

The UK Sports Councils have been especially energetic in this regard. Of particular value is the *Digest of sports statistics for the UK*, now in its second edition (Centre for Leisure Research, 1986), which provides an excellent introduction to the available data, and some of the problems of interpretation and inconsistencies. There are sections on all the main individual sports, which summarize figures on participation, club membership, market size and available facilities. The references provide a guide to further statistical information on individual sports including that produced by the relevant sports governing bodies; a more recent report of this kind is the *Digest of football statistics* (Football Trust, 1988).

The 1986 edition of the *Digest of sports statistics for the UK* also includes an article on sponsorship in sport, pulling together the information available at that date. Sportscan provides regular statistical analyses on this topic and the subject was also covered by market researchers Mintel in their *Sponsorship report* (Mintel, 1986). Sponsorship is also covered in Chapter 8.

The annual reports of the UK Sports Councils provide some data on public sector spending and grants for sports facilities and the current building programmes. Other reports emanating from these sources include a wide-ranging review of the *Economic importance of sport in the UK* commissioned from the Henley Centre (1986), as well as a long list of research reports and special studies (details from The Sports Council's Information Centre in London).

Few other national sports organizations have produced as extensive a range of sports statistics as is available in the UK. But in virtually all the major countries, there are statistics on the membership of sports organizations. An indication of the range of data and sources in Europe some years ago was given in Martin and Mason (1978); more up-to-date comparative data are available in various reports prepared as part of the Council of Europe's continuing review of sports development; some of this material is summarized in the Council's *Sports Information Bulletin* (Council of Europe, 4–5 times a year). Chapter 14, on Europe, provides additional information about Council of Europe publications.

It is important to recognize that much of the published data relates to organized sport and this covers only part of the involvement in sporting activities as a whole. Furthermore, many of the statistics on sports facilities include only those provided by the public sector, notably sports halls, swimming pools and outdoor pitches; in sports and countries where the private sector is an active provider, data on the available facilities are much more sparse.

The nature of national patterns of sports provision is reflected in the sources of statistical data. In the USA, where sports provision is largely in the private and voluntary sectors, extensive information on sports participation and sports markets is provided by the National Sporting Goods Association (NSGA, 1989). In contrast, in France, the official INSEE has carried out special surveys on sporting activities (INSEE, 1988) while, in the Netherlands, a variety of sports-related surveys are reported in the *Sociaal-Cultureel Bericht* (CBS, monthly).

The other sector of active recreation, which is generally well served in terms of specific statistics on participation and facilities, is countryside recreation. Most of the data derive from official or semi-official sources, reflecting again the involvement of the government with national parks, nature reserves and other countryside areas. Examples of the bodies involved with data collation and publication are the Countryside Commissions in the UK, the Department of the Interior and the National Park Service in the USA, and the State Forest Service in the Netherlands.

An aspect of sport and recreation that is not very well documented in statistical terms is levels of spending and market values. The main available data on consumer sports markets are those from commercial or special researchers. A report on the *UK sports market* by Leisure Consultants (1984) gives information on 25 individual sports markets, as well as a comprehensive overview of market trends. The National Sporting Goods Association (NSGA, 1989) covers the U.S. market in some detail; the Institut für Freizeitwirtschaft (IFF, 1987) does the same for Germany. However, these are among relatively few studies to provide any detail of spending breakdown and only highly aggregate figures for sports goods and sports services are published on a regular basis. A recent publication by the Sport and Recreation Information Group (SPRIG, 1990) provides a summary of *Market research sources in sport in the UK*. Other sources are covered by market research guides discussed earlier.

Culture

The heading of Culture includes data on the arts (live, visual, literary, etc.) as well as on newspaper reading and on other media such as broadcasting. Data on this sector of leisure are frequently collected together in specialized publications, a fact that reflects (as in the case of sport) the concern of government bodies with cultural activities and provision.

At the international level, there is a compendium of cultural statistics brought together by Unesco in its *Statistical yearbook* (Unesco, annual). This has sections covering 'Book publishing', 'Newspapers and periodicals', 'Radio and TV', and 'Cinemas and films'. Unesco is also a source of one-off reports and surveys on specific aspects of culture.

In a number of countries, the official statisticians compile regular or occasional reports on cultural topics. The French government has carried out detailed surveys of cultural participation, reported in full by the Ministère de la Culture (1982), and in summary by INSEE (1984). The Norwegian Central Bureau of Statistics has an annual publication *Cultural statistics* (SSB, annual), while in Italy, there is an official *Year book of cultural statistics* (ISTAT, annual); the journal, *Lo Spettacolo* summarizes international as well as Italian cultural data. The Dutch *Sociaal-Cultureel Bericht* (CBS, monthly) contains regular analyses of a variety of data on cultural participation and provision.

Elsewhere the most useful general publications on cultural statistics are from non-official sources. This includes the UK, where the excellent reports *Facts about the arts*, and the more recent quarterly *Cultural Trends*, come from an independent research group, the Policy Studies Institute (J. Myerscough, ed., 1986; A. Feist, and R. Hutchinson, eds., quarterly). The same group have also been responsible for a wide-ranging study on the *Economic importance of the arts in Britain* (Myerscough, 1988).

The government-supported Arts Council of Great Britain has been an important source of research data on audiences for the arts and other topics. In the USA, a variety of agencies, notably the National Endowment for the Arts, have funded similar specialist research studies.

The broadcasting authorities in most countries produce useful data on TV and radio viewing and listening audiences, and their characteristics, as well as on the amount and nature of broadcast output.

Such data are generally available in the form of an annual report or year book; in the UK, the available figures include the number of licence holders, the hours of output of sport and other programmes, and the average time spent viewing different channels (BBC, annual; IBA, annual) Further details about broadcasting statistics can be found in Chapter 8.

Various trade-based organizations compile data on their own particular area of interest; in the UK these include the Audit Bureau of Circulation (for newspapers and magazines), the British Videogram Association (for video cassettes), the British Phonographic Institute (for records and tapes) and the Cinema Advertising Association. This information is often summarized in the relevant trade press. A very useful publication, with an international coverage of such statistics as well as trade news, is the monthly, *Screen Digest* report. There is now a linked Screenfax service providing selective access to a computer database of the published material.

As with the sport and recreation sectors, the most inadequate aspect of the statistics on culture is that of consumer markets and spending. Some data are available in the general commercial leisure reports based mainly on aggregate figures from national accounts and family expenditure surveys (Leisure Consultants, annual; Henley Centre, quarterly). There is also *ad hoc* coverage in special studies like Myerscough (1988), and in market research reports by, for example, Mintel, Euromonitor and KeyNote Publications. Nevertheless, there is a lack both of detailed analysis and time series data in this area.

Other sectors

One important sector of leisure, which has purposely not been covered in detail in this book, is that of holidays and tourism. This is in fact a relatively well-documented area in statistical terms; much of the information comes from national and international tourism bodies and special official surveys. It is worth noting that tourism-related research can be a valuable source of data on specific leisure activities away from home. For example, the English Tourist Board produces regular data on visits to sightseeing attractions (BTA/ETB, annual) as well as occasional surveys on a wide range of holiday and day-trip activities (ETB, 1984; BTA/ETB, 1989). The Central Bureau of Statistics in the Netherlands also has regular surveys on day trips and holidays; the results are published in the *Sociaal-Cultureel Bericht* (CBS, monthly).

The remaining sources of statistical data on other leisure sectors and industries are very fragmented. In addition to looking for possible commercial reports and/or academic analyses, the researcher has two further possibilities. The first is that there may be highly-specific official sources of statistics, based on data gathered for administrative purposes. For example, in many countries activities like gambling and drinking alcohol, are closely monitored by government, and statistics are available on the numbers of establishments and on turnover or other bases for taxation. The existence of such figures is best sought via a *Guide to official statistics* or the general secondary sources described earlier.

The second potential source of specific industry data is the appropriate trade associations or other industry-based organizations. Industries vary greatly in the extent to which they compile useful statistical material. In the UK, the Brewers' Society, the British Radio and Electronic Equipment Manufacturers' Association, and the National Caravan Council are among those preparing useful statistical reports or handbooks. A helpful guide to such industry specific data is the *Sources of unofficial UK statistics* prepared by the University of Warwick Business Information Service (1989).

In other industries, occasional figures quoted in the trade press are all that is to be had. These need to be viewed with a good deal of caution and should be cross-checked against other sources. From time to time, industry bodies have co-operated with academic researchers to produce useful survey reports; the Dixey and Talbot report on bingo (1982) is a notable example. But, as with all sport and leisure statistics, the researcher must be prepared to consult a variety of sources and to use imagination and persistence in seeking out the material needed.

Bibliography

References are given under the subject headings used in the earlier discussion. In addition to listing details for the publications mentioned in the text, some additional statistical sources for the UK, France, Germany, the Netherlands and the USA are included.

General secondary sources

Organization for Economic Co-operation and Development, *Living conditions in OECD countries*, Paris, OECD, 1986.
Central Statistical Office, *Social trends*, London, HMSO, annual (a).
Central Statistical Office, *Annual abstract of statistics*, London HMSO, annual (b).
Institut National de la Statistique et des Études Économiques, *Données Sociales*, Paris, INSEE, 1984.
Institut National de la Statistique et des Études Économiques, *Annuaire statistique de la France*, Paris, INSEE, annual (a).

Statistiches Bundesamt, *Statistisches Jahrbuch*, Stuttgart, Metzler-Poeschel (previously W. Kohlhammer), annual (a).

Centraal Bureau voor de Statistiek, *Statistisch zakboek*, Voorburg, CBS, annual (a) — also version in English.

U.S. Department of Commerce, Bureau of the Census, *Social indicators III*, Washington, Department of Commerce, 1980.

U.S. Department of Commerce, Bureau of the Census, *Statistical handbook of the United States*, Washington, Department of Commerce, annual (a).

CAB International, *Leisure, Recreation and Tourism Abstracts*, Wallingford, CAB, quarterly.

Centre de Recherches et de Documentation sur le Loisir, la Récréation et le Tourisme, *LORETO Revue*, Bruxelles, Centre LORETO, three times a year.

People and activities

Office of Population, Censuses and Surveys, Social Survey Division, *General household survey*, London, HMSO, annual.

Countryside Commission, *National countryside recreation survey, 1984*, Cheltenham, Countryside Commission, 1985.

British Market Research Bureau, *Target Group Index*, London, BMRB, annual.

Opaschowski, H.W. (ed.), *Freizeit-Daten*, Hamburg, BAT Freizeitforschungsinstitut, 1982.

Centraal Bureau voor de Statistiek, *Sociaal-Cultureel Bericht*, Voorburg, CBS, monthly from 1988, previously quarterly.

U.S. Department of the Interior, Heritage Conservation and Recreation Service, *1977 National outdoor recreation survey*, referenced in U.S. Department of Commerce, Bureau of the Census, *Social indicators III*, Washington, Department of Commerce, 1980.

Leisure Studies, the Journal of the Leisure Studies Association, London, E. & F.N. Spon, three times a year.

Loisirs et Société (Society and Leisure), Quebec, Presse de l'Université de Québec, twice a year.

Journal of Leisure Research, Virginia, National Recreation and Parks Association, quarterly.

Brodie, M., *Leisure surveys: a review of the literature*, London, Greater London Council, 1982.

Veal, A.J., *Leisure research & planning: sources of information*, Papers in Leisure Studies No.1, London, The Polytechnic of North London, 1981.

Duffield, B. *et al. A digest of sports statistics for the UK*, 1st edn, London, The Sports Council, 1983.

Time use

Parker, S.R., *Leisure & work*, Leisure & Recreation Studies 2, London, George Allen & Unwin, 1983.

TIME BUDGETS

Szalai, A. (ed.) *The use of time. Daily activities of urban & suburban populations in twelve countries*, The Hague, Mouton, 1972.

Organization for Economic Co-operation & Development, *Living conditions in OECD countries. A compendium of social indicators*, Paris, OECD, 1986.

British Broadcasting Corporation, *The people's activities*, London, BBC, 1965.

British Broadcasting Corporation, *The people's activities and use of time*, London, BBC, 1978.

British Broadcasting Corporation, *Daily life in the 1980's*, 4 volumes, London, BBC Data Publications, 1984.

Gershuny, J. and Thomas, G.S., *Changing patterns of time use*, Brighton, Science Policy Research Unit, 1980.

Henley Centre for Forecasting, *Leisure futures*, London, The Centre, quarterly.

Sociaal en Cultureel Planbureau, *Sociaal en cultureel rapport*, Rijswijk, SCPB, biennial.

Statistisk Sentralbyrå, *Arbeid, fritid og samvaer*, Oslo, SSB, 1983.

Statistisk Sentralbyrå, *Tidsnyttingsundersøkelsen 1980-81*, Oslo, SSB, 1983.

See also the following publications listed in earlier sections: CBS, monthly; INSEE, 1984; Department of Commerce, 1980; H.W. Opaschowshi (ed.), 1982.

TRENDS IN LEISURE TIME

International Labour Office, *Year book of labour statistics*, Geneva ILO, annual.

Statistical Office of the European Communities, *Labour force survey results 1987*, Luxembourg, Eurostat, 1989.

Department of Employment, *Employment Gazette*, London, HMSO, monthly.

Department of Employment, *New earnings survey*, London, HMSO, annual.

Commission of the European Communities, Directorate-General for Employment, Social Affairs and Education, *Adaptations in the labour market with regard to reductions in individual working time*, in *Social Europe*, No. 1/86, Luxembourg, The Commission, 1986.

The Technical Change Centre, *Technical change and reductions in life hours of work*, London, The Centre, 1984.

Markets and spending

OFFICIAL SOURCES AND DATA

Organization for Economic Co-operation & Development, *National accounts, detailed tables, Volume II*, Paris, OECD, annual.

Statistical Office of the European Communities, *National accounts ESA — detailed tables by branch*. Series C: Accounts, survey and statistics, Luxembourg, Eurostat, annual.

Central Statistical Office, *United Kingdom national accounts, The CSO blue book*, London, HMSO, annual (c).

Central Statistical Office, *Family expenditure survey*, London, HMSO, annual (d) (prior to 1988, produced by Department of Employment).

Chartered Institute of Public Finance and Accountancy, *Leisure & recreation statistics estimates*, London, CIPFA, annual.

Interbuild, the 42nd International Building and Construction Exhibition, *Building for Tourism, Leisure & Recreation*, London, *Interbuild87*, 1987.

Central Statistical Office, *Guide to official statistics*, No. 6, London, HMSO, 1989.

Institut National de la Statistique et des Études Économiques, *Rapport sur les comptes de la nation*, Les Collections de l'INSEE Série C, Paris, INSEE, annual (b).

Institut National de la Statistique et des Études Économiques, *La Consommation des Ménages*, Les Collections de l'INSEE Serie M, Paris, INSEE, irregular.

Institut National de la Statistique et des Études Économiques, *Le Catalogue de l'INSEE*, Paris, INSEE, annual (c).

Statistisches Bundesamt, *Fachserie 18 Volkswirtschaftliche Gesamtrechnungen Reihe 1.3 — Konten und Standardtabellen*, Stuttgart, Metzler-Poeschel (previously W. Kohlhammer), annual (b).

Statistisches Bundesamt, *Einkommens- und Verbrauchsstichprobe*, Stuttgart, W. Kohlhammer, irregular.

Statistisches Bundesamt, *Katalog der Statistiken zum Arbeitsgebiet der Bundesstatistik*, Stuttgart, Statistisches Bundesamt, annual (c).

Centraal Bureau voor de Statistiek, *Nationale rekeningen*, Voorburg, CBS, annual.

Centraal Bureau voor de Statistiek, *Budget-onderzoek*, Voorburg, CBS, irregular.

Centraal Bureau voor de Statistiek, *Systematisch overzicht van de CBS publikaties*, Voorburg, CBS, annual.

U.S. Department of Commerce, Bureau of the Census, *Survey of current business* (July issue), Washington, Department of Commerce, annual (b).

U.S. Bureau of Labor Statistics, *Consumer expenditure survey*, Washington, Bureau of Labor Statistics, annual.

U.S. Department of Commerce, Bureau of the Census, *Census catalog and guide*, Washington, Department of Commerce, annual (c).

Harvey, J.M., *Statistics Europe*, 5th edn. Beckenham, CBD Research, 1987.

COMMERCIAL REPORTS AND SERVICES

Leisure Consultants, *Leisure forecasts*, Sudbury, Leisure Consultants, annual.

Henley Centre for Forecasting, *Leisure futures*, London, The Centre, quarterly.

Mintel Publications, *Leisure intelligence*, London, Mintel, quarterly.

Institut für Freizeitwirtschaft, *Wachstumsfelder im Freizeitbereich bis 1995*, Munich, IFF, 1987.

Cambridge Information Group, *Findex, The directory of market research reports, studies and surveys*, Gaithersburg, Cambridge Information Group, annual.

Off-the-Shelf Publications, *Off-the-Shelf, The international catalog of business reports*, New York, Off-the-Shelf, bi-monthly.

Arlington Management Publications, *Marketsearch*, London, Arlington Management Publications, annual.

Marketing Strategies for Industry, *Marketing Surveys Index*, Mitcham, MSI, monthly.

Gofton, K. (ed.), *A Guide to marketing research in the UK*, London, KeyNote Publications, 1987.

Euromonitor Publications, *European directory of marketing information sources*, London, Euromonitor, 1987.

Euromonitor Publications, *International directory of marketing information sources*, London, Euromonitor, 1988.

Foster, P. and Foster, A. (eds.), *On line business sourcebook*, Cleveland, Headland Press, 1989.

See also H. W. Opaschowski (ed.), 1982, referenced under People and Activities.

Specific sectors and industries

SPORT AND ACTIVE RECREATION

The Centre for Leisure Research, *A digest of sports statistics for the UK*, 2nd edn, London, The Sports Council, 1986.

Football Trust, *Digest of football statistics*, London, Football Trust, 1988.

Mintel Publications, *Sponsorship report*, London, Mintel, 1986.

Henley Centre for Forecasting, *The economic importance of sport in the UK*, London, The Sports Council, 1986.

Martin, W.H. and Mason, S., *Leisure markets in Europe*, London, Financial Times Business Publishing Division, 1978.

Council of Europe, *Sports information bulletin*, Brussels, Clearing House, 4–5 times a year.

Martin, W.H. and Mason, S., *UK sports market*, 1984 edition, Sudbury, Leisure Consultants, 1984.

Institut National de la Statistique et des Études Économiques, *Les Pratiques Sportives en 1981*, in *Données Sociales*, Paris, INSEE, 1984.

Institut National de la Statistique et des Études Économiques, *Évolution de la Pratique Sportive des Français 1967-1984*, Les Collections de l'INSEE Serie M 134, Paris, INSEE, 1988.

National Sporting Goods Association, *Sports participation in 1988*, Mount Prospect, Illinois, NSGA, 1989.

National Sporting Goods Association, *Sporting goods market in 1989*, Mount Prospect, Illinois, NSGA, 1989.

Sport and Recreation Information Group, *Market research sources in sport in the UK*, Sheffield, SPRIG, 1990.

See also publications by CBS (monthly) and IFF (1987) referenced in earlier sections.

CULTURE

United Nations Educational, Scientific, & Cultural Organization, *Unesco statistical yearbook*, Paris, Unesco, annual.

Services des Études et Recherches du Ministère de la Culture, *Pratiques Culturelles des Français, Description Démographique Évolution 1937-1981*, Paris, Dalloz, 1982.

Statistisk Sentralbyrå, *Kulturstatistikk*, Oslo, SSB, irregular.

Istituto Centrale di Statistica, *Annuario delle Statistiche Culturali*, Rome, ISTAT, annual.

Lo Spettacolo, Rome, SIAE, quarterly.

Myerscough, J. (ed.), *Facts about the arts*, 1986 edition, London, Policy Studies Institute, 1986.

Feist, A. and Hutchinson, R., *Cultural trends*, London, Policy Studies Institute, quarterly.

Myerscough, J., *The Economic importance of the arts in Britain*, London, Policy Studies Institute, 1988.

British Broadcasting Corporation, *Annual report and handbook*, London, BBC, annual.

Independent Broadcasting Authority, *Television & radio, The IBA's yearbook of independent broadcasting*, London, IBA, annual.

Screen digest, London, Screen Digest Publications, monthly.

See also the following publications by bodies referenced in earlier sections: INSEE, 1984; CBS, monthly; Leisure Consultants, annual; Henley Centre, quarterly; Mintel, quarterly.

OTHER SECTORS

British Tourist Authority/English Tourist Board Research Services, *Sightseeing*, London, BTA/ETB, annual.

English Tourist Board, *Leisure day trips in Great Britain, summer 1981-1982*, London, ETB, 1983.

British Tourist Authority/English Tourist Board Research Services and NOP Market Research, *Activities by the British on holiday in Britain*, London, BTA/ETB, 1989.

The Brewers' Society, *Statistical handbook*, London, Brewers' Society, annual.

The British Radio & Electronic Equipment Manufacturers' Association, *Statistical yearbooks*, London, BREMA, annual.

National Caravan Council, *The British caravan industry statistics*, Aldershot, NCC, annual.

University of Warwick Business Information Service (ed.), *Sources of unofficial UK statistics*, 2nd edn, Aldershot, Gower Publishing Company, 1989.

Dixey, R. with Talbot, M., *Women, leisure & bingo*, Leeds, Trinity & All Saints' College, 1982.

Table 2.4 Material in market research guides — an illustration

publisher's
address
given in full

report title

report content

country covered

pages

price

Note: Only the latest research is included in Marketing Surveys Index – not research which is now years out of date.

alphabetical index

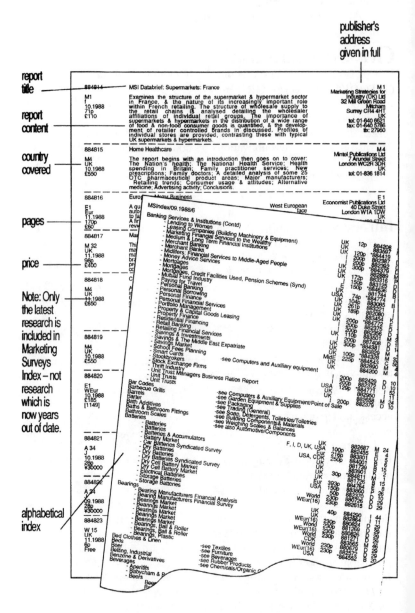

(Reproduced with permission from Marketing Strategies for Industry (UK) Ltd.)

CHAPTER THREE

Government and sport

G. TORKILDSEN, G. GRIFFITHS AND J. CUTTS

Introduction

The UK has its own 'peculiar' brand of mixed economy. So it is with sport. Its organization is broad-based, uncoordinated in large measure. This greatly contrasts with the situation in other countries, many of which have more highly structured national plans and far more government investment and involvement in sport.

The term 'sport' in this context relates not only to active sport, but also to spectator sport and other forms of physical recreation in the public, commercial and voluntary sectors, embracing children's play and physical recreational activities in the countryside, the air and in water. In the UK, sources of information pertaining to these areas are many, varied, uncoordinated and, in many instances, are difficult to gain access to. This chapter illustrates how complex and dispersed the field is.

Like many countries, public provision for sport and recreation in the UK has its origins in nineteenth century legislation relating to public health and training. Subsequent legislation was concerned with physical education in schools and later the economic benefits of dual use of education facilities. The 1960s saw a greater government concern with 'leisure' in its broader perspective with a series of reports and White Papers relating to the youth service, broadcasting, the countryside, the arts, tourism and adult education. Many of these influenced the provision of sporting opportunities. Readers should refer to Chapter 6 for historical sources relating to the development of sport and leisure.

The second report from the Select Committee of the House of Lords on Sport and Leisure [1] published in 1973 was the most significant government report relating to sport in the 1970s. One of the report's recommendations was that the new local authorities, formed under the Local Government Act, should have a Recreation Committee and a Department of Recreation under its own Chief Officer. The recommendation that a Ministry of Recreation be established has never been implemented, but the post of Minister of State for Sport and Recreation was created within the Department of Environment in 1974. In 1991 the post was transferred to the Department of Education and Science.

The report also recognized the need for appropriate management training and in the subsequent White Paper, *Sport and recreation* (1975) [2], the *Recreation management training committee (Yates Committee)* [3] was established to investigate the training requirements of sports and recreation managers. It also recommended that 'recreational priority areas' be established in deprived inner city areas with additional financial assistance from The Sports Council and the Government's own 'Urban Programme'. This philosophy has been further emphasized in more recent reports and White Papers, e.g. *Policy for the inner cities* [4], and *The report of The Scarman Inquiry* [5] into the Brixton disorders.

Current situation

Since the election of the Conservative Government in 1979 there has been a significant change in the relationship between national and local government which has had an effect upon the range of sporting opportunities that is provided directly or indirectly by local authorities. Controls on capital expenditure have severely restricted the provision of new sports centres and swimming pools, whilst constraints on revenue budgets have resulted in greater emphasis being placed upon providing an efficient service which in some cases can be detrimental to providing an effective service.

The Local Government Act 1988 (Competition in Sports and Leisure Facilities) Order 1989 required that local authorities offer the management of their sports and leisure facilities to competitive tendering. Undoubtedly this will result in some economic savings with many of the sports facilities being operated by commercial leisure companies. This will probably encourage an increased growth in commercial sports provision of the more profitable sports, whilst leaving the non-profitable sports to be provided more and more by the voluntary sector.

The introduction of the Education Reform Act 1988, whereby each school (with its Board of Governors) has to be responsible for its own budget, may reduce the range of sporting experiences offered to school children and may well prevent some local sports clubs from using school premises. The present Government's policy of privatizing nationalized industries, based on the assumption that it will provide a more efficient service, is also likely to affect sporting opportunities. For example, under the Water Act 1973 each water authority had the responsibility to provide recreational opportunities. However, with the privatization of the different water authorities, through the Water Act 1989, the established priority of the new companies is to maximize their return on investment. In such circumstances, it is unlikely that the provision of sporting facilities will have a very high level of priority.

A further concern to the current Government has been the behaviour and safety of sporting crowds. Since 1923 there have been eight government reports published relating to crowd safety and control — many commissioned after the disasters at Ibrox (1971), Bradford (1985) and Hillsborough (1989). The most recent report *The Hillsborough Stadium disaster: final report* [6] by Lord Justice Taylor has recommended that all First and Second Division football clubs' stadia should become all-seater grounds by 1995 and the grounds of the Third and Fourth Division clubs by the end of the century. To assist the football clubs to raise the necessary capital funds the Government cut the rate of tax on football pools by 2.5% in an attempt to provide some £100 million over a five-year period.

A further recommendation made by Lord Justice Taylor was that the proposed government legislation to introduce a National Membership Scheme for supporters (under Section 1(5) of the Football Spectators Act 1989) should be discarded and the government has subsequently postponed its introduction.

Central government role for sport

The responsibility for sport at central government level is shared by the following departments:

Department of the Environment. This is responsible for local government and the various roles that it plays with regard to sports and recreation.

Department of Education and Science. This is responsible for sports, arts, education and physical education, the youth service and adult education facilities.

Home Office. This provides licensing for public entertainment, safety of sports buildings and broadcasting.

Ministry of Agriculture, Fisheries and Food. This is responsible for forest recreation and amenity, the use of agricultural land for recreation, etc. Appointed bodies include the Forestry Commission.

Department of Transport. This is responsible for the management of recreation traffic, including transportation of football supporters.

Department of Employment. This is responsible for tourism. Appointed bodies include the British Tourist Authority and the English Tourist Board.

This multi-departmental and largely uncoordinated approach has contributed to the absence of a national plan for sport and leisure. Sporting issues do not command high priority within central government and sport tends to generate a debate in the House of Commons only because of the poor or negative publicity it receives. In the past the Minister of State for Sport has been 'seconded' at times of emergency, e.g. floods, drought, whilst the House of Commons debate on the White Paper *Sport and recreation* attracted only 41 members to the voting lobbies. Further, the completed *Recreation management training committee report* (Yates Committee) remained on the desks of the Ministers concerned for a period of some two years before being released. Sport appears to suffer badly in comparison with the arts.

However, more recently, the government has needed to be more influential in supporting sports organizations in their fight to alleviate racial discrimination (Gleneagles Agreement, 1977), the misuse of drugs (Council of Europe Anti-Doping Charter, 1984) and spectator violence. Legislation was introduced in Scotland in 1980 and in the rest of the UK in 1985, curbing the sale of alcohol at football grounds and new public order legislation has given courts greater powers. Thus sport and politics have become inextricably linked.

Information sources

Central government information sources

The Headquarters Library of the Department of the Environment and the Department of Transport provide some useful publications: *Annual list of publications* [7] is a comprehensive guide which details all publications issued or sponsored by the DoE and the DoT (excluding publications of the research establishments). Entries are divided by broad subject headings and type of publication and include press notices, departmental circulars, statutory instruments and command papers, etc. It is indexed by subject, author and issuing agency. The *Monthly publications list* [8] follows the same format as the annual list but is published on a monthly basis. *Library Bulletin* [9], an abstracting journal of current literature on the environment and transport subjects, was published until 1990. A publication which appears in their Information Series is *Sport and recreation: sources of information* (2nd edn, 1987) compiled by C.M. Lambert. This aims to bring together all the major aspects of provision for physical recreation in the UK.

The Sport and Recreation Division formerly of the Department of the Environment also commission studies that provide examples of good management. Examples of such publications are: *Developing sport and leisure, Good practice in urban regeneration* [10] and *Development and operation of leisure centres (selected case studies)* [11]. In 1991 the Sport and Recreation Division transferred to the Department of Education and Science.

OTHER GOVERNMENT SOURCES OF INFORMATION

Statistical information is available from each government department. However, the Government Statistical Service consists of the statistics divisions of all major departments together with the Business Statistics Office and the Office of Population Censuses and Surveys, with the Central Statistical Office being the coordinating body.

Government statistics, a brief guide to sources [12] is available from the Central Statistical Office's information services division. It gives a brief description of the major government publications containing statistics. Far more detailed information can be obtained from the *Guide to official statistics* [13]. Major publications that have relevance to sport include: *Social trends* [14], *General household survey (GHS)* (1977, 1980, 1983 and 1986 contain leisure data) [15], *Key data* [16] and the *Family expenditure survey* [17].

The *GHS* is a survey of households covering a wide range of social and socio-economic aspects. The leisure survey is held every three years and records participant trends in indoor and outdoor sports and recreation for those aged 16 and over. The respondents are asked to recall participation in the four weeks prior to interview. Although the accuracy of the frequency of participation may be a little suspect, the data provide an invaluable tool for assessing potential sporting demand for a given community.

Social trends provides a broad description of UK society. The 1990 edition included a leisure section that details the availability of leisure participation in social and cultural activities, holiday profiles and levels of disposable income. It includes statistical information provided by or obtained from the *GHS*, British Tourist Authority (BTA), Henley Centre for Forecasting, Department of Employment, Broadcasting Audience Research Board and Family Expenditure Survey.

The various papers relating to parliamentary legislation are an important source of information for any student of sport and its relationship with government. The *HMSO annual catalogue* (also available in daily, weekly and monthly lists) [18] lists all publications published by HMSO. This includes Acts of Parliament, government Green Papers (discussion or consultative documents), White Papers (statements of government intent which precede the introduction of a Bill of Parliament and as such are debated in Parliament) and *Hansard*, but not Statutory Instruments. There are also a number of HMSO Bookshops throughout the country.

Hansard, published daily by HMSO, is the verbatim transcript of debates on current draft legislation (Bills) for both the House of Commons and the House of Lords. Debates on sport-related issues, answers to MP's questions and the Prime Minister's Question time provide useful information on contemporary sport not available from other sources.

HMSO also produce a series of *HMSO sectional lists* [19] which consist mainly of in-print non-parliamentary material. These, together with the *Annual catalogue*, provide a detailed comprehensive guide to all HMSO government publications.

All HMSO publications are available on British Telecom's Prestel service, listed by the date of publication. Details are displayed for one week only. HMSO's bibliographic database is available through Dialog and via the British Library's Blaise-Line. The *Catalogue of British official publications not published by HMSO* is also available via Dialog. HMSO, in conjunction with Chadwyck-Healey, also publish the database on CD-ROM. Called UKOP, it amalgamates the *HMSO catalogue* and the *Catalogue of British official publications not published by HMSO*, plus a number of publications from international organizations, e.g. the Council of Europe.

POLIS (the Parliamentary Online Information System) is hosted by Meridian Systems Management for the House of Commons Library. It is particularly useful for tracing parliamentary questions, and information relating to particular subjects or MPs. Set up in 1979, its subject coverage consists of Parliamentary information (parliamentary questions and Acts) and non-parliamentary material (mainly official publications and material held in the House of Commons Library), plus all European legislation since 1983. Material is arranged in four separate databases: CURRENT, PARL83, PARL79 and EDM databases. Further information can be obtained from Meridian Systems Management in Bromley, Kent.

Statutory bodies

Central government has the ability to appoint (by Royal Charter, legislation or by ministerial direction) statutory bodies, commonly known as quangos. Their nature, functions and powers vary greatly. In some instances, central government plays a decisive role through funding, the appointment of members, approval of policies, etc. and, therefore can directly influence the organizations at national, regional and local levels. There are numerous quangos, but few are concerned with sport and recreation.

THE SPORTS COUNCIL

The Sports Council, the major quango for sport, was established in 1972 by Royal Charter, to develop sport and recreation in the interests of social welfare and the enjoyment of leisure, to encourage the provision of new facilities and stimulate use of existing facilities, and to encourage high standards. Its primary objectives are to increase participation and performance. The English Council has 10 Regional Councils and there are separate Councils for Northern Ireland, Wales and Scotland. All produce their own publications.

From its inception, The Sports Council has claimed to be an autonomous organization that operated independently of central government, apart from receiving its annual grant. In reality, the Council usually represents government policies, for example, in the position it adopted towards the Moscow Olympics and sports tours to South Africa. The Department of the Environment has recently been critical of its overall efficiency and lack of monitoring of the grants that it distributes. In 1985, the Environment Committee of the House of Commons was appointed to examine the expenditure, administration and policy of The Sports Council (amongst others). The Committee examined, in detail, the operational aspects of The Sports Council, its relationship with other agencies, such as the CCPR, and the justification for spending public money on sport. The findings of the Committee and the Government's response were published in 1986 [20, 21] and resulted in The Sports Council commissioning an independent review of its national sports centres, *Review of national sports centres* [22]. This report highlighted the actions necessary to improve the managerial effectiveness and efficiency of the relevant centres. It also produced a consultation document *Which way forward?* [23] which was circulated in 1987 to individuals and organizations connected with sport. The responses to the document generally sought greater coordination and cooperation amongst sports organizations in an attempt to increase general efficiency. However the Government intends to carry out further investigations with a view to reducing the staff complement of The Sports Council.

The Council's Information Centre at its headquarters in London has an extensive reference library, containing approximately 20 000 documents and 350-400 periodicals. The centre aims to provide a service for its own staff, leisure professionals, students and the general public, by answering personal, written and telephone enquiries. The library covers such topics as administration, finance, management, facilities and economics.

Its major publication, *SCAN*, lists selected new publications and articles and is distributed free [24]. Entries, along with brief abstracts, are arranged under headings such as periodicals, handbooks, yearbooks, annual reports, new publications, etc. The lists tend to reflect recent accessions to The Sports Council Information Centre.

The Sports Council has an extensive publications list ranging from basic directories and annual reports to subjects that reflect the Council's main areas of interest. The main categories of publication are as follows:

- Basic information: an extensive range of directories and reports, including the *Digest of sports statistics for the UK* (2nd edn) [25]. As with any directory, they rapidly become out of date and need constant updating.
- Leisure provision: publications ranging from economic, sociological and psychological aspects of leisure to public and private provision and from theory to practice. These publications include *Sport in the community, into the 90s* [26] the Council's strategy for 1988-1993, which supersedes an earlier publication *Sport in the community ... the next ten years* [27]. Such documents provide a wealth of information on levels of sporting participation and the current state of leisure provision.
- Technical material: includes reports produced by The Sports Council's Technical Unit for Sport. These include such publications as the *Small community recreation centres design guide* [28], *Arenas* [29] and the *Handbook of sports and recreational building design* [30]. Also available free of charge are the Technical Unit for Sport *Data sheets*. These cover a large range of sport and leisure facilities and provide valuable design notes for those planning such facilities.
- Health and Fitness: publications relating to the health and fitness boom. These include the *Case for exercise* [31] and *The new case for exercise* [32].
- Finance: publications relating to leisure funding in the UK. These

include *Fund raising for sport – a guide for sports clubs* [33] and the *Economic impact and importance of sport in the UK* [34].

The *Proceedings of the Council's annual recreation management seminar* are published. They provide a valuable source of information on topical subjects related to leisure. Additionally, the Council publishes an *Annual report*, an annual *Corporate plan* and the journal *Sport and Leisure* which appears bi-monthly and again covers topical issues. The Council's factsheet *Keep in touch ... with The Sports Council* [35] lists all current publications and their costs. It does not however, indicate when the publications were originally published and this can be misleading.

In conjunction with the Social Science Research Council (SSRC) (and in later years, the Economic and Social Research Council (ESRC)), The Sports Council commissioned a large number of desk studies that covered aspects of sports and leisure such as: sports participation and policies of different providers. Although these are now dated, they still contain valuable information [36–38].

Regional Councils

The Regional Councils for Sport and Recreation provide a consultation forum for organizations which have a major interest in the development of sport and recreation at a local level, e.g. local authorities, local sports councils, regional water authorities, tourist boards, conservation agencies, landowners, etc. Their aim is to promote the development of sport and recreation at a regional level. The Councils for Sport and Recreation are administered by the 10 Regional Sports Councils, all of whom produce an *Annual report*, a *Regional strategy* and a range of other publications.

The National Sports Councils for Scotland and Wales and the Northern Ireland Sports Council are managed independently of The Sports Council and each produces annual reports, a strategy for the nation and a range of other publications. Worthy of note is the computerized planning model produced by The Scottish Sports Council, which consists of three principal components - Demand, Supply and Catchment Areas. An illustration of how this model can be implemented is given in the publication *Aberdeen Area – urban sports study report of the Working Party* [39]. The model has also been used by the Sports Council for Wales in its publication *National strategy 1986/1996 consultative document* [40].

NATIONAL CHILDREN'S PLAY AND RECREATION UNIT

The National Children's Play and Recreation Unit is being funded by The Sports Council for a fixed period to cater exclusively for children's play. The Unit took over from the government-funded Playboard. The National Play Information Centre offers a collection of over 4000 books, journal articles, over 80 journals, and a growing collection of videos on play provision, theories, activities, education, playground design and child development. Regular mailings outline the work of the Unit affecting children's play and abstracts of recent acquisitions to the Information Centre. They are brief, up-to-date and informative.

THE COUNTRYSIDE COMMISSION

The Countryside Commission was established under the Countryside Act 1968. The Commission is an advisory and promotional body whose duty is to protect and make accessible the countryside in England and Wales. These objectives are achieved through work with other bodies, including local authorities, voluntary bodies and private individuals and organizations.

The Commission publishes a variety of reports, guides, booklets and research registers. A *Catalogue of publications* is available twice yearly [41]. Publications are classified under a variety of headings, including audio-visual materials, maps and related publications.

The Countryside Commission also has a substantial library which provides a current-awareness service in the form of *Selected periodical articles* and the *Library accessions list*.

Other countryside bodies with an influence on sport and recreation are the Forestry Commission, the National Rivers Authority and the Nature Conservancy Council. All three provide information services.

The influence of central government upon local government sports provision

Local authorities are the largest providers of leisure facilities for sport and outdoor physical recreation. Central government has placed an obligation on local authorities (in England and Wales) to provide leisure services in three specific areas: library services; the youth and adult education facilities; and allotments. However they do not indicate what the scale of provision should be and local authorities therefore interpret the needs and demands of their community in different ways and the scale of provision varies enormously from one authority to another.

Successive pieces of legislation in the late 1980s have had the effect of tightening central government's control of local authorities' budgets. The Local Government Housing and Finance Act 1988 which contained provision for the Uniform Business Rate, Compulsory Competitive Tendering (CCT) and the Education Reform Act 1988 collectively, are likely to have dramatic effects on the role of local government and sport.

Each district, metropolitan and county council has documents that relate to municipally-managed sports facilities and schemes. Each year councils publish their annual budget generally called the *Yearly estimates*, in which the likely expenditure levels of the council's services (including sports and recreation facilities) for the previous fiscal year are given, together with the estimated expenditure for the forthcoming year. Within many of these documents the attendance levels achieved in the previous year at swimming pools, sports centres, etc. are also given.

Each local authority has the statutory obligation to produce local plans for its area giving indications of what future developments are proposed or likely to be allowed. This document normally includes a section on sport and leisure.

The Audit Commission for Local Authorities in England and Wales is predominantly concerned with the efficient and effective management of local government services. It has produced financial performance norms for the management of sports and leisure facilities and published documents relating to CCT procedures necessary for improved managerial efficiency, e.g. *Sport for whom? Clarifying the local authority role in sport and recreation* [42] and *Local authority support for sport: a management handbook* [43].

With CCT becoming a reality, the tendering documents providing operational specifications of the service required from contracted management companies are available to potential applicants on the production of a charge which in some cases can be as much as £250. All local authorities annually produce a range of reports for their respective committees. Documents presented at open council meetings are available for public scrutiny under the Access to Information Act 1987. The most interesting tend to be those associated with the planning and design of new leisure facilities, and the individual council's leisure strategy.

The Chartered Institute of Public Finance and Accountancy (CIPFA) publishes annual data relating to the management of sports and leisure facilities in the public sector. These publications include *Leisure usage statistics*, *Charges for leisure services statistics* and *Leisure and recreation statistics (estimates)* [44–46].

The influence of central government on the voluntary and commercial sector sports provision

The voluntary sector is the foundation and remains the backbone of UK sport; introduction of the community charge (to be replaced by a new form of taxation in 1993) and the New Business Rate will probably result in increased operating costs for most sports clubs which may be passed on as higher membership charges, ultimately limiting participation in sport on the grounds of cost.

Sources of information that relate to the national scene are rather dated [47,48] and on a regional basis, the scale and nature of the provision provided by the voluntary sector is included in the Regional Sports Councils' strategic documents. Individual sports clubs normally have a written constitution which insists that an Annual General Meeting be held where an annual report and statement of accounts are produced. Clubs with charitable status are required by law to submit audited accounts to the Charitable Commissioners.

There has also been a significant increase in the commercial sports market and currently this includes sports clubs, squash clubs, indoor tennis, indoor bowls, swimming pools, sports villages and sporting holidays. Again the advent of the CCT legislation will undoubtedly increase the commercial management of municipally-owned sports facilities.

The Government have indirectly assisted the development of the commercial sector by allowing sports and leisure developments to be eligible to the benefits that are normally available for industrial or commercial development, e.g. Government Enterprise Zones and Business Expansion Schemes.

Because of the need by most commercial organizations to conceal confidential data from competitors, readily available sources of information are difficult to obtain. All companies with limited liability have to, by law, lodge their Annual Accounts at Companies House whilst 'plc' companies produce annual reports which are normally readily available upon application. Microfiche copies of these accounts are available for a fee. Research relating to a specific aspect of the commercial leisure industry is very expensive to purchase and the reviews of the commercial leisure industry tend to be few in number and rather dated [49, 50].

Other useful sources of information

There are a number of organizations and sources of information which, although not directly related to government and sport specifically, will have information and published documents relating to the subject.

NCVQ

There are a number of governmentally-supported organizations. One is a relatively new body which has responsibility for vocational qualifications in a whole range of areas, including sport and recreation.

This body, called the National Council for Vocational Qualifications (NCVQ) approves vocational qualifications based on national standards agreed through Industry Lead Bodies (ILBs). The ILB for sport and recreation was organized through the Local Government Training Board (LGTB) and brought together employers, Sports Council representatives, employees and trade union representatives, in order to develop standards for all areas of the industry. In 1991, the LGTB merged with the Local Authority Conditions of Service Advisory Board to form the Local Government Management Board (LGMB). It should be noted that the NCVQ is not an awarding body but simply approves qualifications awarded by City & Guilds, etc. Further details can be obtained through the LGMB. The equivalent body in Scotland is called SCOTVEC.

CCPR

The Central Council of Physical Recreation (CCPR) receives government funding through The Sports Council and is involved in sport at a national and international level. Its publications include the *Committee of enquiry into amateur status and participation in sport – The Palmer report* [51] and an *Annual report* which is a valuable source of information. Better links between The Sports Council, the British Olympic Association and CCPR were partially established through the formation of the British International Sports Committee in 1988, but more needs to be achieved.

PEA and NPFA

A number of other organizations attempt to influence government actions. Two such organizations that have argued for physical education in the curriculum and the importance of playing fields are respectively, the Physical Education Association (PEA) [52], and the National Playing Fields Association (NPFA) [53].

Professional organizations

The professional organizations that represent the interests of leisure professionals such as the Institute of Leisure and Amenity Management (ILAM), the Institute of Baths and Recreation Management (IBRM) and the Institute of Groundsmanship, are a valuable source of information on sport and recreation. Most have an annual conference and produce monthly or bi-monthly journals. The institutes also have their own professional examination structure and organize seminars and courses to assist their student members. Both ILAM and IBRM have produced distant learning packages of some of their course material. ILAM has a library which is available for use by members; the main emphasis of the collection is on leisure.

Academic sector

The Leisure Studies Association (LSA) is primarily an academic association with interests covering the whole spectrum of leisure activity, some relating to government and sport. The Association's official journal is *Leisure Studies*, published by E. & F.N. Spon and they also organize national and international conferences. Chapter 10 provides more information on leisure and other relevant organizations.

Staying with the academic sector, many universities and polytechnics have Departments of Sports Sciences and Leisure Studies which have undertaken research projects for The Sports Council and various local authorities. Loughborough University of Technology and the Polytechnic of North London have undertaken numerous user surveys of sports centres, leisure centres and swimming pools, whilst Birmingham University has produced a range of reports relating to both local government and leisure [54, 55]. The Sir Norman Chester Centre for Football Research, at the University of Leicester, has undertaken a number of projects relating to football for the DoE.

Consultancies

Many of the leading leisure management consultancies have their own databases for retaining information and this is used to produce national performance norms for comparative analysis and for the production of feasibility studies. There is now a wealth of survey and statistical information emanating from such sources as the Henley Centre for Forecasting, CACI, Applied Leisure Marketing and Leisure Consultants.

Abstracting and indexing journals and primary journals

There are a number of journals which are worth checking for material relating to sport and its relationship with government. These include *Leisure Management, Sports Industry, Leisure Week, Leisure Manager, Sport & Leisure* and *Leisure Studies*.

Most of these journals are indexed in *Leisure, Recreation and Tourism Abstracts* and *Sports Documentation Monthly Bulletin*. Refer to Chapter 1 for more information on these abstracting services and relevant online databases, e.g. ACOMPLINE.

Conclusions

Sport is influenced by government at all levels. Statutory and permissive powers, financial opportunities and constraints, planning, community charges and taxes and political bias all influence sport. Yet there is no national strategy, no national plan and government quangos like The Sports Council have diminishing powers and freedom of action. The non-governmental influences – British Olympic Association, Central Council of Physical Recreation, governing bodies of sport and the many thousands of clubs, societies and associations – are also strong influences and remain the backbone of sport in the UK. However, the need for financial and other assistance for the voluntary sector is very evident for sport, as we know it, to survive and prosper. The commercial sector in sport is growing rapidly, not only with new and expanding leisure opportunities, but also through the management of public-sector facilities.

References

Introduction

1. House of Lords (1973) *Second report from the Select Committee of the House of Lords on Sport and Leisure.* HL193, 1972–73. HMSO, London.
2. Command Paper Cmnd 6200 (1975) *Sport and recreation.* HMSO, London.
3. Department of the Environment (1984) *Recreation management training committee: final report.* HMSO, London.
4. Command Paper Cmnd 6845 (1977) *Policy for the inner cities.* HMSO, London.
5. Command Paper Cmnd 8427 (1981) *The Brixton disorders, 10–12 April 1981. Report of the Right Honourable Lord Scarman.* HMSO, London.

Current situation

6. Command Paper Cm 962 (1990) *The Hillsborough Stadium Disaster: final report.* HMSO, London.

Central government role for sport

CENTRAL GOVERNMENT INFORMATION SOURCES

7. Department of the Environment, Department of Transport *Annual list of publications*, annual. DoE, DoT, London.
8. Department of the Environment, Department of Transport. *Publications monthly list*, monthly. DoE, DoT, London.
9. Department of the Environment, Department of Transport *Library Bulletin*. DoE, DoT, London.
10. Department of the Environment (1989) *Developing sport and leisure, good practice in urban regeneration*. HMSO, London.
11. Department of the Environment, *Developing and operation of leisure centres (selected case studies)*. HMSO, London.

OTHER GOVERNMENT SOURCES OF INFORMATION

12. Government Statistical Service, *Government statistics, a brief guide to sources*, annual. HMSO, London.
13. Government Statistical Service, *Guide to official statistics (1990)*. HMSO, London.
14. Central Statistical Office, *Social trends*, annual. HMSO, London.
15. Central Statistical Office (1986) *General household survey*. HMSO, London.
16. Central Statistical Office, *Key data*, annual. HMSO, London.
17. Central Statistical Office, *Family expenditure survey*, annual. HMSO, London.
18. *HMSO annual catalogue*. HMSO, London.
19. *HMSO sectional lists*. HMSO, London.

Statutory bodies

20. House of Commons (1986) *Second report from the Environment Committee, 1985–86*. Sports Council, HMSO, London.
21. House of Commons (1986) *Third special report from the Environmental Committee, 1985-86, Government's response to the Committee's second report*. HMSO, London.
22. L. & R. Leisure Consultants (1987) *Review of national sport centres*. L. & R. Leisure Consultants, London.
23. The Sports Council (1987) *Which way forward?*. Sports Council, London.
24. Sports Council, *SCAN*, selected new publications and articles, monthly. Sports Council, London.
25. Sports Council (1986) *A Digest of sports statistics for the UK*, 2nd edn. Sports Council, London.

26. Sports Council (1988) *Sport in the community, into the 90's. A strategy for sport 1988–1993.* Sports Council, London.
27. Sports Council (1982) *Sport in the community. The next ten years.* Sports Council, London.
28. Sports Council (1989) *Small community recreation centres design guide — briefing, design, performance specification and cost guidance notes for small community recreation centres (SCRC).* Sports Council, London.
29. Sports Council (1989) *Arenas – A planning, design, and management guide*, vols. 1-4. Architectural Press, London.
30. Sports Council (1981) *Handbook of sports and recreational building design*, vols. 1–4. Architectural Press, London.
31. P. Fentem & E.J. Bassey (1977) *The case for exercise. Research working paper.* Sports Council, London.
32. P. Fentem, E.J. Bassey and N. Turnbull (1988) *The new case for exercise.* Sports Council/Health Education Authority, London.
33. H. Griffiths. *Fund raising for sport — a guide for sports clubs.* Sports Council, London.
34. Henley Centre for Forecasting (1986) *The economic importance of sport in the UK. Sports Council,* London.
35. Sports Council *Keep in touch .... with The Sports Council*, updated regularly. Sports Council, London.
36. A. Tomlinson (1979) *The voluntary sector in leisure.* SSRC/Sports Council, London.
37. A.S. Travis (1979) *The state and leisure provision.* SSRC/Sports Council, London.
38. J. Blackie, T. Coppock and B. Duffield (1979) *The leisure planning process.* SSRC/Sports Council, London.
39. Grampian Regional Council (1988) *Aberdeen Area—Urban sports study.* Grampian Regional Council, Aberdeen.
40. Sports Council for Wales (1985) *National strategy 1986/1996 consultative document.* Sports Council for Wales, Cardiff.
41. Countryside Commission *Catalogue of publications*, twice yearly. Countryside Commission, Manchester.

The influence of central government upon local government sports provision

42. Audit Commission (1989) *Sport for whom? Clarifying the local authority role in sport and recreation.* HMSO, London.
43. Audit Commission (1990) *Local authority support for sport: a management handbook.* HMSO, London.
44. CIPFA (1988–89) *Leisure usage statistics.* CIPFA, Statistical Information Service, London.

45. CIPFA (1989–90) *Charges for leisure services statistics.* CIPFA, Statistical Information Service, London.
46. CIPFA (1989–90) *Leisure and recreation statistics (estimates).* CIPFA, Statistical Information Service, London.

The influence of central government on the voluntary and commercial sector sports provision

47. J. Boothy and M. Tungate (1977) *North-East area study working paper 46. Clubs for sports and arts: Results of a survey of facilities, members and activities in Cleveland County.* University of Durham.
48. K.K. Sillitoe (1969) *Government social survey. Planning for leisure.* HMSO, London.
49. J. Roberts (1979) *The commercial sector in leisure.* SSRC/Sports Council, London.
50. J. Roberts (1986) *The commercial sector as a supplier of leisure goods and services.* INLOGOV, Birmingham.

Other useful sources of information

51. *Committee of enquiry into amateur status and participation in sport — The Palmer report* (1988). CCPR, London.
52. Physical Education Association (1987) *Report of a Commission of Enquiry to enquire into the present state and status of physical education (both primary and secondary) in England and Wales.* PEA, London.
53. National Playing Fields Association (1989) *The State of play.* NPFA, London.
54. J. Bennington and J. White (1986) *The future role and organisation of local government. Functional study No. 4. Leisure.* Institute of Local Government Studies (INLOGOV), Birmingham.
55. A.S. Travis *et al.* (1978) *The role of central government in relation to the provision of leisure services in England and Wales.* CURS, Birmingham.

Part II

CHAPTER FOUR

Sports science

M.E. NEVILL[*], S. BIDDLE[**], D.G. KERWIN[†] AND
J.H. CHALLIS[†]

Introduction

Sports science as an academic discipline has emerged only in the second
half of the twentieth century. Whilst strands of the subject area were
evident prior to this time in other disciplines such as physiology,
psychology and biomedical physics, sports science itself has developed
largely as an outgrowth from physical education. Indeed, as far as
investigation in the university sector is concerned, where physical
education itself is a relatively young discipline, sports science is
probably no more than 15–20 years old.

The development of the subject has been highlighted by the number
of sports science conferences being held. In particular, 1989 saw the
First World Congress on Sport Sciences sponsored by the International
Olympic Committee, the proceedings of which have been published by
the United States Olympic Committee. In addition, in the UK, sports
science now forms an important part of the curriculum for both
'Λ'-level Sports Studies and Physical Education, and texts and guides
have begun to be published to cater for this market. The *Sports science
handbook*, compiled by S.P.R. Jenkins (Sunningdale Publication, 1990)
is aimed at colleges and schools. It includes a chronology of the

---

[*] Contributor on Exercise physiology and biochemistry.
[**] Contributor on Sport and exercise psychology.
[†] Contributors on Sport biomechanics.

development of the sports sciences and an encyclopaedia/dictionary of relevant terms. A useful feature is the list of addresses, journals and publishers.

Sports science involves the study of factors which make a significant contribution to human performance during the preparation for, and participation in, sport (Williams, 1978, inaugural lecture Loughborough University). As such, a dual role has emerged for sports scientists. They must remain loyal to their focus of study, i.e. sport, and provide information for academics, sports performers, coaches and other interested parties. In addition, however, the study of élite performers and the healthy population participating in sport and exercise has provided valuable information hitherto unavailable, which has improved the knowledge base in a number of different disciplines such as physiology, physics and medicine.

It has not been satisfactorily resolved which sub-disciplines should fall within sports science, and many would argue that, in addition to the more traditional sub-disciplines of exercise physiology, sports biomechanics and sports psychology, sports science should also include sports sociology and historical aspects of sport. This would be consistent with the widely-held view that investigation within a major discipline is incomplete without appropriate consideration of its social and historical context. However, in this volume, sports sociology and historical aspects of sport are given separate chapters and readers should refer to Chapters 6 and 7. Chapter 5 on Sports Medicine may also provide useful sources. Therefore, the present chapter will confine itself to three core areas of sports science, namely, exercise physiology/biochemistry, biomechanics and sport psychology.

Exercise Physiology and Biochemistry

Introduction

Within medicine and physiology, exercise physiology is used primarily as a tool to further understanding of physiological mechanisms. Within sports science, whilst researchers are interested in physiological mechanisms, they have as their primary concern the investigation of sport and exercise *per se*, the major objective being to further understanding of those factors which underlie and frequently determine performance. There have been major methodological advances in ergometry and biochemical techniques which have allowed a distinctive brand of exercise physiology to emerge within sports science. This centres on investigation of those factors affecting performance and fatigue during laboratory-based exercise, which as closely as possible, simulates the real sporting activity. However, as exercise physiology is practised within a number of different disciplines and the information found in a variety of sources, this review will be wide ranging.

Abstracting services, databases and indexes

Abstracting services covering exercise physiology with a sport bias are largely encompassed within those publications which cover sports science as a whole. Compared to other academic disciplines, they are relatively few in number and recently initiated. However, some valuable services have already emerged. Perhaps the most comprehensive is the *Sports Documentation Monthly Bulletin*, published since 1974 by the University of Birmingham, UK. This bulletin presents conference and journal papers under author and subject index, including an abstract if the author's permission is obtained. In addition, book reviews are included and overall the bulletin should appeal to a wide audience from the coach to the researcher. Also of wide appeal, because of its organization by sport and by subject area within sports science will be *SportSearch* (1986–). However, for the researcher, whilst valuable journals such as *European Journal of Applied Physiology* and *Medicine and Science in Sports and Exercise* are covered, it will be disappointing that the *Journal of Applied Physiology* is omitted. A further valuable publication which has good coverage of exercise physiology is the *Sports Medicine Bulletin* (1987–), a monthly bibliography arranged in subject sections with author and very good subject indexes. Of the databases available the most comprehensive and certainly the best for exercise physiology is the SPORT DISCUS (produced by the Sport Information Resource Centre (SIRC) and distributed by SilverPlatter). This is the compact disc version (1978–) of the SPORT database and provides a search facility by keywords or phrases, giving the full reference, an abstract and an indication of the difficulty of the paper. All major exercise physiology journals are covered. It represents a very comprehensive service and in addition, and importantly, it is easy to use!

The major published index in the field, probably used by all researchers at some stage, is the *Cumulated Index Medicus*. First published in 1879 as *Index Medicus*, the volumes have been produced without interruption to the present time. Since 1960 the annual accumulation of 12 monthly issues has been presented as the *Cumulated Index Medicus*. This is the most comprehensive summary of papers appearing in physiology journals. It is arranged in two major volumes each year with an author and subject index. The subject index is particularly good, being presented as the major subject area, for example, 'Exercise testing' and then further divided into sub-topics, for example 'Adverse effects', 'Instrumentation', 'Methods', 'Standards', etc. However, whilst the *Cumulated Index Medicus* is an exceptionally good indexing system for physiology, it does not, of course, specialize in exercise physiology and researchers should be aware that it will omit publications from journals with a main emphasis on sport. The online version MEDLINE is also useful, although searches can be expensive. Chapter 1 gives a general overview of abstracting and indexing services and online services.

Main reference works

Introductory texts to human physiology and biochemistry

Whilst there are a large number of introductory texts for human physiology one of the best in terms of easy reading and clear explanation is *Human physiology: the mechanisms of body function* by A.J. Vander *et al.* (McGraw-Hill, 1986). As far as biochemistry goes, introductory reading is more difficult, as, even in the most basic texts, background knowledge of chemistry vastly improves understanding. However, *The chemistry of life* (Pelican, 1979) by Steven Rose manages to pass on some of the excitement of biochemistry to the reader with little or no background knowledge. For a more detailed introduction aimed at first-year university students, *Biochemistry* by L. Stryer (Freeman, 1988) is particularly good.

Exercise physiology and exercise biochemistry texts

Within the broad field of exercise physiology, E. Fox's *Sport physiology* (Saunders, 1984) is likely to appeal to a wide audience from undergraduate students to coaches and performers. Similarly, because of its unique sport-by-sport approach and contribution from leading physiologists, the *Physiology of sports* edited by T. Reilly *et al.* (E. & F.N. Spon, 1990) will also appeal widely. However, for in-depth coverage of the area the *Textbook of work physiology: physiological bases of exercise* by the highly respected P.O. Astrand and K. Rodahl (McGraw-Hill, 1986) is probably still the most comprehensive text on the market and also has a list of recommended reading. In addition, *Exercise physiology* by G. Brooks and T. Fahey (Macmillan, 1985) is very readable, dealing extremely well with controversial issues in the subject area and has good sections on health and applied studies.

As far as the biochemistry of exercise is concerned, an excellent reader for the coach and performer and one which specifically applies biochemical knowledge to endurance running and sprinting is *The runner* by E. Newsholme and T. Leech (Fitness Books, 1983). For the researcher essential reading in this area includes the *Biochemistry of exercise III* and *IV* which are part of the *International series on sport sciences* (Human Kinetics, 1982, 1986) and provide, every 3–4 years, an up-to-date summary of the best work in the exercise biochemistry field.

Specialisms within exercise physiology/biochemistry

Aging

The classic work on aging with an exercise physiology perspective still remains 'Aerobic work capacity in men and women with special reference to age' by I. Astrand *(Acta Physiologica Scandinavica,* **49**, *Suppl. 169, 1960).* Another good single text is R. Shephard's *Physical activity and aging* (Croom Helm, 1978). Journals specifically oriented towards the physiological mechanisms associated with aging are a rarity. The major publication is the *Journal of Gerontology*.

Children and exercise

Within this major specialism probably the best single text is *Pediatric sports medicine for the practitioner* by O. Bar-Or (Springer-Verlag, 1983). The best series is *Children and exercise* (Human Kinetics), part of the *International series on sports sciences* published largely in the 1980s. An excellent journal in the field initiated only in 1989 is

Pediatric Exercise Science which devotes itself entirely to the area of children and exercise.

Endurance

The physiological basis of endurance running performance and the physiological and metabolic adaptations to endurance training, are amongst the most widely investigated and best understood aspects of exercise physiology. A prolific author in the field, Dave Costill has produced publications aimed at a wide audience, such as *A scientific approach to distance running* (Track and Field News, 1979) and numerous quality research papers. The specialism as a whole is well covered by key journals such as *Medicine and Science in Sports and Exercise* and the *European Journal of Applied Physiology*.

Environmental

This aspect of exercise physiology is, at present, best covered in the *Journal of Applied Physiology* and *Journal of Physiology*. These cover the two major areas of heat and cold stress and the influence of high and low pressures on performance and on physiological mechanisms. John Sutton's work, found in various issues of the *Journal of Applied Physiology*, simulating the pressure changes during an ascent of Everest and the resulting changes in the physiological responses to exercise, is a good example of recent innovative work in the field.

Health and exercise

Good introductory information is to be found in the more general text *Exercise physiology* by G.A. Brooks and T.D. Fahey (1984) and in several chapters of *Exercise, benefits, limits and adaptations* by Macleod *et al.* (E. & F.N. Spon, 1987). More detailed information is provided in P.O. Astrand and G. Grimby's *Physical activity in health and disease* (*Acta Medica Scandinavica*, Symposium Series, No. 2). Journals relevant to this area include the *Journal of Sports Medicine and Physical Fitness* and *Medicine and Science in Sports and Exercise*. Both The Sports Council (UK) and the Health Education Authority have been responsible for sponsoring a number of research projects in the area of exercise and health, the findings of which have been published. One publication in this category is a select bibliography entitled *Benefits of exercise: the evidence* by P.H. Fentem, N.B. Turnbull and E.J. Bassey (MUP, 1990) which is based on research carried out for the *New case for exercise* (Sports Council and Health Education Authority, 1988). The bibliography contains references collected from various sources over the last 15 years. Its various indexes provide access to a vast number of references which are divided by physiological function into eight major sections. More resources for physical fitness can be found in Chapter 12.

High-intensity exercise, power and strength

These topics are generally given only scant coverage in physiology texts, and the researcher would be best directed to the excellent conference proceedings *Human muscle power*, edited by N.L. Jones *et al.* (Human Kinetics, 1986) which examines human power output and performance from the single fibre to the whole body level. Two further conference proceedings are particularly good on fatigue during high-intensity exercise. *Exercise, benefits, limits and adaptations* edited by D. Macleod *et al.* (E. &. F.N. Spon, 1987) and *Human muscle fatigue: physiological mechanisms*, a collection of papers from the Ciba Foundation Symposium (Pitman Medical, 1981). There is no journal specifically directed at this topic area, but good coverage is given in key journals such as *European Journal of Applied Physiology, Medicine and Science in Sports and Exercise* and in the *Journal of Applied Physiology*.

Nutrition and performance

A good starting point within this broad area of exercise physiology for both coaches, performers and undergraduate students would be Steve Wootton's *Nutrition for sport* (Simon & Schuster, 1988) which provides both practical advice and the physiological/biochemical background upon which that advice is based. Another very practically oriented book, with sound advice, is Nancy Clark's *Sports nutrition guidebook* (Leisure Press, 1990). For the researcher, the *Proceedings of the Nutrition Society* and the *American Journal of Clinical Nutrition* provide the current research in the nutrition area with occasional, but very good, papers on exercise. Those journals which more regularly publish information relating diet and exercise include the *European Journal of Applied Physiology* and *Medicine and Science in Sports and Exercise*.

Special needs

This expanding area of exercise physiology covers the physiological and metabolic responses to exercise and the determinants of performance in athletes with a disability, for example spinal-cord injury, cystic fibrosis, and cerebral palsy. For wheelchair athletes and coaches the most popular publication is *Sports 'n' Spokes*, which provides summaries of research in an easily understood form. However, for the researcher, whilst most of the exercise physiology journals include some papers on athletes with disabilities, the journals specifically aimed at this group include, *Paraplegia, Adapted Physical Activity Quarterly* and the *Scandinavian Journal of Rehabilitation Medicine. Sports Medicine* also gives good coverage.

Review of major journals covering exercise

Physiology and biochemistry

For the coach and performer many of the journals and magazines aimed at one particular sport, e.g. *Squash Player International* and *Canoe Focus*, apply the information from original exercise physiology research papers to questions which concern their readership. These journals are often indexed in *SportSearch*. However, the original research findings are found across a broad spectrum of journals. The number one publication in the field of exercise physiology must be the *Journal of Applied Physiology* which publishes high-quality original papers on a monthly basis with a strong emphasis on human performance. This publication is closely followed in terms of quality by the *European Journal of Applied Physiology*, *Medicine and Science in Sports and Exercise* and *International Journal of Sports Medicine*, all of which tend to concentrate on human physiology, dealing both with physiological mechanisms and factors affecting performance. Journals specifically devoted to Sports Science and to exercise physiology within Sports Science include *Journal of Sports Sciences, Canadian Journal of Sport Sciences* and the *Australian Journal of Science and Medicine in Sport*. Whilst all of these journals cover other aspects of sports science in addition to exercise physiology, the area is given very good coverage. Authors to particularly look out for include Bengt Saltin, the late Lars Hermansen and David Costill in the field of exercise physiology and for exercise biochemistry, Eric Hultman and his co-workers.

Two other journals which tend to present work of an applied nature and therefore, may particularly interest coaches and performers are *The Physician and Sports Medicine* and the *Journal of Sports Medicine and Physical Fitness*. In addition there are a number of journals, which although not dedicated to exercise physiology, often include some excellent papers on exercise. Such journals include the *American Journal of Physiology*, the *Journal of Physiology*, the *Proceedings of the Nutrition Society* and *Ergonomics*.

Professional associations

Those professional associations having a close link with exercise physiology within sports science include The Physiological Society, The British Association of Sports Sciences (BASS) and The American College of Sports Medicine (ACSM). The ACSM was responsible for sponsoring an early publication on sports sciences — the *Encyclopedia of sport sciences and medicine* (Macmillan, 1971). Although out of date now it provides a useful perspective on the development of the subject. Other ASCM publications have been mentioned earlier in the chapter. Moving to the UK, BASS has three special-interest groups which reflect the core subjects associated with sports sciences. In conjunction with the National Coaching Foundation, BASS runs the Sport Science Education Programme. This scheme provides a link between those organizations requiring sports science research in specific areas and those sports scientists who can undertake the research. The British Association of Sports Medicine has an interest in sports science although its main emphasis is on sports medicine.

Other information sources

There are a number of publications of a more general nature which should be mentioned. The excellent *Exercise and Sport Sciences Reviews* — the American College of Sports Medicine Series, produced since 1973 by a variety of publishers from Academic Press to Macmillan, contains a good proportion of exercise physiology reviews specifically directed at factors affecting performance.

In addition, for all those exercise physiologists contemplating exercise testing, extremely valuable if not essential reading is to be found in the following: the American College of Sport and Medicine publication *Guidelines for exercise testing and prescription* (Lea & Febiger, 1986); the BASS's *Position statement on the physiological assessment of the elite competitor* (1988) and the Declaration of Helsinki guidelines for experiments with human subjects (recommendations from which are found in the guidelines for authors in the *Journal of Applied Physiology*). Also of interest concerning the ethics of experimentation is 'Research on healthy volunteers' (*Journal of the Royal College of Physicians of London.*, **20**(4), 1986) and at a very practical level for exercise testing in general, including field tests, *Physiological testing of the elite athlete* by J. MacDougall *et al.* (Movement Publications, 1982).

Certain organizations have responded to the increasing interest in performance testing. The British Olympic Committee Medical Centre based at Northwich Park Hospital and Clinical Research Centre offers a testing service to Olympic athletes and national class competitors. The centre provides data on élite fitness levels and will answer public enquiries. The National Sports Medicine Institute, based at St. Bartholomew's Hospital Medical College houses a Physiological Testing Centre and provides an information service. Finally, the coach education programme of the National Coaching Foundation includes many courses related to sports science.

Sport and Exercise Psychology[*]

Introduction

The study of psychological processes in sport and physical activity is not new.   Nevertheless, it was not until the 1960s that a clearly observable expansion of literature in this area was evident. At the same time, national and international organizations were being formed.

Given that psychology itself can be organized into its many specialisms, it is hardly surprising that the all-encompassing field of 'sport psychology' has, at times, suffered an identity crisis. For the sake of brevity, 'sport psychology' will be defined in terms of three different but overlapping areas: Motor learning, sport psychology and exercise psychology.

MOTOR LEARNING

Motor learning refers to the study of the acquisition of skilled movements, and as such has provided a great deal of information on how people learn and control physical movements, such as sports skills. Motor learning psychology has its origins in neurophysiology, human factors, ergonomics and experimental psychology.

SPORT PSYCHOLOGY

Rejeski and Brawley (1988, p. 239) define sport psychology as 'educational, scientific and professional contributions of psychology to the promotion, maintenance and enhancement of sport-related behaviour', where sport is seen to be 'an institutionalised game occurrence characterised by physical prowess, strategy and chance in combination'. Generally, the focus in sport psychology has been on personality, social psychology, motivation, emotion, and performance enhancement strategies. Sometimes motor learning is included as a sub-section of sport psychology, particularly in the UK. The North Americans tend to refer to motor learning and sport psychology separately.

---

[*]   The author gratefully acknowledges the assistance of Anne Dinan and Treveor Learmouth (University of Exeter Library) in the preparation of this section.

EXERCISE PSYCHOLOGY

Exercise psychology is a relatively new area of study that has seen rapid growth in recent years. Rejeski and Brawley (1988, p. 239) define exercise psychology as 'the application of the educational, scientific and professional contributions of psychology to the promotion, explanation, maintenance and enhancement of behaviours related to physical work capacity'. The exercise psychology literature has a strong health emphasis and makes particular reference to the psychological determinants or correlates of physical activity and the psychological ('mental health') outcomes of physical activity (Biddle and Fox, 1989).

Abstracting and indexing journals

As sport and exercise psychology has become a legitimate area of academic study, two things have happened. There has been a growth in both the sport and exercise science journals, and also the number of sport or exercise-related papers appearing in other psychology journals has increased greatly. This has, of course, meant that the retrieval of such information has become potentially more difficult. However, the existence of indexes, abstracting services and computer online databases means that a system of retrieval exists. Chapter 1 provides a good overview of these kinds of sources. Those wishing to learn more about locating references are advised to read the excellent publication on *How to find out in psychology* (Borchardt & Francis, 1984). The chapters on 'Indexes, abstracts and union lists' and 'Computer-based data retrieval' provide most useful summaries of the available sources.

In terms of psychology itself, *Psychological Abstracts* is recognized as the key bibliographic service for the subject. The online version of this is PSYCINFO, although it contains more than *Psychological Abstracts* as it now includes material from *Dissertation Abstracts* and other sources. It scans nearly 1000 journals and reports annually. Those wishing to use PSYCINFO may need to consult the American Psychological Association's (APA) '*Thesaurus of psychological index terms*', which is available online in PSYCINFO.

The *Social Sciences Citation Index* (SSCI) is a vast retrieval system based on author citations, but will include most of the social science literature needed by those in sport and exercise psychology. The online version is SOCIAL SCISEARCH. Other, more specialized, indexes which may include particular branches of the field include *Biological Abstracts* and *Index Medicus*. Articles with an educational focus may be found in *Education Index* or *British Education Index*. Many of these are also online, and for those interested in the medical aspects of sport and exercise psychology, the MEDLARS and BIOSIS PREVIEWS are useful. MEDLARS includes *Index Medicus* while BIOSIS PREVIEWS includes *Biological Abstracts*. References pertaining to the expanding field of psychological ('mental health') outcomes of sport and exercise may be found in *Mental Health Abstracts* which is also available online. However, it is unlikely to include items not covered by PSYCINFO or *Psychological Abstracts*.

For very up-to-date information, *Current Contents* is an invaluable publication. It is produced on a weekly basis both in printed form and on disk, and has a number of different subject versions. 'Social and behavioural sciences' is the one most relevant to sport and exercise psychologists. Addresses are given for those wishing to write for reprints of articles. A new publication from APA to complement *Psychological Abstracts* is PSYCBOOKS. This is an index of monographs and individual chapters in psychology. While this does provide a useful addition to the usual indexing of articles, it is expensive and prohibitive to many libraries.

Sport and exercise psychologists will not only need to search psychology indexes, but will also need access to sport indexes and databases. In the UK, the University of Birmingham houses the Sports Documentation Centre and this produces *Sports Documentation Monthly Bulletin* of recent journals, reports, etc. In the bulletin some titles are accompanied by abstracts although only a limited number of journals are indexed. The *Microforms publications* from the University of Oregon publishes information on postgraduate dissertations and out-of-print journals and books. The dissertations are rarely worth chasing in large numbers, since the trend is now for the better ones to appear in article form as well.

Perhaps the most comprehensive system now available in sport is *SportSearch* published by the Sport Information Resource Centre (SIRC) in Ottawa, Canada. The online version is SPORT database, available on CD-ROM as SPORT DISCUS. SIRC has recently bought the *SIRLS* (Specialized Information Retrieval and Library Services) collection and associated sport and leisure database. For more information on databases and indexes likely to be relevant to sport and exercise psychology, see Hall (1986), Lockheed Information Systems (1985) and System Development Corporation (1979).

Main reference works

The past twenty years has seen a proliferation of textbooks in sport psychology and motor learning. The exercise psychology literature is primarily in article form.

Motor learning

For those working in sport and leisure, the textbooks on motor learning are strongly 'academic' and are usually written for students at undergraduate or postgraduate level. One of the key texts is Schmidt, *Motor control and learning* (1988). This is widely recognized as the most comprehensive of the motor-learning textbooks written by a well-known authority in the field. It covers the origins and scientific methods of motor-learning research, motor behaviour and control, and motor learning and memory. It is more appropriate for senior undergraduate and postgraduate students, but is written in a clear and lucid style.

Sport psychology

The vast majority of books in this field are overview texts for students. However, in recent years two other types of books have emerged. First, there are the mental training/applied sport psychology books written more for the coach and performer than the academic (e.g. Albinson and Bull, *A mental game plan: a training programme for all sports*, 1988; Nideffer, *Athletes' guide to mental training*, 1985; Railo, *Willing to win*, 1986; Rushall, *Psyching in sport*, 1979; Syer and Connolly, *Sporting body, sporting mind*, 1984; Terry, *The winning mind*, 1989). Secondly, more specialized books have begun to appear on topics such as anxiety (Hackfort & Spielberger, *Anxiety in sports: an international perspective*, 1989), Jones and Hardy, *Stress and performance in sport* (1990), motivation (Carron, *Motivation: implications for coaching and teaching*, 1984), and group dynamics (Carron, *Group dynamics in sport*, 1988). The applied sports psychology books have proved to be popular in appeal although some have been criticized for making over-stated or generalized claims about the efficacy of some mental training techniques. Some are not based on sound psychological principles.

The text *Psychological foundations of sport* (Silva and Weinberg, 1984) is an edited volume of 32 chapters providing the most comprehensive coverage of psychology in one text. Sections include: 'Evolution of sport psychology', 'Personality', 'Anxiety and arousal', 'Motivation', 'Aggression', 'Group dynamics', 'Sport socialisation', and 'Exercise and psychological well-being'.

Exercise psychology

Only a handful of books solely on exercise psychology are available in this area, including Dishman, *Exercise adherence: its impact on public health* (1988). This is a 16-chapter multi-authored text reviewing the major issues of exercise adherence from a public health point of view.

A more recent book is that by Biddle and Mutrie, *Psychology of physical activity and exercise: a health-related perspective* (1991) which deals with the psychological antecedents of exercise. In addition to these more conventional textbooks in sport and exercise psychology and motor learning, *The world sport psychology sourcebook* (Salmela, 1991) provides a useful guide to national and international developments in the field.

Finally, it is often useful to new scholars to seek out key review papers. Those that have reviewed the theoretical field or the development of sport psychology should see Biddle, *Journal of Applied Sport Psychology*, **1**, 23–34 (1989) and Hardy, *Psychology Survey* **7** (1989) for a UK perspective and Browne and Mahoney, *Annual Review of Psychology*, **35**, 605–625, (1984) and Dishman, *Exercise and Sport Sciences Reviews*, **10**, 120–159, (1982) for a view from North America.

Major journals

The number of specialist journals in sport psychology, and associated areas, has increased greatly in recent years. The following journals include refereed research papers in psychology on a regular basis, although these are not exclusively devoted to sport and exercise psychology: *British Journal of Sports Medicine, Canadian Journal of Sport Sciences, Journal of Sports Sciences, Medicine and Science in Sports and Exercise, Pediatric Exercise Science, Research Quarterly for Exercise and Sport* and *Sports Medicine*. There is also a Research Supplement to the *British Journal of Physical Education*.

Specific journals

The following journals are devoted exclusively to motor learning and/or sport and exercise psychology. All are refereed.

INTERNATIONAL JOURNAL OF SPORT PSYCHOLOGY

This is one of the official journals of the International Society of Sport Psychology (ISSP) but has had variable quality of papers since it was first published in the early 1970s. However, from 1988 the reorganization of the editorial and reviewing procedures promises to increase the quality of published research in this journal. Indexed in *Current Contents, Psychological Abstracts* and *Social Sciences Citation Index*, as well as PSYCINFO database.

JOURNAL OF APPLIED SPORT PSYCHOLOGY

This is the official journal of the Association for the Advancement of Applied Sport Psychology (AAASP) and was first published in 1989. To provide a varied and comprehensive literature source, the journal will need to reflect the three sections of the AAASP (performance intervention, health, social psychology).

JOURNAL OF MOTOR BEHAVIOR

This is a relatively long-standing journal devoted more to motor learning than sport psychology. High-quality research papers only are published with strict refereeing standards.

JOURNAL OF SPORT BEHAVIOUR

This covers both psychological and sociological topics and tends to be less rigorous in its approach than most of the other journals listed here.

JOURNAL OF SPORT AND EXERCISE PSYCHOLOGY

This was formerly the *Journal of Sport Psychology*, and was first published in 1979 and quickly established itself as the leading research journal in the field. This has continued with the name change and, as its new title suggests, has broadened its approach to include exercise psychology research. Each issue has the 'Sport psychologist's digest' — useful summary of recently published sport and exercise psychology.

THE SPORT PSYCHOLOGIST

This is the second official journal of the ISSP and was first published in 1987. The journal is published for 'educational' sport psychologists (defined as those who teach psychological skills to sport participants and coaches), and 'clinical' sport psychologists (defined as those who provide clinical services to sport participants and coaches who have psychological dysfunctions; see 'Editorial statement' in *The Sport Psychologist* (1989), **3**, (3)). The journal is also intended for teachers of sport psychology and coaches with a particular interest or expertise in the field. The two major sections of the journal are on 'Applied research' and 'Professional practice'.

In addition to the books and journals listed, a number of organizations have produced their own publications. Those produced by the National Coaching Foundation and the Scottish Sports Council are particularly recommended for coaches. Chapter 13 provides more information.

Professional organizations

The organization of professional groups in sport and exercise psychology is far from simple or logical. The International Society of Sport Psychology (ISSP) is the parent international body and stages the World Congress every four years. In Europe, the national organizations affiliate to the European Sport Psychology Federation (FEPSAC). In the UK, sport psychology is one section of the British Association of Sports Sciences (BASS). This section includes members whose primary interest is in motor learning, exercise psychology and sport psychology. The British Psychological Society (BPS) has not, as an organization, been greatly involved in sport psychology. BASS has an accreditation scheme with an approved list of 'Registered Sport Psychologists'. Further details can be obtained from: Sport Science Education Programme, 4 College Close, Beckett Park, Leeds LS6 3QH. BASS also produces a monograph series on issues in sports science, the first and third of which were on sport psychology (Fazey and Hardy, *The inverted-U hypothesis: a catastrophe for sport psychology?*, 1988; Morris and Bull, *Mental training in sport: an overview*, 1991).

References

Albinson, J.G. and Bull, S.J. (1988) *A mental game plan: a training programme for all sports*. London, Ontario: Spodym Publishers.

Biddle, S.J.H. (1989) Applied sport psychology: a view from Britain. *Journal of Applied Sport Psychology*, **1**, 23–34.

Biddle, S.J.H. and Mutrie, N. (1991) *Psychology of physical activity and exercise: a health-related perspective*. London: Springer-Verlag.

Biddle S.J.H. and Fox K.R. (1989) Exercise and health psychology: Emerging relationships. *British Journal of Medical Psychology*, **62**, 205–216.

Borchardt, D.H. and Francis, R.D. (1984) *How to find out in psychology*. Oxford: Pergamon Press.

Browne, M.A. and Mahoney, M.J. (1984) Sport psychology. *Annual Review of Psychology*, **35**, 605–625.

Carron, A.V. (1980) *Social psychology of sport*. Ithaca, New York: Movement Publications.

Carron, A.V. (1984) *Motivation: Implications for coaching and teaching*. London, Ontario: Sports Dynamics.

Carron A.V. (1988) *Group dynamics in sport*. London, Ontario: Spodym Publishers.

Dishman, R.K. (1982) Contemporary sport psychology. *Exercise and Sport Sciences Reviews*, **10**, 120–159.

Dishman R.K. (1988) (ed.) *Exercise adherence: its impact on public health*. Champaign, IL: Human Kinetics.

Fazey, J. and Hardy, L. (1988) *The inverted–U hypothesis: a catastrophe for sport psychology?* BASS Monograph No. 1. Leeds: British Association of Sports Sciences/National Coaching Foundation.

Hackfort D. and Spielberger, C.D. (1989) (eds.) *Anxiety in sports: an international perspective*. Washington DC: Hemisphere.

Hall, J.L. (1986) *Online bibliographic databases: A directory and sourcebook*, 4th edn. London: Association for Information Management.

Hardy, L. (1989) Sport psychology. In A.M. Colman and J.G. Beaumont (eds.) *Psychology survey 7*. Leicester: BPS Books.

Jones, J.G. and Hardy, L. (1990) (eds) *Stress and performance in sport*. Chichester: John Wiley.

Lockheed Information Systems (1985) *Guide to Dialog databases*. Palo Alto, CA.

Morris, T. and Bull, S.J. (1991) *Mental training in sport: an overview*. BASS Monograph No. 3. Leeds: British Association of Sports Sciences/National Coaching Foundation.

Nideffer, R.M. (1985) *Athletes' guide to mental training*. Champaign, Illinois: Human Kinetics.

Railo, W. (1986) *Willing to win*. Huddersfield: Springfield Books.

Rejeski, W.J. and Brawley, L.R. (1988) Defining the boundaries of sport psychology. *The Sport Psychologist*, **2**, 231–242.

Rushall, B.S. (1979) *Psyching in sport*. London: Pelham.

Salmela, J. (1991) *The world sport psychology sourcebook*, 2nd edn. Champaign, IL: Human Kinetics.

Schmidt, R.A. (1988) *Motor control and learning: A behavioural emphasis*, 2nd edn. Champaign, Illinois: Human Kinetics.

Silva, J. and Weinberg R. (1984) (eds.) *Psychological foundations of sport*. Champaign, Illinois: Human Kinetics.

Syer, J. and Connolly C. (1984) *Sporting body, sporting mind*. Cambridge: Cambridge University Press.

System Development Corporation (1979). *SDC search service quick reference guide*. Santa Monica, CA.

Terry, P. (1989) *The winning mind*. Wellingborough: Thorsons.

Sports biomechanics

Introduction

Sports biomechanics is a relatively new science which has grown out of biomechanics, itself a combination of the methods of enquiry and analysis used in biology, engineering and applied mathematics. It also embraces bio-engineering, animal mechanics and human gait analysis. Sports biomechanics focuses upon the human participation in sport, during both training and competition. In addition, sports biomechanics techniques have been developed and applied in formalized laboratory environments, where more control can be exercised over the data-collection processes. This has been one of the major topics in sports biomechanics since its inception in the late 1960s. During the 1970s, most of the major international and national societies featuring sports biomechanics were established, and regular meetings commenced at which experimental data were presented and discussed. A sub-discipline has emerged within sports biomechanics which concentrates upon investigating aspects of equipment design in relation to performance (e.g. running shoes, track design, pole vault poles, javelins).

In the 1980s much emphasis was placed upon numerical data processing. In particular, methods for improving the quality of kinematic data derived from cine-film were developed. Other improvements in data-recording techniques have included the use of CMOS chip technology for the logging of force and electromyographical (EMG) data during activity and improvements in radio-telemetry for similar purposes. The rapid advancement in very powerful microcomputers has made much of this possible.

There has been, over the last decade, a large amount of research into the development of techniques for quantifying internal forces, muscle movements and segmental energy patterns. However, this work is not new: see for example, Elftman's (1939, 1940) published papers on walking and running which formulated many of the techniques still in use to-day. The major enhancements to his techniques have only been possible with the assistance of modern equipment and algorithms and have enabled optimization techniques to be used extensively in the estimation of muscle forces.

Sports biomechanics is now a subject of study in many undergraduate and postgraduate degree courses in the UK and around the world. It is seen as one of the key subjects in a sports science or sports studies degree programme, and appears in various forms within most higher education courses focusing upon sport, human movement or physical education.

Specialist associations

The British Association of Sports Sciences (BASS)

This has grown from an amalgamation of three sports science groups — Exercise physiology, Sport psychology and Sports biomechanics. Within this society there is an open section which caters for all those interested in the study of sport, but not necessarily within one of the three listed disciplines. The sports biomechanics section holds two meetings each year and produces proceedings which are obtainable from the secretary of the society. Most of its members are lecturers and researchers specializing in sports biomechanics. Interested engineers, coaches and athletes have also attended meetings and made contributions to the proceedings.

The International Society of Biomechanics (ISB)

This grew out of the First International Biomechanics Seminar in 1967, hosted by Wartenweiller in Zurich. This meeting is commonly regarded as the formal beginning of the discipline of biomechanics, although many pioneers had made important contributions as early as the late 1800s. The ISB is now the major international society representing biomechanics and has a sub-section dedicated to sports biomechanics. Bi-annual congresses are held around the world and the proceedings published. The ISB has an electronic mailing forum for discussion and disseminating information. A relatively new sub-section of ISB concentrates on computer simulation in biomechanics. This group has held two major meetings, both immediately prior to the last two ISB congresses and is destined to expand in the future.

The European Society of Biomechanics (ESB)

ESB meets in the intervening years between the ISB congresses. Although sports biomechanics is represented within the conferences, the main emphasis tends to be on medical applications of biomechanics, including orthodontics.

North American Congress of Biomechanics (NACOB)

This is the equivalent of ESB. Sports biomechanics features strongly within this group. Meetings are annual, from which sets of two-page abstracts rather than formal conference proceedings are published. The ISB are now following this lead with Biomechanics XI, The Proceedings of the Amsterdam Congress, being the final full conference report.

Major texts

General biomechanics

Biomechanics of human movement (D.A. Winter, 2nd edn, 1979) is a very good general text on experimental biomechanics. It is a popular and useful text for a sports biomechanics course, but because most of the worked examples are based on the study of human gait, its general applicability is limited.

General sport mechanics

Biomechanics of sports techniques (J. Hay, 1985) probably the most internationally successful book on sports biomechanics, is in its third edition. The first seven chapters provide the theoretical background mechanics, but use sporting examples throughout. Linear and angular motion, together with an introduction to fluid mechanics, are covered. The second part of the book concentrates on sport, and uses the material from the first seven chapters to examine the techniques employed in a variety of sports, including track and field athletics, swimming, gymnastics and ball games.

Shoes and playing surfaces

Sport shoes and playing surfaces (E.C. Frederick, 1984), *Biomechanics of running shoes* (B.M. Nigg, 1986) and *The shoe in sport* (B. Segesser and W. Pforringer, eds., 1990) are compilations of recent research into the nature and characteristics of shoes and floor surfaces in sport. They are edited collections, covering a wide range of topics from Achilles tendon stresses in tennis to re-designing the Harvard University indoor running track. Both are interesting and representative of the rapid growth in knowledge and understanding about the interaction between and athlete and his environment. A less formal and readable book on a similar topic is the *Running shoe book* (P.R. Cavanagh, 1980).

Skeletal system

Basic biomechanics of the skeletal system (V.H. Frankel and M. Nordin, 1990) is an excellent overview for anyone interested in the 'bio' of biomechanics. Bone, tendon and muscle are examined as mechanical structures. The book goes on to examine in detail individual articulations in the body. This is an excellent course text for students of ergonomics, and bio-engineering as well as for students of sports techniques and sports injuries.

Overview of major research themes

Current research in sports biomechanics (B. van Gheluwe and J. Atha, 1987), covers a wide range of topics and includes contributions from the USA, Canada, UK, Germany, Australia, Switzerland and Holland. Muscle elasticity, biomechanical limitations of sprinting, shoe and foot mechanics, physical and theoretical models of human movement, and the quantification of EMG are some of the topics included. This edited collection gives some indication of the scope and variety of work currently being undertaken within the field of sports biomechanics research.

Journals

There is only one journal which deals exclusively with sports biomechanics — the *International Journal of Sport Biomechanics*. It provides a publishing forum for the biomechanical analysis of the Olympic Games, funded by the IOC Medical Commission. The premier journal in biomechanics, which often contains sport-related papers, is the *Journal of Biomechanics*. There are a number of other journals which, although not directly connected with sports biomechanics, do contain related articles. These include *Human Movement Science* and the *Journal of Human Movement Studies*.

A number of journals which are concerned with sports science or sports medicine provide a forum for biomechanical papers. Amongst these are: *International Journal of Sports Medicine; Journal of Sports Sciences; Canadian Journal of Sport Sciences; Research Quarterly for Exercise and Sport; Medicine and Science in Sport and Exercise,* and the *Australian Journal of Science and Medicine in Sport. Exercise and Sport Sciences Reviews* specializes in review articles and each issue contains articles which are concerned with sports biomechanics.

Specialist magazines

There are a large number of specialist magazines which report on coaching for a particular sport or sports. These are generally not peer review journals, but are still a useful source of information. Chapter 13 covers these sources in more detail. They often contain general biomechanical articles relating to sport. Some researchers publish preliminary reports of their academic research in these magazines or simplified versions of research aimed at the practitioner and/or coach. For example, track and field athletics is covered by *Modern Athlete and Coach, Athletics Coach, Track and Field Quarterly Review* and *Track Technique.* Information on all such specialist magazines can be found in *SportSearch,* a monthly indexing journal published by the Sport Information Research Centre (SIRC) which has a good coverage of individual sports magazines.

Abstracting and indexing services

There are a number of abstracting services concerned with sport in general, all of which contain a sports biomechanics section. *Sports Medicine Bulletin* is published monthly by the National Sports Medicine Institute, and has a section on biomechanics which draws from much of the medical literature. A comprehensive list of references in sports medicine, with a section on biomechanics, is provided by *Physical Fitness/Sports Medicine* which is published quarterly. *Sports Documentation Monthly Bulletin* provides references on sports biomechanics from sport-specific related literature. *SportSearch* has already been mentioned. These abstracting services are covered in more detail in Chapter 1.

Finally, mention should be made of two other abstracting and indexing services, which although not connected with sport or biomechanics directly, provide access to much useful information. *Applied Mechanics Reviews* (ASME) carries a general biomechanics section (550) and a sports biomechanics section (556) which provide abstracts. *Index Medicus* has a section for sport, and references to sports biomechanics related work can be found under specific headings. It is also available online and on CD-ROM.

Databases

There are a number of online databases concerned with sport. A general overview of them is provided in Chapter 1. HERACLES is a French service which is growing at a very rapid rate. It provides scientific and practical material on sport, with references from 1973 to the present day. SPOFOR is provided by the Bundesinstitut für Sportwissenschaft in Cologne and contains details of all the main European research projects into sport, including biomechanics. The database is also available at The Sport Council, but cannot be accessed directly. The most comprehensive of the services available is the SPORT database, provided by SIRC (Canada). It contains 230 000 citations to books and theses from 1947, and serials from 1975 to the present day. A sub-set of the information contained on this database is also available in published form in the *Sport bibliography*, which has been published in 13 volumes, 1974–1984, covering all aspects of sport, including sports medicine and biomechanics. The information contained on this database is also available on CD-ROM as SPORT DISCUS (SilverPlatter). At present, this database contains about 8000 biomechanics references from international sources. A search on a general skill like jumping provides about 260 references. Other examples include kicking, with 73, trampolining, 26 and fencing, 13. These figures are based on the 1989 edition.

Bibliographies

There are two major bibliographies in biomechanics. The first is concerned with gait but includes references to running, Vaughan *et al.* (1987) *Biomechanics of human gait: an annotated bibliography.* The second and more comprehensive is a J.G. Hay's (1987) *Bibliography of biomechanics literature.* This is now in its fifth edition, each one being an update of the previous edition. It covers all areas of biomechanics, and divides the literature by individual sports.

Conference proceedings

In addition to the proceedings of the ISB and ESB congresses, scientific conferences which focus upon a single or collection of sports are becoming more common. In 1988, the First World Congress on Football was held in Liverpool, UK, and the proceedings published by Spon. Swimming biomechanics has had a series of international conferences with full proceedings published by Human Kinetics. A regular feature of major sporting competitions like the Olympic and Commonwealth Games has become the pre-games conference. The proceedings of both the *Olympic Scientific Congress* and the *Commonwealth and International Conference on Sport, Physical Education, Dance, Recreation and Health*, are often published in multi-volumes. The latest in this line of specialist conferences is the First World Congress of Golf, published in 1990.

Major techniques in biomechanical analysis

Opto-electronic techniques

Cine-film has been the major research medium in sports biomechanics, mainly because of its versatility and accuracy. More recently, the introduction of charge-couple device video cameras has provided a new visual format which is both useful and convenient for recording and analysing sports skills. Two-dimensional, or planar studies have been popular during the 1970s but in more recent times the emphasis on three-dimensional data analysis has become more prevalent. All these cine-film techniques rely on the principles of photogrammetry, with the direct linear transformation (DLT) technique being currently the most dominant.

The resulting data can be used to quantify movement and as input to calculation procedures for determining velocities and accelerations in both linear and angular forms. This latter process relies upon differentiation of numerical data which has proved to be a major area of research in the field of sports biomechanics. It relies heavily upon electrical engineering techniques of signal processing before reliable data can be obtained. These principles are comprehensively covered, for example by Rabiner and Gold (1975). With the addition of human inertia data, and the application of inverse Newtonian mechanics, forces, momenta and energy can be calculated.

Alongside the developments in traditional visual recording systems, a number of automatic opto-electronic devices have been introduced during the last twenty-five years. The most notable of these are Selspot, Vicon, Elite and CODA. Other units are continually being developed but as all require some form of markers to be placed on the subject, they have not been used extensively in sports biomechanics. Modern developments in the automatic tracking of video images offer exciting possibilities for the future. Systems produced by Peak Performance in the USA represent one important example.

Force transducers

These include force plates, load cells and sports equipment instrumented with strain gauges. The two leading manufacturers are currently AMTI from the USA, who produce strain gauge-based systems and Kistler from Switzerland who specialize in piezo-electric quartz crystal technology. A few of these units have been used to collect force data during international competition, e.g. the World Weightlifting Championships, Sweden, in 1985, and the Calgary Winter Olympic 70-metre ski-jump competition in 1988. Individual load cells have been used for measuring tensions in support cables, loads in gymnastic apparatus and forces in ski boots. Strain gauges have been applied to tennis rackets, cycle cranks, canoe paddles, and even human Achilles tendons in attempts to quantify better the nature and magnitude of forces developed during sport. In most analyses of sport, force data are combined with data from other measurement techniques to describe the activities more fully.

Electromyography (EMG)

This is a measurement technique used for studying the electrical activity in muscle. The electrical signals are picked up via surface-mounted or in-dwelling electrodes. The signals are then processed in a variety of ways to give an indication of the associated muscle activity. Although primarily a laboratory technique it has been used successfully in sport environments for example by Clarys in swimming (1983). Dainty and Norman (1987) include a large amount of detail on EMG and other important techniques in an excellent reference text, *Standardizing biomechanical testing in sport*.

Modelling

The process of modelling, whether physical or mathematical, is growing in popularity. It is the most exciting but most challenging aspect of modern biomechanics research. Representing the inertia characteristics of the human body has been one avenue of research. By taking measurements of athletes' physical dimensions and using these to define geometric solids, descriptions of the mass, moment of inertia and centre of mass locations can be obtained on a very specialized group of the population. Once these data are combined within a simulation model of human movement, again based on mathematical formulae, two major advantages are gained. The fundamental mechanics underlying human motion can be examined in a systematic and controlled way, and the implications of specific strategies can be examined without the need to disturb or endanger the athlete in question. Recent advances in computing technology have aided the progress of theoretical modelling in particular. Notable examples of this type have been produced by Van Gheluwe (1981), Hatze (1981) and Yeadon (1990).

Videos and films

Although the filming of sport has long been popular, it is only recently that filming for scientific purposes has been considered important. In 1982 The Medical Sub-Commission of the International Olympic Committee was founded to provide a 'Research basis for the creation of an Olympic Scientific Film Archive'. Scientific studies of the Olympics has been conducted as early as 1949, but it is only in very recent times that properly formulated, research-based filming and video recording have been undertaken at major events. The results of these data collection processes are distributed in two ways: as scientific papers in academic and sport-specific journals and in various video and cine-film formats. An example of the latter from the 1984 Los Angeles Olympics includes films and videos on men's and women's gymnastics, weightlifting and track and field athletics. All details can be obtained from the IOC Medical Commission, Chateau de Vidy, 1007 Lausanne, Switzerland.

Additional video material on biomechanics related specifically to coaching can be obtained from the National Coaching Foundation, Leeds, UK. The NCF has recently published *Action replay — audio visual resources in sport and recreation*, edited by C. Rankin and S. Chappel (1990). They also publish three titles which deal specifically with sports biomechanics.

References

Cavanagh, P.R. (1980) *The running shoe book*. Mountain View, Anderson World.

Clarys, J.P. (1983) A review of EMG in swimming: explanation of facts and/or feedback information. In A.P. Hollander, P. Huying and G. De Groot (eds.) *Biomechanics and medicine in swimming*, 123–135. Champaign, Illinois: Human Kinetics.

Crowninshield, R.D. (1978) Use of optimization techniques to predict muscle forces. *Transactions ASME Journal of Biomechanical Engineering*, **100**, 88–92.

Dainty, D.A. and Norman R.W. (1987) *Standardizing biomechanical testing in sport*. Champaign, Illinois: Human Kinetics.

Dempster, W.T. (1955) *Space requirements of the seated operator*, Technical Report, 55-159. Wright-Patterson Air Force Base, Ohio: WADC.

Elftman, H. (1939) Forces and energy changes in the leg during walking. *American Journal of Physiology*, **125**, 339–356.

Elftman, H. (1940) The work done by muscles in running. *American Journal of Physiology*, **129**, 672–684.

Frankel, V.H. and Nordin, M. (1990) *Basic biomechanics of the skeletal system*, 2nd edn. Philadelphia: Lea & Febiger.

Frederick, E.C. (1984) *Sport shoes and playing surfaces*. Champaign, Illinois: Human Kinetics.

Hatze, H. (1981) A comprehensive model for human motion simulation and its applications to the take-off phase of the long jump. *Journal of Biomechanics*, **14**, 135–142.

Hay, J.G. (1985) *The biomechanics of sports techniques*, 3rd edn. Englewood Cliffs, N.J.: Prentice-Hall.

Hay, J.G. (1987) *A bibliography of biomechanics literature*, 5th edn. University of Iowa: J.G. Hay.

Nigg, B.M. (1986) *Biomechanics of running shoes*. Champaign, Illinois: Human Kinetics.

Patrico, A.G., Mann, R.W., Simons, S.R. and Mansour, J.M. (1981) An evaluation of the approaches of optimisation models in the prediction of muscle forces during human gait. *Journal of Biomechanics*, **14**, 513–525.

Rabiner, L.R. and Gold B. (1975) *Theory and application of digital signal processing*. Englewood Cliffs, N.J.: Prentice-Hall.

Rankin C. and Chappel, S. (eds.) (1990) *Action replay — audio visual resources in sport and recreation*. National Coaching Foundation and Sheffield Sports Library and Information Service.

Segesser, B. and Pforringer, W. (1990) *The shoe in sport* (translated by T.J. DeKornfeld). London: Woolfe.

Van den Bogert, A. and Woltring, H.J. (1989) BIOMH-L: An electronic mail discussion list for biomechanics and kinesiology. *Journal of Biomechanical Engineering*, **111**, 93–94.

Van Gheluwe, B. (1981) A simulation model for airborne twist in backward somersaults. *Journal of Human Movement Studies*, **3**, 5–20.

Van Gheluwe, B. and Atha, J. (1987) *Current research in sports biomechanics*. Basel: Karger.

Vaughan, C.L., Murphy, G.N. and du Toit, L.L. (1987) *Biomechanics of human gait: an annotated bibliography*. Champaign, Illinois: Human Kinetics.

Winter, D.A. (1979) *Biomechanics of human movement*. Chichester: Wiley Science.

Yeadon, M.R., Atha, J. and Hales, F.D. (1990) The simulation of aerial movement. Part IV: A computer simulation model. *Journal of Bio mechanics*, **23**(1), 85 89.

CHAPTER FIVE

Sports medicine

K. WALTER AND D.S. TUNSTALL PEDOE

History and development

Sports medicine has a long history. The Ancient Greeks and Romans were well aware of the role of exercise in the maintenance of health, and the best physicians were often entrusted with caring for athletes in the Olympic and Gladatorial Games, supervising their training and handling injuries. These attitudes are documented in the first recorded book on sports medicine: *Artis gymnastica apud antiquos celeberrimae, nostris temporibus ignoralae* was published in 1569 by Geronimo Mercuralia and is an illustrated history of Greek and Roman attitudes to diet, bathing and exercise and their effects on health and disease.

Despite this ancient precedent of a close relationship between physician and athlete, and the evolution of sports medicine as a recognized activity in Germany just before the First World War, sports medicine in the UK has been slow to establish itself, and has been regarded as an 'orphan' or a sub-speciality to established areas of expertise such as orthopaedics, cardiology, physiotherapy or nutrition. However, the founding of specialist organizations (see Appendix 1), the creation of a Diploma in Sports Medicine, and the growth of the published literature have been major factors in its emergence as a discipline in its own right.

The twentieth century has also seen much development in sports medicine in the USA. The American Medical Association appointed an *ad hoc* committee on Injuries in Sports in 1951, which later became a standing committee. One of the largest and most productive organizations is the interdisciplinary American College of Sports Medicine, founded in 1954. The American Orthopedic Society for Sports Medicine was established in 1971 and the National Athletic

Trainers Association began in 1938. All these organizations publish high-quality journals which comprise a large proportion of the English-language publications in this field.

Sports medicine is a diverse subject, which requires selective information from and integration with many other disciplines. Not only are the obvious sports injury specialities of orthopaedics and rheumatology involved, but environmental medicine, exercise physiology, cardiology, respiratory medicine, infectious diseases, clinical pharmacology, biomechanics, equipment and training variables can all be part of this catholic discipline. One of the major problems is where 'sports medicine' demarcates from 'sports science'.

This diversity increases the range of publications in which material of interest to the sports medicine practitioner may appear. Sports medicine often features as a 'special issue' of journals, or as sections of books of related interest. It has also caused problems for the cataloguer, and sports medicine documents are usually to be found scattered throughout the library rather than conveniently shelved together.

This chapter will focus on the major publications dedicated to sports medicine and review the secondary sources most useful in locating the relevant literature. Special consideration will be given to sports injuries, physiotherapy, drugs in sport and nutrition. Physiological and psychological aspects are covered in greater detail in Chapter 4.

Journals

English-language journals

Sports medicine journals are often the official publication of a relevant national or international organization. The *American Journal of Sports Medicine* is the official journal of the American Orthopedic Society for Sports Medicine and concentrates on aspects of sports injury diagnosis, aetiology, prevention and management with emphasis on surgical techniques. The American College of Sports Medicine (ACSM) publishes a range of material. *Medicine and Science in Sports and Exercise* includes a range of original articles reporting clinical and physiological investigations. The annual *Exercise and Sports Sciences Reviews* contains extensive reviews on topical subjects and *Sports Medicine Bulletin* is a newsletter-style publication mostly concerned with ACSM membership news. Also originating from the USA is *Physician and Sportsmedicine*, 'a peer reviewed journal on the medical aspects of sports, exercise and fitness'. This popular journal contains articles on current issues in addition to news items and events listings. *Clinics in Sports Medicine* is a relatively new title in the reputed series published by W.B. Saunders Company. Each quarterly issue focuses on a specific topic and contains comprehensive review-type articles. *Sports Medicine Digest* contains short, practical items with editorial comment.

Other English-language journals include the *British Journal of Sports Medicine*, which, with a recently enhanced appearance and content publishes proceedings, news, reviews and original refereed articles. This is the official publication of the British Association of Sport and Medicine (see Appendix 1) and contains material to interest all sections of its membership. The *Journal of Sports Medicine and Physical Fitness* publishes research and practical papers pertaining to applied physiology, sports medicine and sport psychology. The *International Journal of Sports Medicine* has a similarly broad scope and also publishes regular supplements containing conference proceedings or abstracts. *Sports Medicine* is an excellent authoritative journal which includes original investigations and reviews with extensive bibliographies. *Annals of Sports Medicine* which has excellent review articles and some original refereed material has recently ceased publication. The *Australian Journal of Science and Medicine in Sport* and the *New Zealand Journal of Sports Medicine* are both official publications of the appropriate national body and contain original articles and editorial material. A promising recent publication is the annual *Advances in Sports Medicine and Fitness*, which contains detailed, well-referenced review articles.

The appearance of several new titles further illustrates continuing interest in an emerging field. They include:

- *International Journal of Sport Nutrition* (published by Human Kinetics Publishers, Inc)
- *Scandinavian Journal of Medicine & Science in Sports* (published in Denmark by Munksgaard International Publishers)
- *Sports Medicine and Soft Tissue Trauma* (a glossy journal with short items). Published by John Wiley & Sons and sponsored by Lederle Laboratories. Distributed free to general practitioners.
- *Sports Injury Management:* A quarterly series (published by Williams & Wilkins).
- *Sports Training, Medicine and Rehabilitation* (published by Harwood Academic Publishers).

A selection of the general medical journals which regularly include relevant articles is as follows (it should be noted, however, that this list could be extended considerably): *American Journal of Cardiology; Archives of Physical Medicine and Rehabilitation; Australian Family Physician; British Medical Journal; Foot and Ankle; Injury; Instructional Course Lectures; Journal of the American Dietetic Association; Journal of the American Medical Association; Journal of*

Bone and Joint Surgery; Lancet; New England Journal of Medicine; Pediatrics; Practitioner.

Since a large number of the journals are North American it may be useful to consult Chapter 15 for more information on medical journals.

Foreign-language journals

Some of the foreign-language journals which include English abstracts are: *Médecine du Sport; Deutsche Zeitschrift für Sportmedizin; Medicina dello Sport; Medizin und Sport; Schweizerische Zeitschrift für Sportmedizin; Sportverletzung Sportschaden.*

Special interest journals

Of special interest to physiotherapists is the *Journal of Orthopedic and Sports Physical Therapy* (Orthopedic and Sports Physical Therapy Sections of the American Physical Therapy Association – see Appendix 1). Clinical and research papers, together with abstracts, book reviews and news items are included. *Physiotherapy in Sport* is the journal of the Association of Chartered Physiotherapists in Sports Medicine (see Appendix 1) and contains news and short items with some original material. The *Journal of the Canadian Athletic Therapists Association* publishes short articles and membership news. *Sports Therapy* is a new journal published by the Society of Sports Therapists (see Appendix 1). Relevant articles are also found in the mainstream physiotherapy journals such as *Physiotherapy* and *Physical Therapy.*

Among the other specialist journals are the *International Journal of Sports Cardiology*, the official journal of the Italian Society of Sports Cardiology, which publishes original papers in the field of clinical cardiology and cardiovascular physiology applied to sports activities. Clinical and experimental research in sports traumatology is documented in the *Journal of Sports Traumatology and Related Research* (formerly *Italian Journal of Sports Traumatology*) which is the official journal of the Italian Society of Sports Traumatology. Each text is published in both English and Italian. *Chiropractic Sports Medicine*, published by Williams & Wilkins, is dedicated to the advancement of manipulative treatment and biomechanics of sports injuries.

Books and monographs

General textbooks

The *Olympic book of sports medicine* (Oxford: Blackwell Scientific,

1988) edited by A. Dirix, H.G. Knuttgen and K. Tittel, is the first volume of a new *Encyclopaedia of sports medicine*, a collaborative project involving the International Olympic Committee, the International Federation of Sports Medicine and Blackwell Scientific Publications. Fifty chapters span nearly 700 well-presented pages. *Sport and medicine* (London: Butterworths, 1983) by P.N. Sperryn is one of the best introductory texts and *Sports medicine* (2nd edn., London: Edward Arnold, 1976) edited by J.G.P. Williams and P.N. Sperryn is a comprehensive treatise with 29 eminent contributors. It is now rather old but otherwise unrivalled in its scope and coverage. Other general texts include *Essentials of sports medicine* (Edinburgh: Churchill-Livingstone, 1986) by G.R. McLatchie, *Sports fitness and sports injuries* (London: Faber & Faber, 1981) edited by T. Reilly, *Sports medicine* (2nd edn., Baltimore: Urban & Schwarzenberg, 1983) edited by O. Appenzeller and R. Atkinson and *Sports medicine* (Philadelphia: W.B. Saunders Company, 1984) edited by R.H. Strauss.

Medicine and sport science is an irregular series of monographs published by Karger. While mostly of high quality, the price is likely to be prohibitive to many of its potential audience. The 1984 Olympic Scientific Congress Proceedings (Champaign, IL: Human Kinetics, 1986) were published as a set of 10 volumes, with several individual titles of interest to the sports medicine practitioner: *Sport and elite performers* (edited by D.M. Landers); *Sport and aging* (edited by B.D. McPherson); *Sport and human genetics* (edited by R.M. Malina and C. Bouchard); *The dancer as athlete* (edited by C.G. Shell); *Sport for children and youths* (edited by M.R. Weiss and D. Gould); and *Sport, health and nutrition* (edited by F.I. Katch). A promising new series published by F.A. Davis is entitled *Contemporary exercise and sports medicine:* individual titles so far are *Women and exercise* (edited by M.M. Shangold and G. Mirkin), *Drugs and the athlete* (edited by G.I. Wadler and B. Hainline) and *Winter sports medicine* (edited by M.J. Casey).

Sports injuries

J.G.P. Williams's *A colour atlas of injury in sport* (2nd edn., London: Wolfe Medical, 1990) follows the familiar format and standard of the *Wolfe medical atlas* series with over 500 annotated clinical pictures. Also by Williams is *Diagnostic picture tests in injury in sport* (London: Wolfe Medical, 1988), one of another familiar series published by Wolfe, which has questions and answers relating to 200 photographs and radiographs. *Sports injuries and their treatment* (London: Chapman & Hall, 1986), edited by B. Helal, J.B. King and W.J. Grange, is a detailed text with a strong orthopaedic input. Injuries are described by anatomical site, with additional chapters on prevention, footwear, psychology and legal aspects. In contrast, the majority of chapters in *Sports injuries: mechanisms, prevention, and treatment* (Baltimore: Williams & Wilkins, 1985), edited by R.C. Schneider, J.C. Kennedy and M.L. Plant, deal with injuries as they occur in specific sports. Later sections describe the management of different types of injury. *Sports injuries* by M. Read (London: Breslich & Foss, 1984) is a 'self-help' guide for athletes and outlines the principles of diagnosis and rehabilitation with great clarity. Further titles selected from the plethora available are: L. Peterson and P. Renstrom, *Sports injuries: their prevention and treatment* (London: Martin Dunitz, 1986); P.F. Vinger and E.F. Hoerner (eds.), *Sports injuries: the unthwarted epidemic* (2nd edn., Littleton MA: PSG Publishing Co., 1986) and D.S. Muckle, *Injuries in sport* (2nd edn.) Bristol: Wright, 1982). Some textbooks have a more specific anatomic approach such as *Sports medicine of the lower extremity* (New York: Churchill-Livingstone, 1989) edited by S.I. Subotnick, *Athletic injuries to the head, neck and face* (Philadelphia: Lea & Febiger, 1982) edited by J.S. Torg and *Soft tissue injuries in sport* (Oxford: Blackwell Scientific, 1988) by S. Lachmann.

Physiotherapy

Good primary resource material for the sport physiotherapist is rare. The American equivalent to the term 'sport physiotherapy', viz. 'athletic training', often causes confusion in the literature. *Relevant topics in athletic training* (Ithaca, N.Y.: Mouvement Publications, 1978) edited by K. Scriber and E.J. Burke gives basic practical information on a wide spectrum of subjects but is now over 10 years old and hence of limited value. Slightly more recent is *Handbook of athletic training* (Ithaca, N.Y.: Mouvement Publications, 1983) by P. Hossler, which is largely based on the personal experience of the author. *Athletic training and sports medicine* (Chicago, IL: American Academy of Orthopedic Surgeons, 1984) is an essentially practical volume which attempts to consolidate the relationship between trainer and physician. *Rehabilitation of athletic injuries: an atlas of therapeutic exercise* (Chicago: Year Book Medical, 1987) by J.S. Torg, J.V. Vegso and E. Torg, is well described by its title. *Sports injuries: A self help guide* (London: John Murray, 1984) and *Knee health* (London: John Murray, 1988) both by V. Grisogono, attempt to bring a physiotherapist's knowledge to a wider lay audience. Sport physiotherapy facilities and modalities are discussed in *Sports injuries (International perspectives in physical therapy:* **4**) also edited by Grisogono.

Sports nutrition

Nutrition for sport (London: Simon & Schuster, 1988) by S. Wootton in which the author gives practical advice based on theoretical principles, is perhaps the best recent text and has attracted a wide readership. *Eat to compete* (Chicago: Year Book Medical, 1988) by M. Peterson and K. Peterson is aimed at athletes and their advisers. Almost one-third of the book is devoted to appendices on subjects such as the composition of foods, energy expenditure in different activities and diet guidelines. K. Inge and P. Brukner's *Food for sport* (London: Kingswood Press, 1988) is a concise and entertaining text which is similarly intended for the sportsperson. It covers the needs of special groups such as children, diabetics and vegetarians in addition to the diets of competitive athletes. N. Clarke's *Nutrition guidebook* (Champaign, IL: Leisure Press, 1990) is aimed at a similar audience. For more detail, there is much useful material in M.H. Williams' *Nutritional aspects of human physical and athletic performance* (2nd edn., Springfield, IL: Charles C. Thomas, 1985), F.I. Katch and W.D. McArdle's *Nutrition, weight control and exercise* (3rd edn., Philadelphia: Lea & Febiger, 1988) and in W.D. McArdle, F.I. Katch and V.L. Katch's *Exercise physiology: energy, nutrition, and human performance* (2nd edn., Philadelphia: Lea & Febiger, 1986).

Sports cardiology

Cardiovascular aspects of exercise participation in normal and cardiac populations are described in detail in 'Exercise and the heart' (*Cardiology Clinics*, **5**(2), 1987, pp. 147–348) edited by P. Hanson. *Exercise and the heart: clinical concepts* (2nd edn., Chicago: Year Book Medical, 1987) by V.F. Froelicher concentrates on exercise testing whilst *Cardiovascular system and physical exercise* (Boca Raton, FL: CRC Press, 1987) by V.L. Karpman describes the cardiovascular system's physiological adaptations and responses to exercise. *Athletics and the heart* (Chicago: Year Book Medical, 1987) by R. Rost is written for a wider audience and outlines cardiovascular function during exercise, possible cardiac incidents for athletic populations and the value of exercise for the cardiac patient.

Drugs in sport

The controversial issues surrounding drugs in sport have reached media headlines but there are relatively few textbooks which cover the subject well. One of the best edited works is M.H. Williams' *Ergogenic aids in sport* (Champaign, IL: Human Kinetics, 1983). This includes sections on all methods of performance enhancement: nutritional, pharmacological, physiological, psychological and mechanical. R.H. Strauss also pursues this broader approach in *Drugs and performance in sports* (Philadelphia: W.B. Saunders, 1987) with chapters on ethical issues, nutrition and psychology as well as banned substances. The pharmacological actions, therapeutic uses and adverse effects of proscribed drugs are detailed in *Drugs in sport* (London: E. & F.N. Spon, 1988) edited by D.R. Mottram. The effects on performance of commonly used self-medication and 'social' drugs is also assessed. M.G. di Pasquale's *Drug use and detection in amateur sports* (Ontario: M.G.D. Press, 1984) describes the pharmacology, adverse effects and detection of the five categories of drug banned by the International Olympic Committee (IOC). Commercial preparations of these drugs are listed in the text and index. The Sports Council produces a useful information pack entitled *Doping control* which contains booklets on anabolic steroids, IOC doping classes, IOC accredited laboratories and advice on medication for athletes travelling abroad. *Foul play: drug abuse in sports* (Oxford: Blackwell, 1986) by T. Donohoe and N. Johnson is written for a lay audience and contains many anecdotal illustrations.

Special categories

Certain categories of athlete require special consideration, and this is reflected in the literature. Those involved with athletes at the highest level will be interested in *The elite athlete* (Champaign, IL: Life Enhancement, 1985) edited by N.K. Butts, T.T. Gushiken and B. Zarins which has sections on administration, biomechanics, psychology, physiology and nutrition, with contributors from the United States Olympic Committee.

Papers presented at an International Masters Sports Medicine Symposium held in conjunction with the inaugural World Masters Games in 1985 are published in *Sports medicine for the mature athlete* (Indianapolis: Benchmark Press, 1986), edited by R.M. Brock and J.R. Sutton.

There are a number of useful books which deal with those aspects of sports medicine and physiology which are peculiar to women. They include *Female endurance athletes* (Champaign, IL: Human Kinetics, 1986) edited by B.L. Drinkwater, *Sport science perspectives for women* (Champaign, IL: Human Kinetics, 1988), edited by J. Puhl, C.H. Brown and R.O. Voy; *Women and exercise: physiology and sports medicine* (Philadelphia: F.A. Davis, 1988) edited by M.M. Shangold and G. Mirkin, and *Women, sport and performance: a physiological perspective* (Champaign, IL: Human Kinetics, 1985) by C.L. Wells. More specific titles include *Exercise in pregnancy* (Baltimore: Williams & Wilkins, 1986), edited by R. Artal and R.A. Wiswell and *The menstrual cycle*

and physical activity (Champaign, IL: Human Kinetics, 1986) edited by
J.L. Puhl and C.H. Brown.

Children represent another category which needs specialist
knowledge and information. Titles are *Competitive sport for children
and youth: an overview of research and issues* (Champaign, IL: Human
Kinetics, 1988) edited by E.W. Brown and C.F. Branta; *Pediatric and
adolescent sports medicine* (Boston: Little, Brown & Co., 1984) edited
by L.J. Micheli; *Pediatric sports medicine for the practitioner; from
physiologic principles to clinical applications* (New York: Springer,
1983) by O. Bar-Or and *Common sports injuries in children* (New
Jersey: Medical Economics Books, 1987) by R.B. Birrer and D.B.
Brecher.

Indexes and abstracting services

Sports medicine literature can be accessed via a number of well-known
general medical and scientific indexing and abstracting services. *Index
Medicus, Excerpta Medica, Biological Abstracts*, and *Science Citation
Index* are all useful access points. Subject headings tend to be rather
general – for example, descriptors in *Index Medicus* which imply a
'sporting' connection include 'sports medicine', 'sports' (and around 20
specific sports), 'athletic injuries', 'physical education and training' and
'doping in sports'. This can make searching rather time-consuming. For
example, to find an article on 'eye injuries in squash' one has to scan
either all the items under 'eye injuries' or all the items under 'sports', as
squash is not one of the individual sports listed as a keyword in *Medical
subject headings (MeSH)*.

The databases from which *Biological Abstracts* and *Index Medicus*
are produced have also been used to generate bibliographic tools for use
specifically in the fields of sports medicine. *Collected papers on sports
medicine research 1982-1987* published by BIOSIS is a retrospective
bibliography providing over 6000 references to research on medical and
physiological aspects of human sports participation. Its companion
publication *Sports Medicine Research Today* is a monthly
current-awareness service to update the retrospective collection. Over
9000 source titles are monitored for relevant material. A range of
document types are listed in alphabetical order of first author; a subject
arrangement would have been more useful. The subject index is a
KeyWord In Context (KWIC) index of title words with some additional
keywords added to give context. Searching for relevant articles is rather
painstaking, but may result in the retrieval of material (particularly
conference papers and books) not covered by other bibliographies.
Physical Fitness/Sports Medicine is a quarterly index consisting of

citations retrieved from the National Library of Medicine's MEDLINE database. The format, layout and subject headings are the same as *Index Medicus*. It contains no additional material to *Index Medicus* but its advantages over the parent publication are its cost, compactness, and the convenience of having all relevant articles listed together.

Monthly and annual indexes are published by the Sport Information Resource Centre in Canada. *SportSearch* (monthly) lists articles under subject headings which are biased towards individual sports rather than specific injuries. Headings to look under include medicine, nutrition, physiology (together with various sub-headings), injuries and accidents and drugs and doping. *Sport Bibliography* is an annual compilation of articles with the addition of extra sub-headings, published between 1974 and 1984.

Physical Education Index claims comprehensive coverage of dance, health, physical education, physical therapy, recreation, sports and sports medicine. Around 200 journals are indexed and citations listed under subject headings. There are no author or subject indexes. Although this would rarely be used as the only tool in a sports medicine query it is a useful adjunct to other indexes and occasionally reveals additional items. An index of book reviews provides a useful appendix. *Sportdokumentation* (a publication from Germany) has a broad subject and journal coverage with a section devoted to sports medicine. The subject headings and subject index are in German but a large proportion of the citations are from English-language publications. *Year Book of Sports Medicine* is published annually and contains descriptive abstracts and editorial comment on papers selected from 700 academic medical journals.

Two UK current-awareness services provide comprehensive coverage of sports medicine and related fields, and are compiled by two of the country's specialist libraries in this field. *Sports Medicine Bulletin* is published monthly by the National Sports Medicine Institute (see Appendix 1), with some input by the British Library. *Sports Documentation Monthly Bulletin* is produced by the Sports Documentation Centre. It has a broader subject scope and covers all aspects of sports science including sports medicine. Both publications include selected abstracts and are backed up by a photocopy supply service.

Leaflets & posters

Introductory leaflets and posters on aspects of sports medicine are much sought-after items for projects and displays. Unfortunately, this type of material tends to be somewhat ephemeral and hence often difficult to obtain. A good introduction to the literature of the subject is given in the Sport & Recreation Information Group's *Sports medicine* leaflet (*How to find out in sport & recreation, No. 2*). Pharmaceutical companies often publish relevant material as part of their promotional activities – leaflets have recently been produced by Crookes Healthcare (*How to cope with sports injuries*) and Lederle Laboratories (*Pocket guide to sports injury* by G.R. McLatchie). The Sports Council produces two useful leaflets on drugs in sport – *Dying to win* and *Doping control in sport*. *Food for action* is a very useful introductory booklet on sports nutrition published by the National Dairy Council. The Welsh Sports Council produce a series of booklets including *Injuries* and *Medical advisory service*.

Videos

The UK has a dearth of videos designed for the professional sports medicine practitioner. A few basic tapes are available (for example the National Coaching Foundation's *Safety and injury in sport* and *Energy food for sport* but these are aimed primarily at the athlete and coach. In the USA the *Physician and Sportsmedicine* is currently marketing a series of videos with new titles introduced approximately every three months. Recent titles include *Diagnosis of anterior knee pain, Immediate on-site care of head and neck injuries* and *How to diagnose and treat a sprained ankle*. Videos on all aspects of sport are listed in *Action replay – audio visual resources in sport and recreation*, edited by C. Rankin and S. Chappel (Leeds: National Coaching Foundation and Sheffield Sports Information Service, 1990).

Sports injury clinics

Finding a suitable sports injury clinic is a common problem for athletes, their coaches and doctors. Both National Health Service and private clinics exist, and may have varying levels of staff expertise and varying amounts of appropriate equipment. Lists of clinics are available from several organizations: The Sports Council and its regional offices produce both national and area listings; the National Sports Medicine Institute publishes an annual listing of clinics in the London area; the British Association of Sport and Medicine in conjunction with The Sports Council has recently compiled a list of clinics which meet certain basic professional criteria.

Sports injury reporting systems

The collection and collation of sports injury data in the UK has been rather haphazard. Studies of small populations have been carried out but there is no definitive source of sports injury epidemiology statistics. In contrast, the USA has numerous government agencies, sports-related groups and academic centres which perform large-scale documentation of sports injuries. Examples include the Athletic Injury Monitoring System, the National Collegiate Athletic Association Injury Surveillance System, the Interscholastic Athletic Injury Surveillance System and the National Football Head and Neck Injury Registry. Details of these organizations are given in 'Sports Medicine Groups 1990' (*Physician & Sportsmedicine*, **18**(1), 131–142).

Online sources of information

Online is a well-established method of literature searching and has many advantages over the use of hard-copy indexes, with the ability to combine keywords and to simultaneously search a range of years being obvious examples. The advent of CD-ROM has further facilitated access to the literature via user-friendly software and the removal of cost-based time constraints.

There are two international databases, SPORT and MEDLINE, which, when used individually or in combination usually result in the retrieval of some relevant articles in response to a sports medicine search enquiry. They have complementary subject scope and journal coverage and both are available online and on compact disc. One small disadvantage of using SPORT on compact disc as opposed to online is that the compact disc is only updated every six months. Thus the most recent information may be missed. MEDLINE however, is updated monthly on both media.

To fully exploit both SPORT and MEDLINE, a combination of search techniques must often be employed. As with their hard-copy equivalents, the available keywords are not always appropriate. For example, when searching MEDLINE for most sports, sports equipment, some specific joints and ligaments or certain physiological or biomechanical aspects of exercise, there are no suitable *MeSH* descriptors. Similarly, the SPORT thesaurus, although its coverage of both sport and medical aspects is generally comprehensive, does not include all the more specialized medical terms, for example certain therapeutic drugs and surgical procedures. However, another of the advantages of online is the option to search free-text, which locates terms as they appear in the text – e.g. the title or abstract (see Example 1).

Example 1

Search enquiry: Backache in rowers.
Database: MEDLINE.
Host: Datastar.
Rationale: 'Bachache' is a *MeSH* descriptor, but the general term 'sports' is used to index articles on rowing. As this is obviously too general, free-text searching should be used.
Search strategy: Backache.de. and (rower$ or rowing or sculler$ or sculling or oarsm$ or oarswom$) and sports£.

The specificity of the search can thus be improved, provided synonyms, alternative spelling and plurals are considered.

As illustrated in Fig. 5.1, no single database comprehensively covers the literature of sports medicine, and the searcher must be prepared to use a range of databases if a detailed literature search is required. A selection of online sources, all of which contain material relevant to sports medicine is shown in Table 5.1.

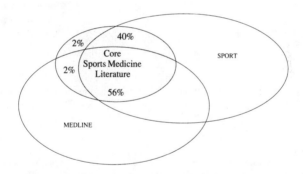

Figure 5.1. Coverage of core sports medicine literature by SPORT and MEDLINE databases. The 'core literature' is taken as the titles listed in the Journals section of this chapter.

TABLE 5.1. A selection of databases relevant to sports medicine

Database	Hosts include	Year	Scope
BIOSIS PREVIEWS Biosciences Information Service	Datastar, Dialog, DIMDI	1969–	Wide range of document types. Good coverage of physiological aspects of sports medicine and sports nutrition.
CAB ABSTRACTS CAB International	Dialog, DIMDI	1972–	Occasionally useful for sports nutrition enquiries.
DISSERTATION ABSTRACTS University Microfilms International	BRS, Dialog	1861–	Comprehensive coverage of American dissertations. Some entries from other countries.
EMBASE (Formerly Excerpta Medica) Excerpta Medica	Datastar, Dialog, DIMDI, SDC	1974–	Good coverage of all aspects of sports medicine, including drugs and nutrition.
FOOD SCIENCE & TECHNOLOGY ABSTRACTS International Food Information Service	Datastar, Dialog, DIMDI	1969–	Occasionally useful for scientific and technical aspects of sports nutrition.
MEDLINE National Library of Medicine	BRS, Datastar, Dialog, DIMDI	1966–	Major online source of sports medicine information, especially clinical aspects.
PSYCHINFO American Psychological Association	BRS, Datastar, Dialog, DIMDI, SDC	1967–	Major source of citations on the psychological aspects of exercise.
SCISEARCH Institute for Scientific Information	Datastar, Dialog	1974–	Large database with some coverage of sports medicine and science.
SPORT LITERATURE BISP	DIMDI	1974–	Good coverage of sports science literature, including sports medicine, with emphasis on German-language material.
SPORT Sport Information Resource Centre	Datastar, Dialog, DIMDI, SDC	1949–	Excellent coverage of all aspects of sport, including sports medicine and science. Good for lower-level material.

Appendix 1 — Useful Organizations

American College of Sports Medicine
P.O. Box 1440, Indianapolis, IN 46206-1440, USA.
Multi-disciplinary, professional and scientific society with large membership. Publishes *Medicine and Science in Sports and Exercise* and *Exercise and Sport Sciences Reviews*. Also publishes occasional advisory position stands.

American Orthopedic Society for Sports Medicine
70 W. Hubbard, Suite 202, Chicago, IL 60610, USA.
Has membership of orthopaedic surgeons involved in sports medicine. Publishes *American Journal of Sports Medicine*.

American Physical Therapy Association — Sports Physical Therapy Section
1 Lytle Place, Suite 415, Cincinnati, OH 45202, USA.
Members are physical therapists with a special interest in sports medicine. Joint publisher of *Journal of Orthopedic and Sports Physical Therapy*.

Association of Chartered Physiotherapists in Sports Medicine
Secretary, 14 Mayfield Court, Mayfield Road, Moseley, Birmingham 1, UK.
A specific interest group of the Chartered Society of Physiotherapy. Publishes *Physiotherapy in Sport*.

British Association of Sport and Medicine
Education Officer, c/o London Sports Medicine Institute, Medical College of St. Bartholomew's Hospital, Charterhouse Square, London EC1M 6BQ, UK.
Publishes *British Journal of Sports Medicine;* holds courses in sports medicine and is the nationally recognized membership organization for doctors and other professionals in sports medicine. Provides information on careers and courses in sports medicine.

British Olympic Medical Centre
Northwich Park Hospital, Watford Road, Harrow, Middlesex, HA1 3UJ, UK.
Major fitness testing centre for Olympic sports.

Canadian Athletic Therapists Association
c/o Sports Medicine Council, 333 River Road, Ottawa, Ontario K1L 8H9, Canada.
Membership organization which publishes *Journal of the Canadian Atheltic Therapists Association*.

Fédération Internationale de Médecine Sportive
c/o Verdurmenstraat 2a, B-2700 Sint-Niklaas, Belgium.
An international organization which promotes scientific research, organizes courses and meetings and publishes relevant material.

National Sports Medicine Institute
   Medical College of St. Bartholomew's Hospital, Charterhouse
   Square London EC1M 6BQ, UK.
Has research library and database and a human performance laboratory for research and
fitness testing. Publishes *Sports Medicine Bulletin* (monthly). Runs a three-year part-time
course for general practitioners and a popular series of open lectures in sports medicine.

National Athletic Trainers Association
   2952 Stemmons Freeway (Inwood Exit), Suite 200, Dallas, TX
   75247, USA.
Membership organization which publishes *Athletic Training*.

Society of Sports Therapists
   Lasyard House, Underhill Street, Bridgnorth, WV16 4BB, UK.
Publishes *Sports Therapy*.

Sports Council
   16, Upper Woburn Place, London WC1H 0QP, UK.
Has an information centre and publishes general sports literature. Produces *Doping
control information pack*.

Sports Nutrition Foundation
   Administrator, c/o London Sports Medicine Institute, Medical
   College of St. Bartholomew's Hospital, Charterhouse Square,
   London EC1M 6BQ, UK.
Publishes a quarterly newsletter and has a slide pack for dieticians.

CHAPTER SIX

History of sport

R.W. COX

Introduction

Subjects chosen for investigation into the history of sport are diverse but generally fall into one or more of three main categories: (1) studies of the emergent role of sport and sport-related activities within society at large, particular communities or institutions; (2) the development of individual forms of activity or games; and (3) biographical studies of individual teams and personalities. The period over which such topics is examined can also vary enormously. Certain individual activities have their origins in the ancient civilizations of the Classical World and the Far East, whilst others are only recent inventions.

What is important for the historian of sport is to identify the most appropriate sources for the subject of research. These are generally those which are accessible, reliable and most revealing of significant information. Sources appropriate for the investigation of different topics will vary immensely and may differ for the study of the same subject at different stages of their development. Whilst a study of the BBC's presentation of the Olympic Games will rely heavily on systematic examination of hours of recorded video tape, a study of the contribution of Thomas Arnold to the emergence of athleticism in the Victorian public school will rely upon careful examination of written records in the form of diaries, sermons, etc. and the contemporary views expressed by those around him.

Sources can broadly be divided into either primary or secondary forms and it is under these headings that sports-history information will be discussed here:

- *Primary sources* are original forms of documentation, presenting facts as they were witnessed first-hand, whilst secondary sources are generally regarded as those expressing the views and interpretations of commentators on past events and personalities. Primary sources can include: written documents, e.g. coaching manuals, diaries, score books, etc.; pictorial records in the form of prints, photographs, films and paintings; oral recordings in the form of disks and magnetic tape; items of clothing and equipment, etc.
- *Secondary sources* include books, journal articles, conference papers, theses, etc.

There are obviously some grey areas between these two divisions, for example a newspaper report of a past event.

To discuss the sources for all sports in all nations throughout history would be an impossible undertaking. The emphasis in this chapter will be on English-language material, covering sport in the UK, especially during the modern period of history. Sports historians researching the development of sport in other countries may be able to adopt similar strategies using parallel publications. Many sources of value to the historian of sport are the same as those used by historians of any other subject and therefore this chapter should be used in conjunction with guides to historical information in general. Before discussing secondary sources quick reference material on sports history will be obtained.

Quick reference material

Encyclopaedias and dictionaries

Useful sports dictionaries and encyclopaedias include: John Arlott's *Oxford companion to sports and games* (London: Oxford University Press, 1975); F.G. Menke's *The encylopaedia of sports* (6th edn.) (Brunswick, N.J.: A.S. Barnes, 1977) and R. Hickok's *New encyclopaedia of sports* (New York: McGraw-Hill, 1977). These sources are often considered the best sports encyclopaedias for background historical information. Typically, the article for each sport begins with a history followed by famous players and outstanding records. D.P. Blaine's *An encyclopaedia of rural sports* (London: Longman, 1840) and H.C. Howard (Earl of Suffolk), H. Peak and F.G. Aflalo's *The encyclopaedia of sport* (London: Lawrence and Bullen, 1911) (both of which ran to more than one edition) are amongst the most useful for the historian researching earlier developments of sport in the UK. There are also a large number of sport-specific encyclopaedias. Robert Hale published a valuable series which included volumes on: Association football, athletics, boxing, cricket, flat racing, motor racing, rugby union football, rugby league football, show jumping, and swimming. More recently, Guinness Superlatives have produced encyclopaedic works which are updated regularly, although often under different series titles. The present *Facts and Feats* series includes, to date, volumes on cricket, golf, motorcycling, mountains and mountaineering, rugby, soccer and yachting. In terms of sports dictionaries, J.A. Cuddon's *Macmillan dictionary of sports and games* (London: Macmillan, 1980) is probably the most useful to the sports historian. Other, more specialist sports dictionaries and encyclopaedias include: R. Bateman's *Encyclopaedia of sports stamps* (London: Stanley Paul, 1969), B. Liddle's *Dictionary of sporting quotations* (London: R.K.P., 1987) and M. Brander's *Dictionary of sporting terms* (London: Adam & Charles Black, 1968). All these and other such publications relating to sport in the UK published before 1987 are listed in R.W. Cox's *Sport in Britain: a bibliography of historical publications, 1800–1988* (Manchester: Manchester University Press, 1991). A review of select mainly North American sports encyclopaedias by D.A. Peele is included in *Reference Service Review*, **10** (Fall 1982), pp. 61–63.

Almanacs, directories, handbooks and yearbooks

Some governing bodies of sport and other publishers produce yearbooks, directories and almanacs. The most famous of these is perhaps *Wisden cricketers' almanack* published annually (currently by John Wisden and Co.) since 1863. It includes details of cricketing records; fixtures for the forthcoming season; up-to-date information on rules, bibliography, deaths of cricketers, etc. To celebrate its centenary in 1984, *An index to Wisden cricketers' almanack, 1864–1984* (London: Queen Anne Press) was compiled by D. Barnard. In 1969 Rothmans started their *Football yearbook*, followed by volumes on *Rugby union* and *Rugby league*. In the mid-1980s, Newnes began a new series of yearbooks in association with certain governing bodies of sport such as the Football Association and the British Board of Boxing Control. Other useful serials of a similar nature include: *Baily's hunting directory* (annual, 1897–), *The golfer's handbook* (annual, 1903–) and the *British rowing almanack* (annual, 1860–). Many more directories exist for Association football, cricket and rugby. C.B.D. Research of Beckenham publish annually a *Guide to current British directories*, which may help the researcher track down additional sources of interest.

Finally, a number of directories of sports grounds have been published in recent years which include brief historical reviews of each of the venues included (e.g. G. Plumptre's *Homes of cricket: the first class grounds of England and Wales* (London: Macdonald, 1988), S. Inglis' *The football grounds of Great Britain* (London: Collins/Willow, 1988) and A. Sampson's *Winning waters* (London: Hale, 1986).

Dates, results, averages and other statistical records

The only chronology of sports history is in German, the *Daten zur Sportgeschichte* series compiled by K.C. Wildt and published in Stuttgart by Verlag Karl Hofmann in the 1970s (Volume 1, *Die alte Welt und Europa bis 1750;* Volume 2, *Europa von 1750 bis 1894*; Volume 3, *Nord und Latinamerika bis 1900*). A number of sports history books include chronologies of significant dates and events in appendices. J. Berryman compiled a lengthy chronology in R.J. Higgs' *Sports: a reference guide* (Westport, CT: Greenwood Press, 1982), R. Bowen includes a chronology of cricket in *Cricket: a history of its growth and development throughout the world* (London: Eyre and Spottiswoode, 1970) and V.A. Titley and N. McWhirter present a chronology of rugby union in their *Centenary history of the Rugby Football Union* (London: Rugby Football Union, 1970).

Statistical publications devoted to sport include: *The Hamlyn A–Z series of records* (which includes volumes on cricket and soccer), *The Guinness book of Olympic records, The Guinness book of British and Empire & Commonwealth games records* and *The Guinness book of sports records, winners and champions.* For recent statistics of sport, including details of participation rates, number of clubs affiliated to the governing bodies, sales figures for equipment, etc. The Sports Council's *Digest of sports statistics for the UK* (2nd edn.) (London: The Sports Council, 1986) may be of some use for information on recent levels of participation and provision. For individual sports there are several useful publications relating to Association football, athletics, cricket, golf and rugby. Those published before the end of 1988 are listed in section A of Cox's the *Sport in Britain: a bibliography of historical publications, 1800–1988* (1991), *vide supra.*

Especially useful for details of attendance figures, scores, league tables, averages, etc. are the publications of The Association of Football Statisticians, The Association of Cricket Statisticians and The Association of Track and Field Statisticians.

Subject bibliographies (including bibliographical essays and bibliographical series)

The literature associated with certain sports is reasonably well documented in the form of bibliographies. Unfortunately, published bibliographies all have limitations and are always out-of-date by the time they appear in print and will need to be updated using some of the reference works listed in this chapter. Certain bibliographies are regularly updated, some of which may be accessed online.

Many bibliographies and bibliographical series on history have been published. By far the most comprehensive is *Historical Abstracts* (Oxford: ABC-Clio), published three times a year, with annual and five-yearly cumulative author and subject indexes since 1955. *Historical Abstracts* includes abstracts of periodical articles, selected conference proceedings, books and dissertations on modern history of all parts of the world (excluding the USA). These are published in two parts: Part A 'Modern Abstracts, 1450–1914'; and Part B, 'Twentieth Century Abstracts'. *Historical Abstracts* can be searched online back to 1973 through Dialog. The Royal Historical Society in conjunction with the American Historical Association, published an extensive series of *Bibliographies of British history* (Oxford: Clarendon Press) which list books and articles, with annotations, published up to the time when the bibliographies themselves were completed.

The Royal Historical Society and the Institute of Historical Research have also produced a valuable bibliographical series entitled *Writings on British history*. These volumes provide a bibliography of books and articles on the history of Great Britain from AD 450 to 1939, published anywhere in the world in any language (except Russian and Japanese) in certain years. This publication is superseded by the Royal Historical Society's *Annual bibliography of British and Irish history* which has been published since 1976 (for the year 1975). A few items on sport have found their way into the publication under the heading 'Intellectual and cultural history', but these reflect only a very select few.

The *Annual bulletin of historical literature* (1976–) and its successor *Historical research: the bulletin of the Institute of Historical Research* (Oxford: Basil Blackwell, 1987–) critically review a selection of the previous year's major publications with different reviewers for each of the different periods and subjects covered. Unfortunately, to date, very few histories of sport have been included although this might change in future years as sports history becomes more popular and accepted as a legitimate branch of social history.

Writings on American history (published annually by the American Historical Association since 1906) provides a sister publication to *Writings on British history* although it has only included periodical articles since 1962. Also useful is *America: history and life*, a database of theses, monographs and periodical articles on all aspects of American life (hardback volumes are published quarterly by Clio Press).

Ongoing bibliographies directly concerned with the history of sport are: 'The annual bibliography of publications on the history of sport' published annually in the December edition of the *International Journal of the History of Sport* (1984–), and published regularly in the *Journal of Sport History* since the first issue in 1974.

There are also a number of bibliographical series devoted to sport which sometimes include items of a historical nature: *Sports bibliography* (Ottawa, Sport Information Resource Centre, 1974–1984) — a 13-volumed index to literature on all aspects of sport. This includes scholarly works in the form of monographs, periodical articles, conference papers and theses accepted for higher degrees (mainly in North America). Volume 7 covers the Humanities and Social Sciences and devotes 30 pages of references on 'Halls of fame', 'Historical research', 'Historiography' and 'History' (in individual countries). In addition to providing author and title indexes this bibliography indicates the academic level of each entry. Documents are assigned a basic, intermediate or advanced level code. The bibliography is the printed version of the SPORT database, which is now available on CD-ROM as SPORT DISCUS (distributed by SilverPlatter Information). The SPORT database is updated by the monthly indexing journal *SportSearch*. For details on all general sport sources see Chapter 1.

SIRLS (Specialized Information Retrieval and Library Services), based at the University of Waterloo in Canada, published *Sport and Leisure: A Journal of Social Science Abstracts* until 1990. They also maintained an online database. SIRC have recently bought the SIRLS database and collection. Up until 1979, SIRLS also maintained standard files which were regularly updated, two of which were devoted to sports history (File 38, *Sociology of sport and leisure — Renaissance to Modern Times* and File 39, *Sociology sport and leisure Renaissance to Modern Times Sociology of sport and leisure — Ancient and Medieval Times*). These files provide useful bibliographies and are still available in a number of libraries.

Completed Research in Health, Physical Education, Recreation, and Dance (published annually since 1953 in Reston, VA, by the American Alliance for Health, Physical Education, Recreation, and Dance) provides an index to theses and dissertations completed in a number of North American universities and periodical articles appearing in a select list of professional physical education journals.

'One-off' bibliographies of note, devoted to specific sports include: F. Lake and A. Wright's *Bibliography of archery* (Manchester: Simon Archery Foundation, 1974), E.W. Padwick's *Bibliography of cricket*

(2nd edn.) (London: The Library Association in association with J.W. McKenzie (Bookseller) on behalf of the Cricket Society, 1984), J.S. Murdock's *Library of golf 1743–1966* (Detroit, MI: Gale Research Co., 1968), T. McNab and P. Lovesey's *Guide to British track and field literature 1275–1968* (London: Athletics Arena, 1969).

More general bibliographies, including references on sport history include: E.B. Wells' *Horsemanship: a bibliography of printed material from the 16th century* (New York: Garland, 1985) and A. Grimshaw's *The horse: a bibliography of British books 1851–1976* (London: The Library Association, 1982).

Students of sports history should be aware of a number of bibliographical essays and literature reviews which review and evaluate rather than simply list important works on a given subject area. These are: W.J. Baker's 'The leisure revolution of Victorian England: A review of recent literature', in *Journal of Sport History*, **6**(3) (Winter 1979), pp. 76–86; J.M. Carter's 'All work and no play? A review of the literature of Medieval sport', in *Canadian Journal of the History of Sport and Physical Education*, **11**(2) (December 1980) pp. 67–72; and R.D. Mandell's 'The Modern Olympic Games: a bibliographical essay', in *Sportwissenschaft*, **6**(1) (1976), pp. 89–97.

Finally, a number of useful bibliographies on sport have been compiled for Fellowships of the Library Association (FLA). Titles highlighting sport include B.C. Skilling's *British canoeing literature, January 1866– January 1966: a bibliography and subject guide*, 1967; E.P. Loder's *Bibliography of the history and organization of horse racing and thoroughbred breeding in Great Britain and Ireland, 1975*; B.J. Read's *Mountaineering, the literature in English: a classified bibliography*, 1976. Some topographical bibliographies accepted for FLA also include many references on sport. FLA theses may be identified using P.J. Taylor's *FLA theses: Abstracts of all Theses Accepted for Fellowship of the Library Association from 1964* (London: British Library, 1979) and for more recent works, the catalogue of the Library Association Library. Again, those related to sport in the UK published before the end of 1988 are listed in R.W. Cox (1991), *vide supra*.

Other reference works

Further reference sources of potential interest to the sports historian include: D. Booker's *Directory of scholars identifying with the history of sport* (4th edn.) (Pennsylvania: North American Society of Sports Historians, 1988) and P. Ray's *Rothmans atlas of world sports* (Aylesbury: Rothmans, 1982). The directory provides details of the names, addresses, research interests, recent publications and professional affiliations of sports historians. Although coverage is international, there is a strong North American bias.

Secondary sources

Monographs

General library collections of special interest to the sports historian include:

- *In the UK*: the British Library (for which printed author and Subject Catalogues already exist and which are available on CD-ROM (Saztec Europe and Chadwyck-Healey), the London Library, Plumstead and Swiss Cottage public libraries (London), and the Mitchell Library (Glasgow)
- *In Canada*: the Metropolitan Library (Toronto), the Sport Information Resource Centre (Ottawa), the library of the University of British Columbia (Vancouver); the Leddy Library, University of Windsor (Ontario), the Weldon Library, University of Western Ontario (London, Ontario) and the University of Waterloo (Waterloo, Ontario)
- *In the USA*: the Library of Congress (Washington, DC), the Huntington Library (San Marino, CA), Princeton University Library and the New York Public Library. A useful list of specialist sports collections in North America is included as an appendix to R.J. Higgs' *Sports: a reference guide* (Westport, CT: Greenwood Press, 1982), pp. 268-286.

Collections of books and periodicals on individual sports, include:

The Library of the Alpine Club, London: mountaineering, skiing and other Alpine sports
The B.P. Library of Motoring, Beaulieu: motor racing
The Kenneth Ritchie Memorial Library, Wimbledon: lawn tennis
The Library of the Cricket Society (London): cricket
The Library of Marylebone Cricket Club (London): cricket
The Horse and Hound Library at the National Equestrian Centre at Stoneleigh: equestrian sports
The National Centre for Athletics Literature (University of Birmingham Library): athletics
The Library of the Cruising Association (London): sailing
The Library of the Fly Fishers' Club (London): angling
The Library of the Fell and Rock Climbing Club (University of Lancaster Library): climbing

The Library of the Rugby Football Union (Twickenham): Rugby
   Union Football
The Library of Rugby League (Leeds): Rugby League football
The Library of the Royal and Ancient Golf Club (St. Andrews): golf

In addition, several public libraries have large or special sports
collections, often linked to local events or popular activities. The Picton
Library in Liverpool, for example, has a large collection of works on the
Grand National steeplechase, and the Central Library in Melton
Mowbray has a special collection on fox hunting. The public libraries in
Chippenham and Mitcham both have large collections of books and
periodicals on cricket. Sheffield Sports Information Service is currently
building a special collection of mountaineering literature to supplement
the valuable Alan Rouse Collection which it has inherited. The John
Rylands University Library, Manchester, houses the Brockbank Cricket
Collection.

In the USA, general sports collections include the International
Sports and Games Research Collection, University of Notre Dame Li-
brary and the Life Sciences Library of the University of Illinois at
Urbana/Champaign. There are literally hundreds specializing in individ-
ual sport such as The Library of the Tennis and Racquets Club, New
York.

All British collections are listed in R.W. Cox's *Sport in Britain: a
bibliography of historical publications, 1880–1988* (1991), *vide supra*
(which also includes details of addresses, telephone numbers, access,
published catalogues, etc.). Useful directories of American sports
libraries, in addition to the general guides listed above, are G. Lewis and
G. Redmond's *Sporting heritage A guide to halls of fame, special
collections and museums in the United States and Canada* (Brunswick,
NJ: A.S. Barnes, 1973) and P. Sodberg and H. Washington's *The big
book of halls of fame in the United States and Canada* (New York: R.R.
Bowker, 1977).

A number of bibliographies of sports books, not based on specific
sports or collections have also been published. These include: E.R.
Gee's *Early American sporting books, 1734–1844* (New York: Haskell
House, 1971); J. C. Phillips' *A bibliography of American sporting books*
(Ann Arbor, MI: Gryphon Books, 1971); R.W. Henderson's *Early
American sport — a check list of books by American and foreign
authors published in America prior to 1860* (3rd edn.) (Rutherford, NJ:
Farleigh Dickinson University Press, 1977) and C. M. van Stockum's
*Sport — an attempt at a bibliography of books and periodicals
published during 1890–1912 in Great Britain, United States, France,
Germany, Austria, Holland, Belgium and Switzerland* (New York: Dodd
and Livingston, 1914).

Details of a selection of scholarly historical monographs are indexed in *Historical Abstracts* and details of a selection of scholarly sports books in *SportSearch*. Highly selective lists of scholarly monographs specifically on sports history are included in details of the NASSH Congress Book Display published in the *NASSH proceedings* each year, 'Recent publications by members' published in the *HISPA Bulletin* and 'Book news' published occasionally in *Journal of Sport History*.

Journal articles

A considerable amount of research is reported in the form of journal articles before it is published in book form. Chapter 1 provides an overview of sports and leisure journals.

Periodicals dealing specifically with sports history, published in the English language include: *The Australian Society of Sports History Bulletin* (published annually by ASSH, 1985–); the *HISPA Bulletin* (published twice a year by the International Association for the History of Sport, 1973–); the *International Journal of Sports History* (*IJSH*) (published three times a year, 1988–; formerly the *British Journal of Sports History* 1984–1987 published by Frank Cass Ltd., London); the *British Society of Sports History Bulletin* (published by the BSSH, 1982–); the *Canadian Journal of the History of Sport* (published twice a year since 1986 by the Department of Human Kinetics at the University of Windsor, Ontario — formerly the *Canadian Journal of the History of Sport and Physical Education*, 1970–1981); the *Journal of Sport History* (published three times a year by the North American Society of Sports Historians); *Sports History* (published privately since 1987, c/o PO Box 183, Leesbury, VA 22074, USA); *Sporting Traditions* (published three times a year since 1984 by the Australian Society of Sport History); and *Ludi Medi Aevi* — Newsletter of the International Society for Medieval Sport (published twice a year by Wampusongs Publishing, Eden, NC, 1989–).

Multi-lingual journals specializing in sports history include: *Nike* (published annually by Weidmannsche Verlagsbuchhandlung, 1989–) and *Stadion* (published occasionally in Cologne, 1976–). *History of Physical Education and Sport Research and Studies* was a Japanese-published multi-lingual Unesco journal devoted to sports history but this ceased publication after the first four volumes (1974–76).

Most of the journals cited above are international, refereed academic journals containing lengthy, in-depth scholarly articles. The bulletins of the ASSH and the BSSH contain short article reviews and more news-based items. There is a tendency for the journals to contain a bias towards the region in which they are published. Only *Nike* is restricted to one particular period of history — Antiquity. *Sports History* (UK) was a typescript journal which mainly reproduced historical documents relating to sport in the UK, but has now ceased publication.

The only journals devoted exclusively to the history of an individual sport are *The Footballer: the Journal of Soccer History and Statistics*, a popular journal of soccer history published quarterly since 1988 by Sports Promotions International and Baseball History. The *Rangers Historian* is a typescript magazine specifically devoted to the history of Glasgow Rangers Football Club. *The Cricketer, Cricket Statistician, Cricket World* and the *Journal of the Cricket Society* regularly carry historical and biographical articles. In February 1990, *Iron Game History* was launched by the Todd-McLean Collection, Department of Kinesiology at the University of Texas, Austin, TX.

Details of articles appearing in sports journals may be identified using indexing journals, most of which have been covered in Chapter 1: Periodical indexes relevant to sports history include *Historical Abstracts, Physical Education Index* (published quarterly, Ben Oak Publishing, Missouri, 1978–), *Sport/Physical Education Index* (published quarterly by Marathon Press, New York, 1978–) *Sports Documentation Monthly Bulletin* (published monthly with annual cumulative indexes by the Sports Documentation Centre, University of Birmingham 1969–). The *Sports Periodical Index* (published monthly in Ann Arbor, by National Information Systems 1985–). With the exception of the *Sports Periodical Index*, these services abstract and index academic periodicals. This policy poses a problem for the historian needing to be informed of popular as well as academic articles. Although the *Sports Periodical Index* currently indexes 130 popular sports magazines, these are confined almost entirely to events in the USA. Cricket which generates perhaps more literature than any other sport is not one of the 80 sports listed. Most of the popular cricket journals mentioned above contain an index.

Two 'one-off' indexes to periodical articles on sports history are included in J. S. Dickinson's 'An annotated bibliography of historical writings related to physical education published in national professional physical education journals and proceedings in North America during the last decade January, 1963 – December, 1972', MS Thesis, University of Oregon, 1973 and R. Thurmond's 'The history of sport and physical education as a field of study in higher education', Ed.D. Dissertation, University of Oklahoma, 1976. Thurmond's dissertation contains a bibliography, with author and subject indexes, of over 1000 articles from eight professional physical education journals published in the period 1894 to 1975.

Conference papers

Proceedings of the Australian Society of Sports History conferences and abstracts of the *Proceedings of the North American Society of Sports Historians* are published annually and listed in the *HISPA Bulletin. Proceedings of the HISPA congress* are published bi-annually in separate volumes and the *Proceedings of the Canadian symposiums on sports history* separately, approximately every three years. Another sports history group occasionally publishing proceedings is the Society on the History of Sport and Physical Education in Asia and the Pacific Region. The *Proceedings of the annual conference of the BSSH* were published separately between 1982 and 1986 but now appear in the society *Bulletin*. The *HISPA Bulletin* reproduces the contents' pages to proceedings of the majority of specialist sports history conferences and the Canadian *Sport bibliography*, indexed selected conference papers.

Theses

Select bibliographies of theses on the history of sport include: T.D. Abernathy's 'Bibliography of Masters and Doctoral studies related to the history of physical education in the United States of America'; M. Adelman's 'Bibliography of Masters and Doctoral studies related to the history of sport and athletics in the United States of America'. Both are published in E.F. Zeigler, M.L. Howell and M. Trekell's *Research in the history, philosophy and international aspects of physical education and sport: bibliographies and techniques* (Champaign, IL: Stipes, 1971). R. Thurmond's 'The history of sport and physical education as a field of study in higher education' (Ed.D. Dissertation, University of Oklahoma, 1976) also contains a bibliography, with author and subject indexes, of over 1500 Masters theses and Doctoral dissertations on the history of sport and physical education submitted to American universities between 1927 and 1975. Other lists of theses include: R.W. Cox's *Theses and dissertations on the history of sport, physical education and recreation accepted for higher degrees and advanced diplomas in British universities, 1900–1981* (Liverpool: Bibliographical Centre for the History of Sport, 1982); *American theses on the history of British sport, physical education and recreation* (Liverpool: Bibliographical Centre for the History of Sport and Physical Education, 1982); B.T.P. Mutimer's *Canadian graduating essays, theses and dissertations relating to the history and philosophy of sport, physical education and recreation* (Trois Rivieres: CAHPER — History of Sport and Physical Activities Committee, 1975); G. Redmond's 'Studies of the history of physical education and sport', in *Bulletin of Physical Education*, **X**,(2) (April 1974), pp. 51–53. Unfortunately, all of these bibliographies are now considerably out of date. General sources for tracing dissertations can be found in Chapter 1.

Primary sources

Manuscript sources

The most important source for listings and locations of manuscript collections in the UK is the National Register of Archives (NRA). It maintains a catalogue of manuscript collections housed within all public and many private repositories throughout the UK and is often the best place to start a search. Catalogues are updated annually in the Royal Commission on Historical Manuscripts' *Accessions to repositories and reports added to the National Register of Archives*. Details of addresses, telephone numbers, opening hours, archivists, and photocopying facilities of particular record offices are included in the Royal Commission's *Record repositories in Great Britain* (8th edn.) (London: HMSO, 1987). A further useful guide is J. Foster and J. Sheppard's *British archives: a guide to archive resources in the United Kingdom* (2nd edn.) (London: Macmillan, 1989). This publication includes many small and private archives not mentioned in the NRA's guide. It contains a useful 'Guide to key subjects' which includes three special collections devoted to sport and 13 others with an interest in, or substantial volume of material on, the subject. Mention should also be made of the *National inventory of documentary sources in the United Kingdom and Ireland* (Cambridge: Chadwyck-Healey, 1987–) a reference guide to published and unpublished 'finding aids' to archives and manuscript collections in county record offices, public libraries and specialist repositories included in the scheme, issued on microfiche by Chadwyck-Healey. The national inventory is being published over a number of years, with approximately 1000–1500 finding aids published each year.

Perhaps the most notable indexes of manuscripts in a collection are the *Lists and indexes of the Public Record Office collections* produced and published by the Lists and Indexes Society. These indexes list all the single items contained within individual files and are an excellent aid to the researcher. They can save many hours of fruitless searching through literally hundreds of different files. Recently, these have been published on some 3500 microfiche. Manuscripts specifically concerned with sport contained within all public and many private collections are listed and indexed in R.W. Cox's *Sport: a guide to historical sources in the UK* (London: The Sports Council, 1983). This index is updated annually in the *British Society of Sports History Bulletin*.

Some sporting organizations have their own collections of manuscripts which they themselves manage and administer. These vary in scope, and accessibility. The MCC, for example, employ their own professional archivist whilst certain other governing bodies of sport have little more than a pile of unsorted documents in a dusty basement or loft. The value of such material varies immensely.

In the USA, the United States General Services Administration National Archive and Record Service produce a *Directory of archive and manuscript repositories in the United States and a union catalogue of manuscripts collections*. Historians of sport in Canada are advised to read T. Nesmiths's 'Sources for the history of sport at the public archives of Canada' in R. Day and P. Lindsay's *Sport history research methodology, Proceedings of a workshop held at the University of Alberta* (May/June 1980), pp. 46–50.

Finally, important and sometimes rare or inaccessible historical documents (published and manuscript) are reproduced in published compilations. Specifically relating to sport are: S.G. Miller's *Arete — Ancient writings, papyri, and inscriptions on the history and ideals of Greek athletics and games* (Chicago: Ares Publishing, 1980), W. Decker's *Some documents on sport and physical education in Ancient Egypt* (Sankt Augustin: Verlag Hans Richarz, 1978) and M. Vale's *The gentleman's recreations — accomplishments and pastimes of the Englishmen, 1580–1630* (Studies in Elizabethan and Renaissance Culture Series, No.1) (Cambridge: D.S. Brewer, 1977). The author compiled a collection of important documents relating to the history of elementary school physical training for publication in the *Journal of Sources in the History of Education*, **4**, (3), (1981). ICSPE sponsored a five-volumed *International compilation of sports historical documents* (Leipzig: German College for Physical Culture) in the 1970s. Most of these are in languages other than English.

Monographs

Monographs providing primary source material may be identified in much the same way as those of a secondary nature, although separate catalogues (of which there are very few directly concerned with sport) will need to be consulted for earlier publications, e.g. A.W. Pollard and G.R. Redgrave's *A short-title catalogue of English books printed in England, Scotland, Ireland, Wales and British America and English books printed in other countries 1475–1640* (2nd edn.) (New York: Index Committee of the Modern Language Association of America, 1972) and its supplement covering the years 1641–1700.

The *Eighteenth and nineteenth century short title catalogues* (London: Avero Publishers Ltd., 1986) provide a union catalogue of all books in English published in the UK, housed in the Bodleian Library, the British Library, the University Library Cambridge, the Library of Trinity College Dublin, the National Library of Scotland and Newcastle-upon-Tyne University Library.

Periodical articles (including newspaper reports)

For identifying runs of nineteenth century periodicals the researcher might usefully consult the *Waterloo directory of periodicals 1824–1900*. For identifying the contents of individual periodicals, W.E. Houghton's *Wellesley index to Victorian periodicals 1824–1900* (5 vols.) (London: R.K.P., 1972–89) is one of the most useful. This publication indexes 50 prominent serials, including such titles as *Contemporary Review* and the *Gentleman's Magazine*. The only periodical directly related to sport is *The Rambler*.

Unfortunately, apart from a brief discussion of major American sporting periodicals in F.L. Mott's five-volume *A history of American magazines*, there is no directory to the many specialist sporting periodicals of the nineteenth and early twentieth centuries (many of which survived for only a few issues), nor indexes to their contents. Since many of these periodicals frequently changed their title, had limited circulation and are unavailable in the major library collections, a union list of early sports periodicals would be of immense assistance to the sports historian.

Among the more prominent general sports periodicals are: the *Badminton Magazine of Sports and Pastimes* (1895–1923); *Baily's Magazine of Sports and Pastimes* (1860–1926); *Bell's Life in London and Sporting Chronicle* (1822–1886); *Illustrated Sporting and Dramatic News* (1874–1974); and *The Field* (1853–). Details of more specialist periodicals sometimes appear in guides to the literature (e.g. A. Grobani's guides to baseball and football literature *op. cit.*), specialist library catalogues (e.g. the published *Kenneth Ritchie Wimbledon Library catalogue* lists many British and foreign periodicals on tennis), bibliographies (e.g. *Padwicks' Bibliography of cricket*) and guides to sources contained within published histories (e.g 'A note on sources' in D. Smith and G. Williams' *Fields of praise: The official history of the Welsh Rugby Football Union, 1881–1981* (Cardiff: University of Wales Press, 1980) which lists many Rugby Union magazines. C.B. Cone's *Hounds in the morning: sundry sports of merry England* (Lexington: University of Kentucky Press, 1981) reproduces a selection of writings from *The Sporting Magazine* 1792–1836.

Of particular interest are newspaper articles since these often carry commentary on important events and printed league tables, match reports, etc. The titles of a large number of sports newspapers and magazines may be identified using: national directories such as *The Times tercentenary handlist of English and Welsh newspapers, magazines and reviews* (London: *The Times*, 1920); directories devoted to specific regions or subjects such as the R. Webber's *World list of national newspapers: a national union list of national newspapers in the libraries of the British Isles* and *Bibliography of British newspapers* and the *Library Association's bibliography of British newspapers* series; union lists such as A.R. Hewitt's *Union list of Commonwealth newspapers in London, Oxford and Cambridge* (London: University of London Institute of Commonwealth Studies, 1962); and catalogues of individual collections. By far the largest collection of newspapers in the UK is the British Library's Newspaper Library at Colindale, London.

Indexes to the contents of individual newspapers are relatively few. Whilst detailed comprehensive indexes exist for *The Times* newspaper since 1790, indexes for certain other daily newspapers are only recent (for example, the *Clover newspaper index* acts as an index to *The Daily Telegraph, The Financial Times, The Guardian*, and *The Observer*, but has only been in existence since 1987) or do not exist at all. The *British Humanities Index* indexes selected items from what are termed 'quality newspapers' and the WORLD REPORTER database gives full-text retrieval of articles from recent years of leading national papers. *The Guardian* has a hand-written index to the early years of the paper which is now held in the Manchester Central Library. Several local studies collections hold indexes to particular newspapers or maintain a clipping service. These may be catalogued separately, or, as part of the main local studies catalogue.

Several compilations of newspaper reports have been published in recent years, for example, The *New York Times scrapbook encyclopedia of sports history* (New York: Arno Press, late 1970s) includes volumes on baseball, basketball, boxing, American football, golf, indoor sports, horse racing/auto sports, soccer/professional hockey, track and field, water sports and winter sports. Collections of sports cuttings from British newspapers include: I. Wooldridge's *Great sporting headlines* (London: William Collins & Sons, 1984), John Lovesey's the *Sunday Times sports book* (London: World's Work, 1979), the annual *Guardian book of sport* and the *Back page: a century of newspaper coverage* series published by Macdonald/Queen Anne Press, and for which volumes so far exist for cricket, football and horse racing. Exclusively concerned with newspaper feature articles associated with the Olympic Games is M. Brant's *The Games: a complete news history* (London: Proteus, 1980).

Finally, a number of important and popular sports magazines have been reprinted to assist the historian. *Bell's Life in London and Sporting Chronicle* for example, has recently been made available on microfilm and is presently being indexed. Greenwood Press have reprinted several American titles such as *American Athlete* and *Cycle Trade Review*, *Annals of Sporting and Fancy Gazette* and *All Outdoors*.

Government publications

CENTRAL GOVERNMENT RECORDS

Material in this category covers that generated by, or for, parliament and various government departments. Such publications can take many forms and are published by HMSO. Other publications, produced by government departments as a result of their work and not expressly intended for parliamentary use, are generally referred to as non-parliamentary publications. Such publications may also take several forms but are not necessarily published by HMSO. More detailed discussion of the different forms of publications, including their role in the legislative process are discussed in P. and G. Ford's *Guide to parliamentary papers: what they are, how to find them, how to use them* (Shannon: Irish University Press, 1972) and J. Olle's *An introduction to British government publications* (London: Association of Assistant Librarians, 1973).

Bibliographic control of HMSO publications is excellent. Daily, monthly and yearly lists are produced, the latter two of which provide detailed subject and title indexes, including where appropriate, the names of persons responsible for producing various reports. Useful guides for the researcher attempting to track down pertinent material are: R. Stavely and M. Piggott's *Government information and the research worker* (2nd edn.) (London: Library Association, 1965), J. Pemberton's *British official publications* (Oxford: Pergamon, 1973) and the *Bibliographical control of official publications*. In 1988, Chadwyck-Healey published a five-volume *Subject catalogue of the House of Commons parliamentary papers, 1801–1900*. This catalogue classifies the *Papers* into one or more of 19 major subject areas such as education, finance, industry, etc. Although sport is not represented in one of these major subject divisions, useful sub-headings (e.g., recreation, horse racing, etc.) help locate more specific items of interest. Reference is made to the *Paper* number, to the session, volume and volume page number for each of the references included. Unlike earlier attempts to create subject indexes, this catalogue attempts to index all documents published in the 5900 volumes of House of Commons' bound series between 1801 and 1900, as well as all those included only in House of Lords series and other locations — Annual Reports, Bills, Memoranda and Statistics, etc.

The Public Record Office holds the manuscript records of central government departments. The records of the Ministry of Education (later the Department of Education and Science) contain a good deal of material. There are, for example, files relating to local education authority facilities for physical training and recreation under the various Acts (in the class ED56) to the evening play centres which operated between the wars (ED65) and the National Fitness Council (ED113). On the public order aspects of sport, there is a good deal of material in the records of the Home Office and the Metropolitan Police. There is information on the diplomatic issues raised by sporting events (for example, the 1936 Olympic Games) in the records of the Foreign Office. Direct government provision of sports facilities and training is largely confined to the armed services and information on this may be located in the records of the War Office, Admiralty and Air Ministry. The financial implications of all this activity are dealt with in the records of the Treasury. Information relating to sport is also to be found in the records of the Ministry of Agriculture, Fisheries & Food, the Board of Trade, etc. Users of the Public Record Office are advised to consult the official *Guide to the contents of the Public Record Office* (London: HMSO). Part One contains a brief history of each government department, law court or other institution, outlining its development and functions. Part Two describes the nature and content of each class of records, including their data span, the number of records and their format, nature and contents and a note of any variation from the standard 30-year closure to public inspection. Part Three is a comprehensively cross-referenced index to Parts One and Two.

For U.S. government publications, the *Monthly Catalog* (published since 1895), is the most complete source. Various cumulative and subject indexes to the *Monthly Catalog* are also published by the Government Printing Office. Numerous documents relating to regulation of sporting monopolies, gambling, etc. are to be found.

LOCAL GOVERNMENT RECORDS

The records of local government may also be of interest. As with central government, it was not until recently that many authorities set up separate committees for sport and recreation. Swimming baths usually came under 'Baths and Wash-houses', outdoor recreation areas under 'Parks, gardens and cemeteries', indoor sport under 'Education', etc. Some local authority facilities are provided by both Education and Recreation Departments in which case relevant information may be found in the minutes of more than one committee.

Copies of annual reports, published minutes of the various committees, etc. are usually held in the local public library, and unpublished documents in the local County or District Record Office. The format and detail contained within these documents varies immensely. Generally, and until recent years it was only the large urban authorities which made provisions for sport and recreation and, therefore, it is only their records which are likely to include much discussion of and policy towards sports provision.

Contemporary literature

Several eminent sports historians have made effective use of contemporary literature as a source for understanding contemporary values and concerns of the period under investigation. Thomas Hughes' *Tom Brown's School Days* and Charles Kingsley's *Westward Ho!* have been cited many times in historical assessments of public school athleticism. In due course, the works of Dick Francis may well be used as graphic descriptions of sporting life in the 1960s and 1970s.

Bibliographies of works of fiction include G. Buin's *Sports pages — a critical bibliography of 20th century novels and stories* (Metuchen, NY: Scarecrow Press). Useful anthologies of writings from selected works include: A.C. Jenkins' the *Sporting life* (London: Blackie, 1974) and V. Scannel's *Sporting literature: an anthology* (London: Oxford University Press, 1987). More concerned with sport in North America are R. J. Higgs' *Laurel and thorn: the athlete in American literature* (Lexington: The University of Kentucky Press, 1981) and the *Sporting spirit: athletes in literature and life* (New York: Harcourt-Brace-Jovanovich, 1977).

Oral recordings

Over the past few decades, oral recordings made of commentaries on important events, interviews, etc. have been preserved in national and local collections, the most prominent of which is the British Library's National Sound Archive. Details of this and other collections in the UK are contained in L. Weerasinghe's *Directory of recorded sound resources in the UK* (London: British Library National Sound Archive, 1989) and A McNulty and A. Troo's *Directory of British oral history collections* (Colchester: Oral History Society, 1981). These may be updated to some extent by checking the announcements on 'Current British research' in each issue of *Oral History*, a periodical published since 1972 by the Oral History Society.

In North America, where considerably more attention has been directed to oral history, large collections of material of a general and specialist nature have been established. Notable collections include the University of Columbia Oral History Collection, the University of

California at Berkeley, Radcliffe College and several of the sporting halls of fame, details of which are included in *Oral History Index*.

Pictorial records

Several guides and directories have been published in recent years which are helpful in locating pictorial (mainly photographic and film) sources of information. These include: R. Eakins' *Picture sources in the UK* (London: Macdonald, 1985), H. and M. Evans' *The picture researcher's handbook: an international guide to picture sources and how to use them* (3rd edn.) (Newton Abbot: David & Charles, 1986); D.N. Bradshaw's *World photographic sources* (New York: Directories, 1984); J. Wall's *Directory of British photographic collections* (London: 1977); The British Association of Picture Libraries and Agencies — *List of members, a subject index and practical guide to libraries and their users* (London: BAPLA, 1980) all of which include sports collections.

In terms of film collections, E. Oliver's *Researcher's guide to British film and television collections* (2nd edn.) (London: British Universities Film Council, 1985) is a useful starting place to locate suitable material. Large film collections in England include: the National Film Archive (part of the British Film Institute), the BBC Film and Video Tape Library and those of the many other major television companies. A large and well-indexed collection of films is the North West Film Archive at Manchester Polytechnic. Details of individual films and videos are listed in the *British national film and video catalogue* (London: British Film Institute, annual 1963–). The Sports Council published a *Catalogue of sports films* (2nd edn.) (London: The Sports Council, 1983) which is not very comprehensive and contains little that will be of use to the sports historian. Some film and television companies specialize in particular sports and maintain an extensive collection. 'Chrisfilms' of Pately Bridge in Yorkshire, for example, have films and videos documenting most of the major championship events in white-water canoeing over the past 25 years.

Large general collections of photographs in the UK include: the photographic library of the Royal Photographic Society; the photograph library of the British Institute of Architects and the Royal Town Planning Institute (pictures of sports buildings and stadia), the BBC Hulton Picture Library (sport in general) and the Mansell Collection (sport in general but particularly between 1900 and 1940). More specialized large collections include the photographic library of the National Portrait Gallery and Aerophoto for aerial photographs. Many national and local newspaper offices, as well as publishers of general and specialist sports periodicals (such as *Sports Illustrated, Canoeist*, etc.) maintain extensive photograph libraries, some of which are catalogued with helpful cross-referencing. Unfortunately for the researcher, many private libraries will only conduct searches themselves and often make a charge for this service. A small number of governing bodies of sport maintain photographic collections, although these vary in size and range.

In recent years, albums illustrating the history of towns and villages have been published which sometimes contain photographs revealing important detail of sporting events. More specifically concerned with sport are N. Wigglesworth's *Victorian and Edwardian boating from old photographs* (London: Batsford, 1986) and J.N.P. Watson's *Victorian and Edwardian field sports from old photographs* (London: Batsford, 1978). Many of these photographs are still in private hands and would not have otherwise been revealed to the researcher. A recent collection of photographs devoted entirely to sport in the Ancient World is R.L. Sturzebecker's *Photo-atlas of athletic cultural archaeological cities in the Greco-Roman world* (published by the author in 1985). This publication contains black-and-white, and colour, photographs of sporting sites.

The most notable collections of paintings and prints in the UK include: the National Art Collection at the Victoria & Albert Museum and the British Museum. Both collections are well indexed by artist and subject matter. The National Portrait Gallery also includes many portrait paintings as well as photographs — boxing, cricket and horse racing being the best represented. J.N.D. Watson's *Collecting sporting art* (London: Sportsman's Press, 1988) lists galleries with sporting collections and the British Sporting Trust, c/o The Tate Gallery, maintains an inventory to sporting paintings in UK galleries. In 1987, together with Boydell and Brewer, they published an *Inventory of sporting art in the public galleries in the UK* edited by G. Pendred. The most extensive collection of British sporting paintings is the one owned by the American Paul Mellon, details of which are included in J. Egerton's *The Paul Mellon Collection, British sporting and animal paintings, 1655–1867* (London: The Tate Gallery, 1978). Notable specialist print and painting collections exist at Lord's Cricket Club and the National Horseracing Museum at Newmarket. The USA has its own National Art Museum of Sport in New York.

It must not be forgotten that many sporting photographs, along with other forms of manuscripts remain in private hands. Many sportsmen and women maintained scrapbooks of newscuttings, and other memorabilia associated with their sporting days. These are often made available to researchers by relatives after the person has died.

Other sources

ARTEFACTS

Several governing bodies of sport, individual clubs, manufacturers of sports equipment and stadia are beginning to take an interest in their heritage and are now building their own collections of historical material. The MCC Museum at Lord's (formerly the Memorial Gallery) is said to be the oldest museum of sport in the UK. Artefacts include bats, balls, trophies, ties, etc. Other sports museums exist at Newmarket (National Horseracing Museum), Twickenham (Museum of Rugby Union), Huddersfield (Rugby League Hall of Fame), Wimbledon (The National Lawn Tennis Museum), Birmingham (National Centre for Athletics Literature) details of which are included in R.W. Cox's *Sport: A guide to historical sources in the UK* (1983), *vide supra*. Plans have recently been announced for a national museum of rowing to be established at Henley.

On a more local level, Liverpool and Manchester United Football Clubs, Old Trafford cricket ground and Wembley Stadium, and York and Aintree racecourses, have their own small historical collections of artefacts which may be consulted with prior approval. Gray's of Cambridge have their own private collection of racquets made by the company since its foundation and similarly Pyrahana Mouldings of Runcorn have a historical collection of canoes. Several such companies are usually prepared to allow the serious researcher to consult their collection with prior permission.

The Museum Association's *Museum Yearbook* provides a useful directory of museums and galleries in the UK with a helpful subject index to special collections. Also included are details of addresses, opening hours and facilities.

In North America there are over two hundred sports museums and halls of fame devoted to individual sports, sports within a particular town or state, sport associated with a particular institution, venue or competition. G. Lewis and G. Redmond's *Sporting heritage – a guide to halls of fame, special collections and museums in the United States and Canada* (New Brunswick, NJ:, A.S. Barnes, 1973), R.J. Higgs' *Sports: reference guide (Westport, CT: Greenwood Press, 1982)* and P. Sodberg and H. Washington's *The big book of halls of fame in the United States and Canada* (New York: R.R. Bowker, 1977) are helpful in identifying those collections likely to be of interest to the researcher.

EPHEMERA

Throughout the world there are many serious collectors of items on specific sports and sporting events. The Ephemera Society periodically produce a list of members with a subject index. There are also a number of specialist collectors' groups in addition to the ones already mentioned in connection with artefacts, such as the British Football Programme Collectors' Club.

PATENTS

A patent protects the right of an individual to benefit from the usefulness of his invention by preventing exploitation of it by others, without permission, for a given period. It describes the invention and often contains diagrams and other illustrations. The usefulness of patents in sports historical research has been shown by I.T. Henderson and D.I. Stirk in their *Golf in the making* (Crawley: Henderson and Stirk, 1979), and by others interested in the impact of new technology on sport. By its very nature, the bulk of this information is technical.

Historians interested in following up this line of enquiry are advised to consult F. Newby's *How to find out about patents* (Oxford: Pergamon, 1967) and the British Patents Office's *About patents as a source of technical information* (London: 1972). The Science Reference Library has a large collection of patents with useful finding aids.

CHAPTER SEVEN

Sociology of sport

J. HORNE

Introduction

The sociology of sport has been a very marginal sub-discipline of
sociology in the UK, as it has even in North America. In a recent
survey, fewer than 4% of members of the British Sociological
Association expressed either past or present research interest and/or
teaching involvement in leisure or sport (*BSA 1988 Members' register*;
London: BSA, 1988). This marginality has been compounded by a
number of factors, amongst which two features of its development and
organization in the UK are worth emphasizing. First its origins have
mainly lay in a few colleges and departments of physical education,
where it was taught by physical educators, sometimes considered to be
'marginal professionals'. Second, as in North America, its development
relied upon a few influential, although in some respects, idiosyncratic
sociologists. In the UK, until the late 1970s, the theoretical backbone of
sociological writing on sport was derived largely from the relatively
neglected 'figurational sociology' of Norbert Elias and Eric Dunning.

   In the last fifteen years or so, however, the sociology of sport (and
leisure, since in the UK, unlike North America, the distinction is not so
clear cut) has been injected with fresh perspectives which have, to an
extent brought more mainstream sociological traditions to focus on the
area. Challenges to what some have regarded as the orthodoxy of sociological sport and leisure studies in the UK have been mounted by new
groupings of researchers and teachers. There are those who have graduated from or been influenced by the Centre for Contemporary Cultural
Studies (CCCS) at the University of Birmingham, with Cultural Studies
as their organizing label; and there is now a substantial body of Feminist-inspired theory and research into sport and leisure. Criticism of

earlier research into sport and leisure has been wide-ranging, in terms of theoretical assumptions, methodologies, as well as the often implicit value stances.

The situation at present is therefore one of a plurality of voices. The sociology of sport may be at a turning point. The sources of finance for academic work in the UK are undergoing major change, whilst at the same time the basic framework of local authority leisure provision is altering, and a series of cracks is opening up in the already crumbling edifice of UK sport – drug-taking, sponsorship, amateurism and apartheid – which may together contribute to an unprecedented transformation of the very subject of study.

Since there is considerable overlap between the sociology of sport and the sociology of leisure, readers should also refer to Chapter 10 on leisure. For more information on resources for the social sciences in North America, consult Chapter 15.

Libraries, databases and abstracting services

Major libraries and abstracting services are well covered in Chapter 1. In the UK, the Sports Documentation Centre, University of Birmingham, is the best single library catering for sport sociology. It also publishes *Sports Documentation Monthly Bulletin*, a monthly abstracting journal which has a useful section devoted to 'Sport sociology'. The Centre has an in-house database which can be accessed via the Centre's librarian.

The largest databases and abstracts which cover the sociology of sport are both Canadian. SIRLS (Specialized Information Retrieval and Library Services), University of Waterloo, Canada, has a library which consists of microfilms and reflects the material held on its online database. SIRLS published the abstracting journal *Sport and Leisure: a Journal of Social Science Abstracts* until 1990. The SIRLS collection and databse has recently been bought by SIRC.

The Sport Information Resource Centre (SIRC) (1600, James Naismith Drive, Gloucester, Ontario, Canada), is the largest library devoted to sport literature in the world. It provides an online database, SPORT which is also available on CD-ROM as SPORT DISCUS. Although this is a general sports database, coverage of sociological references is quite good. The *Sport bibliography*, published in 13 volumes, represents a sub-set of the database for the years 1974–1984. SIRC also publish a current-awareness bulletin, SportSearch, which updates the database in printed form.

A number of databases and associated abstracts also contain sections on sport and leisure: *Sociological Abstracts* (Sociological Abstracts

Inc.), *LRTA*, (co-produced with the World Leisure and Recreation Association, CAB International (CABI)) and *Social SciSearch* (ISI) which corresponds to the printed *Social Sciences Citation Index*. It is worth noting that the *Social Sciences Citation Index* is a very helpful tool, although it takes some getting used to. Citation indexing enables researchers to search forward from a known source (article or book) to later articles which cite that source in their footnotes or references. It is up-to-date, but one drawback is that it concentrates on the 'core' journals in each field and can therefore be restrictive as new titles may be ignored for some time after initial publication.

Social SciSearch, as well as being accessible online commercially and in the UK, on the Janet Network via BIDS, is also available on CD-ROM. A number of other databases are also available on CD. Whilst many North American academic institutions search online, not all British institutions (and few social scientists) routinely use online searches. Cost is the major factor here. Additionally the quantity of the response is unpredictable. Although data from online databases can be downloaded straight away, or returned within a week of requesting the search at a cheaper rate, there is a danger of retrieving information which is redundant unless the keywords of the search are precisely defined. Although even less widely used at present, but growing in popularity all the time, is CD-ROM. This format of the databases permits much greater user control. Initial capital cost and the annual subscription are quite high, but for example, the twice yearly updated SPORT DISCUS is very user-friendly, enabling the researcher a greater amount of time to consider different keywords.

Other hard-copy indexes include: *British Humanities Index*, (Library Association Publishing), which covers such publications as *New Statesman and Society, The Spectator, The Guardian, The Times Index* (Times Newspapers Ltd.) – which indexes all *Times* publications and supplements – and *Research Index* (Business Surveys Ltd.) – which covers over 100 periodicals and the national press from a business angle, but nonetheless has a section on sport and leisure. *The Times* on the other hand, is widely acknowledged as providing a very broad coverage of sport and so *The Times Index* is particularly helpful when trying to gather information about a minority sport, e.g. Stoolball – see *The Times*, 24 March, 1989.

Handbooks & bibliographies

A number of handbooks and guides to academic research in the field of sport and leisure have been published in recent years. Although difficult to define precisely, a handbook falls somewhere between an encyclopaedia and a textbook in terms of material included. Surveys of research specialisms are often introductory, but they still provide a guide. Amongst the most useful are the following: J. Knight and S. Parker (1978) *A Bibliography of British publications on leisure*, LSA, London; M. Collins and A. Dye (1981) *Sports research in the UK*, The Sports Council, London; S. Parker (1985) *International handbook of leisure studies and research*, LSA, London; A. Graefe and S. Parker (eds.) (1987) *Recreation and leisure: an introductory handbook*, E. & F.N. Spon, London. The last is an expanded version of S. Parker's work (1985), which contains many more entries relating to research in sport and leisure in North America. There are some useful, if a little dated, 'pen portraits' of areas of research in the UK (e.g. 'The economics of leisure', 'The sociology of sport', 'Leisure and the media', 'The politics of leisure', 'Women and leisure', and so on).

In the sociology of sport, R. Pearton and S. Parker (1972) *The sociology of sport: a bibliographical review* (British Sociological Association, Sociology of Sport Group, Paper No. 1, April, 1972) was the first attempt in the UK to bring together in one place a list of specific sources in the subject area. It remains of interest in so far as it demonstrates the paucity of such material in the early 1970s (there were less than 100 entries). In 1968, G. Luschen had produced *The sociology of sport: a trend report and bibliography* (Special issue of *Current Sociology*, **XV**(3), Mouton, The Hague/Paris) with considerably more entries. This became the basis for the 5000 plus entries in the 'International classified bibliography on sociology of sport' contained in G. Luschen and G. Sage (eds.) (1981) *Handbook of social science of sport*, Stipes Publishing Inc., IL, USA. Paul Redekop (1988) has recently produced *Sociology of sport: an annotated bibliography* (New York, Garland). Largely focused on North American sources and adopting a rather strict definition of the 'sociological', it is nonetheless of considerable use as an initial source.

Encyclopaedias

Little information on the sociology of sport has been included in encyclopaedias or dictionaries of sociology or sport. *The international encyclopedia of social sciences* (D. Sills, ed., 1968) has the entry for sport, '*see* Leisure' – written by J. Dumazedier. The more recent *Handbook of sociology* (E. Shils, ed., 1988) has no entry. Nor do *The Macmillan student encyclopedia of sociology* (M. Mann, ed., Macmillan, 1983) or *The Penguin dictionary of sociology* (N. Abercrombie, S. Hill and B. Turner, Penguin, 1988, 2nd edn.). The recently published *Collins' dictionary of sociology* (eds. D. and J.J. Collins, 1991) is an exception. None of the general encyclopaedias of sport (e.g. J. Arlott, ed., 1975, *The Oxford companion to sport and games*, Oxford; J. Cuddon, 1980, *The Macmillan dictionary of sport and games*, Macmillan) have relevant entries.

Monographs, textbooks and collections of articles in sociology of sport/leisure

The sociology of sport has developed throughout the world, but it is usually acknowledged that its main site of growth has been the USA and Canada. A marked feature of publications in these countries is the early emergence of textbooks which provided a stronger basis for institutional development than elsewhere.

The first textbook was written by Harry Edwards (*Sociology of sport*, Dorsey, IL, USA, 1973), although a critical account of sport in society had been written earlier by Paul Hoch (*Rip off the big game*, Doubleday, New York, 1972). As the subject became more widely taught in U.S. colleges, additional textbooks and collections of articles appeared. These included J. Loy and G. Kenyon (eds.) (1969, 2nd edn, 1981) *Sport, culture and society*, and J. Coakley (4th edn, 1990) *Sport in society*, Times Mirror/Mosby, St Louis, MO. Other significant collections of essays and monographs by U.S., French, Canadian, German and Australian sociologists which mark stages in the spread and development of the sub-discipline include: J.-M. Brohm (1978) *Sport: a prison of measured time*, Ink Links, London (translated from French, first published 1976); R. Gruneau (1983) *Class, sports and social development*, University of Massachusetts Press, Amherst, MA; A. Guttmann (1978) *From ritual to record*, Columbia University Press, New York; J. Harvey and H. Cantelon (eds.) (1988) *Not just a game: essays in Canadian sport sociology*, University of Ottawa Press, Canada; G. Lawrence and D. Rowe (eds.) (1986) *Power play: essays in the sociology of Australian sport*, Hall & Iremonger, Sydney, Australia; and B. Rigauer (1981) *Sport and work*, Columbia University Press, New York (translated from German, first published 1969).

UK-based sociology of sport can be said to have gone through three phases which have mainly followed those of its parent discipline. The earliest work has often, although not necessarily accurately, been referred to as 'functionalist'. This would include the work of Parker on leisure and Elias and Dunning on sport and leisure (E. Dunning, ed., 1971, *The Sociology of sport*, Frank Cass; S. Parker *et al.*, 1975, *Sport and leisure in contemporary society*, LSA/BSA Conference Proceedings, LSA, London). Various critical texts then developed out of neo-Marxist and interpretive sociology, cultural studies and

Feminist-inspired writing: A. Tomlinson (ed.) (1981), *Leisure and social control*, Chelsea School of Human Movement, Brighton Polytechnic: *Proceedings of BSA/LSA Workshop held at the Centre for Contemporary Cultural Studies, University of Birmingham;* J.A. Hargreaves (ed.) (1982), *Sport, culture and ideology*, Routledge & Kegan Paul, London (*Proceedings of a Conference held at the Roehampton Institute of Higher Education, London, 1980*); G. Whannel (1983) *Blowing the whistle*, Pluto, London; and A. Tomlinson and G. Whannel (eds.) (1984), *Five ring circus*, Pluto, London.

In the final phase, a number of theoretical perspectives are present – a phase of 'multi-paradigmatic rivalry' or methodological pluralism, depending on one's point of view: C. Rojek (1985), *Capitalism and leisure theory*, Tavistock, London; J. Clarke and C. Critcher (1985), *The Devil makes work*, Macmillan, London; John Hargreaves (1986), *Sport, power and culture*, Polity, Cambridge; J. Mangan and R. Small (eds.) (1985), *Sport, culture, society*, E. & F.N. Spon, London (*Proceedings of the VIII Commonwealth & International Conference on Sport, PE, Dance, Recreation and Health, Glasgow, July 1986*); E. Dunning and N. Elias (1986), *Quest for excitement*, Basil Blackwell, Oxford; R. Deem (1986), *All work and no play?: the sociology of women and leisure*, Open University Press, Milton Keynes; J. Horne *et al.* (eds.) (1987), 'Sport, leisure and social relations', *Sociological Review*, Monograph No. 33, Routledge & Kegan Paul, London; E. Wimbush and M. Talbot (eds.) (1988), *Relative freedoms: women and leisure*, Open University Press, Milton Keynes.

Specific areas of research – reviews, survey articles and monographs

No claim for completeness is made in this section; however, the aim is to give a brief guide to useful summaries or reviews of sociological work which have been undertaken in specific areas of research by UK-based sociologists accomplished within the UK context. Review articles can save much time, combining as they often do a survey of the field, a review of literature, and a critique.

In the UK, the best overview of theories and methods in the sociology of sport is still probably John Hargreaves (1982) 'Sport, culture and ideology' in J.A. Hargreaves (ed.) (1982) *Sport, culture and ideology*, Routledge & Kegan Paul. The study of football and football hooliganism has been a major field for sociologists of sport in the UK. The most useful references are: J. Williams *et al.* (1984) *Hooligans abroad*, Routledge & Kegan Paul (revised edition, 1989); M. Melnick (1986) 'The mythology of football hooliganism: a closer look at the

British experience', in *International Review for the Sociology of Sport*, **21**(1), pp. 1–21; I. Taylor (1987) 'Putting the boot into a working class sport: British soccer after Bradford and Brussels', in *Sociology of Sport Journal*, **4**(2), June 1987, pp. 171–191; and E. Dunning *et al.* (1988) *The roots of football hooliganism,* Routledge & Kegan Paul, London. Another large field is the study of sport and the mass media. The most stimulating work includes: E. Buscombe (ed.) (1975), *Football on television*, BFI Monograph No. 4, London; G. Whannel (1986), 'The unholy alliance: notes on television and the remaking of British sport, 1965–1985', in *Leisure Studies*, **5**, pp. 129–145; and for an excellent overview of research in the British context see: C. Critcher (1987) 'Media spectacles: sport and mass communication', in A. Cashdan and M. Jordin (eds.), *Studies in communication*, Basil Blackwell, Oxford.

A good overview of research into race, ethnicity and sport is contained in: J. Parry (1989) *Participation by black and ethnic minorities in sport and recreation,* London Research Centre. One attempt to apply and develop some North American approaches to the subject with respect to English soccer is by J. Maguire (1988) 'Race and position assignment in English soccer: a preliminary analysis of ethnicity and sport in Britain', in *Sociology of Sport Journal*, **5**, pp. 257–269. The sociological study of gender is concerned with males and masculinity as well as women and femininity. An early attempt to look at the former in the context of sport was by K. Sheard and E. Dunning (1973) 'The Rugby football club as a type of "male preserve"', in *International Review of Sport Sociology*, **8**(1) pp. 5–24. S. Scraton (1987) 'Boys muscle in where angels fear to tread – girls' sub-cultures and physical activities', in J. Horne *et al.* (1987), *Sport, leisure and social relations*, Routledge & Kegan Paul, London, cites evidence that gender continues to structure involvement in sport. J. Graydon (1983) '"But it's more than a game. It's an institution." Feminist perspectives on sport', in *Feminist Review*, No. 13, Spring, contains a useful overview of different Feminist approaches to sport, whilst A. White and C. Brackenridge (1985) 'Who rules sport? Gender divisions in the power structure of British sports organisations from 1960', in *International Review of Sociology of Sport*, **20**(1 & 2), provide data on the gender imbalance in governing bodies of sport and E. Green *et al.* (1987) *Leisure and gender,* The Sports Council/Economic and Social Research Council, present a very clear picture of gender inequality in sport and leisure participation and opportunity. Finally, UK sociology of sport contains many historical studies and contemporary descriptions of social class divisions in participation in sport: see John Hargreaves (1986), *Sport, power and culture,* Polity, Cambridge; A. Tomlinson (1987) 'Playing away from home: leisure, disadvantage and issues of income and access', in P. Golding (ed.) *Excluding the poor,* CPAG, London; and for an excellent sociological history of Rugby football, see E. Dunning and K. Sheard (1979) *Barbarians, gentleman and players*, Martin Robertson, Oxford. For more historical sources, refer to Chapter 6.

Periodicals & journals

Chapter 1 provides a general overview of journals whilst individual sport magazines which may be relevant for sociologists are reviewed in Chapter 8.

Journals primarily devoted to sport sociology

The following three journals are devoted primarily to articles on the sociology of sport and can be highly recommended:

- *Sociology of Sport Journal.* Since 1984, *SSJ* has been published quarterly by Human Kinetics Publishers in the USA in association with the North American Society for the Sociology of Sport (NASSS). Each issue contains articles, sometimes on related themes, research reports, essays from outside North America, book reviews and a very useful annotated bibliography derived from the SIRLS database covering a specific subject area (e.g. 'Sport and deviance', 'Sport and stratification', etc.). Members of NASSS receive *SSJ* with their membership.

- *International Review for the Sociology of Sport* (formerly *International Review of Sport Sociology*). Since 1966 *IRSS* has been published quarterly and edited on behalf of the International Committee for Sociology of Sport (ICSS), a sub-committee of the International Council of Sport Science and Physical Education (ICSSPE) and of the International Sociological Association (ISA), affiliated with Unesco. Members of ICSS receive IRSS with their membership.

- *Journal of Sport and Social Issues.* Published twice a year by the Center for the Study of Sport in Society (CSSS), at Northeastern University, Boston, USA. Although this journal tends to focus on issues primarily of concern to North American sport sociologists it is nonetheless an invaluable source on specific topics. Until May 1990, a subscription to the *Journal* also included an additional publication, *Arena Review*, which provided a forum for guest editors to produce issues on a single theme (e.g. the special issue on 'The formal organization of sport' (Guest Editor: Prof. T. Slack), **12**(2), November, 1988). The Center now provides the *CCSS Digest* containing new articles on sport which appear in newspapers and periodicals throughout North America, statistical data on current issues and opinion pieces, as part of the *Journal* subscription package.

Journals often publishing sport sociology articles

The following are sport/leisure-related journals which often include articles on the sociology of sport. It is indicative of the position of sociology of sport and leisure in the UK that only two of the following are actually published there. North American and European journals nonetheless offer an opportunity for UK-based sociologists of sport to contribute to databases:

- *Loisir et Société (Society and Leisure)* was founded by the Committee on Leisure Research of the International Sociological Association in 1978; it is published twice a year by the Département des sciences du Loisir, Université du Québec à Trois-Rivieres, Canada.
- *Leisure Studies.* Since 1981 *LS* has been published three times a year by E. & F.N. Spon Ltd. A reduced subscription rate is available to members of the Leisure Studies Association (LSA)
- *Quest.* This is published three times a year by Human Kinetics for the National Association for Physical Education in Higher Education (NAPEHE). Prior to 1987, a bi-annual publication. Members of NAPEHE receive *Quest* with their membership.
- *Physical Education Review.* This is the journal of the North Western (England) Physical Education Association. Published twice a year, this journal contains some interesting articles on applied research in the field.

Journals occasionally publishing sport sociology articles

Sport and leisure journals that sometimes publish papers related to the sociology of sport and leisure include: *International Journal of the History of Sport; Journal of Sport History* (has occasional special issues or themes, such as 'The Black athlete in American sport', **15**(3), Winter 1988); *Stadion; Research Quarterly for Exercise and Sport; Canadian Journal of History of Sport; Journal of Philosophy of Sport; Sport Place International;* and *Leisure Sciences.*

Sociological and other journals that occasionally publish articles on the sociology of sport and leisure are: *Theory, Culture & Society,* published by Sage Publications; *Sociology, the Journal of the British Sociological Association; British Journal of Sociology; Sociological Review; International Social Science Journal; Journal of Popular Culture;* and *Feminist Review.*

Finally, a potentially important reference work which provides annual 'state-of-the-art reviews' in all aspects of sports sciences is *Exercise and Sport Sciences Reviews*. Published since 1973 by the American College of Sports Medicine, articles by sociologists have featured in many of the 17 volumes published to date (e.g. P. Donnelly 'Sport subcultures', in *ESSR*, **XIII**, 1985).

CONSUMER MAGAZINES

Some characteristics of sports consumer magazines are discussed in *A digest of sports statistics for the UK* (Sports Council, 1986). For example, in terms of circulation, the top five sports magazines in 1985-6 were: *Shoot* (football); *Motor Cycle News; Golf News; Angling News;* and *Camping and Caravanning*. In the Top 20, sports with affluent followers and involving high expenditure on equipment, such as golf, yachting, motor sports and field sports, were all well represented. Such specific titles attract the bulk of advertising and hence are more likely to be financially viable. For this and other reasons, the UK market has not been able to sustain a general sport magazine equivalent to *Sports Illustrated* published in the USA, which has a weekly circulation in excess of two million and is one of the most widely cited sources, according to SIRC. The closest to such a generalist magazine available in the UK is probably The Sports Council's monthly *Sport and Leisure*.

An important development, worthy of sociological research in itself, is the growth of the 'alternative' football supporters magazines or 'fanzines'. These magazines, produced by enthusiasts and distributed mainly by means other than mainstream commercial channels, have emerged primarily in the late 1980s. Currently, there are over 200 football fanzines, ranging from the general (*When Saturday Comes, Balls!*, etc.) to those associated with specific clubs. An alternative cricket magazine has also been produced (*Sticky Wicket*). Many of these are available from the specialist sports bookshop, SportsPages, Caxton Walk, 94/96 Charing Cross Road, London, WC2H 0JG.

In terms of newspapers and general current affairs magazines *New Statesman and Society* (formerly *New Society*), *Marxism Today, New Socialist* and *The Spectator* all feature articles on sport occasionally. The first two often feature examples of the new 'sociological sports journalism' which has emerged from the influence of Cultural Studies on sports writing in the UK, whilst *New Socialist* had a regular column on sport. The 'quality' press (i.e. *The Times, The Guardian, The Daily Telegraph, The Independent* and their Sunday equivalents) often contain in-depth articles on aspects of sport which are of interest to the sociologist. All forms of popular sports media, however, can be criticized for continuing misrepresentation and trivialization of women's sports and sportswomen. The 'tabloid' press remains a prime example of this, as well as the portrayal of sport and sport-related issues to a mass readership in general.

Part of the problem for the sociologist of sport is that so much information is available through the sports pages of newspapers and magazines that it is quite difficult to cover all the material available. A comprehensive digest of relevant articles, along the lines of that produced by the CSSS in Boston for North America, would be a tremendous addition to the UK source-base.

Professional associations

There are two professional associations specifically focused on the sociology of sport. These are:

- North American Society for the Sociology of Sport (NASS) which provides a newsletter and the *Sociology of Sport Journal* as part of the subscription, and has held an annual conference since 1980.
- International Committee for Sociology of Sport (ICSS) which provides a twice-yearly bulletin, the *International Review for the Sociology of Sport*, and organizes conferences on a regular basis.

The main UK-based associations which offer a supportive environment for sociology of sport/leisure are:

- Leisure Studies Association (LSA) which holds an annual conference, produces a quarterly newsletter, and offers a reduced subscription to *Leisure Studies Journal*. The LSA has routinely published the proceedings from its annual conference.
- Sport and Recreation Study Group of the British Sociological Association. The BSA holds an annual conference, and members receive a newsletter and the journal *Sociology*, and are entitled to membership of various 'Study Groups', including the Sport and Recreation Study Group.
- The British Association for Sports History (BASH) holds an annual meeting and papers are circulated through a newsletter and proceedings.
- The British Association of Sports Sciences (BASS) is forming a sociology 'Interest Group'.

Official organizations and sports governing bodies

The Sports Council publish many documents and papers of general relevance, including their own *Annual report*. In addition to the two strategy documents published in the 1980s, which contained a considerable amount of information (*Sport in the community*, 1982 and *Into the '90s*, 1988, both London), The Sports Council, in conjunction with the Economic and Social Research Council funded a research programme into various aspects of sport and leisure in the late 1970s and 1980s. This has led to the publication of 25 'state-of-the-art-reviews' (SOTARS or 'blue books' – e.g. A. Tomlinson (1979), *Leisure and the role of clubs and voluntary groups*) as well as the research reports which have contributed much to the enlargement of the sociology of sport/leisure literature. The Sports Council also has an information department with a small library.

Regional Sports Councils also produce reports, for example The West Midlands Council for Sport and Recreation (1988) *Sport and young people* and *Women and sport*, and A. White and J. Coakley (1986) *Making decisions*, Greater London & South East Region Sports Council.

The Central Council for Physical Recreation (CCPR) produces some fascinating material which contains very good summaries of basic research into sport and recreation, for example the CCPR (1983) *Committee of enquiry into sports sponsorship* (The Howell Report) and the CCPR (1988) *Committee of enquiry into amateur status and participation in sport* (The Palmer Report).

Governing bodies of sport (e.g. based at places such as Lord's, Wimbledon, Newmarket, Twickenham, Cardiff Arms Park, etc.) often have libraries and permanent exhibitions which may provide useful data. It is worth checking in advance with the librarian about access.

Statistical sources

Undoubtedly, the sociologist of sport could do with more readily available and digestible data. Much information that is collected about sport and leisure is highly valued by commercial interests and as such the price is often prohibitive. Apart from the Henley Centre for Forecasting, The Sports Council and CCPR-funded research for basic leisure participation data, the sociologist is reliant upon the *General household survey (GHS)*. The general shortcomings of this source are well known, but J. Smith (1987) 'Men and women at play: gender, life cycle and leisure' (in J. Horne *et al.*, eds., *Sport, leisure and social relations*, R.K.P.), discusses them in the context of an attempt at secondary data analysis. *Social trends*, the annual collection of official statistics published by the Central Statistical Office, includes a chapter on 'Leisure' which derives from the *GHS* and a few other sources. CIPFA statistics are of use when considering the financing of sport and leisure, but again need to be used with caution (see C. Gratton and P. Taylor, 1988, *Leisure in Britain*, Leisure Management, for discussion of this and other sources of statistical data). For further details on statistics refer to Chapter 2.

Two additional sources of leisure and sport statistics are: The Sports Council/Centre for Leisure Research (1986), *A digest of sport statistics for the UK*, The Sports Council, London; Sir Norman Chester Centre/Football Trust *Annual digest of football statistics*, Football Trust/Centre for Football Research, University of Leicester.

Attitudinal surveys

There is surprisingly little information about public attitudes toward sport in the UK. There is no equivalent to the massive U.S. *Miller Lite report on American attitudes toward sports* (Miller Lite, Milwaukee, WI, 1983). Some statistics on public attitudes toward sport can be gleaned from two sources. The BBC Broadcasting Research Department publish their research findings annually. These have occasionally contained information about public attitudes toward broadcast sport (see for example, V. Marles (1984) 'The public and sport', in *Annual Review of BBC Research Findings*, **10**, BBC, London). In addition, a programme of research conducted by the University of Liverpool Health and Leisure Research Group, co-ordinated by the sociologist Professor Ken Roberts, has begun to yield data on a large sample of participants and non-participants in sport (see for example, J. Minten and K. Roberts (1987) 'Sport in Great Britain', in T. Kamporst and K. Roberts, (eds.), *Trends in sport: multinational perspectives,* Giordano Bruno, Amersfoort, The Netherlands).

Teaching and audio-visual materials

As we have seen, unlike the situation in the USA, there is, as yet, no specifically UK 'textbook' in sociology of sport. There are a number of resources available however which can enhance the teaching of the subject.

The Teaching Resource Center of the American Sociological Association published *Syllabi and instructional materials for courses on sociology of sport* in the mid-1980s (see W. Whit, 1985, ASA, Washington, DC). This consists of course outlines, student assignments, tests, class projects and exercises contributed by sociology of sport lecturers in North America and amounts to nearly 300 pages of useful information. It is currently being revised and updated. For a discussion and outline of teaching methods and strategies, J. McKay and K. Pearson (1984) 'Objectives, strategies, and ethics in teaching introductory courses in sociology of sport', *Quest*, **36**(2), pp. 134–147, is a very helpful article.

Illustrating some issues in the sociology of sport through films and/or video recordings can be quite successful. Sports films drawing on UK sporting traditions are rare (*Chariots of Fire* and *Gregory's Girl* in the 1980s were exceptions to the rule). There are however a few feature films which retain some interest, e.g. *The Bad News Bears* (baseball), *Pumping Iron* (body building), *Raging Bull, The Rocky* series (boxing) and, possibly the best insight into professional sport, *The Hustler*.

In the late 1980s both Channel 4 and BBC2 television began to produce serious sports magazine programmes which probe into the politics of sport (e.g. *Running Late*, C4; *On The Line*, BBC2). Whilst general sports coverage on ITV appears to be suffering from satellite television competition, C4 has produced a unique position for itself through coverage of American football, sumo wrestling and the Tour de France. An invaluable guide to sport on C4 has been written by G. Whannel (1988) *Channel 4 Sport*, C4, London.

CHAPTER EIGHT

Individual sports

S. HALL

Introduction

This chapter provides an overview of information sources on specific sports activities. The range of individual activities defined as sports is considerable and open to debate and the sources of information many and diverse. In such and overview it is inevitable that many activities are mentioned briefly, some may be not at all by name, but the sources mentioned should hopefully cover all such activities in one form or another.

The range of information that might be required on any sport is considerable. It can include information on the administration of the activity, participation statistics, design of facilities, rules of the game, events information, results and records, coaching information, and details of equipment. The result of such a multi-disciplinary subject area is that information sources can be very disparate, resulting in duplication of some areas and scant coverage in others.

This chapter has a bias towards activities and sources within the UK, but overseas sources will be included where possible.

Collections

General sports library collections

There are many library collections around the world that have substantial collections on individual sports although they vary as to the amount of public use that is encouraged. Many of these are reviewed in Chapter 1.

The Sport Information Resource Centre in Canada has a collection which includes material on top-level, international and Olympic sport. The Centre also co-ordinates the SPORT database which includes many references on individual activities. There is little use of the Centre by the public and limited use by students.

Other centres around the world that have considerable collections on individual sports are the United States Olympic Committee, the Deutsche Sporthochschule in Cologne (Germany), and the National Sport Information Centre (Australia).

United Kingdom collections

There are four Sports Councils in the UK and each has a reference library and information centre: (1) The Sports Council; (2) The Scottish Sports Council, The Sports Council for Northern Ireland and The Sports Council for Wales.

1. The Sports Council, which covers England, has a reference library of over 20 000 items at its London headquarters which is open to the public. A large part of the collection deals with information on individual sports. There is a collection of handbooks produced by the governing bodies of individual sports in England or the UK and international governing body handbooks. Annual reports and other governing body publications are also taken, giving information on the administration of the various sports. A large journal collection includes over 100 titles on individual activities, and many more general titles. The library also includes publications on the design, construction and management of sports facilities and information on the history of individual activities, coaching methods, Olympic sports, participation data and general interest books on individual sports.

A current-awareness journal — *SCAN* — is produced monthly and is available free of charge. This lists new publications received in the Information Centre, including journal articles. A calendar of major sporting events is produced twice a year, in February and September. This is also available free of charge. Bibliographies on individual sports can be produced on request, giving details of material held in the Centre. The nine Sports Council regional offices in England have small reference libraries which can be consulted by appointment. Their information is more regionally based but does include some information on individual sports.

2. The Scottish Sports Council, The Sports Council for Northern Ireland, and The Sports Council for Wales also have reference collections and information centres. Although smaller in scale than The Sports Council they have journals, governing body handbooks

and other information pertaining to the organization of specific sports in their countries.

Full details of services provided can be obtained from the addresses in Appendix 1.

Public libraries in the UK in general vary in their provision of sports information. Most will have encyclopaedias or directories (not always up to date) and books on how to play the game together with biographies of sportsmen and women and they will frequently get involved with the provision of participation information. They are a good source of information on local sports clubs and local authority facilities. Some are involved in the provision of community information through local viewdata services whereby information is made available via public access viewdata terminals. A menu system enables users to search for information by subject and the systems will usually include local sports information including events, clubs and facilities. Sheffield Sports Information Service, which is part of Sheffield Public Library Service, provides a specialist service which is available to all other public library authorities.

Greenwich Public Libraries in London have a specialist collection on sport including indoor and outdoor sports, mountaineering and camping, automobile sports, rowing, sailing and equestrian sports.

Library collections on specific activities

There are a number of relatively small collections of material on individual activities but there can be access problems. An exception to this is the National Centre for Athletics Literature housed at the University of Birmingham Library. This collection of books, journals, programmes and taped interviews with track and field stars is available to those interested in track and field history by appointment. Two private libraries which can be visited by appointment are the MCC Library at Lord's and the Kenneth Ritchie Memorial Library at Wimbledon. Both collections represent the best sources of information in the UK for cricket and tennis respectively, housing books, journals, programmes, score cards and other ephemeral material.

Each sport has at least one governing body which organizes and administers the sport. It is responsible for the competition structure, coaching and development of the sport, affiliates to the appropriate international body and generally sets the rules and guidelines by which the sport is played. However, the majority of these have no organized archive or library collection. Some governing bodies have deposited their archives at the National Sports Archive at Liverpool University.

The governing bodies who do claim to have archives and libraries do not always make them generally available. Many governing bodies are run by voluntary officials and do not have full-time offices. Some governing bodies do have small libraries and are prepared to make access available to genuine enquirers usually by appointment. The Amateur Rowing Association, The Amateur Swimming Association, The British Hang Gliding Association, The Croquet Association, Hurlingham Polo Association, Ladies' Golf Union and Rugby Football Union all have collections of less than 1000 items that can be consulted. The Royal and Ancient Golf Club of St Andrews, The Ramblers' Association and The Football Association have collections of between 1000 and 5000 items which are available for consultation by appointment. More libraries are listed in Chapter 6.

Information sources

Indexing and abstracting services

There are a number of indexing and abstracting journals which include references on individual sports, although few are sport specific. An overview of all relevant abstracting and indexing services can be found in Chapter 1. The Sports Council's abstracting service *SCAN* includes details of monographs, journal articles and governing body handbooks and annual reports received in the Information Centre.

The National Coaching Foundation (NCF) publishes a series called *Sporting Updates*. These are produced using references from the NCF database, and from selected references contributed by the Sports Documentation Centre at the University of Birmingham. Content is mainly coaching and sports-science related and current titles dealing with individual activities are *Athletics* (covering track and field events, distance running and orienteering), *Racket sports* (covering tennis, squash, badminton and table tennis), *Swimming* (covering all aspects of swimming and diving), *Team sports* (covering indoor and outdoor team sports, including soccer, rugby, netball, volleyball, basketball and hockey).

The Sports Documentation Monthly Bulletin, produced by the Sports Documentation Centre at the University of Birmingham includes a section on individual sports and activities organized in alphabetical order by sport. Some entries have abstracts.

Leisure, Recreation and Tourism Abstracts is produced by CAB International Information Services and includes abstracts on recreation and sport. Those for individual activities are limited into broad subject areas of: outdoor activities; water recreation; winter recreation; animal sports; ball games; athletics; physical fitness; motoring, cycling and aerosports; other activities. Individual activities are listed by name in the index.

SportSearch is a current-awareness tool produced monthly by the Sport Information Resource Centre in Canada. It monitors nearly 300 sport and physical education periodicals published in English or French and also lists books and book chapters and conference proceedings. Entries are divided by broad subject headings which include individual sports. Abstracts are included and a list of forthcoming conferences is given.

Physical Education Index is a subject index to periodicals covering dance, health, physical education, physical therapy, recreation, sports and sports medicine published quarterly by the BenOak Publishing Company in the USA. The subject divisions include individual activities, but abstracts are not included.

The overlap in coverage of these indexing and abstracting journals is considerable, particularly for the English language. All have slightly different emphases and none covers all aspects of individual sports.

Journals

Again, it has to be said that the range of journal titles dealing with individual sports activities is very large. Every activity you can think of has at least one title, although these can range from a small governing body newsletter to a mass-marketed, glossy, independently-published magazine. Some activities have a whole range of titles covering them. Association football, for example, has *FIFA Magazine*, the journal of the international governing body, a publication *Football in Schools*, produced by the English Schools Football Association, commercial journals such as *Shoot!* and *Football Today*, general 'fanzines' such as *When Saturday Comes*, as well as fanzines for individual clubs — all this for a sport which probably gets more coverage in daily newspapers than any other.

The journal list in Table 8.1 covers those taken at the Sports Council's Information Centre — it is not comprehensive but it is given to show the wide range available. These journals are often difficult to trace. The *SPRIG union catalogue of periodicals in sport and recreation*, edited by M. Shoebridge in 1988 provides some locations in the UK for this kind of material. In addition, some libraries produce lists of their journal holdings.

Bibliographies

A general bibliography covered in more detail in Chapter 1, is the 13 volume *SPORT Bibliography*, published by SIRC (1974 — 1984). A large proportion covers individual sports.

TABLE 8.1. A range of sports journals representing individual sports

Amateur Golf	Fighters (martial arts)	Quarterback
Amateur Rowing Association Club News	First Down (American football)	Rambler
Athletics Coach	Flight Line (microlight flying)	Rider
Athletics Today	Football in Schools	Riding Monthly
Athletics Weekly	Football Today	Rowing
Badminton Now	Golf Monthly	Rugby World
Ballroom Dancing Times	Golf World	Running
Basketball Monthly	The Great Outdoors	Sailplane & Gliding
Basketball News	Groundswell (surfing)	Scottish Diver
British Archer	The Gymnast	Sea Angler
Camping and Walking	High Magazine	Shooting Times
Canoeist	Hockey Digest	Skywings (hang gliding)
Climber	Hockey Field	Snooker Scene
Combat (martial arts)	Horse & Hound	Sport Parachutist
Compass Sport	IAAF Bulletin	Squash News
Coarse Fishing Handbook	IAAF Newsletter	The Squash Player
Cricket World	International Swimming and Water Polo	Swimming Times
Cricketer International	Karting	Table Tennis News
Croquet	Lacrosse Talk	Tennis
Cycletouring	Motor Sport	Tennis World
Cycling	Motorcycle Sport	Triathlete
Darts World	National Rifle Association Journal	Volleyball World
Descent (caving)	Netball	Water Ski International
Diver	Olympic Wrestling	Winning — Bicycle Racing Illustrated
Fencing	On Board (boardsailing)	World Bowls
FIFA Magazine	Open Rugby	World Gymnastics
FIFA News	Pull (clay pigeon shooting)	Yachts & Yachting

A wide range of bibliographies are available on individual sports although they can vary in content and coverage. Some examples are: the *Guide to British track and field literature 1275–1968* which includes annotations, keywords and author index; a *Bibliography of archery* which lists materials on the use of the bow and arrow for hunting, war and recreation from earliest times; *Baseball: a comprehensive bibliography* including over 21 000 sources; and a *Bibliography of cricket* by E.W. Padwick.

Many of these publications are compiled by enthusiasts and can often be difficult to trace, especially when they are published either by the individual or by the governing body concerned.

Encyclopaedias, almanacs and dictionaries

It is unfortunate that many of the general encyclopaedias on sport are no longer in print. One of the best (certainly for the reference librarian!) is the *Oxford companion to sports and games*. Edited by John Arlott, this publication gives a general history of each activity and a description of the facilities and equipment required together with the basic rules. Other entries cover famous individuals, and trophies.

The *Macmillan dictionary of sports and games* is a similar publication, although more individual sporting terms are included. Each sport or game is defined and described and accompanied by an historical summary of its evolution, a synopsis of the rules and numerous references to notable players, events and records. Famous associations, clubs, competitions, courses, institutions, grounds, races, teams and trophies all have entries. In addition there is a wide selection of technical, semi-technical, colloquial and slang terms used in sports and games throughout the world.

Guinness Publishing cover a number of sports in their two series *Guide to facts and feats* and *Records, facts and champions*. Sports covered include angling, American football, cricket, flat racing, judo, karate, motor racing, Rugby, sea fishing, show jumping, snooker, soccer and steeplechasing. They also publish *Olympic Games records* edited by Stan Greenberg which includes the results of all the Olympic Games to 1988.

More and more sports are having almanacs and yearbooks published. *Wisden's* for cricket is probably the best known of these, but the *Rothmans yearbook* series now covers a number of sports: football, rugby union, rugby league, snooker and amateur football. They all give similar information, a review of the year, current results, articles on individuals, as well as historical results and details of clubs in the particular sport. Golf has a similar publication in the guise of the *Benson & Hedges golfer's handbook*. This lists golf clubs in the UK and

Europe, gives results of important competitions, and reviews the sport for the previous year.

Videos

The number and range of sports videos now available is immense. They range from videos of matches and events to instructional videos explaining how to improve technique. A new publication available listing sports videos is produced by the National Coaching Foundation and the Sheffield Sports Information Service. Entitled *Action replay* the first edition gives details of over 900 videos commercially available for purchase in the UK. Details of running time and information on the content of the video are given with details of the distributor.

Video reviews are often included in specific sports magazines and the journal *Sport and Leisure* also includes video reviews whenever possible.

Statistics

Statistics in sport can cover a number of aspects of an individual sport including results, participation, sponsorship and television coverage.

Results

The encyclopaedias and almanacs included in the previous section will frequently contain comprehensive retrospective results information. Some sports have separate associations for statistics in their activity. The Association of Track and Field Statisticians member associations produce athletics statistics each year and an overall publication *Athletics 1990, the international track and field annual* is the latest covering track and field results from around the world. In the UK the National Union of Track Statisticians produces a yearbook, *British athletics*, in conjunction with the British Amateur Athletic Board and the Amateur Athletic Association, which gives a statistical review of the previous year. The National Union of Track Statisticians have also published *A statistical history of UK track and field athletics* which includes information up to 31 December 1989.

The International Swimming Statisticians Association publish the *World swimming annual each year which includes the world and European records, world lists, best times and world rankings for the previous year. Many governing bodies include results from the previous year in their annual handbook. For example, the European Squash Rackets Federation handbook* (annual) includes the results of European events and the Squash Rackets Association (England) includes results of senior and junior tournaments and leagues.

In the general reference books field, *Whitaker's Almanack* includes a summary of sport for most of the previous year giving details of records broken and championship results for sports such as athletics, swimming, skiing, angling, Association football, badminton, basketball, bowls, boxing, cricket, cycling, equestrian sports, fives, fencing, golf, greyhound racing, gymnastics, hockey, horseracing, ice skating, judo, tennis, motor cycling, motor racing, netball, polo, rackets, real tennis, rowing, rugby league, rugby union, shooting, snooker and billiards, speedway, squash rackets, swimming, table tennis and yachting.

Some results information can be found on British Telecom's Prestel service, and on Oracle and Ceefax. There is also a SPORTSLINE facility (originally provided by BT) which can be accessed by dialling 0898 121121, but it is limited to horse racing. COMPUTER SPORTSWORLD, produced by Chronicle Publishing Company provides online access to game results for North American professional sports and horse-racing results.

Participation statistics

The problems of establishing how many people participate in an individual activity are immense, and when it comes to trying to compare statistics from different countries, the problems are even greater. Some countries have a licensing system whereby regular participants hold licences resulting in readily available statistics, whereas in others, detailed statistics on participation in individual activities are not easily found.

The Council of Europe Clearing House published available statistics from various European countries in two issues of the *Sports information bulletin* (Nos. 12 and 13, 1988). Part One included statistics from Austria, Denmark, Luxemburg, the Republic of Ireland, Iceland, Italy, the Netherlands, Switzerland and Turkey. Part Two covers Belgium, Cyprus, Germany, Finland, France, Norway, Spain and the UK. The statistics vary from membership statistics for the individual sports associations to data collected from individual surveys or part of larger omnibus surveys.

In the UK there are a number of sources available on participation statistics. Many reports use information available from the *General household survey (GHS)*, an annual sample survey of the general population aged over 16 and resident in private households in Great Britain undertaken by the Office of Population Censuses and Surveys Social Survey Division. The *GHS* does not include questions on sport each year and the last published results are for the *GHS* of 1986. The

1987 survey does include sports questions, but when published will not be comparable directly with the 1987 figures owing to changes in the 1987 survey methodology. The *GHS* only includes statistics on certain outdoor and indoor activities but it does give some guidance on overall participation and for the more common activities.

The four Sports Councils have taken *GHS* figures, the Continuous Household Survey in Northern Ireland and put them together with membership statistics from governing bodies and other individual surveys to produce a profile for individual activities, the *Digest of Sports Statistics*. The latest (second) published edition is 1986, but a third edition is due to be published in 1991. Although far from being the complete answer to the problems of sports participation statistics, the *Digest* does at least try to bring statistics from various sources together. There are now many commercially published reports on sports statistics, some of them draw on the figures given in the *Digest* and *GHS*, and some undertake sample surveys.

The Henley Centre for Forecasting produce a quarterly publication, *Leisure Futures*, giving an assessment of people's use of leisure time and leisure spending. Mintel's *Leisure Intelligence* quarterly reviews various aspects of the leisure market including sport. Mintel also publish other reports such as the *British sportsman in 1986*, and *British lifestyle 1989*. Leisure Consultants publish *Leisure Forecasts*, covering entertainment and sport, twice a year which review current trends and makes future projections.

There are occasionally one-off reports into participation in individual activities, often carried out on behalf of the governing body. For example, Sports Marketing Surveys undertook a survey of participation in squash on behalf of the Squash Rackets Association in 1985, and a national angling survey was carried out by National Opinion Polls in 1970 and 1980.

A discipline that makes use of sports statistics and can be an additional source is sports geography. Publications relating to this discipline frequently show statistics in the form of maps, for example John Bale's book *Sports geography* and the journal *Sport Place International*. The publication *Sports en France* is an atlas of sport in France and includes maps showing the geographic spread of sports participation.

Allied to participation statistics and also used for marketing purposes are studies on the sports and sports equipment market. There are a variety of reports available, apart from those by Mintel, Henley Centre and Leisure Consultants already mentioned. KeyNote Publications produce *Sports equipment*, an overview of the industry sector in the UK, the markets import and export figures and profiles of the major companies. They also publish a market review of the sports equipment market looking at sales of equipment in individual sports. ICC Financial Surveys publish *Sports equipment — manufacturers and distributors* which provides financial and market profiles on quoted and unquoted companies within the industry sector.

Sponsorship and television statistics

Because of the inevitable link between obtaining sponsorship and television coverage, many publications dealing with sponsorship also include details of television coverage. Although companies are obviously keen for their sports sponsorship activities to be recognized, some of them are less willing to divulge the amount of sponsorship money committed to sport. There are publications that collate sponsorship information giving details of amounts sponsored and the sports events concerned. The journal *Sponsorship News* gives details of sponsorship deals as announced and also has a directory each month of sponsorship services and products.

RSL Sportscan is published twice a year and gives details of sponsorships and reviews trends in the industry. It also gives statistics on television coverage of particular events and reviews trends in television coverage.

Sporting Profiles produced quarterly by AGB Sponsorship Services looks at the other side of the television coin — viewing figures. It also gives details of TV coverage, but concentrates on providing profiles of individual activities, giving a range of details including the number of viewers broken down by sex and age, minutes transmitted, sponsors and the most popular programme within a sport.

There are many more publications on sports statistics than can be covered in an overview such as this. However it should be noted that many are very expensive. A list of references can be obtained from The Sports Council's Information Centre. The Sport and Recreation Information Group have published a report, *Market research sources in sport in the UK* which may also be of interest. Readers should also refer to Chapter 2 for more information on statistics.

History

Many individual sports have a very long history and have gone through many changes. However, information sources on the history of sport are disparate and it can be difficult to find the answer to some historical questions. One useful source is *Sport: a guide to historical sources in the UK*, by R.W. Cox.

The general history of individual sports is frequently covered in many of the encyclopaedias already mentioned, but there are also many separate publications on the history of sport in general and on specific activities.

The *Rothmans atlas of world sport* shows the origins and evolutionary paths of various sports activities throughout the world as well as describing the history of individual sports in a particular country.

In the UK many governing bodies have reached their centenary and have produced publications outlining the history of the sport and the organization concerned. The *Centenary history of the Rugby Football Union* was published in 1970 and the *Official centenary history of the Amateur Athletic Association* in 1980. Individual clubs in particular sports have also celebrated centenaries. Golf club centenary publications are commonly produced giving details of the history of the club concerned. However, these publications are frequently not commercially published and are harder to trace than centenary publications of Association football clubs, which are commercially available.

Many other sports have histories written about them, frequently by enthusiasts of the activity. Examples of these are: *Cricket: a history of its growth and development throughout the world*, by Rowland Bowen; *Golf in Britain, a social history from the beginnings to the present day* by Geoffrey Cousins; *The roots of rugby league*, by Trevor Delaney; *Modern British fencing*, Edmund Gray and *The History of hockey*, by Nevill Miroy.

There are specific organizations concerned with the history of sport. The British Society of Sports History was formed in 1982 to stimulate, promote and co-ordinate interest in the historical study of sport, physical education, recreation and leisure. The Society produces an annual bulletin and organizes an annual conference.

The *International Journal of the History of Sport* is published three times a year and includes articles, bibliographies and book reviews on all aspects of sports history. Chapter 6 contains further information about historical sources of interest to individual sports.

The rules of sport and how to play the game

The rules of the individual sports are set by the international and national governing bodies of sport and any disputes of the rules should finally be referred to the appropriate organization. There are however a number of sources for basic rules and descriptions of how to play individual sports.

Official rules of sports and games gives details of rules and dimensions for 28 sports: archery, athletics, badminton, basketball, bowls, cricket, croquet, golf croquet, Eton and Rugby fives, football (association, British American, rugby union and rugby league), golf, ice hockey, men's and women's lacrosse, netball, real tennis and rackets, rounders, squash, tennis, table tennis, volleyball, and water polo.

The *Know the game* series includes numerous titles but the format is basically the same for all giving details of basic skills in the sport concerned and selected rules. A similar series is the *Take up sport* series, which includes over 20 activities and for each sport contains sections on getting started, basic skills, explaining the terminology and gives details of awards schemes and useful addresses.

There are of course many more individual titles published on a wide range of activities. Books on improving techniques, and training for an individual activity such as golf are readily available in bookshops although if in London, a visit to SportsPages bookshop is recommended. Titles on all kinds of sporting activity are available in this specialist bookshop. Some of these titles are referred to in Chapter 13.

Appendix 1: Addresses

This list contains the addresses of organizations and publishers referred to in this chapter. A useful address book with a wide scope is The Sports Council's *Address book* which is updated on a regular basis, and can be obtained, free of charge, from The Sports Council's Information Centre.

Amateur Rowing Association
    The Priory
    6 Lower Mall
    Hammersmith
    London W6 9DJ

Amateur Swimming Association
    Harold Fern House
    Derby Square
    Loughborough
    Leicestershire LE11 0AL

Association of Track and Field
    Statisticians
    Secretary: D. Martin
    Poste Restante
    Larkhill Post Office
    Larkhill
    Salisbury SP4 8PY

Ben Oak Publishing Company
    P.O. Box 474
    Cape Girardeau
    MO 63702-0474
    USA

Black Oak Press Inc.
  2624 Black Oak Drive
  Stillwater
  OK 74074
  USA

British Hang Gliding Association
  Cranfield Airfield
  Cranfield
  Bedford MK43 0YR

British Society of Sports History
  Department of Physical
  Education
  Queens University of Belfast
  Botanic Park
  Belfast BT9 5EX

CAB International Information
  Services
  Wallingford
  Oxfordshire OX10 8DE

Charterhouse Business
  Publications
  P.O. Box 66
  Wokingham
  Berkshire RG11 4RQ

Council of Europe Clearing House
  Espace du Vingt-Sept
  Septembre
  Boulevard Leopold II
  44 1080 Brussels
  Belgium

Croquet Association
  Hurlingham Club
  Ranelagh Gardens
  London SW6 3PR

Deutsche Sporthochschule
  Postfach 450327
  Carl Diem weig
  D-5000
  Cologne 41
  Germany

Football Association
  16 Lancaster Gate
  London W2 3LW

Guinness Publishing Ltd
  33 London Road
  Enfield
  Middlesex EN2 6DJ

Henley Centre for Forecasting Ltd
  2 Tudor Street
  Blackfriars
  London EC4Y 0AA

Hurlingham Polo Association
  Winterlake
  Kirtlington
  Oxford OX5 3HG

International Swimming
  Statisticians Association
  via Flaminia Nuova 290
  00191 Rome
  Italy

Kenneth Ritchie Memorial Library
  Church Road
  Wimbledon
  London SW19 5AE

KeyNote Publications Ltd
  28/42 Banner Street
  London EC1V 8QE

Ladies' Golf Union
  The Scores
  St Andrews
  Fife KY16 9AT

Leisure Consultants
  Lint Growis
  Foxearth
  Sudbury
  Suffolk CO10 7JX

Marylebone Cricket Club Library
  Lord's Cricket Ground
  London NW8 8QN

Mintel Publications Ltd
  18–19 Long Lane
  London EC1A 9HE

National Centre for Athletics
  Literature
  Main Library
  University of Birmingham
  Edgbaston
  Birmingham B15 2TT

National Coaching Foundation
  4 College Close
  Beckett Park
  Leeds LS6 3OH

National Opinion Polls
  Tower House
  Southampton Row
  London WC2

National Sports Archive
  Archive Unit
  University of Liverpool
  P.O. Box 147
  Liverpool L6 3BX

National Sport Information Centre
  Australian Sports Commission
  P.O. Box 176
  Belconnen
  ACT 2616
  Australia

National Union of Track
  Statisticians
  32 Almond Road
  Leighton Buzzard
  Bedfordshire LU7 8UW

Office of Population Censuses
  and Surveys
  Social Survey Division
  St Catherine's House
  10 Kingsway
  London WC2B 6JP

Ramblers' Association
  1–5 Wandsworth Road
  London SW8 2XX

Research Services Ltd
  Station House
  Harrow Road
  Wembley HA9 6DE

Royal and Ancient Golf Club of
  St Andrews
  St Andrews
  Fife KY16 9JD

Ruby Football Union
  Whitton Road
  Twickenham
  Middlesex TW1 1DZ

Scottish Sports Council
  Information Centre
  Caledonian House
  South Gyle
  Edinburgh EH12 9DQ

Sport Information Resource
  Centre
  Centre de Documentation pour
  le Sport
  1600 Promenade
  James Naismith Drive
  Gloucester
  Ontario
  Canada K1B 5N4

Sport and Recreation Information
  Group
  c/o National Sports Medicine
  Institute
  Medical College of St
  Bartholomew's Hospital
  Charterhouse Square
  London EC1M 6BQ

The Sports Council
  Information Centre
  16 Upper Woburn Place
  London WC1H 0QP

The Sports Council for Northern
  Ireland
  Information Centre
  House of Sport
  Upper Malone Road
  Belfast BR9 5LA

The Sports Council for Wales
  Information Centre
  National Sports Centre for
  Wales
  Sophia Gardens
  Cardiff CF1 9SW

Sports Documentation Centre
  Main Library
  University of Birmingham
  Edgbaston
  Birmingham B15 2TT

Sports Library and Information
  Service
  Central Library
  Surrey Street
  Sheffield S1 1XZ

Sports Marketing Surveys Ltd
  Byfleet Business Centre
  Chertsey Road
  Byfleet
  Surrey KT14 7AW

SportsPages
  95/96 Caxton Walk
  Charing Cross Road
  London WC2H 0JG

United States Olympic Committee
  1750 East Boulder Street
  Colorado Springs
  CO 80909
  USA

References

Abstracting and indexing services

Leisure, Recreation and Tourism Abstracts
  CAB International Information Services
  ISSN 0261 1392
  Quarterly

SCAN — selected new publications and articles
  The Sports Council
  Information Service
  Monthly

Sporting Updates
  Athletics, racket sports, swimming, team sports
  National Coaching Foundation
  ISSN 0958 4382
  Quarterly

Sports Documentation Monthly Bulletin
  Sports Documentation Centre, University of Birmingham
  ISSN 0142 1794
  Monthly

Journals

FIFA Magazine
  Hitzigweg 11
  CH-8030
  Zurich
  Switzerland

Football in Schools
  P.O. Box 39
  Hartlepool
  Cleveland TS24 1SJ

Football Today
  Dartmouth House
  Birmingham Road
  West Bromwich
  West Midlands B71 4JQ

Shoot!
  Holborn Publishing Group
  King's Reach Tower
  Stamford Street
  London SE1 9LS

When Saturday Comes
  4th Floor
  Pear Tree Court
  London EC1R 0DS

Bibliographies

*Baseball: a comprehensive
  bibliography*,
  M.J. Smith Jr,
  Jefferson, USA, McFarlane &
  Co., 1986.

Bibliography of archery,
  F. Lake and H. Wright,
  Manchester, The Simon
  Archery Foundation, 1974.

Bibliography of cricket (2nd edn.),
  E. W. Padwick (ed.),
  London, Library Association,
  1984.

*Guide to British track and field
  literature, 1275–1968*,
  P. Lovesy and T. McNab,
  London, Athletics Arena, 1969.

Encyclopaedias, almanacs and dictionaries

*Benson & Hedges golfer's
  handbook 1990*
  Macmillan, 1990
  ISBN 0 333 51862 4

*Macmillan dictionary of sports &
  games*
  J.A. Cuddon (ed.),
  Macmillan, 1980
  ISBN 0 333 19163 3

Olympic Games, the records
  S. Greenberg (ed.),
  Guinness Superlatives Ltd,
  1975
  ISBN 00 85112 896 3

*Oxford companion to sports and
  games*
  John Arlott (ed.),
  Oxford University Press, 1975
  ISBN 0 19 211538 3

*Rothmans football yearbook
  1990–91*
  Jack Rollin (ed.)
  Queen Anne Press, 1990
  ISBN 0 356 17911 7

*Rothmans Rugby League
  yearbook 1990–91*
  R. Fletcher and D. Howes
  Queen Anne Press, 1990
  ISBN 0 356 17851 X

*Rothmans Rugby Union yearbook
  1990–91*
  S. Jones (ed.), Statistician: J.
  Griffiths
  Queen Anne Press, 1990
  ISBN 0 356 19162 1

Whitaker's almanack 1990
  H. Marsden (ed.),
  J. Whitaker & Sons Ltd, 1989
  ISBN 0 85021 197 2

*Wisden's cricketers' almanack
  1990*
  G. Wright (ed.),
  John Wisden & Co. Ltd, 1990
  ISBN 0 947766 15 4

Videos

Action replay, audio visual resources in sport and recreation
C. Rankin and S. Chappel
Leeds, National Coaching Foundation and Sheffield Sport Information Service, 1990

Sport and Leisure
The Sports Council.
Bi-monthly

Statistics

Athletics 1990, the international track and field annual
P. Matthews (ed.)
Sports World Publications Ltd, 1990
ISBN 1 871396 026

British athletics 1990
P. Matthews (ed.), National Union of Track Statisticians
BAAB/AAA, 1990
ISBN 0 85134 096 2

Digest of sport statistics (2nd edn.)
Centre for Leisure Research
Sports Council, 1986
ISBN 0 906577 232 3

European Squash Rackets Federation handbook 1990
European Squash Rackets Federation, 1990

General household survey 1986
Office of Population Censuses and Surveys
Social Survey Division
HMSO, 1989
ISBN 0 11 691248 0

Leisure Forecasts
Twice yearly
Leisure Consultants

Leisure Futures
Quarterly
Henley Centre for Forecasting
ISSN 0263 7774

Leisure Intelligence
Quarterly
Mintel Productions Ltd

Market research sources in sport in the UK
J. Edwards and S. Kearney
Sport and Recreation Information Group, 1990

Market review — UK sports market
KeyNote Publishing, 1987
ISBN 1 85056 508 6

RSL Sportscan
Twice yearly
Research Service Ltd

Sponsorship News
Monthly
Charterhouse Business Publications

Sport Place International — an international magazine of sports geography
Thrice yearly
Black Oak Press Inc,
ISSN 0888 9589

Sports en France
D. Mathieu and J. Praicheux
Paris, France, Fayard-Reclus, 1987
ISBN 2 213 02007 8

*Sports equipment — an industry
sector overview* (7th edn.)
KeyNote Publications Ltd,
1988
ISBN 1 85056 504 X

Sports geography
J. Bale
E. & F.N. Spon, 1989
ISBN 00 419 14390 4

Sports information bulletin No. 12
(March 1988) & No. 13 (June
1988)
Council of Europe Clearing
House

Squash participation survey
Sports Marketing Surveys
Squash Rackets Association,
1985

*Squash Rackets Association
annual 1990–91*
K. Scott (ed.)
London, Squash Rackets
Association, 1990
ISBN 0 900698 13 6

*A statistical history of UK track
and field athletics*
A. Huxtable (ed.)
National Union of Track
Statisticians, 1990
ISBN 0 904 612 11 2

Whitaker's almanack 1990
H. Marsden (ed.)
J. Whitaker & Sons Ltd, 1989
ISBN 0 85021 197 2

World swimming annual 1989
L. Saini
Rome, International Swimming
Statisticians Association, 1989

History

*British Society of Sports History
Bulletin*
British Society of Sports
History. Annual

*Centenary history of the Rugby
Football Union*
U.A. Titley and R. McWhirter
London, Rugby Football
Union, 1970

*Cricket: a history of its growth
and development throughout
the world*
R. Bowen
London, Eyre & Spottiswoode,
1970

*Golf in Britain, a social history
from the beginnings to the
present day*
G. Cousins
London, Routledge and Kegan
Paul, 1975
ISBN 0 7100 8029 X

The history of hockey
N. Miroy
Staines, Lifeline, 1986

*International Journal of History
and Sport*
Thrice yearly
Frank Cass & Co. Ltd.

*Modern British fencing
A history of the Amateur
Fencing Association
1964–1981*
E. Gray
London, Amateur Fencing
Association, 1984

The roots of rugby league
T. R. Delaney
Keighley, T. Delaney, 1984

Rothmans atlas of world sport
  P. Ray (ed.)
  London, Rothmans
  Publications Ltd, 1982

*Sport: a guide to historical
  sources in the UK*
  R. W. Cox
  London, The Sports Council,
  1983

Rules of sport and how to play the game

*Official rules of sports and games
  1988–89* (17th edn.)
  R. Moore (ed.)
  London, Kingswood Press,
  1987

Know the game series
  A. & C. Black Ltd

Take up sport series
  Springfield Books Ltd

Part III

CHAPTER NINE

The Olympic Games

W. WILSON AND G. GHENT

Introduction

The modern Olympic Games began in Athens, Greece, in 1896 owing
primarily to the efforts of Baron Pierre de Coubertin, a French
aristocrat. Staged under the auspices of the International Olympic
Committee (IOC), the Games are held at four-year intervals called
Olympiads. The schedule has been interrupted three times by war — in
1916, 1940 and 1944.

The first Olympic Winter Games took place in 1924 in Chamonix,
France. Historically, the Winter Games have been held in the same year
as the commonly called 'Summer' Games. Beginning with the 1994
Winter Games in Lillehammer, Norway, however, the IOC will stagger
the schedule so that winter and summer competitions are held two years
apart from each other.

The Games have grown and changed dramatically since 1896. At the
Athens Games (1896) there were only 311 athletes from 13 nations
competing in nine sports. In 1988, Seoul hosted competition in 23 sports
in which 9581 athletes from 160 countries participated.

The early competitions were almost exclusively a white male
bastion. In the ensuing years, women and people of other races have
slowly but steadily increased their presence in the Olympic Movement.
Another major change has been the gradual erosion of the concept of
amateurism as an increasing number of Olympic sports have permitted
the participation of state-supported or professional athletes.

As the Games have become a worldwide spectacle, they have been at
the centre of political controversies. Adolf Hitler attempted to use the
1936 Games as a showcase for the new Germany; dozens of Mexican
students were shot by government troops during protests prior to the

1968 Mexico City Games; and Palestinian terrorists murdered 11 Israeli athletes in Munich in 1972. The Games of 1956, 1976, 1980, 1984 and 1988 were the objects of boycotts by nations wishing to express displeasure over larger political issues.

As the Olympic Movement nears the end of its first century, the IOC faces a number of difficult issues including the control of drug use by athletes, the sheer size and scope of the competition, and the continuing issue of amateurism versus professionalism. In addition, the accusation that the Games themselves are becoming too commercially orientated have been levelled against the IOC in recent years.

The IOC is the governing body which sanctions the Games. The committee maintains a staff and headquarters in Lausanne, Switzerland. The Committee itself is comprised of more than 90 members representing over 70 countries. An IOC member must speak French or English and reside in a country which has a National Olympic Committee recognized by the IOC. No nation may have more than two representatives on the committee. Members who were elected after 1965 must retire at age 75; members elected earlier have a lifetime tenure.

The members elect a president and executive board chosen from among the membership. The executive board, comprised of the president, four vice-presidents, and six other members, has broad powers. It appoints the IOC director, manages the committee finances, keeps IOC records, and sets the agenda for the IOC general sessions. Most session decisions are taken on the recommendation of the executive board.

Other important players in the Olympic Movement are the International Sports Federations (IFs), National Olympic Committee (NOCs) and Olympic organizing committees. The IFs are the worldwide governing bodies of their respective sports. As of 1989 the IOC recognized 30 IFs whose sports were represented in the Olympic programme.

To compete in the Olympic Games, a nation's NOC must be recognized by the IOC. Each NOC is responsible for organizing its country's Olympic team. The actual planning and staging of the Games is the responsibility of local organizing committees. Local organizing committees are selected by the IOC after a competitive bidding process. Typically, several cities will compete for the privilege of hosting the Games. Most organizing committees are quasi-governmental groups.

Bibliographies and indexing/abstracting services

The printed literature which documents the history, issues, and statistical information on the Olympic Games and the Olympic Movement is voluminous, especially from mid-century to date. In this chapter, we will survey works published predominantly in the last two decades, some of which are still in print. Other specialized, but more fugitive sources, also will be included since they represent a current, new direction in publishing.

According to Richard Mandell, bibliographical works which document the Olympic Games prior to the 1970s are mainly the purview of German scholars and physical education practitioners. His outstanding, critical review of these earlier sources was published in a periodical article entitled 'The Modern Olympic Games', *Sportwissenschaft*, **6**(1), 1976, pp. 89–98. Mandell provides the reader with an historical context and critical commentary of the various works of dedicated bibliographers such as Karl Lennartz, *Bibliographie: Geschichte der Leibesübungen*, Bd.5, *Olympische Spiele* (Köln: Der Pädagogischen Hochschule Rheinland, 1971) and Hans Lenk, *Werte, Ziele, Wirklichkeit der modernen Olympischen Spiele* (Stuttgart, Verlag Karl Hofmann, 1964). Karl Lennartz's work is available in the 2nd edition (Bonn, Verlag Karl Hofmann, 1983). In addition to citing bibliographic works, Mandell identifies the classical writers of the Olympic Movement such as author Carl Diem who wrote seminal works on the Olympic philosophy, e.g. *The Olympic idea: discourses and essays* (Schorndorf: Verlag Karl Hofmann, 1970).

The most comprehensive and systematic bibliography of recent origin is Bill Mallon's *The Olympics: a bibliography* (New York, Garland, 1984). This is one of the best and most comprehensive sources to date which lists the publications, official reports, serial titles from the International Olympic Committee, the national Olympic committees and major publications from the individual organizing committees. His bibliography also includes some of the doctoral dissertations and Olympic films on many aspects of the Olympic Games.

For the general reader, two excellent bibliographical articles by Evelyn Meyer are, 'The Modern Olympic Games: a select bibliography of bibliographies', *Reference Services Review,* **12**, Summer, 1984, pp. 95–101 and 'The Olympic Games and world politics: a selected annotated bibliography', RQ, **23** Spring, 1984, pp. 297–305. In the latter source, Meyer outlines the major political happenings at the Olympic Games from 1936 to 1983, and in the former, her annotated listing of important English-language works in American legal journals is an excellent contribution to the issue of nations boycotting the Olympic Games.

Of interest to scholars is the finding list to the Avery Brundage Collection (he was IOC President from 1952 to 1972) which is held at the University of Illinois. The University of Western Ontario, Amateur Athletic Foundation of Los Angeles and California State University, Long Beach, also hold a microfilm copy of the collection. Maynard Brichford's *The Avery Brundage Collection, 1908–1975* (Schorndorf,

Verlag Karl Hofmann, 1977) is a good systematic outline to a complex collection of primary and secondary material.

The study of the modern Olympic Games is not considered complete unless the ancient Olympic Games and athletics is pursued. Nigel Crowther compiled a very comprehensive listing of 1234 books and periodical articles entitled, 'Studies in Greek athletics', published in two issues of the periodical, *Classical World*, **78**(5), May–June 1985, pp. 497–559 and **79**(2), November–December 1985, pp. 73–135.

Since the late 1970s the appearance of one powerful indexing/abstracting service has made access to a good portion of the existing English- and foreign-language Olympic literature more readily available. As mentioned in Chapter 1, the large international database, SPORT, produced by the Sport Information Resource Centre (Gloucester, Ontario) and its CD-ROM counterpart, SPORT DISCUS, contain references to 2575 citations (as of December 1989) on the administrative, historical, social, political and sport sciences aspects of the Olympic Games and Olympic Movement. There are many other indexes too numerous to list which provide access to the world's major newspapers or the political and news magazine articles. These will provide access, in English and the major European languages, to articles on preparation for an Olympiad or Winter Olympic Games, events held during the Games, and the aftermath of the Games on the host city.

History and politics of the modern Olympic Games

The monographic literature on modern Olympic history is an uneven mix produced by journalists, amateur historians and professional scholars. Typical of the journalistic approach is Bill Henry's *An approved history of the Olympic Games* (Los Angeles, Southern California Committee for the Olympic Games, 1984). The book is arranged chronologically. Each chapter presents a short description of the organizational effort associated with each Olympiad and then describes in greater detail the sports competition. A list of medal winners appears at the end of each chapter. Similar works are Dick Schaap's *An illustrated history of the Olympics* (3rd edn., New York, Alfred A. Knopf, 1975) and *A history of the Olympics* (New York, Galahad Books, 1980).

A number of Olympic athletes and officials have written their memoirs. The best of these is *My Olympic years* (London, Secker & Warburg, 1983) by Lord Killanin, who was IOC president from 1972 to 1980.

The task of presenting a comprehensive analytical history that is international in scope and weaves together the many themes surrounding

the Olympic Games is a difficult one. Consequently most scholarly
works tend to focus on single Olympiads, single issues or individual
personalities. John MacAloon's *This great symbol: Pierre de Coubertin
and the origins of the modern Olympic Games* (Chicago, University of
Chicago Press, 1981) and Richard Mandell's *The first modern Olympics*
(Berkeley, University of California Press, 1976) are well-researched histories of De Coubertin and the early Olympic Movement. Mandell's
Nazi Olympics (New York, Macmillan, 1971) is a classic in sport historiography. The history of the Olympic Movement in the USA is well
documented in a dissertation by Robert Lehr, *The American Olympic
Committee, 1896–1940: from chaos to order* (Pennsylvania State
University, 1985) (available from University Microfilm International,
Ann Arbor, MI, order No. AAC8606355). *Tales of gold* (Chicago, Contemporary Books, 1987) by Lewis Carlson and John Fogarty is a compilation of oral history of 58 Olympic medal winners who competed
between 1912 and 1984.

Allan Guttmann's *The Games must go on: Avery Brundage and the
Olympic Movement* (New York, Columbia University Press, 1984)
successfully combines history and biography in examining the career of
the man who served as IOC president for two decades and was involved
actively in United States Olympic affairs prior to that. Because
Brundage's career spanned such a long period, Guttmann's book is
broader in scope than most scholarly publications. John Lucas' *The
modern Olympic Games* (South Brunswick, NJ, A.S. Barnes, 1980) is
even more comprehensive.

The role of female and Black athletes has attracted the attention of
several writers. The most thorough treatment of women in the Olympic
Games is Mary Leigh Henson's doctoral dissertation 'The Evolution of
Women's Participation in the Summer Olympic Games, 1900–1948'
(Ohio State University, 1974) (available from UMI, order No.
AAC7503121). *Black Olympians* (Los Angeles, California Afro-Ameri-
can Museum, 1984) is a history of African–American athletes published
in conjunction with a 1984–85 museum exhibition in Los Angeles.
Harry Edwards' *Revolt of the Black athlete* (New York, Free Press,
1970) deals in large part with efforts to organize an African American
boycott of the 1968 Games. Bernice Lee Adkins' dissertation 'The Development of Negro Olympic Talent' (Indiana University, 1967) (available from UMI, order No. AAC6712908) focuses on athletes who
competed at Tennessee State University before going on to compete in
the Olympics.

Film and video footage also provides a rich historical resource.
Olympic films and videos exist in a variety of forms including serious
documentaries, promotional pieces commissioned by NOCs, highlight

videos culled from television coverage of the Games, and official films produced by local organizing committees.

Probably the most famous Olympic film is Leni Riefenstahl's *Olympia* (video recording) (International Historical Films, 1985), a two-part documentary of the 1936 Berlin Games. Riefenstahl's film is memorable both for its depiction of the Nazi fervour surrounding the Games and for its cinematic technique. Other well-known films are David Wolper's *Visions of Eight* (video recording) (New York, Axon Video, 1988) and Bud Greenspan's *16 Days of Glory* (video recording) (New York, Cappy Productions, 1986). *Visions of Eight* is a compilation of the work of eight internationally renowned directors who filmed the 1972 Munich Games. Greenspan's *16 Days of Glory* presents stylish and emotional portraits of athletes who competed in Los Angeles in 1984. Greenspan has applied the same formula to two subsequent productions: *Calgary '88: 16 Days of Glory* (video recording) (Santa Monica, CA, Cappy Productions, 1989) and *Seoul '88: 16 Days of Glory* (video recording) (New York, Cappy Productions, 1989). Another of Greenspan's projects, the *Olympiad* series (video recording) (New York, Cappy Productions in co-operation with CTV Television, 1988) is certainly the most complete Olympic series available. Produced in 22 parts, *Olympiad* covers the full scope of modern Olympic history while simultaneously addressing a variety of topics such as women gold medal winners, Soviet athletes, Jesse Owens in Berlin, African runners, East German athletes, great sprinters and the greatest moments of the Olympic Winter Games.

Many writers have dealt with what can be broadly described as the political aspects of the Olympics. One of the most sophisticated examples of this sort is John Hoberman's *Olympic crisis: sport politics and the moral order* (New Rochelle, NY, Aristide D. Caratzas, 1986), a critique of the 'moral poverty of the Olympic Movement' in which Hoberman argues that the Olympic Movement has turned a blind eye to the human rights abuses in countries that are members of the Olympic Family. Richard Espy's *The politics of the Olympic Games* (Berkeley, University of California Press, 1979) analyses the role of the Games in international relations as does David Kanin's *A political history of the Olympic Games* (Boulder, CO, Westview, 1981). *The 1984 Olympic Scientific Congress Proceedings, volume 7: sport and politics* (Champaign, IL, Human Kinetics, 1986) edited by Gerald Redmond includes a section of eight papers on the Olympic Games. Bill Shaikin's *Sport and politics: the Olympics and the Los Angeles Games* (New York, Praeger, 1988) looks specifically at the 1984 Los Angeles Games and other political issues.

The internal politics of the Olympic Movement, and the relationship between the Olympic Games and larger political issues, have inspired several doctoral dissertations. These include C. Cartwright Young's 'United States Olympic Politics: A Public Policy Case Study' (University of Missouri, 1982) (available from UMI, order No. AAC8226224), Robin Tait's 'The Politization of the Modern Olympic Games' (University of Oregon, 1984) (available from UMI, order No. AAC8414869), Alan Platt's 'The Olympic Games and their Political Aspects: 1952–1972 (Kent State University, 1976) (available from UMI, order No. AAC7703840), Udoriri Okafor's 'The Interaction of Sport and Politics as a Dilemma of the Modern Olympic Games' (Ohio State University, 1979) (available from UMI, order No. AAC7922535), Laurence Barton's 'The American Olympic Boycott of 1980: The Amalgam of Diplomacy and Propaganda in Influencing Public Opinion' (Boston University, 1983) (available from UMI, order No. AAC8309745) and Derick Hulme's 'The Viability of International Sport as a Political Weapon: the 1980 U.S. Olympic Boycott' (Fletcher School of Law and Diplomacy, 1988) (available from UMI, order No. AAC8816731).

Some publishers have relied on anthologies as a way of addressing a wide spectrum of Olympic issues within a single volume. Three good anthologies are *The Olympic Games in transition* (Champaign, IL, Human Kinetics, 1988) edited by Jeffery Segrave and Donald Chu, *The modern Olympics* (Cornwall, NY, Leisure Press, 1976) edited by Peter Graham and Horst Ueberhorst and *Five ring circus: money, power and politics at the Olympic Games* (London, Pluto Press, 1984) edited by Alan Tomlinson and Garry Whannel.

An extension of the study of the modern Olympic Games, is the study of the Ancient Greek athletic festivals and games at Olympia which influenced revival of the Olympic Games in 1896. The well-respected works of learned historians are essential reading. These include, H.A. Harris, *Greek athletes and athletics* (London, Hutchinson, 1964) and E. Norman Gardiner, *Athletics in the Ancient world* (reprinted, Chicago, Ares Publishers, 1978). The study of athletics in Ancient Greece has had more recent examination by classical historian David C. Young, *The Olympic myth of Greek amateur athletics* (Chicago, Ares Publishers, 1985), which sets forth the thesis that Greek athletes were professional in the modern sense of the word. Other more recently published introductory works include Judith Swaddling's *The Ancient Olympic Games* (London, British Museum Publications Limited, 1980) and Elie Fallu *et al.*, *Les jeux Olympiques dans l'antiquité* (Montreal, Editions Paulines, 1976). General historical sources, cited in Chapter 6 may contain information of relevance to the Olympic Games.

Other important sources of information about the Olympic Games are the *Reports of the International Olympic Academy* held in Athens,

Greece (Lausanne, IOC, annual 1961–) and the proceedings of various National Olympic Academies. Although usually attended by Olympic devotees and true believers, these academies often feature carefully researched papers, and on occasion, even critical ones.

Specific conference proceedings presenting a wide range of view-points are found in *The Olympic Movement and the mass media: past and present issues: conference proceedings: the University of Calgary, Alberta, Canada, February 15–19, 1987* (Calgary Hurford Enterprises, 1989) and *SISMO 84: rapport officiel* (Lausanne, International Olympic Committee, 1984). The Calgary conference features more than 40 papers on such topics as the symbolic relationship between the Olympic Movement and various types of media, portrayal of female athletes, the symbolic and ideological content of Olympic coverage, marketing the Games, and future prospects. The SISMO 84 conference deals with most aspects of broadcasting major sporting events with specific emphasis on the Olympic Games. Panel discussions and papers focus on organizational problems and facilities available to broadcasters, the financial and legal aspects of international broadcasting and future trends.

Most contemporary Olympic serial publications are self-serving house organs of Olympic groups. *Sport Intern* (Munich, Karl-Heinz Huba) is a notable exception. Published in Munich a minimum of 24 times a year, *Sport Intern* is an 'insider' newsletter, featuring stories about the political and financial machinations of international sport.

Statistics and records

Sources of Olympic statistics and records abound. Popular histories such as Henry's *An approved history of the Olympic Games* (Los Angeles, Southern California Committee for the Olympic Games, 1981) typically provide lists of medal winners.

There are, however, more detailed sources. *Lexikon der 14 000 Olympioken/Who's who at the Olympics* (Graz, Leykam Verlag, 1983) by Erich Kamper is a remarkable compilation. It provides brief biographical data on 14 000 medal winners whose names are arranged alphabetically. The book also lists medal winners chronologically and offers a variety of lists such as athletes who have won the most medals, individual events of each sport, discontinued events, and sites and dates of the Olympic Games. Kamper also has written *Encyclopedia of the Olympic Games* (New York, McGraw-Hill, 1972), which contains: a record of the first six finishers in every event ever held including discontinued ones, the full names of all members of teams placing in the top six; results of Olympic art competitions; and a 32-page set of footnotes in English, French and German correcting myths and errors which have developed during the course of the modern Games.

David Wallechinsky's *The complete book of the Olympics* (New York, Penguin, 1988) provides results of every event from every Games and accompanying text. Wallechinsky lists not only medal winners but the results of many other competitors as well. A country-by-country medal count is also provided for each Games.

Olympic Games: the records (London, Guinness, 1987) by Stan Greenberg is similar to the Wallechinsky book, but lists only the top three finishers. Bill Mallon's *Olympic record book* (New York, Garland, 1988) provides an array of records including Olympic records plus records by Games, sport and nation. An especially valuable feature is the section giving a brief historical overview of each nation's Olympic history.

Some statistical sources present results for single sports. *The Olympic Games: complete track and field results 1896–1988* (New York, Facts on File, 1988) by Barry Hugman and Peter Arnold gives brief results information for every track and field competitor in Olympic history, supplemented by text. Ian Morrison's *Boxing: the records* (London, Guinness, 1988), although general in nature, contains a good section of the Olympic boxing results and records. Vladan Mihajlavic's *80 years of weightlifting in the world and Europe: 1896–1976* (Budapest, International Weightlifting Federation, 1977) presents general and Olympic data.

Another statistical approach which has been used, is to focus on a single Olympiad. *Olympic Review* (see below) provides complete summaries of medal winners. The official reports of organizing committees are, of course, excellent sources not only for data on medal winners but all competitors. Many of the larger National Olympic Committees typically publish commemorative books after each Olympiad providing good statistical information. In recent years, some organizing committees have issued results books apart from the official report; see, for example, *The Seoul Olympian results* (Seoul, Seoul Olympic Organizing Committee, 1988) and *Olympic record* (Los Angeles, Los Angeles Olympic Organizing Committee, 1984).

Publications of Olympic organizations

The most authoritative sources of descriptive information about the Olympic Games are publications of the International Olympic Committee, Olympic organization committees and National Olympic committees.

Five regular and irregular IOC serial titles are particularly good sources of information. *The Olympic Charter* spells out the organizational structure of the Olympic Movement, Olympic rules and bye-laws. *Olympic Movement* published most recently in 1987 presents a clear, concise outline of the structure of the IOC, its purpose, objectives, relationship to other sport organizations, as well as brief information on Olympic history, and prominent personalities. The annual *The Olympic Movement directory* gives names, addresses, phone numbers of all IOC members as well as entries for NOC and major sports governing bodies affiliated to the Olympic Games. *Olympic Review*, issued ten times year, is a forum for historical, although rarely critical, articles and current news. *Olympic Message*, a quarterly, maintains a similar non-critical tone, while presenting articles on current affairs affecting the Olympic Movement.

NOCs publish a variety of information. Many NOCs publish annuals that provide addresses, telephone numbers, and important dates on the sports calendar. NOCs also publish periodicals covering the Olympic efforts in their countries. As might be expected, these tend to be self-congratulatory. However, biographical features about athletes and reports on major competitions can sometimes provide information not found elsewhere. For example, see *The Olympian* (Colorado Springs, CO, The United States Olympic Committee; monthly), *Olympic Panorama* (Moscow, USSR Olympic Committee; quarterly) and *Information Bulletin* (Athens, Hellenic Olympic Committee, quarterly).

Most IFs regularly publish serials that range from newsletters, to glossy magazines, to detailed annual guides. These can be excellent sources of biographical, organizational and statistical information. For instance, one of the larger IFs based in London, England, the International Amateur Athletic Federation, publishes *IAAF Magazine* (monthly), *IAAF Newsletter* (bi-monthly), *IAAF Directory* (annual), *IAAF Handbook* (biennially) and many other publications.

Organizing committees which are awarded the right to stage the Olympic Games generate dozens of publications. Prior to the awarding of the Games, the organizing committee publishes a bid book, a technical manual and sometimes video programmes for the information of the IOC members. After the Games are awarded, organizing committees publish regular progress reports to the IOC, publicity and general information brochures, ticket information, press guides catalogues of cultural events associated with the Games, one or more magazines, graphics manuals, a plethora of guides outlining transportation, medical and language services, programmes for each sport competition, and of course, the final report called the *Official report*. The size and sophistication of the *Official report* vary but this IOC-required publication must provide a detailed accounting of the organization and financing of the Games and results of the competition. Of the *Official reports* from the last two decades, Montreal 1976, Los Angeles 1984 and the Olympic Winter Games, Sapporo 1972 and Calgary 1988, are the most comprehensive and objective. The major problem which arises with these organizing committee publications is that they can be very difficult to acquire. Organizing committees usually publish only enough copies to satisfy the needs of the Olympic Family and few libraries, excluding some NOC libraries around the world, have comprehensive collections (see the section on Libraries and Archives, below, for additional details).

Olympic finances

The Olympic Games have become a large-scale financial phenomenon. Publications about the financial aspects of the Games emanate from both private and governmental sources.

Several reports have examined the financing of specific Games. For example, *The report of inquiry into the cost of the 21st Olympiad* (Quebec, Commission Royale Enquête, 1977), also known as the Malouf Commission Report, is a three-volume report on the cost over runs of the Montreal Games. The 1984 Los Angeles Games generated a surplus of $230 million. Accounts of the methods by which this was achieved appear in: *Olympic retrospective: the Games of Los Angeles* (Los Angeles, Los Angeles Olympic Organizing Committee, 1985) edited by Richard Perelman; *Made in America: his own story* (New York, William Morrow and Company, Inc., 1985) by Peter Ueberroth with Richard Levin and Amy Quinn; and Kenneth Reich's *Making it happen: Peter Ueberroth and the 1984 Olympics* (Santa Barbara, CA, Capra Press, 1986). More recently, the city of Birmingham, England, in conjunction with its unsuccessful bid to host the Games, commissioned a study entitled *Birmingham Olympics 1992: feasibility study for Birmingham City Council. Vol.1, Technical report;* Vol. 2, *Economic report* (Birmingham, Oye Arup for the Birmingham City Council, June 1985). Finally in this vein, researchers should bear in mind that official reports of Olympics organization committees sometimes are excellent sources of financial information. This is particularly true of more recent Olympiads.

A second category of studies examines the broader economic impact of the Olympic Games on the communities which host them. Studies of this sort include: *Hosting the Olympics: the long term impact, report of the conference*, organized by East Asian and Architecture and Planning Program, Massachusetts Institute of Technology (and the) Graduate School of Environmental Studies, Seoul National University (Seoul, 1988); The Canadian Ministry for Fitness and Amateur Sport's *Economic Impact of the 1988 Winter Olympic Games (15th), 1986*;

Economic Associate's *Executive summary community economic impact of the 1984 Olympic Games in Los Angeles and Southern California* (Chicago, Economic Research Associates, 1986); and *Economic impacts of the XV Olympic Winter Games* (Calgary, City of Calgary and Alberta Tourism and Small Business, 1985).

A third type of financial writing focuses on how nations can provide long-term financial support to their Olympic teams. The *Report of the President's Commission on Olympic Sports 1975–1977. Vol.1: Exclusive summary and major conclusions and recommendations. Vol.2: Findings of fact and supporting material*, is an important historical document which established the framework of the federal government's role in the U.S. Olympic effort. More recently, in 1989, the United States Olympic Committee issued *Report of the Olympic Overview Commission, United States Olympic Committee Executive Board Meeting, February 19, 1989, Portland, Oregon* (Colorado Springs, CO, United States Olympic Committee, 1989). Popularly known as the Steinbrenner Commission Report, it discusses ways to govern and finance Olympic sports in the USA more effectively.

Libraries and archives

Several collections of Olympic materials exist through the world.

North America

There are several outstanding archival collections.

- The University of Illinois' Avery Brundage Collection encompasses 139 cubic feet of correspondence and papers of Avery Brundage. These materials, housed in the university's archives, cover the years 1908 to 1975. In addition, books and official reports collected by Brundage are kept in the University of Illinois Applied Life Studies Library.
- The University of California at Los Angeles has an extensive archival collection of 1984 materials produced by the Los Angeles Olympic Organizing Committee (LAOOC). Internal correspondence, reports, strategy papers, press releases, public publications, 1400 videos and 100 000 colour slides are among the items that comprise the collection.
- The State University of New York, Pittsburgh, maintains a much smaller collection of materials about the 1980 Lake Placid Winter Games.
- The City of Calgary in Alberta, Canada, preserves the archives from the 1988 Winter Olympic Games through a legacy grant.

Among the public libraries in the USA with significant collections are the New York Public Library and the Los Angeles Public Library.

The Amateur Athletic Foundation of Los Angeles has a large collection of Olympic material including official reports of each Olympiad, publications of organizing committees, 6000 historical photographs, oral histories of 50 Southern Californian Olympians, recordings of interviews with LAOOC officials, bid books, approximately 400 video volumes, the Avery Brundage Collection on microfilm, and general works and periodicals on the Olympic Games.

Chapter 15 contains further information on resources for the Olympic Games specific to North America.

The most complete library and archive of materials belongs to the International Olympic Committee's Olympic Museum in Lausanne, Switzerland. The museum includes archival documents, official reports, bid books, general books about the Games, periodicals, an excellent collection of works by and about De Coubertin, photographs, and video and film footage dating back to 1912. Researchers should write or telephone the museum before travelling to Lausanne.

The larger NOCs maintain archives. Materials in NOC collections include minutes of meetings, internal documents of the committee, back issues of serial publications, oral histories, official reports, and historical films and photographs. The Canadian Olympic Association Library in Montreal and the United States Olympic Committee collection in Colorado Springs are strong sources of Olympic information in North America.

Europe

In Europe, the outstanding NOC libraries include the British Olympic Association in London which has a comprehensive collection of official reports, as well as publications emanating from the organizing committees. The Comitato Olimpico Nazionale Italiano in Rome contains 32 000 volumes and not only includes an outstanding collection of Olympic-related materials, but also has a sport history library with works dating back to the sixteenth century.

Other European libraries well known for collections on all aspects of sports also include notable Olympic collections. The Sport Museum of Finland (Suomen Urheilumuseo) in Helsinki is a 20 000 volume collection of sport history materials in the Finnish language as well as the major European languages. This library also houses over 50 000 photographs, many with Olympic themes.

A smaller library, dedicated to track and field athletics, but with a substantial collection on the Olympic Games, is the National Centre for Athletics Literature, located at the University of Birmingham Library.

The Centre has books, journals and taped interviews with British Olympians. It also houses the Harold Abrahams Collection.

In Cologne, the Deutsche Sporthochschule has over 2600 volumes, mainly German-language monographs relating to the Olympics, included in its 240 000 volume library. The archival material is found at the Carl-Diem-Institut Library where the special strength includes materials on the 1972 Olympiad in Munich. The most comprehensive collection of archival material for the 1972 Olympiad can be found in the Bundesarchiv in Koblenz which has correspondence and records from 1966 to 1973. The Zentralen Staatsarchiv in Potsdam holds a fairly complete collection of archival material from the 1936 Olympiad in Berlin.

Finally, researchers should be aware that commercial film and photograph libraries have extensive collections. Two such film libraries are Cappy Productions in New York and Sherman Grinberg Film Libraries in Hollywood, California. Photograph libraries with Olympic pictures include Allsport in London and Los Angeles, Bettman Archives in New York, Duomo in New York and Long Photography in Los Angeles. Most commercial libraries charge a research fee and high prices for the publication or broadcast of their footage and photographs.

CHAPTER TEN

Leisure

M. LEIGHFIELD

Introduction

Leisure is traditionally regarded as a time of fun, relaxation, recreation, doing nothing – just enjoying oneself. The range of activities is enormous, including the arts, entertainment, indoor and outdoor recreation, sport, tourism and the media. To try to cover the sources of information for such an array of activities in one short chapter is impossible; therefore this chapter will concentrate on the information sources relating to the social, economic and environmental aspects of leisure and recreation. Information on individual activities and the location of facilities can be obtained either from the national organizations associated with the activity, or through the computer-based community information services run by local authorities or private concerns, e.g. Berkshire Viewdata or Online Leisure. Details of UK organizations and facilities can be found in the *Leisure Services year book* (Longmans, annual) and *The Sports Council's Address book* (The Sports Council, annual).

Although the majority of the sources cited in this chapter are from English-speaking countries, a selection from non-English speaking countries is also included. It is helpful to note that the historical roots of leisure and recreation studies varies: for example, North America was very much influenced by the park and recreation movement, in the UK the approach was more sociological, while in Europe the emphasis is cultural, highlighting free time and animation.

Research directories

In many subject areas the most useful starting point would be with research directories; however, there are no comprehensive or up-to-date
published listings for research specifically on leisure and recreation.
Each of the central government agencies concerned with leisure policy
in the UK produces listings covering those areas with which it is most
involved, but these rely on individual research workers keeping sponsoring agencies up to date with their research progress. The most useful
are: The Countryside Recreation Research Advisory Group's *Countryside recreation research: the programmes of the CRRAG agencies*,
which publishes for each participating agency, a list of those projects
relevant to countryside recreation research. It is an annual publication.
Details of proposed work, relevant publications and databases are included, and a contact point identified for further information.

Another publication specific to leisure is the *International handbook
of leisure studies and research* (1985), edited by S.J. Parker and
published by the Leisure Studies Association. Although now rather out
of date, it aims to provide information about the state of research and
publications in individual countries.

A publication listing current research in higher education institutions
in the UK which covers leisure-related dissertations and theses is the
annual British Library's *Current research in Britain* (formerly *Research
in universities, polytechnics and colleges*). Although published in four
volumes the most useful are those devoted to social sciences and the
humanities. *Dissertation Abstracts International* provides a way of
keeping up to date with research trends worldwide. This includes
abstracts of doctoral dissertations by nearly 500 participating
institutions, mainly in North America but also in numerous other
countries. The most useful volumes are: Section A, Humanities and
Social Sciences which includes a section headed 'Recreation'; and
Section C, Worldwide (formerly *European Abstracts*). The abstracts are
also available online and on CD-ROM. A similar publication for the UK
is Aslib's *Index to theses with abstracts* (Aslib, annual). Chapter 1 gives
more detail on guides to research and dissertations.

Textbooks

The approaches to the study of leisure are diverse, ranging over many
academic disciplines, as well as from the viewpoint of policymakers,
providers and practitioners. The result is a large and increasing number
of textbooks. Unfortunately there is, as yet, no up-to-date published
bibliography of books related solely to the study of leisure, its policy-

making and practice. A small selection of books are noted with the suggestion that publishers of these books be contacted along with colleges running courses on leisure for further information and coursebook lists. *Toward a society of leisure* (J. Dumazedier, 1962) established the study of the sociology of leisure independent from that of work. Since then the theory of leisure has been explored in works such as: *Of time, work and leisure* (S. DeGrazia, 1962); *Leisure theory and policy* (M. Kaplan, 1978); *Capitalism and leisure theory* (C. Rojek, 1985); *Leisure and the future* (A.J. Veal, 1987) and *Understanding leisure* (L. Haywood, F. Kew and P. Bramham, 1989). A number of books cover specific leisure needs: *Youth and leisure* (K. Roberts, 1983), *Leisure and the family life cycle* (R. and R. Rapoport, 1975) and *Relative freedoms – women and leisure* (edited by M. Talbot and E. Wimbush). The provision and management of leisure services are well served by textbooks such as *Leisure and recreation management* (G. Torkildsen, 1986) and *Leisure industries* (C. Gratton and P. Taylor, 1987) and by the publications issued by the Institute of Leisure and Amenity Management (ILAM) in the UK, National Recreation and Parks Association (NRPA) in the USA, Canadian Parks and Recreation Association (CPRA) in Canada, and other national bodies. One of the most active publishers in the UK in the leisure field are E. & F.N. Spon, whilst in the USA, Leisure Press, a division of Human Kinetics has an active publications list.

Abstracting services

This type of publication, which provides summaries of the literature of a specific subject, is generally regarded as the most useful of the information sources, as the abstracts provide both a general overview of trends in the subject as a whole as well as enabling people to keep abreast with developments in their own particular area of interest. Chapter 1 presents a general overview of abstracting services.

The major abstracting source for information on leisure and recreation is *Leisure, rEcreation & Tourism Abstracts* (*LRTA*), published by CAB International. It is the only international service covering publications on the many aspects of leisure, recreation, sport, tourism and the arts. All types of publications are abstracted: books, journal articles, conference papers, working papers, monographs and theses. With the co-operation of the World Leisure and Recreation Association, literature from countries worldwide regardless of language are included. The abstracts are all in English, with English abstracts provided for items written in a language other than English. The journal is issued quarterly and approximately 2500 abstracts are published each year. Author, subject and geographical indexes are included in each copy and are cumulated annually. A document-delivery service is available for the majority of items.

The Canadian service *Sport and Leisure: a Journal of Social Science Abstracts* (formerly the *Sociology of Leisure and Sport Abstracts*) specializes in the sociological aspects of sport, leisure and recreation with a strong coverage of North American literature. A wide range of publications is included: books, journal articles, conference papers and working papers. It has recently ceased publication. Both these journals, *LRTA* and *Sport and Leisure*, produce associated online databases which are described later below.

In addition there is *LORETO (Loisir, Récréation, Tourisme)*. Published three times a year, it contains abstracts of leisure, recreation literature and publications written in French and Spanish. The abstracts are written in the original language and arranged by subject.

The Dutch were the most far sighted in realizing the need for an information service on leisure and recreation and began publishing *REDOC (Recreation Documentation)* in 1967. This monthly journal produces abstracts in Dutch of relevant publications on leisure, recreation, sport and tourism, mainly from the Netherlands and the Flemish-speaking area of Belgium. No indexes are included.

Bibliographies

Few bibliographies have been issued on leisure in general; most deal with specific aspects such as the somewhat out of date *Interdisciplinary bibliography and tourism and leisure research; contributions to general and regional tourism and leisure research, 1979–1984* (edited by A. Steinecke, 1984) which contains over 1400 references to a variety of publications written in a wide range of languages. These provide a structural and systematic overview of general and regional dimensions of leisure and tourism research in different countries. Bibliographies covering other aspects of leisure include *Recreation for the disabled* (The Countryside Commission, 1986), and *Sport and recreation for the disabled* (The Sports Council, 1990) and *Women in sport: a select bibliography* (edited by M. Shoebridge, 1988). *Sport for youth* (1977–1984) and the *Recreational impact of sport and leisure* are international bibliographies issued by the International Association for Sports Information, in 1985 and 1989, respectively.

A useful source of bibliographies relating to recreation in the USA is the National Technical Information Service of the U.S. Department of Commerce. Two examples are *Recreational facilities: water resources 1977–1984* and *Recreational boating 1979–1984*. Further bibliographies illustrating the range of topics covered by leisure are *Gambling: a bibliography*, from the New Zealand Department of Internal Affairs (edited by R. Tan, 1986) and *Cycling: a selection of material based on the DOE/DTP library*, UK (edited by C. Lambert, 1984).

Online databases

A quick way of obtaining access to thousands of references is by searching online databases. The multi-concept enquiry can be easily handled and references obtained in minutes. Most major libraries offer this facility. The main databases containing bibliographical information on leisure are: LEISURE RECREATION & TOURISM ABSTRACTS and the SIRLS database, SPORT AND LEISURE. The LRTA online database contains the records published in the printed journal (see above). It can be accessed from most countries and is available on the following international online database hosts: Dialog, ESA/IRS, CAN/OLE, BRS and two Japanese hosts: JICST, Tsukuba-Daiguku. The SPORT AND LEISURE information retrieval system with its specialism in the sociology of leisure has recently been bought by SIRC, who already produce the SPORT database. Users wishing to access the SIRLS database should contact SIRC at 1600 Promenade, James Naismith Drive, Gloucester, Ontario.

Databases such as SPORT, SOCIOLOGICAL ABSTRACTS, PSYCHOLOGICAL ABSTRACTS, MANAGEMENT ABSTRACTS and ACOMPLINE also contain relevant material and are available on the major online database hosts. They are all described more fully in Chapter 1.

Journals

The best way of keeping up to date with theory and practice is through the core journals. The content of the journals is influenced by the country or region in which they are published, although most of these journals try to include some coverage of other countries. *Leisure Sciences* and the *Journal of Leisure Research* are both published in the USA and consequently have a North American bias. *Leisure Studies* is issued in the UK but includes articles from European countries as well as from North America. Additional academic journals are: *Loisir et Société* (Canada), published in French with English and Spanish summaries; *Vrije Tijd en Samenleving* (Netherlands), in Dutch; *Journal of Leisure and Recreation Studies* (Japanese Society of Leisure and

Recreation Studies), in Japanese; *Tiempo Libre* (Puerto Rico) is published in Spanish, with a remit to cover Latin America.

In addition to journals covering the research aspects of leisure, there are those that deal with the more practical aspects of leisure and recreation management. In the UK the two main journals are *Leisure Manager* (the professional journal of ILAM) and *Leisure Management.* The latter also circulates a weekly free classified newsletter. Other notable publications for practitioners are *Recreation Canada, Australian Parks & Recreation* and *Parks and Recreation* (USA). Two journals dealing with a specific area of leisure are the *Therapeutic Recreation Journal* and *Journal of Leisurability*, both covering leisure for the disabled.

Magazines such as *Leisure Week* and *Sports Industry* are aimed specifically at those sports and fitness professionals who have control of budgets. Many are published in a newspaper format, and they appear more frequently than the other journals and magazines, but are often transitory. They are frequently complemented by annual publications like *Sports Industry Annual* (Sports Business, annual) and *Harper's Sports and Leisure: Guide to the Trade* (Harper's Sports and Leisure, annual).

Statistics-related publications

There are a number of services which provide information and descriptive statistics on people's free-time activity patterns and associated spending. For the UK these include: *Leisure Futures* which examines economic and social data, time budgets, total leisure spending and key areas in individual leisure sectors; *Leisure Intelligence* which provides market reports, consumer research and monitors activity trends; and *Leisure Forecasts* which cover key market indicators and consumer spending in four areas – entertainment and sport, hobbies and pastimes, catering and holidays and the media, and also provides an overview of leisure as whole. This type of publication is examined in more depth in Chapter 2.

The Countryside Commission produce a free publication on statistics entitled *Compendium of recreation statistics 1984–1986*, with a 1989 addendum. The Sports Councils of England, Scotland, Wales and Northern Ireland all publish annual reports as does The Countryside Commission. Such reports provide useful information about activities, projects, finance, etc. *Digest of sports statistics for the UK* (2nd edn., The Sports Council, 1986) undertaken by the Centre for Leisure Research for The Sports Council provides useful data about leisure pursuits related to specific sports and activities.

Conference proceedings

Papers presented at conferences and seminars can provide useful insights into current topics of interest as well as future key issues. The number of conferences on leisure topics is increasing annually. The *World Leisure And Recreation Association* (WLRA) which organizes conferences approximately every 3–4 years. In 1980 it issued *Proceedings of the First International Link Conference, Belgium*, which discussed the need for information on leisure and recreation. This is somewhat out of date but it was the first attempt to address the problem of finding reliable information on these topics. The European Leisure and Recreation Association (ELRA) also holds regular international conferences, the most recent being on *Cities for the future* (ELRA, 1989), which discussed the future of leisure and recreation in urban areas.

In the UK, the Leisure Studies Association holds an annual meeting and an international conference every three years. The topics are varied, but usually include leisure and the environment, the arts, policy matters, health and education. Approximately 16 conference publications have been issued to date. The Countryside Recreation Research Advisory Group (CRRAG) also holds an annual conference on topics relating to rural recreation. For information on current policy, provision and management of leisure activities and facilities, major conference proceedings are issued by ILAM. Again the topics covered are wide, dealing with all aspects likely to be needed by providers of activities and facilities. The Sports Council, with its wide remit, often organizes conferences which have relevance to leisure. The Sports Council Recreation Management Conference (annual) focuses on a wide range of topical leisure issues and attracts a very wide audience. The proceedings are published each year.

Most national organizations such as the Australian Parks and Recreation Association and Deutsches Gesellschaft für Freizeit publish the proceedings of their conferences and meetings and these can be useful for obtaining a perspective of developments in a particular country.

Further useful sources

The Sports Council in the UK produces a range of relevant publications, ranging over facility provision, technical aspects, health and fitness and participation in particular sports. The nine Regional Sports Councils in England publish strategies, results of demonstration projects and other initiatives. Between 1977 and 1987, The Sports Council/Social Science

Research Council Joint Panel on Leisure and Recreation Research (later The Sports Council/Economic and Social Research Council) undertook a number of research projects which were subsequently published as *State of the art reviews*. Although some of the information is out of date, the reports provide an insight into the perceptions of policymakers on various issues, and provide very useful sources of information on topics such as policymaking, trends, motivation, ethnic groups and participation.

Some local authorities publish market research, statistics and development plans that are relevant to leisure, e.g. *Kelmscott Leisure Centre: market research 1986* (1986, Waltham Forest Recreation Services). Since leisure impinges on so many aspects of life, a number of organizations not directly related to leisure publish relevant material. These include groups involved with the disabled and elderly, e.g. The Royal Association for Disability and Rehabilitation, The Centre for Policy on Aging, The Beth Johnson Foundation, organizations undertaking research in planning like the School for Advanced Urban Studies (University of Bristol), the Institute of Local Government Studies (University of Birmingham) and outdoor pursuits' organizations like Operation Raleigh and The Duke of Edinburgh's Award Scheme.

Organizations

Particularly fruitful sources of information are relevant international and national organizations. The World Leisure and Recreation Association (WLRA) is the major international organization. It not only issues a journal, *World Leisure and Recreation*, but also a newsletter on AIDS and recreation, and assorted publications including the *International directory of academic institutions in leisure, recreation and related fields* (WLRA, 1986). This *Directory*, although now out of date, provides a useful guide to the place of leisure in education in 42 countries. It gives a brief overview of the educational system, describes the place of leisure and recreation in that system and surveys relevant institutions and national organizations.

The European Leisure and Recreation Association has recently moved its headquarters to the ILAM, UK, and intends to issue a multilingual newsletter as well as other appropriate publications. The Latin American Leisure and Recreation Association (ALATIR) publishes its conference proceedings as well as an occasional newsletter. All are in Spanish.

Most countries have national organizations, for example, in the UK the two main ones are the Leisure Studies Association (whose membership is mainly academic and which publishes a series of very informative national and international conference proceedings and is involved with the journal *Leisure Studies*) and ILAM (which not only issues the journal *Leisure Manager*, but also a growing series of monographs relevant to management and practice).

Further examples of national organizations are: National Recreation and Parks Association (USA), Canadian Parks/Recreation Association; Australian Parks and Recreation Association; Deutsches Gesellschaft für Freizeit; Japanese Society of Leisure and Recreation Studies.

Library collections

As colleges develop courses on leisure and related topics, so do relevant resources available in their libraries reflect this expansion of subject coverage. A range of information can therefore be found in most local colleges, plus universities and polytechnics. Oxford Polytechnic, has a particularly good collection.

However, two libraries in particular specialize in these topics in the UK: ILAM and The Sports Council's Information Centre in London. ILAM concentrates on the more practical aspects of provision of facilities and activities, and is in the process of developing a unit devoted to open space, its provision, maintenance and use. The Sports Council has extensive collections covering provision, and maintenance, including technical aspects of facility design as well as motivational and participation information. The National Children's Play and Recreation Unit, funded by The Sports Council houses a library devoted to the provision and theory of play. In addition, the library of The Countryside Commission contains sources on recreation in the countryside, particularly as a competing activity for land use. A useful guide to relevant journals held by UK libraries is the Sports and Recreation Information Group's *Union catalogue of periodicals in sport and recreation* (1988). Details of relevant journals on sport, leisure and recreation held in over 40 libraries in the UK are provided.

References

General

Countryside recreation research: the programmes of the CRRAG agencies. The Countryside Commission. CRRAG: School for Advanced Studies: University of Bristol.

Current research in Britain. British Library: Wetherby: West Yorkshire.

Dissertation Abstracts International. University Microfilms Ltd: Ann Arbor, MI, USA.

Index to theses with abstracts. Aslib & Expert Information: London.

Leisure Services year book. Longmans: Burnt Mill, Harlow, Essex.

Parker, S.J. (ed.) (1985) International handbook of leisure and research. LSA: London.

The Sports Council's Address book. Information Centre. The Sports Council, 16 Upper Woburn Place, London WC1H 0QP

Textbooks

DeGrazia, S. (1962) *Of time, work and leisure.* Twentieth Century Fund: New York.

Dumazedier, J. (1962) *Toward a society of leisure.* The Free Press: New York.

Gratton, C. and Taylor, P. (1987) *Leisure industries.* Comedia Consultancy: London.

Haywood, L. Kew, F. and Bramham, P. (1989) *Understanding leisure.* Hutchinson: London.

Kaplan, M. (1978) *Leisure theory and policy.* J. Wiley: London.

Rapoport, R. and R. (1975) *Leisure and the family life cycle.* Routledge and Kegan Paul: London.

Roberts, K. (1983) *Youth and leisure.* Allen & Unwin: London.

Rojek, C. (1985) *Capitalism and leisure theory.* Tavistock: London.

Talbot, M. and Wimbush, E. (eds.) (1988) *Relative freedoms – women and leisure.* Open University: Milton Keynes.

Torkildsen, G. (1986) *Leisure and recreation management.* E. & F.N. Spon: London.

Veal, A.J. (1987) *Leisure and the future.* Allen & Unwin: London.

Abstracting and indexing journals

Leisure, Recreation & Tourism Abstracts. CAB International: Wallingford, Oxon OX10 8DE, UK. Quarterly.

LORETO. Centre de Recherches et de Documentation sur le Loisir, la Recreation et le Tourism, Direction Générale de la Culture: Galerie Ravenstein 78, 1000 Brussels, Belgium. Thrice yearly.

REDOC. Stichting Recreatie: s'Gravenhage, Netherlands. Monthly.

Sport and Leisure. University of Waterloo Press: Waterloo, Ontario, Canada N2L 3GI. Thrice yearly. Ceased publication 1990.

Bibliographies

The Countryside Commission. *Recreation for the disabled* (CCP21), (1986) The Countryside Commission: Cheltenham.

International Association for Sports Information (1985) *Sport for youth 1977–1984*. Documentation and Information Division, Italian Olympic Committee: Rome.

International Association for Sports Information (1989) *Environmental impact of sport and recreation*. Sports Documentation Centre, University of Birmingham: Birmingham.

Lambert, C.M. (ed.) (1984) *Cycling: a selection of material based on DOE/DTP library*. Library Bibliography Services No. 211, Department of the Environment/Department of Transport: London.

U.S. Department of Commerce, National Technical Information Service, *Recreational facilities: water resources 1977–1984; Recreational boating 1974-1984*. NTIS: Springfield, VA.

Shoebridge, M. (ed.) (1988) *Women in sport: a select bibliography*. Mansell: London.

The Sports Council (1990) *Sport and recreation for the disabled* (Select Bibliography N0. 4). The Sports Council, London.

Steinecke, A. (ed.) (1984) *Interdisciplinary bibliography on tourism and leisure research. Contributions to general and regional tourism and leisure research, 1979–1984, Berlin, Germany*. Institut für Geographie der Technischen Universtät: Berlin.

Tan, R. (ed.) (1986) *Gambling: a bibliography*. Student paper No.1. New Zealand Department of Internal Affairs.

Journals

Harper's Sports & Leisure: Guide to the Trade (1989). Harper's Sports & Leisure, Unit 2, Mill Hill Industrial Estate, Flower Lane, London NW7 2HU.

Journal of Leisurability. Leisurability Publications Inc., 36 Bessemer Court, Unit 3, Concord, Ontario, Canada. Quarterly.

Journal of Leisure and Recreation Studies. Japanese Society of Leisure and Recreation Studies, Kishikinen-Taiikukaikan, 1-1-1 Tinnan, Shibuya-ku, Tokyo 150, Japan. Annual.

Journal of Leisure Research. NRPA, 12th Floor, 3101 Park Center Drive, Alexandria, VA 22302, USA. Quarterly.

Therapeutic Recreation Journal. National Therapeutic Recreation Society, 3101 Park Center Drive, Alexandria, VA 22303, USA. Quarterly.

Leisure Management. Leisure Publications Ltd., 1st Floor, 40 Bancroft, Hitchen, Herts S95 1YL. Monthly.

Leisure Manager. Institute of Leisure and Amenity Management, ILAM House, Lower Basildon, Reading, Berks RG8 9NE. Monthly.

Leisure Sciences. Crane, Russak & Co. Inc., 3 East 44th St., New York, NY 10017, USA. Quarterly.

Leisure Studies. E. & F.N. Spon, 11 New Fetter Lane, London EC4. Thrice yearly.

Leisure Week. Centaur Publishing Ltd., 50 Poland Street, London W1V 4AX.

Loisir et Société. Les Presses de l'Université du Québec, CP250, Sillery, Quebec, Canada G1T 2R1. Twice yearly.

Sports Industry Annual. Sport Business, 50 Poland Street, London W1V 4AX.

Sports Industry. P.O Box 13, Hereford House, Bridle Path, Croydon, CR9 4NL. 10 per year.

Tiempo Libre. Centro de Estudio del Tiempo Libre, American University of Puerto Rico, Apartado 2037, Bayaman, Puerto Rico 00621.

Vrije Tijd en Samenleving. Postbus 80547, 2508 GH Den Haag, Netherlands. Quarterly.

Statistics-related publications

The Countryside Commission. *Compendium of recreation statistics 1984–1986.* The Countryside Commission: Cheltenham.

Leisure Forecasts. Leisure Consultants, Lint Growis, Foxearth, Sudbury, Suffolk. Updates twice yearly.

Leisure Futures. Henley Centre for Forecasting, 2 Tudor Street, London EC47 0AA. Quarterly.

Leisure Intelligence. Mintel, 18–19 Long Lane, London EC1A 9HE. Quarterly.

The Sports Council *A digest of sports statistics for the UK* (2nd edn.) *(1986).* The Sports Council: London.

Conference proceedings

Countryside Recreation Research, *Changing land use and recreation* (conference proceedings) (1989) CRRAG: School of Advanced Studies, University of Bristol.

ELRA, *Cities for the future* (conference proceedings) (1989) Stichting Recreatie: s'Gravenhage, Netherlands.

WLRA, *Proceedings of the First International Link Conference, Belgium* (1980). WLRA: Canada.

Further useful sources

Amies, P. and Davies, I. (1986) *Kelmscott Leisure Centre: market research 1986.* Waltham Forest Recreation Services: London.

The Sports Council. *State of the art reviews.* ESRC/SC Joint Committee, The Sports Council, 16 Upper Woburn Place, London WC1H 0QP.

Organizations

Australian Parks and Recreation Association (USA). 3101 Park Center Drive, Alexandria VA 22302, USA.

Canadian Parks and Recreation Association. 333 River Road, Vanier City, Ontario KL1 8H9, Canada.

Deutsches Gesellschaft für Freizeit. Neuenhausplatz 10, 4006 Erkrath-Unterfeldhaus, Germany.

European Leisure and Recreation Association. ILAM, ILAM House, Lower Basildon, Reading, Berks RG8 9NE.

Institute of Leisure and Amenity Management (ILAM), ILAM House, Lower Basildon, Reading, Berks RG8 9NE.

Japanese Society of Leisure and Recreation Studies, Kishikinen-Taiiku-kaikan, 1-1-1 Tinnan, Shibuya-ku, Tokyo 150, Japan.

Latin American Leisure and Recreation Association. c/o Prof. R. Ortegan Yanez, Asociación Colombiana de Recreación, Calle 62 No. 17-26, A.A. 12977, Bogotá, Colombia.

Leisure Studies Association. c/o Chelsea School for Human Movement, Brighton Polytechnic, Eastbourne, Sussex.

National Recreation and Parks Association (USA). 3101 Park Center Drive, Alexandria, VA 22302, USA.

World Leisure and Recreation Association, P.O. Box 309, Sharbot Lake, Ontario, Canada K0H 2PO.

Library collections

Shoebridge, M. (1988) *Union catalogue of periodicals in sport and recreation*. Sport and Recreation Group: London.

CHAPTER ELEVEN

Physical education

M. WHITEHEAD AND L. HODGKINSON WITH THE
BEDFORD COLLEGE OF HIGHER EDUCATION
RESOURCES CONSORTIUM

Introduction

Definitions abound, but physical education can be described as athletic
activities organized and used to promote the education, health and all-
round development of children and young people. Physical education
has been a part of education in the UK for well over a century: first, in
the form of team games in the public schools then as drill or physical
training in Board of Schools and finally, from the early 1950s, in all
schools under its current nomenclature. Although the system in the UK
has influenced physical education throughout the world, it is very difficult to make comparisons between different countries because work in
each country has developed differently.

The literature needed by those researching or teaching physical education is very wide ranging, being drawn from a number of disciplines.
Because the subject is so wide there are few handbooks, encyclopaedias, etc. However, researchers can draw on general sources and
these will be considered, followed by the literature relating to specific
aspects. Detailed analysis of worldwide sources would involve more research than is possible within the confines of this volume so the
emphasis will be on physical education in the UK, with international
comparisons where appropriate.

Online, abstracting and indexing services

The main information source for physical education is the international SPORT database produced by the Sport Information Resource Centre (SIRC), Canada. The printed version was published in eight volumes in 1981, as *Sport bibliography*, with supplementary volumes covering material published up to 1985; *Sport and Fitness Index* acted as an updating tool between publication of the annual volumes. *SportSearch*, a monthly current-awareness journal has been published since 1985. Material is arranged alphabetically by subject and many entries include an abstract. SPORT is available online through a variety of hosts all of which are listed in Chapter 1. The database is also available on CD-ROM, as SPORT DISCUS from SilverPlatter. A high proportion of the material is North American, but the main UK physical education journals are indexed. The database also includes many books, conference papers and theses.

Staying in North America, *Physical Education Index*, published by BenOak Publishing Company from 1978 onwards, consists mainly of North American material, although some UK journals are indexed. It covers literature on dance, health, physical therapy, recreation, sports and sports medicine. References do not include abstracts. Cross-references contribute to its ease of use.

In the UK, the Physical Education Association of Great Britain and Northern Ireland (PEA) published a specialist physical education indexing journal called *Bibliographical Index on Physical and Health Education, Sport and Allied Subjects* from 1975 to 1982. However, the most important British source is now *Sports Documentation Monthly Bulletin* which has been produced by the Sports Documentation Centre at the University of Birmingham since 1971. With its international coverage, much of its content is relevant to the physical education teacher: for example, there are sections on exercise physiology, physical fitness, special needs, individual sports and activities, in addition to physical education. Both periodical articles and conference papers are indexed, and a number of abstracts are included.

Dance Current Awareness Bulletin, produced by the National Resource Centre for Dance at the University of Surrey since 1983, provides an annotated index to dance journals, in addition to information about resources, and conferences and events.

Relevant material can also be found in publications covering related disciplines. Again, these are listed in Chapter 1. *British Education Index*, published by Leeds University Press (1954–), indexes the main British physical education journals and, more usefully, gives access to articles about physical education in education journals. It is available online through Dialog. *Current Index to Journals in Education* (1969–)

published by Orynx Press, and *Resources in Education* (1966–) and is-sued by the U.S. Government Printing Office, are both sponsored by the Educational Resources Information Center (ERIC), U.S. Department of Education. These two publications are also widely available online as ERIC, and on CD-ROM. Much material on physical education is in-cluded, mainly of North American origin. A number of other online databases contain material of interest: for example, MEDLINE and PSY-CINFO. Both of these databases are also available in printed version.

Theses

The University of Oregon has published *Microform publications: Health, Physical Education and Recreation* since 1949. A supplement listing new titles is issued twice a year; the material is mainly North American. All Microform Publications titles are now indexed in the SPORT database. Since 1959, the American Alliance for Health, Physical Education, Recreation, and Dance has published an annual volume of *Completed Research in Health, Physical Education, Recreation, and Dance.* This covers a substantial number of American universities and abstracts are included. In the UK, the Librarians of Institutes and Schools of Education published *PERDAS, 1950–1980: a list of theses, dissertations and projects on physical education, recreation, dance, ath-letics and sport, presented at United Kingdom universities,* compiled by J.S. Keighley (1981). This list is arranged alphabetically by author's surname; a subject index is provided. It is a useful publication which in-cludes material difficult to trace, for example work completed for diplomas. The publication warrants an update. Research in physical education can also be traced in general reference sources. The most comprehensive guide to theses is *Dissertation Abstracts International* published by UMI, which gives details, including abstracts, of theses ac-cepted in American and many European universities. Again this is available online and on CD-ROM.

The main UK source is *Index to Theses Accepted for Higher Degrees with Abstracts* published by Aslib and Expert Information Ltd. Since late 1986 abstracts have been included.

Videotext services

The Sports Council have contributed to Prestel since 1977; their frames now provide a significant amount of information. Most of the frames have been structured to give information on participation and the A–Z of sport takes up many of the frames. Additionally, information is given on local authority and national sports centres, on the function and work of The Sports Council, on publications, major sporting events, careers, courses, coaching and conferences. Schools and colleges can also access The Sports Council frames on the British Telecom education network Campus 2000, on a Campus Plus subscription. (Campus 2000, PO Box 7, 214 Grays Inn Road, London WC1X 8EZ.)

Journals

There are a large number of physical education journals, and many more that are not specifically concerned with physical education, but containing relevant articles. Obviously, physical education differs in each country, so a journal published in the USA may not be as relevant in Europe. However, experience shows that trends begun in the USA are on occasions, adopted elsewhere, consequently North American journals often contain relevant information.

For general information about journals, the Sport and Recreation Information Group's *Union catalogue of periodicals in sport and recreation* (1988), edited by M. Shoebridge, provides details of a large number of physical education titles, both UK and foreign. It also indicates their locations in over 40 UK libraries. Other academic and special libraries often produce lists of their periodical holdings which can be of use.

International journals

The *International Journal of Physical Education* reports news from a number of international associations: for example, the International Council of Sport Science and Physical Education (ICSSPE); the International Association for Physical Education in Higher Education (AIESEP); the International Federation of Physical Education (FIEP); the International Association of Physical Education and Sport for Girls and Women (IAPESGW); the International Committee on Sport Pedagogy (ICSP); and the International Society for Comparative Physical Education and Sport (ISCPES). As well as reporting on the programmes of these associations, the journal includes a wide range of articles which cover broad issues of international interest such as the Olympic Games and crowd control at football matches and research articles relating to, for example, acquisition of skill and pedagogy.

The *Journal of the International Council for Health, Physical Education and Recreation*, the official journal of ICHPER, is another journal which covers a wide range of subjects, not always about physical education but of some relevance.

The *FIEP Bulletin*, a long-established journal which began publishing in 1930, also covers a very wide field of interest. For example, a single issue could include pre-school work, fitness, historical topics, comparative issues and pupil attitudes to physical education. It includes a comprehensive calendar of international events.

Major UK journals

The *British Journal of Physical Education*, published by the Physical Education Association of Great Britain (PEA), has experienced many title changes since it first appeared in 1908 as the *Journal of Scientific Physical Training*. It contains short articles of a practical nature and occasionally articles of a more 'philosophical' nature and provides a forum for the PEA to debate current moves in education which relate to physical education. It also carries a comprehensive list of events and information on books, resources and equipment. A supplement *Primary PE Focus* has been issued since summer 1990.

The *Bulletin of Physical Education* (1945–) published by the British Association of Advisers and Lecturers in Physical Education (BAALPE), contains a variety of articles on small-scale school-based evaluations and recommends particular teaching content and methods. It is not refereed and as a result the articles are variable in quality.

The North Western Counties Physical Education Association publish *Physical Education Review*. It is a refereed journal which includes articles on a wide range of areas: curriculum development; philosophy, comparative, etc. It is perhaps of more value to those training rather than teachers.

The *Scottish Journal of Physical Education* has been published since 1973 by the Scottish Physical Education Association. General aspects in physical education are covered but a large proportion of the articles relate to the situation in Scotland which has its own National Curriculum in physical education.

Sports Teacher, published by the National Council for Schools' Sports since 1982, includes a range of practically-based articles on subjects such as sports injuries, sportsmanship and material for teaching, and a wealth of general information on courses, books, resources for teaching, equipment and competitions. The content reflects views of both educationalists and governing bodies.

The Sports Council's magazine, *Sport and Leisure* began publication in 1949. Its main emphasis is on sport in the community. It is a valuable source of information on courses and equipment. A more specialist journal, *Movement and Dance*, is a continuation of the *Laban Art of Movement and Dance Magazine*, which began publication in 1947. Its main concern is with the history, development and philosophy of the work of Rudolph Laban, but articles on dance therapy are a useful source of material for students and teachers.

Adventure Education carries articles of use to the outdoor physical education specialist. It has been published since 1984 by the National Association for Outdoor Education.

North American journals

Journal of Physical Education, Recreation, and Dance, the journal of the American Alliance for Health, Physical Education, Recreation, and Dance (AAHPERD), is the longest established journal related to physical education published in the USA. It first appeared in 1930 and has had many title changes since that time. It is primarily aimed at teachers and concentrates on issues related to work in school.

Another less formal AAHPERD publication is *Update* which appears as a newspaper providing current information on future events, and publicizes a whole range of resources. Directed at the American reader it is of general interest and value.

The *Physical Educator* published by Phi Epsilon Kappa Fraternity (1940–) is directed at teachers and coaches and reports relevant research and gives practical advice.

The *Journal of Teaching in Physical Education* (1981–) is a valuable journal for lecturers and students doing small-scale research into teaching.

The Canadian Association for Health, Physical Education and Recreation's *CAHPER Journal* (1933–) is a broadly-based, practically-focused journal, covering topics such as special needs, medical issues, sociological topics, material for teaching and reports on small-scale research.

Pediatric Exercise Science (1989–) is an authoritative and valuable contribution to the literature. As the journal of the North American Society of Pediatric Exercise Medicine it is concerned with a broad range of medical/scientific aspects of the younger child's movement and involvement in physical education and sport.

Journal of Sport Behavior (1978–) is primarily a vehicle for the publication of research of an empirical nature. Perhaps of more relevance to coaches, lecturers and students than to teachers.

Specifically of interest to the special needs teacher is *Adapted Physical Activity Quarterly*, a title introduced by Human Kinetics in 1984.

The *Journal of Comparative Physical Education and Sport* caters for the ever-growing interest in comparative aspects of physical education. It is the journal of the International Society for Comparative Physical Education and Sport.

Other international journals

These include:

ACHPER National Journal (1983–) Australia
Education Physique et Sport (1959–) France
Geneeskunde en Sport (1978–) Netherlands
Leibesübungen-Leibeserziehung (1973–) Austria
New Zealand Journal of Health, Physical Education and Recreation
(1954–) New Zealand
Sportunterricht (1973–) Germany

A number of the sources quoted in this section are listed in a useful leaflet on physical education, produced as No. 4 in the Sport and Recreation Information Group's *How to find out in sport and recreation* series (SPRIG, 1990).

Historical and philosophical aspects of physical education

Philosophy

There are more books on the philosophy of sport than on the philosophy of physical education and most have been published in North America. Two compendia are of value. Both contain a large number of articles dealing with philosophical issues in sport: E.W. Gerber and W.J. Morgan (eds.) *Sport and the body: a philosophical symposium* (2nd edn.) (Lea and Febiger, 1979); and W.J. Morgan and K.V. Meier (eds.), *Philosophic inquiry in sport* (Human Kinetics, 1988). Both books contain sections of relevance to physical educationalists. In the UK, Peter Arnold has made a valuable contribution to the physical education area with his two books: *Meaning in movement, sport and physical education* (Heinemann, 1979) and *Education, movement and the curriculum* (Falmer, 1988). D. Best's *Expression in movement and the arts* (Lepus, 1974) and *Feeling and reason in the arts* (Allen & Unwin, 1985) are also important texts. Although somewhat dated, H. Whiting and D. Masterson (eds.) *Readings in the aesthetics of sport* (Lepus, 1974) contains some useful articles. On the topic of ethical issues, P. McIntosh's *Fair play* (Heinemann, 1979) makes some interesting comments.

While books looking specifically at the philosophy of physical education are few in number, articles on this topic are printed regularly in many of the journals listed earlier in this chapter. Other useful sources of articles are journals of philosophy of education such as the *Journal of Philosophy of Education.*

History

The history of physical education reflects the broader social and educational changes that have taken place since the beginning of the twentieth century. Its examination is best undertaken alongside a study of this broader context and reference to general history texts is recommended.

PRIMARY SOURCES

Primary sources of the history of physical education are to be found in the form of government and other publications which detail recommended aims and activities at the time of their publication. The government, through the Board of Education produced syllabi for physical training/education as far back as 1902. These were updated in 1904, 1909, 1919 and 1933. The early versions were for the elementary school only, whilst the 1933 syllabus is divided into two parts – one for junior and one for senior pupils. These publications show the prevailing attitudes to physical education in the Board schools at that time and detail exercises to be performed in strict unison by the children. The work is very clearly focused on medical and therapeutic principles. They were all published by HMSO in the UK.

Later publications from the Department of Education and Science (DES) are less in the form of 'series of exercises' and more focused on general principles to guide planning. These are *Physical education in the primary school. Part I: Moving and growing* (1952) and *Part II: Planning the programme* (1953), Ministry of Education and Central Office of Information. *Movement: physical education in the primary years* (DES, 1972) is now a text of some historical interest as it was produced at the height of the 'child-centred' movement. This traces the physical development of the child from birth, discusses the role of physical education in the primary years and then looks at teaching different aspects of the subject.

Valuable adjuncts to these government publications are what would now be considered out-of-date texts on teaching the subject. Particularly interesting here are M. Randall's *Modern ideas on physical education* (Bell & Sons, 1952) and A. Bilbrough and P. Jones' *Developing patterns in physical education* (University of London Press, 1973). A particularly useful publication is the *Journal of Sources in Educational History*, 4(3), 1981, which is devoted to the physical education curriculum in UK public elementary schools between 1870 and 1944.

Additional primary source material can be found in archival material. The PEA has an archive, based at Liverpool University and most long-established colleges, such as Bedford, have their own archives. One way of locating physical education historical material is to look through non-published material such as theses and dissertations. Valuable here are two occasional papers written by R.W. Cox *Theses and dissertations on the history of sport, physical education, recreation and dance approved for higher degrees and advanced diplomas in British universities 1900–1981* and *American theses on the history of British sport and physical education.* Both were published in 1982 by the Bibliographical Centre for the History of Sport, Physical Education and Recreation, University of Liverpool. Another source is the City of Leeds and Carnegie College's *Catalogue of the Carnegie historical collection of books on physical education, sport and recreation and health education published before 1946,* compiled by Joan Newiss in 1969.

SECONDARY SOURCES

Secondary sources can be divided broadly into two categories. The first concerns the development of the subject itself while the second considers the history of training teachers of physical education. Most valuable in the first category are: P. McIntosh's *Physical education in England since 1800* (revised Bell, 1968) and P. McIntosh *et al. Landmarks in the history of physical education* (3rd edn.,Routledge and Kegan Paul, 1981).

The second category includes valuable reference to pioneers in physical education in the UK. There were as many women of note as men, and it was, in fact, the women who had the most significant impact on training. Two texts to be recommended here are J. May's *Madame Bergman-Österberg: pioneer of physical education and games for girls and women* (Harrap, 1969) and *Nine pioneers in physical education* (PEA, 1964). For those particularly interested in the development of the training of women specialist physical education teachers, S. Fletcher *Women first: the female tradition in English physical education 1880– 1980* (Athlone, 1984) gives an easy-to-read account in relation to changing social and cultural climates. Reflecting the North American situation is M. Lee's *Memories of a bloomer girl (1894–1924)* (AAHPER, 1977).

Conference reports represent another useful historical source. For example, the 1982 Annual Conference of the History of Education Society of Great Britain focused on the nation's fitness. The conference proceedings – *The Fitness of the Nation: Physical and Health Education in the Nineteenth and Twentieth Centuries,* edited by Nicholas Parry and David McNair — published by the History of Education Society (1983).

Current trends in physical education

Since the publication of the syllabi at the start of the century there have been two major government publications on physical education. These are *Curriculum 11–16* (1979) and *Physical education from 5–16* (1989). The first is a pamphlet published as a supplementary paper to an earlier edition of *Curriculum 11–16* published in 1978, and contains brief comments on a number of curricular subjects. The second publication is the long-awaited edition of *HMI curriculum matters* relating to physical education. It is currently the most authoritative document on physical education but, unlike others in the series, *Physical education from 5–16* does not propose new ways forward, but rather surveys the current trends in the subject area. *Sport and young people, partnership and action* (1988), however, makes clear proposals for the future. Produced by the School Sport Forum, a body set up by the Department of Education and Science and the Department of the Environment to look into the state of sport and physical education in schools in England and Wales, it is a readily accessible publication covering areas like equal opportunities, competition and assessment. A similar publication was produced by the ILEA in 1988 under the leadership of Peter McIntosh. *My favourite subject* contains 76 recommendations and sections on primary work, health and fitness, co-operation between school and community, etc.

The PEA, the Secondary Head Teachers Association and Coventry LEA have also produced statements on the developing trends in physical education. The forerunner of the National Curriculum Council, the Schools Curriculum Development Council produced some useful physical education documents, some of which have arisen from seminars.

There are few central texts which consider the overall current position of physical education. J. Kane's *Physical education in secondary schools* (Routledge, 1974) and G. Underwood's *The physical education curriculum in the secondary school* (Falmer, 1983) both provide overviews. A recent book looking generally at physical education is L. Almond (ed.) *The place of physical education in schools* (Kogan Page, 1989). This book, which contains the views of a number of experienced and committed physical educationalists, is of value both as a source of information and as the focus for debate, in, for example, initial training or in-service work.

The primary age range is no better served by texts looking broadly at this area of the curriculum. In 1976 the PEA set up a primary school study group which produced a volume of essays entitled *Physical education within primary education*, edited by M. Mawer and M. Sleap and published by the PEA. A recent publication of value is A. Williams' (ed.) *Issues in physical education for the primary years* (Falmer, 1989) which includes the multicultural and gender aspects of physical education.

The most recent texts in the UK have been produced with the National Curriculum very much in mind. Physical education has been designated as a Foundation subject and in due course the National Curriculum in physical education will be drawn up. There is a Professional Development Officer with responsibility for physical education and the Physical Education Working Group produced its Interim Report in February 1991. Official information about the development of the subject in the National Curriculum can be obtained from the National Curriculum Council, 15–17 New Street, York YO1 2RA.

In the absence of general texts, conference proceedings can provide useful information. Many of the associations listed at the end of this chapter run annual conferences, often centred around a particular theme, e.g. the ICHPER conference. Two regularly-held conferences that include a volume on physical education are the *Commonwealth and International Conference on Sport, Physical Education, Dance, Recreation and Health* and the *Olympic Scientific Congress.*

Physical education for all — equal opportunities

Physical education has been accused of elitism, favouring the physically able and white middle/upper class males. In response to a concern in the profession to counterbalance this somewhat elitist image, there has recently been more research and writing in this area, although it is not yet substantial. The issue of enabling pupils with learning difficulties to benefit from physical education has attracted considerable attention in the USA and a Public Law (94-142) was passed which made it mandatory for individual educational programmes to be developed and to include provision for physical education. This provided the impetus for mainstreaming thousands of children. In the UK, this concept has also attracted interest, particularly as a result of the Warnock Report in 1978.

For those working with these children there are two approaches. The first is to consult texts on special needs generally. To be recommended here are D. Stott's *Helping children with learning difficulties* (Ward Lock, 1978) and A. Cohen and L. Cohen (eds.) *Special educational needs in the ordinary school: a source book for teachers* (Harper and Row, 1986). Also useful are journals such as *Special Children* available from 6–7 Hockley Hill, Hockley, Birmingham, B18 5AA, and the

British Journal of Special Education produced by the National Council for Special Education.

The second approach is to consult texts specifically focused on physical education for children with learning difficulties. Two bibliographies of resources can be recommended. One was compiled by L. Groves and C. Midgley for the PEA Special Needs Committee (1986). Entitled *Physical education and recreation for people with special needs*, it covers printed material, films and videos. The other bibliography, produced by the Sport Information Resource Centre in Canada is called *Sport and recreation for the disabled* and contains 4000 references to material published in the period 1984–1989. An additional source of information is a disk that forms part of the 1989 BAALPE publication, entitled *Physical education for children with special needs in mainstream education,* and obtainable from White Line Press, 60 Bradford Road, Stanningley, Leeds LS28 6EF.

Some publications cover the facilities required for the disabled and list various organizations. *Give us the chance; sport and physical recreation with people with a mental handicap* (The Disabled Living Foundation, 1989) includes a wealth of information on relevant organizations, periodicals, audio tapes, films and videotapes.

Gender issues in physical education have attracted more attention in the last ten years since there has been a growing debate over the appropriateness or otherwise of mixed sex physical education. Until the mid-1970s, single-sex physical education was generally taken for granted. The USA addressed this problem earlier than the UK by introducing Title IX of the Educational Amendments Act 1972 which stated that no one in the USA should be excluded from participation in educational programmes on the basis of sex. The introduction of Title IX is still having repercussions for women in the USA. Perhaps the best sources of information on this subject can be found in journals which carry articles on such issues as dance for boys, discrimination against girls in mixed physical education and the potential dangers of teaching games such as hockey and rugby in mixed classes. The *Journal of Physical Education, Recreation, and Dance* covers the American situation. Texts in this area include O. Leaman, *Sit on the sidelines and watch the boys play: sex differentiation in physical education* (Longman, 1984) and *Providing equal opportunities for girls and boys in physical education: a report from the ILEA Study Group 1982–84* (ILEA, 1984). John Evans has edited two collections that look at a range of sociological issues in physical education. These are *Physical education, sport and schooling: studies in the sociology of physical education* (Falmer, 1986) and *Teachers, teaching and control in physical education* (Falmer, 1988). Coventry Education Authority have produced a number of publications on ethnicity. They can be obtained from the Elm Bank Teachers' Centre, Mile Lane, Coventry CV1 2LQ.

Teaching and assessment of physical education

A key text here is M. Mosston and S. Ashworth's *Teaching physical education* (3rd edn.) (Merrill, 1986). The authors propose a systematic analysis of teaching from which they develop a series of teaching strategies. BAALPE has produced a book based on Mosston's work, entitled *Teaching and learning strategies in physical education* (1989) available from Whiteline Press.

There is a wide range of American texts on the teaching of the subject. Three can be particularly recommended. These are C.A. Bucher and C.R. Koenig's *Methods and materials for secondary school physical education* (6th edn.) (Mosby, 1983), D. Siedentop's *Developing teaching skills in physical education* (2nd edn.) (Mayfield Publishing, 1983) and W.G. Anderson's *Analysis of teaching physical education* (Mosby, 1980). Together these three texts provide a complete overview of the teaching of physical education.

A recently-produced UK text concerned with methods of analysing teaching is edited by G. Underwood, and is entitled *Teaching and learning in physical education: a social psychological perspective* (Falmer, 1988). It investigates the teaching of physical education and focuses on teaching strategies and pupil behaviour.

A valuable publication, *Physical education: recent curriculum developments* was produced in 1988 by the National Curriculum Council, under the chairmanship of Joyce Allen. It considers developments in the south of England, is well indexed by subject area, LEA and keyword, and briefly sets out recent initiatives taken by schools.

Many local authorities have produced their own curriculum guidelines for different aspects of physical education. These are generally very useful documents as they contain a wealth of ideas for teaching. A list of currently available guidelines can be obtained from BAALPE and includes publications from Avon, Coventry, Essex, ILEA, Lancashire, Northamptonshire and Rotherham.

Health and well-being

Health-based physical education or health-related fitness has developed considerably over the last few years, both in Europe and North America. It is pupil-centred, espouses equal opportunity for all, and could well be seen to pave the way for The Sports Council's 'Sport for All' programme. Acknowledgement of the current importance of this area of work in physical education was indicated in the setting up of the Health and Physical Education Project at Loughborough University in 1985 by the Health Education Authority (HEA) and the PEA. This project produces a Newsletter which is circulated with the *British Journal of Physical Education*. It provides many examples of the practical application of this work in schools and advertizes the project's latest books and resources. The HEA also provide up-to-date information on health issues and resources through their *Health Education Journal*.

Other centres which have pioneered work in this area are the Universities of Exeter and Hull. *Health and fitness in the curriculum; Perspectives*, No. 31 (1987) was produced by the School of Education, University of Exeter. The University of Hull has developed the Happy Heart Project. This project, also funded by the HEA and the PEA, involves mainly work with the primary age range.

Lancashire County Council Education Committee produced a discussion document entitled *Health related fitness in the school physical education programme* (1984). The Sports Council's and HEA's *The new case for exercise* (1988) covers health and fitness issues related to youth and middle life, and also addresses the hazards of exercise.

Other useful texts include D. Ashton and B. Davies' *Why exercise?: expert medical advice to help you enjoy a healthier life* (Blackwell, 1986) which looks at the rationale for health-related fitness with an emphasis on the physiological benefits of exercise, E. Newsholme and T. Leech's *The runner: energy and endurance* (Fitness Books, 1983) which makes an interesting comparison between the sprinter and the marathon athlete in terms of physiological responses and adaptations to exercise. S. Biddle's *Foundations of health-related fitness in physical education* (Ling, 1987) is a practical publication. Also useful is *Heartfacts: a Cambridge resource pack* by David Applin (Cambridge Science Books, 1988). The American Alliance of Health, Physical Education, Recreation, and Dance, the American College of Sports Medicine and the Council of Europe's Eurofit project have published documents on testing physical fitness.

Testing and measuring equipment and wall charts of weight training exercises can be obtained from Sport and Leisure Marketing Ltd., Unit 2, New Inn Bridge Estate, 998 Foleshill Road, Coventry CV6 6NE. A video and resource pack is available from The North Western Physical Education Association. This looks at the justification for health-related fitness and gives a range of examples of how this work can be carried out in school. For information write to Mr. J.M. Young, 2 Vanderbyl Avenue, Spital, Bebington, Wirral, Merseyside L62 2AP.

Teaching physical education activities

The national governing body and the schools' association of each activity represent prime sources of information on teaching all the different aspects of physical education. The addresses of the governing bodies can be obtained from The Sports Council Information Centre's *Address book*, which is updated regularly. Addresses of schools' associations can be obtained from The Secretary, National Council for Schools Sports, 21 Northampton Road, Croydon, Surrey, CR0 7HB. In many instances these associations produce their own publications (journals and texts), visual materials and teaching aids and also run courses for teaching/coaching the activity. Information of this nature is frequently updated and readers are advised to contact the associations direct for further information. Material published by the National Coaching Foundation is also of value to teachers.

A valuable source for video material for teaching activities   is Pergamon Educational Productions list, *Videos for P.E. and outdoor education*, Hennock Road, Exeter, EX2 8RP.

There are also a large number of texts relating to curricular games. These can be traced through *British Books in Print*, (Whitaker's) *Books in Print* (Bowker) and *British National Bibliography* (British Library). National Associations can provide information relating to outdoor pursuits. The National Advice and Information Centre for Outdoor Education based at Doncaster Metropolitan Institute of Higher Education, High Melton, is a useful resource centre for outdoor education, along with some of the academic libraries like Charlotte Mason College, Liverpool Polytechnic and Moray House College, Edinburgh.

Dance and aerobics have attracted a large number of publications. Useful texts for aerobics can be obtained from the London Central YMCA Training and Development Department, 112 Great Russell Street, London WC1B 3NQ. A number of local authorities publish guidelines specifically on dance and the HMI produced a report entitled *Dance in secondary schools* in 1983. The National Resource Centre for Dance, based at Surrey University, provides an information service, whilst the National Dance Teachers Association can supply a variety of information including dance teaching networks. A new development in dance resources has been *Dance Laser Disk* which offers multi- perspective, close ups, slow motion features, graphic display of time and space information, Labanation display option, teaching points recorded on a second audio track, automatic replay, a manual and accompanying worksheets. Further information can be obtained from the Interactive Video Project Director, Bedford College of Higher Education, 37 Lansdowne Road, Bedford MK40 2BZ.

Safety and law in physical education

Safety has always been an important consideration in physical education teaching. However, the increase in the number of court cases, first in the USA and now in the UK, related to accidents that have occurred in physical education classes means that greater attention is now being paid to this area. This increase is reflected in the journals, particularly those published in North America.

A regularly updated publication is produced by BAALPE, *Safe practice in physical education*. Many governing bodies publish their own codes of safety together with legal advice for coaches and teachers. The DES produce *The safety series* – a collection of six booklets on safety aspects in education. Two relevant titles cover outdoor education (1989) and physical education (1973). Both are published by HMSO. Recently there have been a number of conferences concerned with safety issues in physical education. The proceedings from these are often valuable, for example the *Proceedings of the 1988 Association of Polytechnic Physical Education Lecturers (APPEL) Conference: P.E./P.R. Safety framework in institutions of higher education.* Also useful is the Canadian Association for Health, Physical Education and Recreation's *Physical activity and legal liability* by D. Moriarty (1980). A number of books that deal with specific aspects of the law are relevant to physical educationalists, e.g. D. Harris, *et al. Compensation and support for illness and injury* (Oxford University Press, 1984) and R. Tiernan *Tort in a nutshell* (2nd edn.) (Sweet & Maxwell, 1990).

Examinations and examining bodies in physical education

The first examinations in the UK to be developed in physical education formed part of the CSE programme. These were introduced in 1972. In 1986 GCSE examinations were established and in the same year two 'A'-Levels were piloted in selected centres. Both were examined for the first time in 1988.

GCSE and 'A'–Level Physical Education include both practical and theoretical work. For more information on the theoretical aspects, the reader should refer to other chapters, e.g. Sports Science (Chapter 4) and Sociology of Sport (Chapter 7). However, most of the texts listed are directed to the teacher rather than the pupil. To date there are relatively few texts designed for pupils although more are being commissioned. P. Beashel and J. Taylor have written two accessible and useful books; these are *Sport examined* (1986) and *Sport assignments* (1988), both published by Macmillan Education. Also valuable are the following: C.W. Hawkins's *Physical education for first examinations* (Blackie, 1985); R. Hawkey's *Sport science* (2nd edn.) (Hodder and Stoughton, 1991); D. Davis *et al. Physical education: theory and practice* (Macmillan, 1986); B. Tancred's *Health related fitness* (Hodder and Stoughton, 1987); *Sports science handbook*, compiled by S.P.R. Jenkins (Sunningdale Publications, 1990). A new text for 'A'-Level, R. Davis's *Physical education and the study of sport* (Wolfe Publishing, 1991) has recently appeared.

In addition there are two packs of material that contain a range of useful material: L. Jackson's *The sport, recreation and leisure pack* (Framework Press, 1987) is designed principally for vocational courses, such as City and Guilds 481 levels 1 and 2, TRADEC level 1, CPVE and BTEC First and National Diploma in Leisure Studies. It is, however, appropriate for GCSE work in schools. The other pack is entitled *On your marks* (1988), an educational pack published by the Community Unit, TVS, Television Centre, Southampton SO9 5HZ. It consists of a video, a teachers' booklet, teaching activities and posters and is appropriate for secondary school work such as GCSE, CPVE and TVEI.

Four Examination Boards offer GCSE for both physical education and dance. These are: The Southern Examining Association, c/o South East Regional Examinations Board, Beloe House, 2/10 Mount Ephriam Road, Tunbridge Wells, Kent TN1 1EU; the Midland Examining Group, c/o West Midlands Examinations Board, Norfolk House, Smallbrook Queensway, Birmingham B5 4NJ; the Northern Examining Association, c/o Joint Matriculation Board, Manchester M15 6EU; the London and East Anglian Examining Group, 'The Lindens', Lexden Road, Colchester CO3 3RL.

The Northern Ireland Schools Examinations Council, Beechill House, 42 Beechill Road, Belfast BT8 4RS and The Welsh Joint Education Committee, 245 Western Avenue, Cardiff CF5 2YX, offer GCSE for physical education.

'A'-Levels in Sports Studies and physical education are offered by The Associated Examining Board, Stag Hill House, Guildford, Surrey GU2 5XJ. An 'A'-Level in Dance is offered by The London Regional Examining Board, 104 Wandsworth High Street, London SW18 4LF.

There are three other Examining Bodies relevant here. The Business and Technician Education Council validate BTEC First, National and Higher National Certificate/Diploma courses in Leisure Studies. Details may be obtained from Central House, Upper Woburn Place, London WC1H 0HH. The City and Guilds of London Institute run a Certificate in Recreation and Leisure Studies and may be contacted at 46 Britannia Street, London WC1X 9RG. The Scottish Examination Board at Iron-mills Road, Dalkeith, Midlothian EH22 1LE administer Physical

Education – Standard Grade Examinations at Foundation, General and Credit Levels.

Up-to-date information on boards and addresses can be obtained from The Schools Examination and Assessment Council (SEAC) Newcombe House, 45 Notting Hill Gate, London W11 3JB. They are also listed in two publications: *The Education Authorities' directory and annual*, published by the School Government Publishing Company and the *Education year book* published by Longman.

Teacher training in physical education

There are two routes into teaching physical education at secondary school level: these are through a four-year B.Ed. Degree course or by completion of a one-year Postgraduate Certificate in Education course. The latter route normally requires entrants to hold a degree in Sports Science or Sports Studies. There are 13 institutions in the UK running a four-year B.Ed. and 10 running the PGCE.

Applications for PGCE are dealt with through the Graduate Teacher Training Registry, 3 Crawford Place, London W1H 2BN. For B.Ed. courses in universities, application is through UCCA, P.O. Box 28, Cheltenham, Glos. GL50 1HY, and for B.Ed. Courses in Colleges and Polytechnics, PCAS P.O. Box 67, Cheltenham, Glos. GL50 3SF. These centres will also supply booklets which list all courses and the addresses of all the institutions cited.

Information on training in the USA can be found in *The physical education gold book*. This is a directory of Physical Educators in Higher Education in North America. It is published by Human Kinetics. Unfortunately it is now rather out of date with the latest edition covering 1987–89.

Professional organizations

There are a considerable number of associations related to physical education, most of which produce newsletters, journals or handbooks. They also hold meetings, and run courses and conferences. Many of the international associations which were founded at a time when physical education was very much confined to the teaching of physical education in schools or teacher training, have extended their interests to include sports sciences and sport sociology. Details can be obtained from the individual associations, but it should be noted that the nature of some of the organizations means that the contact addresses tend to change frequently.

International associations

These include the International Council for Health, Physical Education and Recreation (ICHPER), 1900 Association Drive, Reston, VA 22091 and Fédération Internationale d'Éducation Physique, c/o John Andrews, 4 Cleevecroft Avenue, Bishops Cleeve, Cheltenham, Glos. GL52 4JZ

North American associations

The American Alliance for Health, Physical Education, Recreation, and Dance is at 1900 Association Drive, Reston, VA 22091, The Canadian Association for Health, Physical Education, Recreation and Dance, is at Place R. Tait McKenzie, 1600 James Naismith Drive, Gloucester, Ontario KIB 5N4.

UK associations

Association of Polytechnic Physical Education Lecturers, c/o General Secretary, 98 Blackpool Old Road, Poulton-Le-Fylde, Lancashire.

British Association of Advisers and Lecturers in Physical Education, c/o General Secretary, Nelson House, 6 The Beacon, Exmouth, Devon EX8 2AG.

British Council of Physical Education, c/o Honourary Secretary, Liverpool Institute of Higher Education, P.O. Box 6, Woolton Road, Liverpool L16 8ND.

British Universities Physical Education Association, c/o Honorary Secretary Dept. of Physical Education, University of Edinburgh.

Council for Dance Education and Training, c/o Director, Council for Dance Education and Training, 5 Tavistock Place, London WC1H 9SF.

Independent Schools Physical Education Association, c/o General Secretary, Cricket Lodge, Westbury, Sherborne, DT9 3QY.

National Association of Teachers in Further and Higher Education: Physical Education Section, c/o General Secretary, Doncaster Metropolitan Institute of Higher Education, High Milton, Doncaster DN5 7SZ. Dance Section, c/o General Secretary, Copse End, Conyngham Lane, Bridge, Kent CT4 5JX.

National Dance Teachers Association, c/o Honorary Secretary, 30 Farrer House, Deptford Church Street, Deptford, London SE8 3DY.

North Western Counties Physical Education Association, c/o Publications Secretary, 2 Vanderbyl Avenue, Spital, Bebington, Wirral, Merseyside L62 2AP.

The Physical Education Association of Great Britain and Northern Ireland, c/o General Secretary, 162 Kings Cross Road, London WC1X 9DH.

Scottish Physical Education Association, c/o General Secretary, Balcan-
qual Cottage, Glenfarg, Perthshire PH2 9QD.

Standing Conference on Dance in Education, c/o Chair, West Sussex Institute of Higher Education, College Lane, Chichester PO19 4PE.

Standing Conference on Physical Education in Teacher Education, c/o
Secretary, West Sussex Institute of Higher Education, College Lane,
Chichester PO19 4PE.

CHAPTER TWELVE

Physical fitness

T. MERCER*

Introduction

Whilst the study of physical fitness is not new, the latter half of the twentieth century has witnessed a vigorous expansion of interest in the area. This has led to considerable evolution of traditional definitions of physical fitness, as both academic and professional communities strive towards the achievement of a consensus definition and understanding of the concept. This evolution is well documented in two brief review articles by Caspersen, Powell and Christenson (1985) and Pate (1988). The former defines physical fitness as a set of attributes that people have or achieve that relates to the ability to perform physical activity.

Physical fitness can be divided into health-related or skill-related fitness. Health-related fitness covers cardio-respiratory endurance, muscular endurance, muscular strength, body composition and flexibility, and is directly relevant to public health issues. The skill-related components which incorporate agility, balance, co-ordination, speed, power and reaction time, are generally linked with athletic ability in its widest sense, and are often referred to as motor performance, sports fitness, or performance fitness. This distinction is apparent throughout most of the literature and will be adhered to throughout this chapter. For more technical aspects of movement and physiology readers should refer to Chapter 4.

* The assistance of Sheelagh Rowbottom (Staffordshire Polytechnic Library) is gratefully acknowledged.

The emergence of physical fitness as a legitimate area of academic study has occurred, primarily as a result of the continued development of undergraduate and postgraduate level courses in physical education, sports science, sports studies, and exercise science. In addition, physical fitness has become a focus of attention for other groups, most notably ergonomists, health educators, and epidemiologists. This interest has led to a proliferation of both learned and popular journals examining physical fitness, and to articles on physical fitness appearing in non-specialist journals. Although the bibliographic control of the literature of physical fitness is not as good as it is for some of the established scientific subjects, the potential problems of information retrieval have been alleviated somewhat by the development of a range of abstracting and indexing services and computer databases.

Abstracting and indexing journals

Readers unfamiliar with such information retrieval services are recommended to consult Chapter 1 and *Sports and fitness: an information guide* (Prytherch, 1988). The chapter in the latter, describing Abstracts and Indexes may prove a reasonable starting point and guide. Additional information may be obtained by referring to Dialog Information Services (1989) and Lockheed Information Systems (1985).

The principal sources of information can be obtained through the specialized sport abstracting/indexing services of the UK, USA and Canada. In the UK, *Sports Documentation Monthly Bulletin*, produced by the Sports Documentation Centre, University of Birmingham, presents a list of recent journal articles and conference papers. Although it includes some abstracts and both English and foreign material, it is somewhat limited by its emphasis on research journals.

A more irregularly issued, but potentially wider-ranging information source, is The Sports Council Information Centre's publication *SCAN: Selected New Publications and Articles*. It is particularly useful in that it lists books, handbooks, reports, etc. However, the information presented is frequently out of date, even for a bibliographic service.

The key indexing journal from the USA is *Physical Fitness/Sports Medicine*. This is the quarterly publication of the President's Council on Physical Fitness and Sports, produced in co-operation with the National Library of Medicine. Focusing mainly upon exercise physiology, sports injuries, physical conditioning and the medical aspects of exercise, this extensive index culls its information from MEDLINE, the online database of the National Library of Medicine. *SportSearch* updates the SPORT database in printed form. It indexes around 250, predominantly English-language, journals.

A more lightweight but very useful American publication is the quarterly *Physical Education Index*. Including only English-language sources, this index nonetheless provides good coverage of many aspects of physical education related to physical fitness and also incorporates a useful review of new books at the end of each issue.

Alongside these sports/fitness dedicated databases and indexes there are also a number of other relevant information retrieval sources available. Of particular importance for up-to-the-minute information is the *Current Contents* series (ISI), weekly publications which cover a number of different subjects. Applied Sciences, Biology, and Biomedical/Life Sciences are likely to be the most informative for physical fitness. These are also available on floppy disk.

More general indexes such as the *British Education Index* and the *American Education Index* may also be of use, but information stored therein is likely to be in *Physical Education Index* as well.

Online services

The Sport Information Resource Centre (SIRC) based in Canada provides the SPORT database, which has the best coverage of physical fitness literature. It is available on a number of commercial hosts; again refer to Chapter 1 for more details.

With the increasing interest in the health-related aspects of physical fitness the HEALTH PERIODICALS database (Information Access Co.) with its broad coverage in health, medicine, fitness and nutrition, and BIOSIS PREVIEWS (BIOSIS) are useful sources. MEDLINE (National Medical Library) also provide some fitness material.

Major texts

Health-related fitness

The range of material available in this field is immense, with an ever-increasing number of texts being written for both professional and lay readership. For the purpose of this brief review, only those texts written for a professional readership have been examined.

C.R. Corbin and R. Lindsey's *Concepts of physical fitness with laboratories* (6th edn.) (Dubuque, Iowa: W.C. Brown, 1988), first published in 1970, has evolved into a cornerstone resource for the teaching of health-related fitness in introductory courses at undergraduate level in the USA. The text is organized around the themes of physical fitness concepts, programmes of exercise, important fitness factors and planning for fitness. Each chapter is presented in an outline format detailing the why, how and what of exercise for fitness. This text, although basic, is well illustrated, informative, and accessible to a lay readership. Corbin and Lindsey (1985) have also authored an accompanying *Instructor's manual* which is a useful source of information, in that it provides an extremely comprehensive resource list of print and non-print based teaching materials.

E.T. Howley and B.D. Franks' *Health/fitness instructor's handbook* (Champaign: Human Kinetics, 1986) is an extremely comprehensive source of fitness information designed specifically to cover all aspects of the American College of Sports Medicine Health/Fitness Instructor certification programme (the certification programme is now available in the UK). However, with the necessary inclusion, for 'student' ACSM Health/Fitness Instructors, of chapters on 'Basic exercise science' and 'ECG and medications', the book does crossover into the domain of physiological fitness. Consequently, the material included makes it more likely to be an appropriate resource for an undergraduate readership in the Exercise Science/Physical Education field and/or graduate fitness professionals.

C. Bouchard, R.J. Shephard, T. Stephens, J.R. Sutton and B.D. McPherson's *Exercise, fitness, and health: a consensus of current knowledge* (Champaign: Human Kinetics, 1990) presents the thoughts and discussions of some 87 eminent exercise scientists, presented at the *1988 International Conference on Exercise, Fitness, & Health, Toronto, Canada*. It comprises over 60 chapters incorporating review articles, complementary discussion papers and an introductory consensus statement. The book is subdivided into six sections which summarize existing knowledge on the relationships between exercise, fitness, and health. This is achieved specifically through examination of current knowledge about the following: the assessment and determinants of physical activity, fitness, and health; human adaptation to physical activity; physical activity and fitness in disease; physical activity and fitness in growth, reproductive health, and ageing; and the risks of exercising. This book is the definitive of its type and is clearly a crucial resource for all serious students of physical fitness. The scale of the material included makes it an excellent resource for senior undergraduate and post-graduate students in the Exercise Sciences, and an essential reference text for all libraries.

S.J.H. Biddle (ed.) *Foundations of health-related fitness in physical education* (London: Ling Publishing, 1987) is a useful introductory resource for anyone interested in the teaching of health-related fitness in schools. The text is sub-divided into four sections which provide a philosophy and rationale for health-related fitness, a basic knowledge base in each of the main components of the subject, a focus upon teaching and a consideration of key issues. The book is well written and informative and includes chapters by many leading authorities in this field.

Information on the mechanics of health-related fitness testing is covered in quite a large number of documents. Amongst these, L.A. Golding, C.R. Myers and W.E. Sinning's *Y's way to physical fitness* (1989) is a good source and is particularly useful in giving information about the YMCA's publications. M.L. Pollock, J.H. Wilmore and S.M. Fox's *Exercise and health in disease* (1984) is particularly recommended for the clarity of descriptions and explanations offered. The American Alliance for Health, Physical Education, Recreation, and Dance (1980, 1984, 1988) is also an excellent source of information on health-related fitness testing, particularly in children. Useful information about community-based fitness testing can be obtained by reference to Canada Fitness Survey (1983) and the Health Promotion Authority for Wales (1987b).

Performance-related fitness

The majority of texts in this area of interest are sport-specific. However R. Hazeldine's *Fitness for sport* (1987) and F. Dick's *Sports training principles* (1989) both provide a useful general introduction to the foundations of performance-related fitness. In the UK the National Coaching Foundation produce excellent resource material, related to the development of performance-related fitness. These include study packs, including videos, and pamphlet material, e.g. *Development of strength and speed*, which are available from the trading arm of the NCF-Coachwise Ltd. For more information on the NCF refer to Chapter 13.

Published conference proceedings, recording the research interests and activity of kinathropometrists (Day, 1986; Reilly, Watkins and Borms, 1986) can prove extremely useful sources of information for those interested in sports-specific fitness assessment. Such information however tends to be heavily weighted towards analysis and validation of methods of performance assessment, rather than simple advocacy or description of protocols. For more information about this field of study readers are directed to the paper by Beunen and Borms (1990). This outlines the roots, development and possible future for this academic discipline and explains the importance of valid assessment of physical performance capacity. A reasonably well-established source of information and protocols, for performance-related fitness assessment of schoolchildren, can be obtained from the Council of Europe's *Eurofit: handbook for the Eurofit test of physical fitness* (CONI, 1988).

Major academic journals

Although physical fitness is not the sole focus of attention of any major academic journal, a large number of journals regularly publish refereed research papers and review articles focusing on physical fitness. Included amongst these are the *British Journal of Sports Medicine, British Journal of Physical Education Research Supplement, Canadian Journal of Sport Sciences, European Journal of Applied Physiology, International Journal of Sports Medicine, Journal of Sports Medicine and Physical Fitness, Journal of Sports Sciences, Medicine and Science in Sports and Exercise, Pediatric Exercise Science, The Physician and Sportsmedicine, Research Quarterly for Exercise and Sport* and *Sports Medicine*. A selection of these major journals is reviewed.

Medicine and Science in Sports and Exercise

This is the official journal of the American College of Sports Medicine (ACSM) and it has consistently provided a platform for the publication of high-quality research papers in the field of sport and exercise science for almost 30 years. Although the last decade has witnessed a shift towards publication of more papers addressing physiological issues rather than physical fitness *per se*, it remains a key resource for all serious students of physical fitness. Published bi-monthly, with a supplement to the April edition (abstracts of ACSM annual conference).

Research Quarterly for Exercise and Sport

One of the official journals of the American Alliance for Health, Physical Education, Recreation, and Dance, this journal has been at the forefront of the academic study of physical fitness for over 50 years. Published quarterly, it has recently introduced changes to both the editorial process and the journal style with a view to accelerating the review-publication process and improving the level of scholarly discourse. The last decade has seen an increasing number of articles published in this journal with a health-related fitness emphasis. However, articles examining performance-related fitness continue to be published.

Pediatric Exercise Science

This journal, first published in 1989, is the official journal of the North American Society of Pediatric Exercise Medicine (NASPEM). In a short time it has established itself as the definitive, up-to-date source of information concerning the physical fitness of children. Published quarterly, each issue comprises a particularly useful Research Digest of key paediatric exercise science abstracts published in other journals, review articles and original research articles. Selected issues also include NAS-PEM conference abstracts. This journal should be essential reading for those concerned with physical fitness of children and adolescents.

The Physician and Sportsmedicine

Published monthly, this journal provides a highly accessible source of information concerning physical fitness. Mirroring the growing interest in health-related fitness, almost every issue carries a useful review or original article in this area. In addition to this it includes a long-running feature 'Exercise Adviser' which provides a succinct synopsis of some key aspect of physical fitness/exercise behaviour. Recent editions have also seen the inclusion of a new feature focusing on nutrition and fitness.

Professional journals

A wide variety of professionally-oriented periodicals also exist which provide specially 'tailored' information on physical fitness. These can be broadly subdivided into three categories which focus upon health-related fitness and physical education, performance-related fitness and coach education, and the fitness instruction/fitness industry sector.

Journal titles associated with the first category include, from the UK, the *British Journal of Physical Education, Bulletin of Physical Education* and *Physical Education Review.* From North America, there is the *Canadian Association of Health, Physical Education and Recreation Journal* (CAHPER), and the *Journal of Physical Education, Recreation, and Dance (JOPERD)*, which is published by the American Alliance for Health, Physical Education, Recreation, and Dance (AAHPERD).

Examples of titles associated with performance-related fitness include: *Coaching Focus* (UK), *National Strength Conditioning Association Journal* (USA), *Science Periodical on Research & Technology in Sports* (SPORTS) (Canada) and *Sports Coach* (Australia).

Information sources for the Fitness Industry/Fitness Instructor readership ranges from specialist periodicals such as *Bodytalk* (UK) and *American Fitness Quarterly*, through to occasional articles in more general publications such as *Leisure Management, Sports Industry* and *Sport & Leisure* (all UK). In addition to these sources, many of the professional associations in this field also produce Instructor Newsletters and magazines, although it must be stressed that these vary considerably in quality.

Additional sources of information

In addition to the information available from standard sources information relating to many aspects of physical fitness in the population at large is available from organizations and professional associations. In the UK such alternative sources would include: the Health Education Authority; The Sports Councils of England, Scotland, Wales and Northern Ireland; the Welsh Heart Programme Directorate; the YMCA; professional associations such as the Physical Education Association; and the National Coaching Foundation. Other organisations which are not directly related to physical fitness occasionally publish useful documents, e.g. the King Edward's Fund for London, the Coronary Prevention Group. A number of Regional Health Authorities have also published relevant documents (West Midlands Regional Health Authority, 1988).

Internationally, organizations such as the Council of Europe, Fitness Canada, the American College of Sports Medicine and the American Alliance for Health, Physical Education, Recreation, and Dance, and the President's Council on Physical Fitness have also contributed significantly towards an improved understanding of physical fitness.

Health Education Authority (HEA)

This organization has been involved in the initiation and support of key projects aimed at promoting health-related fitness in the UK. Central to the work of the HEA in this field has been the 'Look after Yourself' project which comprises a complete Health and Fitness instructional programme with accompanying resource materials. The project has grown in stature and now incorporates a nationally validated Tutor Certification programme. More information about the project can be obtained from The 'Look After Yourself' Project Centre, Christ Church College, Canterbury, Kent CT1 1QU.

In conjunction with The Sports Council and the Physical Education Association (PEA), the HEA has generated a variety of important resource materials. The Fitness and Health Advisory Group, which serves both the HEA and The Sports Council, and issues occasional factsheets like Fitness and Health Advisory Group *Children's exercise, health and fitness fact sheet* (1988), is responsible for the initiation of a national fitness survey – the Allied Dunbar National Fitness Survey. This survey has generated a considerable amount of information relating to the relationship between exercise, fitness and the individual's health and well-being. The data, using a sample of 6000 adults in the population of England, are gathered via a questionnaire carried out in the home and a battery of fitness tests and measurements carried out in a mobile laboratory. The survey is based at the School of Sport and Exercise Sciences, University of Birmingham, Edgbaston, Birmingham B15 2TT.

The HEA also supports the work of the HEA/PEA project based at Loughborough University, UK. *The Health & Physical Education project newsletter* appears four times a year. Newsletter No. 19 (HEA/PEA, 1988) is an especially useful resource as it contains a list of print and non-print resources related to health-based physical education and health-related fitness. The HEA itself produces an excellent resource list, *Exercise: a resource list* (HEA, 1990) of both print and non-print sources of information pertaining to exercise and health-related fitness. It is available from the Health Education Authority, Hamilton House, Mabledon Place, London WC1H 9TX.

Heartbeat Wales

The Welsh Heart Programme – Heartbeat Wales – is another source of information on health-related physical fitness. This UK regional demonstration project for coronary heart disease prevention has generated a significant amount of information about the health-related fitness status and knowledge of the Welsh population. Results are communicated via a series of Technical Reports. Of these, the report describing health-related fitness in Wales (Health Promotion Authority for Wales, 1987a) is particularly useful. For further information contact the Health Promotion Authority for Wales, Brunel House, Fitzalan Road, Cardiff CF2 1EB.

National Coaching Foundation (NCF)

This is the key organization in the UK for those with an interest in performance-related fitness. Based at 4 College Close, Beckett Park, Leeds LS6 3QH, the NCF has developed a wide range of study courses, resource materials and information services to support coach education in the UK. Of particular relevance to those with an interest in physical fitness is the level 1 study pack and accompanying video *The body in action*, and the level 2 courses *Developing Endurance, Developing Flexibility* and *Development of Strength and Speed*. In support of this educational programme the NCF also produces *Sporting Updates,* a range of indexing journals that focus on specific sports. One title in this series is devoted to health-related fitness. The NCF also issue *Coaching Focus* three times a year.

The policies and programmes of the NCF are implemented by a nationwide network of National Coaching Centres. Serving the principal regions of the UK these centres are important resource bases providing access to libraries and learning centres, information and advisory services, and research and consultancy services.

Council of Europe, Eurofit

The Sport Research programme of the Council of Europe has held a number of seminars concerned with physical fitness. These led to the publication of the *Eurofit: handbook for the Eurofit test of physical fitness* (CONI, 1988) The handbook, prepared by the five coordinators of the Eurofit project, contains nine tests for use with schoolchildren.

Canada Fitness Survey (CFS)

This 1981 survey, initiated and funded by Fitness Canada, and undertaken by the Canadian Fitness and Lifestyle Research Institute, obtained data on 15 519 persons between the ages of 7 and 69 years from 11 884 households identified by Statistics Canada, located in both rural and urban areas of each province. Published data relates principally to performance in the Canadian Standardised Test of Fitness. Aside from generating the largest available population database on fitness performance standards, CFS (1983), a number of reports and resource documents examining fitness, activity and health within specific population sub-groups (aged, women, youth, disabled) have also been published. For more information on these publications contact: Canada Fitness Survey, 506–294 Albert Street, Ottawa, Ontario K1P 6E6. CFS's successor, the Campbell's Survey on well-being in Canada was conducted in 1988. Published in 1990, *The well-being of Canadians: highlights of the 1988 Campbell's Survey* presents the 1988 data and is a longitudinal follow-up to the 1991 survey.

The 'parent' body, Fitness Canada, is also an excellent source of information and materials for those with an interest in health-related fitness. For a detailed description of the resources produced by this body, consult Fitness and Amateur Sport — Women's Programme & CFS (1984, p. 44). The contact address is: Fitness and Amateur Sport, 365 Laurier Avenue West, Ottawa, Ontario. K1A 0X6.

American College of Sports Medicine (ACSM)

Aside from the publication of the journal *Medicine and Science in Sports and Exercise*, the ACSM contributes to the information base in physical fitness through the release of highly informative position papers and complementary lay-summaries. Of these, the most relevant to those seeking information about physical fitness, is the recently updated and extended position stand on 'The Recommended Quantity and Quality of Exercise for Developing and Maintaining Cardiorespiratory and Muscular Fitness in Healthy Adults' (ACSM, 1990). The ACSM is also committed to health and fitness instructor education and certification programmes worldwide.

President's Council on Physical Fitness and Sports

Established in 1956, the President's Council co-operates with state and local governments to: develop physical fitness programmes; help schools and clubs with programmes; develop special fitness tests; disseminate information via print, television and video. They publish the indexing journal *Physical Fitness/Sports Medicine*. The Council also collaborated with the National Children and Youth Fitness Study, carried out under the auspices of the Office of Disease Prevention and Health Promotion (ODPHP). The findings of this study are well narrated in the *Journal of Physical Education, Recreation, and Dance*, **56**(1), January 1985, with a more detailed report available from the National Technical Information Service.

American Alliance of Health, Physical Education, Recreation, and Dance (AAHPERD)

The Alliance is an educational organization which conducts programmes in health, physical education and leisure activities. It has developed a number of test manuals and fitness programmes. Both *JOPERD* and its other publications on fitness make a significant contribution to the literature of physical fitness. AAHPERD was also a major collaborator in the National Children and Youth Fitness Survey.

YMCA

The YMCA (USA) is the largest provider of health and fitness programmes in the USA. The Association provides a wide range of promotional literature and publications on fitness.

Professional associations

There are an increasing number of professional associations actively supporting the promotion of exercise and physical fitness. This in turn has led to a growth in information available for the practitioner, particularly with regard to safe supervision and practice of exercise, One long-standing organization in the UK is the Physical Education Association (PEA), an excellent source of information. In addition to publishing the *British Journal of Physical Education* and the *Health and Physical Education Newsletter*, the Association also validate and run a Certificate in Exercise and Health Studies, in conjunction with Polytechnic of East London. A PEA Research Centre is also based at the University of Exeter, UK, through which the Association issue position statements (PEA, 1988) and organize conferences and workshops.

Other associations and organizations involved in Exercise Teacher Education and Certification include: Aerobics and Fitness Association of America (AFAA), Aerobics Fitness Teachers Association (AFTA), Association of Exercise Teachers (ASSET), International Dance-Exercise Association (IDEA), Keep Fit Association (KFA), Royal Society of Arts (RSA: validating and examining body, UK) and the YMCA. The range of information available from these types of associations will vary immensely but some produce a regular journal or newsletter, market videos and books, as well as organizing seminars and workshops. However, examination of all of these organizations is outside the scope of this chapter. Those seeking more detailed information related to Exercise Teacher Training Education & Certification, including addresses etc., should refer to Clough (1988a, b, c) and Heaner (1990).

References

AAHPERD (1984) *Health-related physical fitness test: technical manual.* Reston, VA: AAHPERD.

AAHPERD (1985) *Health-related physical fitness test manual.* Reston, VA: AAHPERD.

AAHPERD (1988) *Physical best: The American Alliance physical fitness education and assessment programme.* Reston, VA: AAHPERD.

American College of Sports Medicine (1990) The recommended quality and quantity of exercise for developing and maintaining cardiorespiratory and muscular fitness in healthy adults. *Medicine and Science in Sports and Exercise*, **20**(2), 265–274.

Andersen, K.L., Shephard, R.J., Denolin, H., Varnauskas, E. and Masironi, R. (1971) *Fundamentals of exercise testing.* Geneva: World Health Organization.

Beunen, G. and Borms, J. (1990) Kinanthropometry: roots, developments and future. *Journal of Sports Sciences*, **8**, 1–15.

Biddle, S.J.H. (1987) *Foundations of health-related fitness in physical education.* London: Ling Publishing.

Bouchard, C., Shephard, R.J., Stephens, T., Sutton, J.R and McPherson, B.D. (1990) *Exercise, fitness, and health: a consensus of current knowledge.* Champaign, IL: Human Kinetics.

Canada Fitness Survey (1983) *Fitness and lifestyle in Canada.* Ottawa: CFS.

Caspersen, C.J., Powell, K.E. and Christenson, G.M. (1985) Physical activity, exercise and physical fitness: definitions and distinctions for health-related research. *Public Health Reports*, **100**(2), 126–131.

Clough, J. (1988a) Health and fitness: staff training. *Leisure Management*, **8**(5), 45, 53.

Clough, J. (1988b) Class teachers: staff training. *Leisure Management*, **8**(6), 77–78.

Clough, J. (1988c) Training courses: health club management. *Leisure Management*, **8**(7), 63–65.

Corbin, C.B. and Lindsey, R. (1985) *Concepts of physical fitness with laboratories: Instructor's manual* (5th edn.). Dubuque, IO: Wm. C. Brown.

Corbin, C.B. and Lindsey, R. (1988) *Concepts of physical fitness with laboratories* (6th edn.). Dubuque, IO: Wm. C. Brown.

Day, J.A.P. (ed.) (1986) *Perspectives in Kinanthropometry*. Champaign, IL: Human Kinetics.

Dialog Information Services (1989) *Dialog database catalog*. California: Dialog Information Services.

Dick, F. (1989) *Sports training principles* (2nd edn.). London: Lepus Books.

Eurofit: handbook for the Eurofit test of physical fitness (1988) Rome: Comitato Olimpico Nazionale Italiano.

Fitness and Amateur Sport – Women's Programme & Canada Fitness Survey (1984) *Changing times: women and physical activity*. Ottawa: Canada Fitness Survey.

Fitness and Health Advisory Group (1988) *Children's exercise, health and fitness fact sheet*. London: The Sports Council.

Gledhill, N. (1990) Discussion: assessment of fitness. In C. Bouchard *et al.* (eds.) *Exercise, fitness, and health: a consensus of current knowledge*, pp. 121–126. Champaign, IL: Human Kinetics.

Golding, L.A., Myers, C.R. and Sinning, W.E. (eds.) (1989) *Y's way to physical fitness*. Champaign, IL: Human Kinetics.

Hazeldine, R. (1987) *Fitness for sport*. Marlborough: Crowood Press.

Health Education Authority (1990) *Exercise: a resource list*. London: HEA.

Health Education Authority/Physical Education Association (1988) *Health and Physical Education Project Newsletter*, No. 19. Loughborough: HEA/PEA.

Health Promotion Authority for Wales (1987a) *Exercise for health: Heartbeat Wales technical report* 17. Cardiff: HPAW.

Health Promotion Authority for Wales (1987b) *Fitness testing: Heartbeat Wales technical report* 18. Cardiff: HPAW.

Heaner, M. (1990). Instructor certification: aerobic dance. *Fitness & Health Magazine*, **7**(5), May, 49–50.

Howley, E.T. and Franks, B.D. (1986) *Health/fitness instructor's handbook*. Champaign: Human Kinetics.

Lockheed Information Systems (1985) *Guide to Dialog databases*. Palo Alto, CA: Lockheed Information Systems.

Pate, R.R. (1988) The evolving definition of physical fitness. *Quest*, **40**, 174–179.

Physical Education Association (1988) Health-related fitness testing and monitoring in schools. *British Journal of Physical Education*, **19**(4/5), 194–195.

Pollock, M.L., Wilmore, J.H. and Fox, S.M. (1984) *Exercise in health and disease*. Philadelphia, PA: Saunders.

Prytherch, R. (1988) *Sports and fitness: an information guide*. Aldershot: Gower.

Reilly, T., Watkins, J. and Borms, J. (eds.) (1986) *Kinanthropometry III*. London: E. & F.N. Spon.

Stephens, T. and Craig, C.L. (1990) *The well-being of Canadians: highlights of the 1988 Campbell's survey*. Ottawa, Ontario: Canadian Fitness and Lifestyle Research Institute.

CHAPTER THIRTEEN

Coaching

C. RANKIN

Introduction

Coaching is a very complex business, and can be considered as both an art and a science. The good coach will play many roles — teacher, friend, scientist, motivator — and needs to acquire a wide range of knowledge and expertise. This can be considered in four main areas: sport-specific knowledge; performance-related knowledge; management and vocational skills; teaching and coaching methodology. The practitioner will require access to a range of information sources taken from a wide range of subjects, such as exercise physiology, biomechanics, psychology and pedagogy. The complexity and range of the material required by coaches makes the bibliographic control of the literature difficult, a task not helped by the absence of any international organization responsible for sports coaching. The idea for such an organization has been suggested, but as yet individual countries tend to operate in isolation.

Organizations

National Coaching Foundation

In the UK the National Coaching Foundation (NCF) is the main organization providing educational resources for coaches. Established by The Sports Council in 1983, the objectives of the organization are to promote the education, instruction and training at national and local levels of honorary and professional coaches, and other interested persons, in performance-related knowledge. This is achieved through a nationwide network of National Coaching Centres which provide a range of courses, workshops and seminars, supported by publications, videos and information services. A trading company, Coachwise, has been set up to increase awareness of, and sell coaching products, all profits being channelled back into the work of the NCF.

The NCF Information Centre houses a collection of literature on performance sport and coach education. Information on coach education systems in other countries is also being collected, and information exchanges set up with a number of overseas organizations. The journal collection of over 80 titles includes coaching material from international sources. A number of in-house bibliographic databases on sport and recreation are also being developed. The range of information services available includes fact sheets, literature searches and the *Sporting Update* current-awareness bulletins which are published quarterly. A current-awareness service is also being developed specifically for gymnastics coaches, with selected bibliographic records being published in *GRASP*, the technical journal of the British Amateur Gymnastic Association.

National governing bodies (NGBs)

Until recently coach education in the UK was undertaken solely by the national governing bodies of sport (NGBs) — each had its own award structure and there was no uniform pattern of training. The NGBs can now select from the NCF 'market stall' of courses and packages, and integrate them into their own training programmes where appropriate. The NGBs oversee the administration, the rules and regulations of the sport. Many also operate membership schemes, competitions and events, and coaching and proficiency award schemes. Many NGBs, for example the British Amateur Gymnastics Association, have substantial collections of technical material available for use by their coaching staff. However, access to these resources is not easy unless coaches actually visit the particular organization.

Published information on coaching awards can be obtained directly from the NGB, as each will produce its own syllabus and assessment method. Some NGBs have sophisticated, well-developed coaching award schemes that have evolved over a period of time. A number of the more recently established organizations are just formulating this type of structure, and bringing on board new knowledge. A useful publication giving information about NGBs is the Central Council of Physical Recreation (CCPR) *A guide to governing body coaching awards* (1987), which gives details of English NGB awards. An up-to-date list of governing body contact points for UK and English organizations is available in The Sports Council's *Address book* — an annual publication issued by The Sports Council (England). The Scottish Sports Council, the Sports Council for Wales and the Sports Council for Northern Ireland also produce address lists for their governing bodies.

British Institute of Sports Coaches (BISC)

The 'professionalization' of coaches took a step forward in the UK with the launch of The British Institute of Sports Coaches (BISC) in January 1990. Formerly the British Association of National Coaches, the organization offers a forum for coaches from all disciplines to share experiences and expertise, and debate matters of common interest. BISC has established a nationally recognized *Register of approved coaches* in conjunction with the governing bodies of sport. It is working towards quality and ethical control of coaching across sports, through the publication of a *Coaching manifesto* and *Codes of ethics and practice* which will be binding on all members. In conjunction with the NCF, BISC encourages education and further training by promoting and validating courses of study which will be relevant to the real needs of coaches. Coaches can contact BISC for information on insurance, employment and legal advice. A newsletter *Sportscoach* is also produced, and BISC now publish the proceedings of the bi-annual *International Congress on the Growing Child in Competitive Sport.*

Northern Ireland Institute of Coaching (NIIC)

Another example of a member organization for coaches is the Northern Ireland Institute of Coaching (NIIC) founded in 1980 to co-ordinate existing physical and human resources for the further development of sports coaching at all levels in the province. The NIIC maintains a register of coaches and instructors, and membership is open to organizations and individuals. An annual conference of sport is held, and the published proceedings are available from the NIIC.

British Association of Sports Sciences (BASS)

Today's sports coaches and performers require the best possible information on sport and science topics, e.g. fitness training, mental preparation, nutrition and diet. Close co-operation between the practising coach and the sport scientist is essential if real progress is to be made, and the gap between theory and practice bridged. Coaches and performers need access to appropriate sport science facilities and expertise. The British Association of Sports Sciences (BASS) and the NCF have been working together to provide a sports science service for UK sport. Details of this Sport Science Education Programme have been published in the form of an annual report. BASS have established an accreditation scheme in physiology, psychology and biomechanics, and have a register of experts willing to assist with governing body projects. Proceedings of the annual BASS conference are published and a quarterly newsletter is circulated to members.

Coaching organizations for specific sports

A number of sports also have member organizations specifically for coaches such as the Association of Cricket Coaches, and the Swimming Coaches Association. These organizations offer support services and publications and a contact point for members.

Overseas associations

USA

A number of overseas countries provide coach education and development programmes, and resource materials published to support these programmes can be of value to working in other countries. A well-known example is the American Coaching Effectiveness Programme (ACEP) which is funded through Human Kinetics Publishers. Founded in 1981, ACEP is a multi-level coaching, education and certification programme divided into three levels. The Leader level is aimed at volunteer coaches, undergraduate coaching students and any coaches who have not had any training in the sport sciences during the last five years. The Master series level is designed for experienced coaches and for undergraduate and graduate degree students. The Professional level is for elite coaches and provides sport science information tailored to individual sports. The United States Olympic Committee (USOC) offers a variety of services to NGB-affiliated coaches. The Education Services Department works closely with the Sports Medicine and Sport Science Programmes to provide services and materials. The Library/Information Centre at the Colorado Springs Olympic complex houses several thousand books and over 300 journals related to all aspects of sports medicine and science. Coaches have access to computerized information retrieval services and inter-library loan facilities. USOC sponsors a variety of education conferences, workshops and seminars.

CANADA

The Coaching Association of Canada aims to increase coaching effectiveness in all sports and to encourage the development of coaching. The National Coaching Certification Program is a five-level system which trains coaches in the theory, technical and practical aspects of coaching and has an extensive list of publications to support the award schemes. The Canadian Sport Information Resource Centre (SIRC) is renowned as the largest resource centre for sport in the world and offers a range of information services to users, in particular to coaches based at the Canadian Sport and Fitness Administration Centre. SIRC produce the international SPORT database and publish *SportSearch* current-awareness service — both are discussed in more detail in Chapter 1, and later in this chapter. On a more general note, sport in Canada and the USA are reviewed in Chapter 15.

AUSTRALIA

The Australian Coaching Council also offers a National Coaching Accreditation Scheme, and Australian coaches are able to access the services of the National Sport Information Centre at the Australian Institute of Sport. Sport in Australia is covered in greater detail in Chapter 16.

EUROPE

Coach education programmes are also operating in a number of European countries. Two examples are Germany and Finland.

Germany

The German College of Physical Culture (DHfK) in Leipzig is a central teaching and research institution concentrating on the education of coaches and sport scientists. Experienced coaches can undergo periods of study by correspondence course, and the College's Institute of Further Education offers refresher courses for coaches every four years. Intensive training courses are also available for overseas coaches. The College publishes textbooks, educational aids and other scientific materials. A number of texts have been published in English and are available through the Sportverlag publishers. The College library publishes sport bibliographies. However, since German unification the service offered in what was the GDR, has changed considerably. One immediate change has been the reduction in the number of coaches.

Finland

By comparison, the Finnish Sports Institute at Vierumäki offers a range of sports facilities and services to the sporting community. It also houses a training college for coaches, instructors and sports administrators. Vierumäki offers a national coaching certificate and examinations relating to individual sports. The Finnish Central Sports Federation produce resource materials to support the training of coaches. Further information on sport in Europe can be found in Chapter 14.

Abstracting and indexing journals

The *Sporting Update* series of current-awareness bulletins launched by
the NCF in January 1990 provides a range of published services specifically aimed at coaches, teachers and instructors. There are six titles in
the series to date including coaching, team sports, racket sports, swimming, athletics and health-related fitness. Published quarterly, they
provide access to a wide range of journal articles, reports, conference
papers and books. Items for inclusion are selected from information
added to the NCF's bibliographic coaching database. Volume 1 also
contained references contributed by the Sports Documentation Centre.
Information is arranged under broad subject headings and each issue
contains an author and a subject index.

Sports Documentation Monthly Bulletin is produced by the Sports
Documentation Centre at the University of Birmingham. It lists recent
periodical articles appearing in UK and foreign journals on all aspects
of sport, but with an emphasis on sports science. From 1980 onwards,
conference papers are included. Each article or conference paper is
arranged under broad subject headings. An annual cumulated index is
published at the end of each year. This service covers a wide range of
academic sources, and is of particular value to the coach who wishes to
locate research articles.

Coaches need to be concerned with the physical well-being of their
performers and the *Sports Medicine Bulletin* can provide them with
access to knowledge on sports injuries and management methods for
rehabilitation and recovery. This is a monthly bibliography of articles
relevant to the fields of sports medicine and applied physiology and is
produced jointly by the National Sports Medicine Institute and the
British Library Medical Information Service. The bulletin is divided
into subject sections, and includes an author and subject index.

Physical Fitness/Sports Medicine, published by the President's
Council on Physical Fitness, is a quarterly publication consisting of articles and conference papers retrieved from the MEDLARS computerized
database of the National Library of Medicine. It covers exercise physiology, sports injuries, physical conditioning and the medical aspects of
exercise. The subject headings correspond to those used in MEDLARS.
Articles are arranged by subject, but there is no abstract and only an
author index.

SportSearch, produced by the Sport Information Resource Centre
(SIRC) in Canada is a current-awareness tool; it monitors nearly 300
sport and physical education periodicals published in English and
French. Between 1985 and 1987 this publication displayed only the
contents pages of journals. In 1988 the format changed, and entries are
now arranged in alphabetical order by title, under broad subject head-

ings. Each document is classified according to the intended audience level ranging from basic through intermediate to advanced or research level material. *SportSearch* lists books and book chapters, conference proceedings and other publications where individual contributors are identified. This is a valuable bibliographic tool for information professionals and for students, but may not be of particular interest to the practising coach who usually requires sport-specific information.

Abstracting and indexing journals on related subject areas may also be of interest — for example, *Education Index, Index Medicus* and *Psychological Abstracts.*

Journals and magazines

There are a considerable number of journals published worldwide on the subject of sport, many of which are listed in Chapter 1. They tend to vary from the news and results type magazine to the scholarly journal, but few of these are specific to coaching. Journals, magazines and periodicals on coaching can be considered in broad areas: those which deal with coaching in general terms and are therefore of potential interest to a wide range of coaches, those which cover a particular sport in some depth, and newsletters which act as a communication channel.

A number of core journals are of potential interest to a wide range of coaches, as they cover performance-related knowledge. *Coaching Focus*, for example, is published three times per year by the NCF. It is not intended as an 'academic' journal, but to present issues for discussion with a balance between theory and practice. Each issue takes a specific theme and contributions are invited from authors on the basis of their background interest and particular expertise. Topics covered include drugs in sport, nutrition and sports performance, and competitive sport. The journal forms part of an NCF information subscription package called Coaching Focus Gold.

The *Coaching Director* published by the Australian Coaching Council (ACC), aims to communicate ideas and issues relating to the National Coaching Accreditation Scheme. It provides a medium for contact between National Coaching Directors from different sports. The publication includes summaries of policy decisions at ACC meetings and is a useful resource for comparative information on coach education programmes. *Sports Coach*, Australia's coaching magazine is published by the ACC on behalf of the Australian Sports Commission. The articles cover a wide range of sports and are aimed at the practising coach. Some issues concentrate on a particular theme, for example children in sport, and usually include information on policy. Coaches are encouraged to take advantage of the *Journal Documentation Service* offered by the National Sport Information Centre. This is a listing of sport orientated articles backed up by a photocopy supply service. The *Sportscan* information search service is available to accredited coaches under the National Accreditation Scheme. *EXCEL* is a quarterly journal which publishes material on sports science and medicine and is based on information gathered at the Australian Institute of Sport. As the articles report on actual research projects they offer practical technical information, but are still written in terminology that the coach can understand.

National Strength and Conditioning Association Journal, a bimonthly publication from the USA, includes a sports performance series which features a particular sport or skill. This usually gives detailed kinesiological and biomechanical analysis and is well illustrated. There are regular features on exercise methods, and the articles are of a practical nature. The bias is towards American collegiate sports, but these provide useful comparative information on training programmes. *SPORTS* (Sports Periodical on Research and Technology in Sport) published by the Coaching Association of Canada is specifically geared to the needs of top-level coaches. Each issue of this monthly publication covers a single topic and the aim is to help coaches improve their understanding of physiological and psychological processes as they relate to athletic performance. Topics include sports medicine and sports injuries, nutrition, psychology, training, biomechanics, exercise physiology and administration. Binders are available for storing the series, and a back issues service is offered.

Although not a core journal, *Applied Research in Coaching and Athletics* aims to cater for the layperson. Previously a quarterly publication, it now appears as an annual. It covers a wide range of sports science subjects, but has a North American bias.

There are a number of non-English language journals which could be useful to the coach. These include *Leistungssport* published by the Deutscher Sportbund (Germany), *Revue de l'Amicale des Entraîneurs Français d'Athlétisme* the journal of the AEFA and *Scuola dello Sport; Revista di Cultura Sportiva, Tecnica Scientifica* published by the Comitato Olimpico Nazionale Italiano (CONI). The high cost of translations for English speakers could mean that this type of material is not a readily available information source.

There are other scholarly journals which contain articles of potential interest to the coach. These include: *Physician and Sportsmedicine* (with a free review every two months sponsored by Nike — *Sports Research Review*); *Journal of Sports Sciences*; *Journal of Sport and Exercise Psychology*; *Sport Psychologist* and the *International Journal of Sport Biomechanics*. These are aimed at other professions and therefore are written in technical language which may not be easily understood by the non-subject expert.

A large number of journals concentrate on one particular sport but are specifically aimed at the coach. Many journals originate from the governing body of the sport, and are intended primarily for their members. A number of these are professionally printed and distributed. For example: *Serve and Volley* (Lawn Tennis Association); *Hockey Field* (the Hockey Association); *Table Tennis News* (English Table Tennis Association). They will usually have a 'coaching corner' or coaching news section as part of the publication.

Some governing bodies produce in-house publications directly aimed at coaches of the sport. These can be difficult to trace as they may not be 'officially' published and are often produced and distributed by one person. For example, the British Cycling Coaching Scheme produce *Coaching News* as a regular newsletter for members. This often contains extracts of articles originally published in other sources. Another example is *Volleycoach* distributed by the English Volleyball Association. The Badminton Association of England and the Rugby Football Union Coaching Scheme also circulate coaching bulletins to their members. Usually these very valuable publications can be obtained by keeping in touch with the Director of Coaching for the sport. The *SPRIG Union catalogue of periodicals in sport and recreation* (SPRIG, 1988), the main guide for sports periodicals, does not include many of these titles, and other periodical guides are not very helpful in locating this valuable grey literature. Chapter 8 gives more information on individual sports titles.

Some other useful titles in this group are listed below:

Coaches & Coaching is the official publication of the Lawn Tennis Association Coaching Department. The majority of the articles are written by tennis coaches and include practical advice and information such as coaching tips and practice drills. The publication is directly aimed at tennis coaches and as such is uncluttered by the advertisements prevalent in some of the more glossy tennis magazines.

Coaching Women's Basketball is the official journal of the Women's Basketball Coaches Association (USA) published jointly bi-monthly with Human Kinetics Inc. It includes interviews with top coaches, game-winning techniques and tactics, mental training programmes and guidance on legal matters.

Coaching Volleyball is the official bi-monthly journal of the American Volleyball Coaches Association. It aims to keep coaches up to date on the latest strategies, techniques and issues, current sports medicine and sports science research.

Athletics Coach, published quarterly by the British Amateur Athletic Association, contains contributions from national athletics coaches and the material is of benefit to practising coaches. Occasionally articles are included on event analysis and competition results.

New Studies in Athletics is the IAAF quarterly magazine for technical research, coaching information and bibliographic documentation. It contains more high-level technical articles, and often includes translations from other technical athletics journals.

Swimming Technique is a quarterly publication designed for coaches and swimmers interested in information on stroke mechanics, physiology, psychology and programme administration. The journal includes an abstract review section. Swimming coaches in the UK may also use *Swimming Magazine*, the official journal of the Amateur Swimming Association. Although not specifically aimed at coaches this journal usually has a technical feature section.

There are also quite a number of newsletter type publications in the coaching world. They are a valuable resource because, although newsy and ephemeral, they concentrate on performance sport. They tend to include some information about the parent organization and details of conferences and events, courses, products and services and sometimes results of competition.

The NCF publish *SuperCoach* three times a year with the aim of increasing awareness and promoting new courses and products. *Performance* is the newsletter of The Scottish Sports Council, and was launched in October 1989 to tie in with the Council's new corporate image. The Sports Council for Wales publish *In Touch*, and the Northern Ireland Institute of Coaching issue the quarterly *NIIC NEWS*. *The Coaches Coach* is the newsletter of the American Coaching Effectiveness Program (ACEP) and aims to keep ACEP instructors up to date and involved in the programme. The Australian Coaching Council also publish a newsletter that is widely circulated.

Manuals and books

Many governing bodies of sport in the UK produce training manuals and guides for coaches. These may be an integral part of the coaching award (for example, the Lawn Tennis Association publication *Tennis practices* by C. Applewhaite). A number of governing bodies have extended their publication list to include materials aimed at teachers. For example, the English Basketball Association has produced a curriculum guide which aims to provide the school teacher with advice on good practice in the teaching of basketball to all age groups and abilities. This guide is concerned more with the introduction of the game to all participants, rather than the development of excellence for the few.

The NCF produces a range of resource materials for coaches which are not sport-specific. The *Introductory study pack* series has been written by prominent sport educators and aims to introduce beginner coaches to the art and science of good coaching. Titles range from *Coach in action*, to *Mind over matter*. Each *Introductory study pack* has a complementary video, and the NCF has produced a tutor pack to enable the material to be presented as a taught course. Many local authorities are using these packs for in-service training, and governing bodies of sport are able to adapt the material to make it sport-specific for their own coaches.

The NCF also publishes a series of three Coaching handbooks aimed at the club level coach and covering the *Coach at work*, *Safety first for coaches* and *Physiology and performance*. The *How to* coach series of coaching handbooks has been jointly commissioned by Collins and the NCF and is aimed at beginners. Designed as practical working manuals they contain information on planning a lesson structure, introducing basic skills and techniques, developing a tactical approach to the game, fault finding and corrective practices. The first four titles covering swimming, badminton, cricket, and tennis were published in 1990 and further titles are planned.

The Crowood Press publish the *Skills of the game* series which includes over 30 titles covering the most popular sports. Rules, equipment and skills are explained for the beginner. Sections are also given on advanced techniques, tactics, fitness training and skills practices. Each book is written by a top coach in the sport.

The *steps to success activity* series is published by Human Kinetics Publishers. The series aims to teach sport skills, and, for each activity there is a learning guide for participants and an instructor's guide for group instruction. The instructor's guides are comprehensive texts for individualizing and improving instruction. Each includes management and safety guidelines, rating charts for identifying students' skill levels, specification of equipment needs and a complete test bank of written questions. The participant books are a resource for the students and include sequential illustrations for correct execution of all basic skills, specific goals for measuring performance and summary checklists of keys to correct technique. To date the series has covered swimming, golf, archery, tennis, softball, volleyball and tenpin bowling.

The *Take up* series published by Springfield Books is a good introduction to a wide variety of sports. As well as explaining the basic rules clearly, the authors give hints on techniques and strategies. Each book has been written by an acknowledged expert in the sport. Titles published to date include the following sports: swimming, badminton, tennis, golf, football, cricket, rock climbing, squash, netball, canoeing, athletics and Rugby.

The Coaching Association of Canada has a well-established National Coaching Certification Program and produces a range of manuals for each level of the scheme, for example *Volleyball coaches manual level 1, Squash coaching manual level 2,* etc. *FOCUS* (Fundamentals of Coaching and Understanding Sport) is a series of booklets developed as a result of presentations from Community Coaching Conferences and are aimed at novice coaches and parents of young athletes. Titles in the series include *Building your own coaching profile, Fun in sport* and *Introducing mental imagery to young athletes.* The Coaching Association of Canada produce a *Sport book catalogue* on a regular basis which lists these and other publications and products available for purchase by mail order.

The Australian Coaching Council is also developing this type of resource to support coach education. The level 1 manual *You're the coach: an introduction to coaching,* covers planning, training principles and teaching basic sports skills. The level 2 manual *Towards better coaching: the art and science of sports coaching* includes sport psychology, physiology, skill acquisition, biomechanics and sports medicine. A home study course for the level 2 general principles course has been produced entitled *A self-directed course for towards better coaching.* A catalogue containing descriptions of publications and videos produced by the various programmes of the Australian Sports Commission is available from the National Sport Information Centre.

Online and CD-ROM

Full details of both abstracting journals and online services are given in Chapter 1. The most useful database for coaches is the SPORT database which is produced by the Sport Information Resource Centre (SIRC). It was established in 1973 by the Coaching Association of Canada specifically for coaches. Online access to the SPORT database is possible worldwide. The database contains references to literature on individual sports (including education, training and equipment) and sports medicine (including nutrition, injuries and treatment). For source material in English and French, a full range of publications is covered, including newsletters, theses and conference papers. For other languages only the more technical articles are covered. At present the database contains approximately 270 000 bibliographic citations with over 1500 citations being added each month.

Although this major database has been available to coaches for some years, relatively little use has been made of it by coaches because of the cost of online searching, and problems of access to the necessary telecommunications and computer equipment. The advent of the CD-ROM version, SPORT DISCUS, is beginning to extend use of this database to a much wider audience. It is available from SilverPlatter on an annual subscription basis. However the North American bias means that a considerable amount of the material is not particularly relevant to coaches in this country. In addition, it is not always easy to obtain copies of references cited in the database.

Viewdata

Viewdata services uses a telephone line in the home or office to give access to an extensive range of information and services. The Sports Council are information providers to British Telecom's Prestel system and include details of governing bodies of sport and their coaching awards. The NCF provide a service for coaches on Prestel, including national coaching centre contacts, information on courses and quizzes. A special magazine feature, Coaches Clipboard, is updated on a regular basis. The individual coach is perhaps unlikely to access this type of system, but it is a useful resource for those involved in providing information services.

There are also a number of viewdata services run by local authorities, such as the well-established Berkshire Viewdata and SHEAF which operates in the Sheffield area. These can provide information at a very local level for example club and coaching contacts.

Videos

Video is a medium that is particularly suited to sport. Many coaches will use video recordings of their performers to help analyze and improve performance. The coach may want to learn more about techniques and skills, and the 'appliance of sport science'. The use of video can be an integral part of a coaching session when used to demonstrate particular skills, or tactics and match play. Many governing bodies of sport produce and distribute their own videos. The English Volleyball Association and the English Basketball Association have both produced videos with an accompanying curriculum guide aimed at helping schools with the new GCSE courses. The NCF produce a series of videos which aim to introduce coaches to the principles of good coaching. These videos are not sport-specific, but complement the NCF's *Introductory study pack* series described above.

You can now buy many sporting videos from High Street stores, and the good coach can select extracts for use as teaching points. However, although serendipity may often pay off, not many people have the time to use this browsing technique on a regular basis. Video titles are frequently advertised in sport-specific magazines and journals.

There is a demand for information on sports videos, yet this resource is not well documented. The NCF and Sheffield Sports Information Service have collaborated to produce and publish *Action replay: a guide to audio-visual resources in sport and recreation* (1990). The aim of this publication is to provide details of all sporting videos available through distributors in the UK. Videos are arranged under broad subject headings, and there is a subject and author index.

Part IV

CHAPTER FOURTEEN

European information sources

M. SHOEBRIDGE AND A. REMANS

Introduction

In the last two decades sport has undergone considerable development. What had been a competitive and elitist activity has now become more participative. One in four Europeans regularly practice some kind of physical activity, and with the many publicity campaigns emphasizing health and physical fitness, plus a general increase in leisure time, this percentage is rising every year. However, whilst the participative aspects of sport and leisure have been emphasized Europe-wide, many countries of Eastern Europe have, until the recent political changes, tended to ignore mass leisure and concentrate their resources on top-level sport. Consequently, there is often little participation information available to compare with that collected in the UK and Canada and the public viewdata systems giving information about leisure facilities are not well developed.

Apart from the interest in general European sports policy there has always been demand for information about sport in specific European countries, a demand which may well increase with the arrival of a Single European Market in 1992. Whilst there is usually information available in the native language, relatively little exists in English, making it difficult for those researchers who do not possess language skills. This is particularly significant for those studying sport at GCSE and 'A'-Level. Comparative data are also difficult to obtain, either because it does not exist or because of the language barrier.

The emphasis in this chapter will be on continental Europe. There are a number of well-established libraries and information services for sports information in Europe, e.g. the Library of the Federal School for Sport at Macolin, Switzerland, the Library of the Institute for Physical Education at Leuven, Belgium, and Libraries in Cologne, Leipzig and Jyväskylä (Finland), but only the information sources of France, Germany, Finland, Sweden, Norway, Yugoslavia and Italy will be covered in any detail. Obviously, the political changes taking place in Europe since 1989 make it difficult to be definitive about the situation in some individual countries.

A number of the general sources referred to in Chapter 1 provide information on Europe. More detailed information about financial or statistical data relating to Europe is given in Chapter 2.

It is sometimes possible to obtain general information from the embassy of a particular country, but this rarely amounts to more than a colour brochure. Some of the European-based organizations provide information relating to sport. A detailed analysis of sport policy in Europe reveals that the European Community publishes little related to sport and leisure, but highlights the important role of the Council of Europe in the area of sports information, in particular in publishing conventions, recommendations, charters and conference proceedings.

Council of Europe publications

The Council of Europe is an international organization of 23 European countries: Austria, Belgium, Cyprus, Denmark, Finland, France, Germany, Greece, Iceland, Ireland, Italy, Liechtenstein, Luxemburg, Malta, the Netherlands, Norway, Portugal, Spain, Sweden, Switzerland, San Marino, Turkey and the UK. Other countries such as Hungary, Poland and Yugoslavia have all acceded to the European Cultural Convention and thus participate fully in the Council's work on sport. The Council was founded after the Second World War to promote greater unity in Europe, to improve the living conditions of Europeans, and to protect democracy and human rights. A useful summary of the work carried out by the Council of Europe in the area of sport over the last 20 years has been written by J. Marchand, a professional French sports journalist. Entitled *Sport for all in Europe* (1990), it is published by HMSO in the UK on behalf of the Council of Europe.

In order to draw up guidelines for its policy in this area, the Council of Europe has established a number of bodies. The European Ministers' Conference for Sport meets every three years. The Steering Committee for the Development of Sport (CDDS), a group of governmental and non-governmental experts, has the task of implementing the ministers' guidelines. It draws up the annual work programme and organizes seminars, workshops and courses on sports-related issues. It is assisted in its work by two committees: the Committee of Experts on Sports Research (DS-SR), which co-ordinates research projects and monitors documentation and information on sports research through a European databank, and the Committee of Experts on Sports Information (DS-SI) which supervizes the collection of national data through the 'Sport for All' Clearing House, a specialized information centre, set up in 1974, in Brussels.

The Council of Europe's sports policy is laid down in the *European 'Sport for All' Charter* (2nd edn., 1980, Europe CDDS (79)28-E). This basic document, defined by the European Ministers' Conference in 1975 in Brussels, provides a common framework for the actions of governments and other authorities. The sports policy of the Council is intended to promote sport in all its forms from physical activity carried out during spare time for recreation and relaxation purposes, to high level competitive sport. Largely inspired by the European Charter, Unesco published its *International charter of physical education and sport* in 1978 (Paris, Unesco).

The Council of Europe explores ways of protecting sport from international problems in order to preserve its traditional ethic of fair play and sportsmanship. Two important policy documents which are referred to as conventions are binding on those who signed the declaration.

● The *European Convention on spectator violence and misbehaviour at sports events and in particular of football matches* (1989), is now operational in many European countries. It provides for the maintenance of order within stadia and along access routes, separation of rival supporters, supervision of ticket sales, expulsion of trouble-makers, and restrictions on the sale of alcohol. The Convention also makes recommendations on security controls and stadia design.

● The *European Anti-doping Convention — explanatory report* (1989, Council of Europe, T-DO(89)2) contains measures to combat doping: the establishment of doping control laboratories of a high technical standard, promotion of preventive measures and educational campaigns, and penalties for athletes caught using drugs.

Both these Conventions were established after discussions with other international bodies such as the International Olympic Committee, the Union of European Football Associations, Unesco, and the General Association of International Sports Federations.

Finally, the *European Charter for 'Sport for All': disabled persons* (1987, Council of Europe) is a result of the Council's efforts to encourage the involvement of groups who traditionally take little or no part in sport. The Charter also contains interesting information for sport facility providers — the second part of the document contains guidelines to promote access to and use of recreation facilities by disabled persons.

Of relevance to all those responsible for making sports policy in both governmental and non-governmental organizations at a national level, are the reports of the European Ministers' Conferences for Sport. Six conferences have taken place between 1975 and 1989. The report of the *First Conference of European Ministers responsible for sport* (1975, Brussels, Clearing House) reflects the unity the European Ministers achieved concerning the 'Sport for All' Charter. Subsequent conferences have explored similar themes and discussed important issues of the day. At the Fourth conference in Malta in 1984, for the first time specific resolutions were made concerning doping (Resolution 1) and spectator violence (Resolution 6), and co-operation with sports authorities in individual countries has increased since then.

Since 1975, 43 resolutions have been adopted by the European Ministers' Conference for Sport. All the resolutions from the period between the Brussels Conference in 1975 and that held in Dublin in 1986 are collected in a special publication — *Texts approved by the European Ministers' Conference for Sport 1975–1986* (1986, Council of Europe MSL-5(86)B5-E). A number of background and working papers related to these Conferences are available through the Sport Section of the Council of Europe.

The sports research programme of the Council of Europe has held five seminars concerned with developing a fitness battery. Reports of the seminars were published. Later *Eurofit: handbook for the Eurofit test of physical fitness* (1988, Rome, CONI) was published, which offers a useful benchmark for schools, clubs and medical centres to assess physical fitness in children. Other publications specific to particular target groups include *Sport for the mentally handicapped* (1983, Council of Europe), *Sport for young school leavers*, (1979, Stockholm, Swedish Sports Federation), *Sport for immigrants* (1979, Lisbon, Instituto Nacional dos Desportos), the *Greater involvement of women in sport* (1981, Dublin, Department of Education) and *Sport for children* (1982, Oslo, Ministry for Cultural and Scientific Affairs).

There are a significant number of publications covering other aspects of sport and leisure. In addition the Council of Europe has published comparative and cross-national research. *Rationalising sports policies. Sport in its social context: international comparison* (1978, council of Europe, CDDS(78)10-E) attempted a statistical, cross-national comparison using non-standard data sources and brought an international dimension to the analysis of the problems of encouraging mass participation in sport. For researchers as well as policymakers, it offers a way of measuring participation but warns of the complexity of such international data and comparisons.

A useful publication of the 'Sport for All' Clearing House, is *Sport: acronyms* (1984). Two further reports published by the Committee on Culture and Education of the Parliamentary Assembly of the Council of Europe are *European sports co-operation* (1984, Council of Europe, Document 5270) and *Olympic Games and the outlook for their future* (1980, Document 4585). Both these reports are based on resolutions of the Parliamentary Assembly.

Finally, two major reference works for those interested in sport at international level are *Sports structures in the countries of the Council of Europe* (1987, Brussels, 'Sport for All' Clearing House) which describes the structures and organization of sport in 21 countries, and the *European inventory of sports information and documentation centres* (1990, Brussels, 'Sport for All' Clearing House). This latter publication lists the important sports information and documentation centres in 24 European countries, with information arranged under the headings: general background; information and documentation; publications and services; information retrieval and users; international exchange; data processing.

The *Sports Information Bulletin*, issued four times a year by the 'Sport for All' Clearing House, was originally distributed on cards but now appears in pamphlet form. It is based on national data sent to the Clearing House by the members of the Experts Committee for Sports Information. The contents cover sports legislation, participation and promotion, ethics, economic aspects of sport, sports facilities and the Council of Europe and sport. Individual issues cover specific areas. Recent examples are 'Sport for All' initiatives in 1989 in eight countries, doping substances and doping methods in 13 countries, and the Single European Act and Sport. Unfortunately, the lack of an index makes the bulletin difficult to search, especially retrospectively.

The European Sports Research Project Database aims to co-ordinate European sports research projects. In order to ensure consistency, a standardized European questionnaire was drafted to co-ordinate the input and output of the research databank. The database can be consulted by applying to The Sports Council in the UK and through the Bundesinstitut für Sportwissenschaft (BISp) in Cologne. The latter make a version available as SPOFOR on DIMDI. BISp also published the first printed volume in 1978, which covered the years 1976–77 and contained 738 research projects. More information on BISp is given on p. 273 The second register, which concentrated on sports medicine, was published in Brussels in 1982, and covered the years 1978-79. Three other volumes were planned — history, sports sciences and sports psychology but these never materialized. Although these documents are now out of date, they do offer the users some idea of the contents and working methods of this on-going sports research database.

A related document published by BISp in conjunction with the Council of Europe is the *Directory of sport research institutes* (1990). It lists the institutions and personnel involved in sports science in 11 countries of the Council of Europe.

EEC publications

Sport and leisure are not subjects which figure highly in the current European Community action programmes. The Treaty of Rome, which gave birth to the European Economic Community, makes no specific reference to sport or leisure; neither does the amending treaty, the Single European Act. However, harmonization plans currently afoot as part of the Single European Market programme may affect sport, since the Treaty of Rome refers to the 'free' movement of workers, which, according to the European Commission (the policy planning body) applies to professional athletes such as footballers as much as to any other category of workers.

At the moment, the only legislation being initiated relating to sport and recreation is that by the European Parliament's Committee on Youth, Culture, Education, Information and Sport, whose role is to look at legislative proposals as part of the Parliament's consultative role. This Committee also has the right to decide the topics it chooses to investigate and produces what are known as own initiatives reports. A number of these have emerged in the sport and leisure area. Once they are adopted by the Committee the report is presented by the rapporteur to a plenary session. If it is accepted, it becomes an opinion of the European Parliament and may include suggestions for action to be undertaken by the Commission, e.g. the 'Resolution on the violence at the Heysel Stadium on 29 May 1985'. This calls on the Commission to draft a directive aimed at improving the safety of players and spectators.

The text of these reports, together with any proposed or adopted EC legislation is published in the *Official Journal of the European Communities*. The contents of the *OJ* are held on the Community's legal database, CELEX. An easy way of accessing this database in through JUSTIS on CD-ROM (detailed in the section on online services, p. 268).

Finally, another body involved in sport in Europe and which is not very well known is the European Sports Conference. This body is a consultative conference made up of representatives of national sports organizations and governmental sports institutions from a number of European countries. It includes representatives from countries which are not directly associated with the Council of Europe. Its aim is to adhere to the principles laid down in the Final Act of the Helsinki Conference on Security and Cooperation in Europe. It holds a conference every two years, the proceedings of which are published, and appoints a number of working groups to look at specific topics. The *European sports conference charter* was published in 1989.

Abstracting and indexing journals

Of the major abstracting and indexing journals, *Sports Documentation Monthly Bulletin* indexes a large number of foreign-language journals and provides an English-language abstract for most foreign-language entries. It has a separate section on comparative sport. *SportSearch* also lists a small number of references under individual countries. *Leisure, Recreation and Tourism Abstracts* provides a good source for European leisure literature, in particular conference proceedings. More information on these and other abstracting services can be found in Chapter 1.

Online services

Basic guides to online services should be consulted for the latest information regarding databases. Some guides are listed in Chapter 1 but readers should also consult T. Hanson's *Directory of European Community and related databases* (1991, European Information Association). Another directory of particular use is *Euronet Diane, directory of databases and databanks*. This directory is extracted from the DIANEGUIDE database on ECHO, the European Community Host Organization, the most up-to-date version being available online from ECHO. The printed directory contains seven references under the subject heading sport, but readers should note that not all the sport-related databases are actually listed in the index under this category.

The European Sports Research Project Database has already been mentioned in the section on the Council of Europe. Of the bibliographic databases, the SPORT database contains 20% non-English language material a large proportion of which is European, since some European countries contribute their national data to the database. SPORT DISCUS the CD-ROM version of the database yielded over 1220 occurrences of the word 'Europe' in 871 records when the June 1990 disc was searched, but there are over 2000 records in the database indexed under 'European'. In addition there are many records indexed under the individual European countries. LRTA, the online version of *Leisure,*

Recreation and Tourism Abstracts, and ABI/Inform are also useful sources. Two European databases specific to sport and leisure, which are accessed internationally — SPOLIT (Germany) and HERACLES (France) — are covered in more detail in the sections on individual countries, as are the sport-related databases in the Spanish language.

Two important databases available on CD-ROM are UKOP and JUSTIS.

- UKOP. This is particularly useful because, besides containing all UK official publications since 1980, regardless of publishing body, it also contains the publications of 12 major international organizations distributed in the UK by HMSO, one of which is the Council of Europe. Access to records is by personal and corporate author, title, series, publication year, session year, keyword, ISBN and price. A search of the disc in January 1991 found 757 references to sport and 162 to leisure when both words were used as a keyword, but only four references when Sport and Europe were used together (see Figure 14.1 for a sample UKOP record).

- The JUSTIS CD-ROM is marketed in the UK by Context and contains the contents of CELEX (online legal database of the EEC), the official database of European law. It is full text from 1952, and contains law reports, indexes, newsletters and encyclopaedias and provides a European Community law file. It is particularly useful for sport, and a search carried out in January 1991 revealed 125 references to sport and 31 to leisure, and 40 when Sport and Europe were combined, all from the *Official Journal* (see Figure 14.2).

General information sources

Of some limited use is the *International list of information sources in the field of physical education and sport 1975–1987*, published by the International Association for Sports Information in 1988. This co-operative list was produced by a number of mainly European countries, and lists the major bibliographies published in each country during the period concerned. Unfortunately, its unselective approach, lack of English abstracts and poor indexing make it of limited value. The *List* can be obtained from the IASI Secretary, Albert Remans, at the Clearing House, Espace du Vignot-Sept Septembre, Boulevard Leopold II 44 1080 Brussels, Belgium.

For anyone wishing to investigate 'Sport for All' programmes, *'Sport for All' programmes throughout the world*, a report prepared by Peter McIntosh for the International Council of Sport and Physical Education

Council of Europe
Anti-doping Convention/Council of Europe. – Strasbourg:
  Council of Europe: HMSO [distributor], 1989. – Cover
  sub-title: Strasbourg, 16.11.1989'. – Doping in sport. –
  This treaty has been signed by the UK government. – Parallel
  texts in English and French. – Parallel title: Convention
  contre le dopage. – 19p.; 29 cm. – European treaty series /
  Council of Europe 135. – ISBN 92 8711 782 9: 2.70 (hard
  copy)

Figure 14.1   Record from UKOP

(1980), although now out of date, provides information on national
projects in a number of European countries.

As in many other areas, up-to-date research registers are very hard to
come by. The shortcomings of the European Sports Research Project
Database have already been covered in the section on the Council of
Europe. *Dissertation Abstracts International, series C* 'Worldwide'
covers some European universities, but the coverage of sport is
minimal.

There are a number of multi-lingual dictionaries which might be of
use when using non-English language material, e.g. two by E. Beyer
(ed.) *Wörterbuch der Sportwissenschaft [Dictionary of sport science]*
(1987), and *Trilingual dictionary of sport science* (1979), both
published by Hoffmann Verlag.

International directory of sport organizations (1984, IASI) edited by
R. Timmer and J. Recla, although out of date, gives a useful overview.
It is published by an international organization which draws a large
number of its members from European countries — the International
Association for Sports Information (IASI). IASI's other publications
include a *bulletin*, the *International list of information sources in the
field of physical education and sport 1975–1987* (1988) which has been
cited above, and a number of international bibliographies which cite
European references, e.g. *Environmental impact of sport and
recreation*, edited by M. Shoebridge and published by the Sports
Documentation Centre, University of Birmingham in 1989.

Individual countries

Denmark

A number of Scandinavian countries have well-developed sports

JUSTIS – CELEX – Official Legal Database of the European Communities
DOCNUM   : 585lp0408   (The whole document)
PUBREF   : Official Journal no C175, 15/07/85 p. 0211

TITLE
Resolution on the violence at the football match in brussels on 29 May 1985

DOCNUM	: 585lp0408
AUTHOR	: European parliament; *; cassanmagnago-cerretti; brok; on behalf of the european people's party (79); larive-groenendaal; arndt; on behalf of the socialist group (53); plumb; on behalf of the european democratic group (79); papapietro; on behalf of the communist and allies group (73);
FORM	: Own-initiative resolution
TYPDOC	: 5; Preparatory Documents; 1985; ip
PUBREF	: Official Journal no. C 175, 15/07/85 p. 0211
DESCRIPT	: Sport violence belgium information of the public proposal People's europe education public hearing safety standard
ABSTRACT	: ++++ The ep called on the commision to propose urgently a directive, so that sporting events could take place in conditions which ensured personal safety for both players and spectators. It expected that the milan summit would recognize the need for common action in sporting matters, especially in the struggle against violence.
PUB	: 1985/07/15
DOC	: 1985/06/13;
VOTE	: 1985/06/13;
DESPATCH	; 1985/06/14;
DEBATE	: 1985/06/13;
ADDRESS	: Member states – heads of state or government; council; commision; council of europe; international and european football federations;
LEGISLA	: Second legislature;
DATES	: Of document . . . . : 13/06/1985; date of vote of vote . . . . : 13/06/1985 of transmission . . . . : 14/06/1985 of debate . . . . : 13/06/1985

Figure 14.2   Sample record from JUSTIS

information services. The sports librarians in these countries co-operate through NORSIB.

Odense University Library has a good collection on sport-related subjects and contributes to the SPORT database. The main sport library is the Biblioteket Danmarks Højskole for Legemsovelser (Library of the Danish Institute of Physical Education), which has a large collection of books and audio-visual material.

Finland

Sport plays an important part in the consciousness of the Finnish nation. The Finnish Sports Act, passed in 1980, lays down that the state and local authorities are primarily responsible for granting financial aid and providing sports facilities for physical activities. A useful introductory text is *Sports and physical education in Finland* (1987), published by the Government Printing Centre and the Finnish Society for Research in Sport and Physical Education. There is also a new English-language journal, *Motion: Sport in Finland*, published bi-monthly by the Finnish Society for Research in Sport and Physical Education. The major collections and information services are located at the University of Jyväskylä and the Sport Library of Finland.

The University of Jyväskylä Library has the largest sports science collection in Finland, having been mandated as the central library for physical education since 1977. Its role is to provide information about Finnish and foreign literature to both Finnish researchers and information services outside Finland. Also located at Jyväskylä is the Research Center for Physical Culture and Health Information Service (LIKES). Working in close co-operation with the University Library, the Centre services the Foundation for the Promotion of Physical Culture and Health, and provides a national and international enquiry service.

The Sport Library of Finland is located in the Olympic Stadium in Helsinki and forms part of the Foundation of the Sport Museum of Finland. The Foundation consists of the Library, Archives and Museum, thus providing a comprehensive sports information service in one building. The library is open to the public, lends its books and journals and offers an external enquiry service. Publications include *Sportenta* (see below), and a list of periodicals held in the Sport Library and the Finnish Sports Institute libraries. Since one of their client groups is journalists, the Library also provides a special service concerning major sports events to the sports media.

There are three major abstracting journals published in Finland, two in Finnish and one in English. *Suomen liikunta — ja urheilukirjallisuus [Finnish literature on physical education and sport]* has been published annually since 1983 by the University of Jyväsyalä Library. It covers material concerned with sport, physical education and public health published in Finland, and is mainly Finnish language. It is available online as FINSPORT (see below), a sub-database of KATI.

Current research in sports sciences in Finland: abstracts (1982 – published in Helsinki by the Finnish Society for the Research in Sport and Physical Education is in English. This bi-annual publication contains abstracts of selected current research projects in Finnish sport sciences and physical education which were in progress or completed during the relevant years.

Sportenta [*Current sport literature*] began publication in 1986 and is produced by the Sport Library of Finland. It is multi-lingual and indexes both Finnish and foreign-language periodicals.

There is a national online database called FINSPORT which contains all monographs, research reports, periodical articles and theses in the Finnish language and which relate to sport, physical education and public health. FINSPORT is a sub-database of KATI which is hosted by the Finnish State Computer Centre. It can be accessed outside Finland, and searches can be carried out on request by most Finnish libraries, including all the information services mentioned in this section.

The Foundation of the Sport Museum of Finland is building up a database of the library's material and, in co-operation with the Finnish State Computer Centre, is attempting to develop a database of the eight best competitors from the track and field events in the Olympic Games, World Championships and European Championships.

There are no local viewdata services in Finland, but the marketing arm of the Central Sports Federation offers, a system called Telesport via a network owned by the Finnish Central Post Office. Further printed information about leisure facilities, etc. is provided at a local level by the municipal sports committees.

France

The major library and information service for sport in France is provided by the Documentation Service of the Institut National du Sport et de l'Éducation Physique (INSEP), in Paris. The Library has a large collection of books, periodicals and audio-visual material, offers a translation service, publishes an indexing journal and contributes to HERACLES, the French national sport database.

HERACLES is available commercially on l'Européene de données via the Minitel system. Co-ordinated by INSEP it is produced by Sportdoc, a co-operative of a number of French sports libraries. HERACLES contains over 45 000 references to both scientific and practical source material, some with abstracts. *Mensuel Signaletique* is the printed version of the online service. All entries are in the French language, arranged in subject order. There is a subject index, a list of forthcoming conferences and a list of books received in the INSEP library. INSEP can provide photocopies of references included in *Mensuel Signaletique*.

Germany

The Federal Republic of Germany and the German Democratic

Republic both had well established sports information networks before unification in October 1990 and there was considerable co-operation between the various institutions. It is difficult to be certain if all the institutions and publications that existed before unification will continue, but some rationalization will occur.

There are three major sports information services in Germany.

- The Zentral bibliothek der Sportwissenschaften is the Library of the Deutschen Sporthochschule (German Sports Academy) at Carl-Diem-Weg 6, 5000 Köln 41. Founded in 1947, it houses over 250 000 volumes, over 1400 periodicals, theses, films and videos. It has a good collection of bibliographies and maintains a German press-cuttings service.
- The 'Documentation and Information' Department of the Bundesinstitut für Sportwissenschaft (BISp) (Federal Institute of Sports Sciences), is also located in Köln, at Carl-Diem-Weg 4, 5000 Köln 41, and has a small library of approximately 24 000 books and 450 periodicals. The main emphasis at BISp is on the dissemination of information via the Institute's databases, publications and enquiry service.
- The Zentralbibliothek für Körperkultur und Sport an der Deutschen Hochschule für Körperkultur (German Academy for Physical Culture) in Leipzig. Established in 1950, the library co-operated with the Zentrum für Wissenschaftsinformation Körperkultur und Sport (Centre for Scientific Information, Physical Culture and Sport). The Academy was closed in 1990 and the operation moved to Leipzig University.

There are two German-language indexing services. *Körperkultur und sport: überblicksinformation Sportwissenschäftliche Beitragen, aus der Deutschen Demokratischen Republik*, has been produced by the Zentrum für Wissenschafts- information, Körperkultur und Sport im Forschungsinstitüt für Körperkultur und Sport in Leipzig for a number of years and contains approximately 400 references which correspond to the SPOWIS database. It is not clear what the future of this publication will be.

Sportdokumentation, published by the Fedcral Institute of Sport Science (BISp) every three months updates the SPOLIT database in printed form. Each issue contains more than 1000 references and has a detailed index.

Many individual journals cover all aspects of sport, although not so many relate to leisure. Not all the journals are of the same quality. Some major international titles are also published in Germany, e.g. *International Journal of Sports Medicine* and the *International Review for the Sociology of Sport*. Journals historically published in the GDR include *Theorie und Praxis der Körperkultur*, which contained theoretical and practical information and ceased publication in 1990, *Medizin und Sport* aimed at physicians, and *Körpererziehung*, which is aimed at physical education teachers. *Wissenschäftliche Zeitschrift der DHfK* has been a vehicle for universities to publish their academic scientific papers. Journals originating from the FRG include *Leistungssport, Sportpädagogik, and Sportunterricht* .

The main online service in the German language is the SPOLIT database provided by BISp and hosted by DIMDI. The database, with over 55 000 references, all with abstracts, covers a wide range of material with a considerable amount of information in English (the ratio between German and foreign-language material being 40:60). A considerable amount of the literature on SPOLIT also appears in the Canadian SPORT database because BISp contributed to the SPORT database until Autumn 1989. SPOLIT is now available on CD-ROM, published by the Ingrid Czwalina Publishing House. It is updated on an annual basis. The other databases maintained by BISp on DIMDI are SPOFOR (European Sports Research Projects), which provides up-to-date information about sports science projects in what was formerly the FRG, Austria and Switzerland, and SPOMED (medical data of top athletes). The Zentrum für Wissenschaftsinformation in Leipzig also has a database with about 120 000 references, without abstracts, but it is not available online.

A number of lists of audio-visual material relating to sport exist. These include *Audiovisuelle Medien Sport*, published by the Institut für Film und Bild in Wissenschaft und Unterricht. Hoffmann publishes *Arbeitsstreifen und Tonfilme* which lists films and videos. Both list videos in subject order.

To find out more information about sports organizations, readers should consult the following lists and yearbooks which are updated periodically: *Das Sportmanagement Taschenbuch* (Munster: Philippka); *Deutscher Sportbund: Jahrbuch des Sports.* (Niedernhausen: Schors); H. Haag and K. Hein *Informationswege zur Theorie und Praxis des Sports* (Schornddorf: Hoffmann); and *Taschenbuch des öffentlichen Lebens* (Bonn: Festlandverlag).

Italy

The structure of sport in Italy is governed by Comitato Olimpico Nazionale Italiano (the Italian National Olympic Committee, CONI) and the various sports federations of which there are 39, all recognized by CONI. CONI is responsible to the Ministry of Tourism and plays an important role in information provision in Italy through its various departments.

The Sport Documentation Centre, housed at the Scuola dello Sport (School of Sport), is located at the Onesti Sport Centre, Via dei Campi Sportivi 48, 00197 Rome. The Centre issues an abstracting journal on an irregular basis and, since 1990, has been contributing Italian language material to the SPORT database in Canada.

The National Sport Library is another section of the Scuola dello Sport. It has over 25 000 books and periodicals. there are associated libraries in Annone (Veneto) and Siracusa (Sicily). Another source of information is the Documentation and infomation division of CONI, which is particularly concerned with sport policy. Requests for information in this area should be directed to the Divisione Documentazione e informazione, located at CONI's headquaters, Foro Italico, 00194 Rome. There are a number of major international journals published in English, with a tendency towards the sports sciences, e.g. the *International Journal of Sport Psychology, International Journal of Sports Cardiology, International Journal of Sports Traumatology, Journal of Sports Medicine and Physical Fitness* and *Medicina dello Sport* (in Italian, with English abstracts). There are a number of useful titles in Italian concerned with coaching individual sports. Some English abstracts are found in *Athleticastudi, New Studies in Athletics* and *Scuola dello Sport/Rivista di Cultura Sportiva*.

There are no online databases that cover facilities. Information about sports or recreational facilities can be requested (preferably in Italian), directly from the CONI regional delegations or from CONI provincial committees. For the addresses and telephone numbers of regional delegations contact CONI's headquarters at the Foro Italico.

Norway

The state supports and encourages sport in Norway. The Norwegian University of Sport and Physical Education, supported by the Ministry of Cultural and Scientific Affairs, plays a major role in providing sports information through its library, the Norges Idrettshogskole Biblioteket (NIH). The Library has a large collection of books, periodicals and audio-visual material and provides a very effective enquiry service which includes answering requests from outside Norway.

Although there is no national sport database, there are two general databases, UBO:BOK which began in 1983 and contains monograph literature, and BIBSYS, a union database of a number of universities and colleges. Started in 1980, it contains Norwegian and international material. More specific to sport the NIH has been developing an in-house database called NIHBOK since 1986. It contains references to Norwegian and international books and periodical articles. Like many European countries, there is little attention paid to providing leisure information and consequently there are no local viewdata services giving information about facilities and clubs.

There are two basic indexing journals, both published by the NIH. *Litt om litt fra biblioteket* [NIH] [*Current literature from the library at the Norwegian University of Sport and Physical Education*] (1970–). This multi-lingual indexing journal is arranged in subject order, contains no abstracts or index and is more useful for Norwegian speakers. *Norsk idretslitteratur* [*Norwegian literature on physical education*] (1971–) is an annual bibliography which deals exclusively with works by Norwegian authors, whether living in Norway or abroad. There are a large number of journals published in Norwegian mostly concerned with individual sports. NIH occasionally publish a list of their current holdings.

Poland

The main information service in Poland is located at the Centrum Informacji Naukowej at the Akademia Wychowania Fizycznego 01-813 Warszawa ul Marymoncha 31. There are other libraries attached to various academies throughout the country.

Poland does not publish any abstracting services or support a national database, but there are a number of scientific journals which appear rather sporadically. These include *Wychowanie Fizyczne i Sport* (concerned with physical education and sport) and *Sport Wyczynowy* both in Polish and *Scientific yearbook: studies in the theory of physical education*. The latter, which appears in English, is not as well established as the other titles.

Spain

Administration of sport in Spain has been decentralized over the last decade. This has led to the emergence of new information centres to join those already in existence. Two of the more well-established libraries are located in Madrid – the Instituto Nacional de Educación Física (National Institute for Physical Education) and the Instituto de Ciencias de la Educación Física y el Deporte (the Higher Sports Council). Both have library collections of monographs, periodicals, audio-visual material and have international links. Two new regional centres have emerged. The International Sports University of Andalusia at Malaga (Unisport Andalucia) was formed in 1984 and is developing a library and enquiry and translation service. The Centre publishes a current contents-type bulletin. Barcelona, venue for the 1992 Olympic Games, has established the Biblioteca de L'Esport (Sports Library of Barcelona). Set up in 1986, it houses books, periodicals, theses, posters and audio-visual material and is developing a publications programme.

A number of online databases are available, but not commercially. They can be accessed via PIC (Puntos de Información Cultural) through the Ministerio de Cultura. The list includes: FUTB-FÚTBOL INTERNACIONAL which describes over 700 soccer matches from Spanish national and international matches; DESP, PRIMEROS PUESTOS DEL DEPORTE ESPAÑOL – which provides information about the position of the teams, etc. in national competitions; OLIM, *OLYPIADAS* – results and classifications of competitions and trials in the modern Olympics.

Sweden

Sport in Sweden is governed by the Swedish Sports Confederation, a body that allocates grants from the Ministry of Agriculture to special federations for information, education and development. The sports information network is not very well developed and attracts little public funding. The major sports libraries are the Biblioteket vid Gymnastik-och idrottshögskolan (University College of Physical Education), postal address Box 5626 114 86 Stockholm, Sweden. The library was established in the nineteenth century and contains over 40 000 books. The Biblioteket vid Sveriges Riksidrottsforbund (Library of the Swedish Sports Confederation) located at Idrottens Hus, 123 87 Farsta, Stockholm, is much smaller. There is a certain amount of co-operation between these two libraries. One project involves establishing a local database, using CDS-ISIS, called IDROTT which will contain material (including audio-visual) held in the two libraries. This will provide a useful resource since there is no specific online database for sport and recreation. A general database, LIBRIS contains references to Swedish monographs, theses and research reports since 1968. The Library of the University of Orebro has a substantial collection of books on physical education.

No printed abstracting or indexing journals are published in Sweden. For information about Swedish sports research readers should consult *Sport research abstracts 1981–1986* (1986) published by the Swedish Sports Research Council and updated irregularly.

Yugoslavia

The major information and research centre for sport and recreation in Yugoslavia is located at the Sport Indok Centar, Kneza Viseslava 72, 11030 Belgrade. Its function is to provide a national and international information service. There are a number of other libraries in major towns which also specialize in sport.

Yugoslavia has an indexing journal, *Biblografija fizicke kultura* which is published in Serbo-Croatian, with English titles and covers professional and scientific Yugoslav literature in physical culture. There are a number of sports periodical titles, some of which have English translations. Mainly concerned with sports sciences and coaching, they include *Fizicka kultura, Kineziologija, Telesna kultura* and *Trener*.

CHAPTER FIFTEEN

North American information sources

B. MILLMAN AND L. WHEELER

Introduction

North American sources for information on sport and leisure are numerous, and available in a wide variety of forms. Every level of government, every occupation involved with sport or leisure, and each individual sport or leisure activity interest group has its own organization, journal or newsletter, or collection of documents to facilitate its mandate. Thus, only general sources which are influential or unique are included, and sport-specific sources are excluded from consideration.

Several areas of particular information strength in Canada and the USA should be noted. Most important are the North American-produced databases and online services which facilitate access to sport and leisure literature and which form the core resource of this type for researchers worldwide. Another area of strength lies in the plethora of sport- and leisure-related organizations which offer valuable information networks for their members. Some have been mentioned throughout the chapter, particularly in the section 'Major Serial Titles', but because of their number, have not been listed in a separate section.

Sport, rather than leisure, seems to be the predominant focus in North America, and the number of information sources available for each reflects this emphasis. A quick glance through the chapter indicates that traditional reference works, such as encyclopedias and dictionaries (at least for general coverage of sport and leisure) are not a prolific information source in North America, while journals abound.

Major libraries and information centres

Canada

SPORT INFORMATION RESOURCE CENTRE (SIRC), SUITE 107, SUITE 204,
1600 JAMES NAISMITH DRIVE, GLOUCESTER, ONTARIO, K1B 5N4

The Sport Information Resource Centre (SIRC) is a world leader in the
identification, collection and distribution of information on sport,
coaching, physical education, physical fitness, and sports medicine.
Established in 1973 by the Coaching Association of Canada, SIRC was
incorporated as a non-profit organization in 1985. The resource
collection of SIRC includes more than 29 000 books, subscriptions to
over 1200 periodicals as well as over 9000 microforms including copies
of materials identified by the International Institute for Sport and
Human Performance, and the College of Human Development and
Performance at the University of Oregon. SIRC produces a wide variety
of information products, of which the foremost in importance is the
bibliographic SPORT Database.

SIRLS (SPECIALIZED INFORMATION RETRIEVAL AND LIBRARY
SERVICES), UNIVERSITY OF WATERLOO, WATERLOO, ONTARIO, N2L 3G1

SIRLS is known internationally for its SPORT & LEISURE database and
document collection, which collects research literature covering the
social science subject areas of sport, leisure and recreation (including
play, games and dance). The bibliographic database has approximately
18 500 abstracted citations. SIRLS ceased operation in early 1991. In
June 1991, SIRC acquired both the SPORT & LEISURE database and the
SIRLS document collection. SIRC plans to incorporate the SIRLS
database in the SPORT database.

LEISURE STUDIES DATA BANK, FACULTY OF HUMAN KINETICS AND
LEISURE STUDIES, UNIVERSITY OF WATERLOO, WATERLOO, ONTARIO,
N2L 3G1

Founded in 1972, the Leisure Studies Data Bank (LSDB) maintains
over 120 data sets of leisure, tourism, sport, fitness, outdoor recreation
time use and related topics. While most of the files are national or
provincial in scope, international surveys are also housed. The datafiles
are stored on magnetic computer tape in the form of raw data, converted
data, or as SPSS (Statistical Package for the Social Sciences) system
files. Staff at LSDB provide results of statistical analyses of the data
sets, or can download subsets of large files onto diskettes for use at

distant sites. Some data sets can be purchased also. A descriptive catalogue of the data sets held at LSDB is available free of charge.

JOHN W. DAVIES LIBRARY – CANADA'S SPORTS HALL OF FAME,
EXHIBITION PLACE, TORONTO, ONTARIO, M6K 3C3

This specialized library contains books, papers and newspaper clipping files on Canada's top athletes, members of the Sports Hall of Fame (both athletes and builders of sports), and sport-specific events. Of interest are the Olympic Collection, which dates from 1928, Commonwealth Games and Pan American Games materials, and archival material on particular Canadian athletes.

RECREATION RESOURCE CENTRE OF NOVA SCOTIA, ACADIA
UNIVERSITY, WOLFVILLE, NOVA SCOTIA, B0P 1X0

Formerly known as the Centre of Leisure Studies, this library houses up to approximately 40 000 documents of all types relating to sport, leisure, recreation and physical activity, mostly Canadian in emphasis. Forty-four general subject headings and approximately 600 sub-headings provide subject access. Documents tend to support administrative and leadership programmes. Photocopies of documents can be obtained, and online access to external users is expected in the next year. The quarterly *Bulletin* lists current holdings, and is available to anyone on the Centre's mailing list.

ATHLETE INFORMATION BUREAU (AIB), SUITE 204, 1600 JAMES NAISMITH
DRIVE, GLOUCESTER, ONTARIO, K1B 5N4

Created in 1975, the AIB's prime mandate is to promote Canada's high-performance amateur athletes and programmes by providing publications, comprehensive data on carded and national team athletes, overseas coverage of events featuring Canadian athletes, photographs and transparencies to serve the media as well as Canadian national sport organizations. The AIB database includes biographical files, competitive histories and medal-winning achievements of Canada's national team athletes and coaches in 39 sports. Written, telephone, or in-person requests for database printouts on particular athletes, or for copies of photographs are accepted by the AIB.

CANADIAN OLYMPIC ASSOCIATION LIBRARY/INFORMATION SERVICES
CENTRE, OLYMPIC HOUSE CITÉ DU HAVRE, MONTRÉAL, QUÉBEC, H3C 3E4

The Canadian Olympic Association Library specializes in collecting and disseminating information with an international focus on the

Olympic and Pan American Games, and on amateur sport in Canada. The library contains approximately 1200 items which can be used by the public in person, or by written, telephone, or Fax request.

USA

CENTER FOR THE STUDY OF SPORT IN SOCIETY RESOURCE CENTER, NORTHEASTERN UNIVERSITY, 360 HUNTINGTON AVENUE, BOSTON, MASSACHUSETTS, 02115

The Center for the Study of Sport in Society (CSSS), primarily concerned with educating athletes for a meaningful life after retirement from sports, has set up a number of programmes (the University Degree Completion Program, and The School Outreach Program), in conjunction with the university, to further this goal. The Resource Center at CSSS concentrates its efforts on culling 25 major newspapers from across the USA for articles dealing with sport and athletes in society. From this information base, Resource Center staff prepare packets of information on particular topics (e.g. drugs, discrimination), available for purchase to students at all levels, teachers, coaches, parents, and others involved in the administration of sport programmes.

MICROFORM PUBLICATIONS – COLLEGE OF HUMAN DEVELOPMENT AND PERFORMANCE, UNIVERSITY OF OREGON, 1479 MOSS STREET, EUGENE, OREGON, 97403

Microform Publications is a unique facility which identifies, collects and prepares microfiche copies of North American Doctoral dissertations and Master's theses. This collection of more than 7000 microforms covers over 40 years of graduate research in the subject areas of health, physical education, recreation, sport sciences and dance. The service also provides microfiche copies of some scholarly books and journals. A listing of current additions can be found in the *Microform Publications Supplement*, published twice a year. The Supplement is cumulated at periodic intervals to form the *Health, Physical Education and Recreation Microform Publications Bulletin*. The SPORT database provides a comprehensive online index to this unique collection.

PAUL ZIFFREN SPORT RESOURCE CENTER, AMATEUR ATHLETIC FOUNDATION OF LOS ANGELES, 2141 WEST ADAMS BOULEVARD, LOS ANGELES, CALIFORNIA, 90018

The Sport Resource Center of the Amateur Athletic Foundation of Los

Angeles is available to users worldwide, primarily through telephone and written requests. The Center collects material on all sports, usually of practical value to coaches and athletes, or of historical or sociological import. The main focus of the collection is material on the Olympic Games (for example, all the official reports of the Olympiades from 1896 forward, as well as the Avery Brundage Collection, a compilation of papers and correspondence over more than 60 years.) Holdings include 250 popular and scholarly journal subscriptions, 1000 videos of an historical and instructional nature, 40 000 black-and-white photographs (primarily from baseball, football and basketball), 70 000 programmes and media guides from sports events, up to 20 000 volumes, and from 1990, 5000 colour slides per year of major sport events and personalities with a North American focus.

Databases and online services

The SPORT database, produced by the Sport Information Resource Centre (SIRC), Ottawa, is one of the most important sources for the world's practical and research literature dealing with all aspects of sport and fitness. Recognized by the International Association for Sports Information (IASI) and by the International Council for Sport Science and Physical Education (ICSSPE) as the international database for sport, this database indexes documentation for such topics as biomechanics, coaching, exercise physiology, motor learning, physical education, physical fitness, sport and special groups, social science and sport, sport psychology, sports medicine and training. At present, the SPORT database contains over 270 000 bibliographic references, some with abstracts, to magazine and journal articles, books, theses, conference proceedings and other published research. Each indexed document has been assigned a level of research difficulty (B – basic; I – intermediate; A – advanced). Material published since 1975 is covered, plus the University of Oregon theses collection dating from 1949. Updated monthly, the SPORT database is currently accessible online on BRS, DataStar, CAN/OLE and Dialog. It is also available on CD-ROM as the SPORT DISCUS from SilverPlatter, and is updated semi-annually. SIRC publishes two search aids: the *SPORT thesaurus* and the *SPORT database user aid*.

The SPORT & LEISURE database, produced by SIRLS, University of Waterloo, originated in 1970, and contains approximately 18 500 abstracted references. SIRLS ceased operation in early 1991. SIRC, which acquired both the database and document collections, plans to make the SPORT & LEISURE database available as a distinct file on the SPORT DISCUS, the CD-ROM version of the SPORT database, by January

1992. Records from the SPORT & LEISURE database will be available through the online version of the SPORT database in 1992.

COMPUTER SPORTS WORLD, produced by The Chronicle Publishing Company, provides online access to game results and related statistics for American professional sports (baseball, basketball, football and hockey), as well as race results and handicapping information for thoroughbred racing.

There are a multitude of North American-produced databases which can be useful in tracking down sport- and recreation-related material in non-sport publications. These databases include COMPENDEX (engineering), ERIC (education), DISSERTATION ABSTRACTS ONLINE (American theses), HISTORICAL ABSTRACTS, MAGAZINE INDEX, MEDLINE and related databases on the MEDLARS network, the MERCK INDEX (chemical and drug information), PSYCINFO (psychology) and SOCIAL SCISEARCH (social science). Management-related databases such as ABI/INFORM, MANAGEMENT CONTENTS and CBCA (Canadian Business and Current Affairs) can also prove useful for certain topics. Carswell's INDEX TO CANADIAN LEGAL LITERATURE ONLINE and LEGAL RESOURCE INDEX provide a valuable online index to legal information, some of which is sport-related. Directory-type databases such as DAC (Directory of Associations in Canada), ENCYCLOPEDIA OF ASSOCIATIONS and PETERSON'S COLLEGE DATABASE can also be helpful. The catalogues of the Library of Congress, the National Library of Canada and the Canada Institute for Scientific and Technical Information are also available online and can be of some assistance. A valuable information source for rehabilitation products and technical aids for the disabled is ABLEDATA, produced by the National Institute on Disability and Rehabilitation Research.

Newspapers online

Another, often overlooked, resource for sport or leisure information (particularly biographical, historical or political) is newspapers, and by far the most efficient method of finding specific information is online searching.

CANADA

In Canada, the major online newspaper coverage is on INFOGLOBE, which is produced by *The Globe and Mail* newspaper in Toronto, and by the online services of INFOMART (Toronto), which gives access to the Southam newspapers including *The Toronto Star, The Montreal Gazette, The Calgary Herald, The Edmonton Journal, The Ottawa Citizen* and *The Vancouver Sun.* Online newspapers are usually searchable by keyword and free text, and are usually updated daily.

USA

In the USA, THE NEW YORK TIMES online database makes the entire *New York Times* newspaper searchable online, while *NEXIS* has more than 100 newspapers, magazines, wire services, newsletters and trade journals searchable online, and NATIONAL NEWSPAPERS INDEX carries the index to *The New York Times, The Wall Street Journal, The Christian Science Monitor, The Washington Post* and *The Los Angeles Times.* Of special interest is the DOW JONES NEWS/RETRIEVAL SPORTS REPORT database which carries current sports news stories, statistics and scores of most professional, college and amateur sports.

Abstracting and indexing journals

Sport and Leisure: A Journal of Social Science Abstracts was the only abstracting service in North America which deals exclusively with the social science subject areas of sport, leisure, physical education, and recreation, and in particular, with the sociological, psychological, historical, philosophical, economical, anthropological, and political aspects of these disciplines. The journal was published three times per year by the University of Waterloo Press but has now ceased publication.

The quarterly *Physical education index* began in 1978 and is published by BenOak Publishing Company (Missouri). It scans periodical literature from the USA (with some coverage of foreign periodicals), for the subject areas of dance, health, physical education, physical therapy, recreation, sports and sports medicine. Arranged by subject, it provides full bibliographic information for each item. While periodical titles are abbreviated in the references, a separate section, 'Abbreviations of Periodicals Indexed', provides the full journal title and is complemented by another section listing journal addresses. *The Physical Education Index* has annual cumulations and provides a section for book reviews.

Published by SIRC, *SportSearch* is a current-awareness index covering an extensive range of sport- and fitness-related documentation. *SportSearch* continues SIRC's print indexing service which first started in 1974 as *Sport Articles 1974–1977,* then became the *Sport and Recreation Index (1978–1984),* and finally became the *Sport and Fitness Index (1984–1985).* Published ten times a year, *SportSearch* provides broad subject access to English- and French-language periodical literature, books and chapters, conference proceedings and theses. A guide to forthcoming conferences as well as a listing of selected journal publishers and addresses is included. Although *SportSearch* is not cumulated in print form, it can be cumulated by searching the SPORT database.

The American Alliance for Health, Physical Education, Recreation, and Dance (Virginia), publishes an annual guide entitled, *Completed Research in Health, Physical Education, Recreation, and Dance*, which includes international sources. The emphasis is on American theses, including those from Simon Fraser University and the University of British Columbia in Canada, which have been completed during the previous year. Preceded by a basic subject index, each bibliographic reference is accompanied by an abstract. A listing of reporting colleges and universities can be found at the end of each issue.

Current Contents – Social and Behavioral Sciences (CCSBS), and *Current Contents – Life Sciences (CCLS)* are published by the Institute for Scientific Information, Philadelphia, Pennsylvania, and present the contents pages of over 1340 of the world's most important journals in the social and behavioral sciences, and over 1180 journals in the life sciences. Both *CCSBS* and *CCLS* are weekly indexing services and both contain the following weekly features: Current Book Contents, Title Word Index, Author Index and Address Directory, and Publishers' Address Directory.

CCSBS contains 100–150 journal contents pages weekly: *CCLS* contains 150–250, also weekly. While the journals covered are primarily of a research nature, and do not cover all of the major journals dealing with sport of leisure (only nine form the list of journals evaluated in this chapter), *Current Contents* alerts the researcher to articles in journals often overlooked as sources for sport and leisure information. Because sport and leisure literature is sometimes difficult to pinpoint by the title keywords, a spot check of particular journals or a quick browsing of the entire issue are good methods of searching these resources.

The new online version of *Current Contents – Life Sciences* provides weekly diskettes which contain the same bibliographic information that is available in the print version. Searching is by keyword in the title, by author, or by browsing particular subject disciplines or journal contents. Although a subscription to this online version is costly (U.S. $495 in 1990), search time is considerably faster, and the diskette format takes considerably less space to store.

Three other useful North American abstracting services are *Sociological Abstracts, Psychological Abstracts* and *Index Medicus. Sociological Abstracts* is published by Sociological Abstracts Inc. (California) and is co-sponsored by the International Sociological Association. There are five issues per year, plus a cumulative index. Abstracts are arranged alphabetically within each subject category; there are 33 main subject categories and numerous sub-categories. Sport and leisure materials are found primarily under the main heading 'Mass Phenomena', and the sub-headings, 'Sociology of sports', and 'Sociology of leisure/tourism'. Access is by author, subject and source indexes. *Sociological Abstracts* is also available in an online version through the vendors BRS, Dialog and DataStar, and a CD-ROM version can also be obtained.

Psychological Abstracts is published monthly by the American Psychological Association (Arlington, Virginia). Of the 17 subject sections, one is devoted to 'Sport psychology and leisure'. Abstracts are arranged alphabetically by first author within the subject sections. Subject index terms are taken from the *Thesaurus of psychological index terms* (1988). The online version, PSYCINFO (available through Dialog, BRS, Orbit, DataStar and DIMDI), includes references to theses and dissertations not found in the print version. A CD-ROM version, called PSYCLIT, can also be purchased through subscription.

Index Medicus, produced by the National Library of Medicine (Bethesda, Maryland) and the U.S. Department of Health and Human Services, is a good source of information for the physiological aspects of sport. It is a monthly bibliographic listing of references to current articles from approximately 2750 of the world's biomedical journals. There is a separate volume each month for author access, and an annual cumulated version of all monthly volumes.

A subset of *Index Medicus*, entitled *Physical Fitness/Sports Medicine*, began in 1978 and is published quarterly by the President's Council on Physical Fitness and Sports (Washington, D.C.). Arranged by subject, this index consists of bibliographic references retrieved from the MEDLARS database of the National Library of Medicine, and covers more than 3000 selected periodicals, as well as papers presented at selected congresses. The abbreviated periodical titles are listed with full journal title equivalent at the end of each issue. This index contains a second section arranged by author's surname.

The online version of *Index Medicus*, MEDLINE, contains the INTERNATIONAL NURSING INDEX and the INDEX TO DENTAL LITERATURE, as well as the MEDLARS database of the National Library of Medicine. MEDLINE is accessible through Dialog, BRS, NLM, DIMDI and BlaiseLine. A CD-ROM version of MEDLINE is also available.

Major serial titles

There is a multitude of sport, fitness, recreation and leisure periodical literature produced in North America, ranging from small newsletters to research journals. In a brief survey of this kind, it is impossible to review each of the numerous North American titles currently published.

Sport

SOCIAL SCIENCES

Many of the major North American serials covering the social sciences of sport are scholarly journals sponsored by professional organizations, or published by academics sharing common research interests.

Covering the history of sport are the *Journal of Sport History*, published by the North American Society for Sport History, and the *Canadian Journal of History of Sport*, published at the University of Windsor, Ontario, by the editors, Metcalfe and Salter. Both journals are refereed (anonymously evaluated), have impressive editorial boards, and contain extensive book review sections along with three to six research articles per issue. Although neither journal is limited to just North American authorship or North American topics, the authorship and subject coverage in both tend to be primarily North American. The *Journal of Sport History* has a bibliographical section called Journal Surveys which provides abstracts of journal articles covering various sport history topics, and a new section beginning with *Journal of Sport History*, **16**(1) entitled Film, Media and Museum Reviews, the intention of which 'is to provide historical criticism of the interpretation of sport history presented by various media (movies, television documentaries, museum reviews, genre essays, research holdings) to the general public'. This section should help to fill a gap in the information resources for non-book materials.

Several journals cover the sociological research into sport: *Sociology of Sport Journal*, published by Human Kinetics Publishers, Inc. (Champaign, Illinois) and offered as part of the membership to the North American Society for the Sociology of Sport; *Journal of Sport and Social Issues, Arena Review,* and *CSSS Digest* all published by the Center for the Study of Sport in Society, Northeastern University, Boston; and the *Journal of Sport Behavior*, sponsored by the United States Sports Academy.

The *Sociology of Sport Journal*, the *Journal of Sport and Social Issues* and the *Journal of Sport Behavior* are refereed journals. The *Sociology of Sport Journal* provides the most extensive coverage of the three. It is published quarterly and includes sections covering 'Research Notes and Comments', 'Book Reviews' and an 'Annotated Bibliography' on one special topic per issue produced by SIRLS SPORT AND LEISURE database.

Arena Review which ceased publication in 1990, was interesting in that the articles in each issue covered a specific topic with a guest editor to introduce the topic in each issue. *CSSS (Centre for the Study of Sport in Society) Digest* has yet another unique format – that of a small newspaper – complete with headlines, catchy news items dealing with sport in society, and a 'cover' story. The 'News Summary' section identifies noteworthy newspaper items, copies of which can be obtained from the Center. This serial could be considered the 'applied' aspect of sport sociology, while the other three journals cover the 'academic' research.

The most important North American journals covering the psychology of sport are the *Journal of Sport and Exercise Psychology* and *The Sport Psychologist* (both published by Human Kinetics Publishers, Inc. and both refereed). While the *Journal of Sport and Exercise Psychology* is designed to stimulate and communicate research and theory in all areas of sport and exercise psychology, *The Sport Psychologist* is published for educational and clinical sport psychologists. Thus, while one covers the academic research being done (primarily in North America), the other covers the applied aspects of sport psychology. The *Journal of Sport and Exercise Psychology* has a 'Digest' section alerting its readers to recent journal articles, as well as a book review section, while *The Sport Psychologist* takes a more applied approach and offers a 'Bulletin Board' of newsworthy items from international sources, and an 'Events and Conferences' section.

Other, more specialized social science topics are covered by the following journals: *Journal of the Philosophy of Sport*, a refereed journal published annually for the Philosophic Society for the Study of Sport by Human Kinetics Publishers; *Aethlon: The Journal of Sport Literature* (refereed) offered bi-annually with a membership to the Sport Literature Association and published by San Diego State University Press; *Sport Place International* (an international magazine of sports geography), published three times per year by Black Oak Press, Oklahoma; *Athletic Business*, a monthly commercial magazine published by Athletic Business Publications Inc., Madison, Wisconsin; and the *Journal of Sport Management*, published bi-annually by Human Kinetics Publishers. Because these journals serve more esoteric research interests, they are alone in their fields in North America, and tend toward international appeal. Although most of the articles in *Aethlon: The Journal of Sport Literature* are by North American authors and researchers, the journal boasts an impressive list of 'associate international editors'. *Sport Place International* likewise has an international editorial board, and the articles reflect international coverage and interests. Articles in the *Journal of the Philosophy of Sport* are also authored by an international group of researchers. *Athletic Business*, which is not research-oriented, focuses on the areas of sporting equipment and athletic facilities. An annual feature is the 'February Buyer's Guide', listing equipment manufacturers, suppliers of facility components, architects, builders and consultants, and a directory of associations. The official journal of the North American Society for Sport Management, the *Journal of Sport Management*, focuses on the theory and application of management to sport and related disciplines. Articles include abstracts and references. There is a regular section, 'Sport Management Digest', which scans relevant management articles, as well as a book review section entitled, 'Off the Press'.

SPORTS MEDICINE/PHYSICAL SCIENCES

There are a number of sport medicine journals currently being published in North America. *Clinics in Sports Medicine*, from W.B. Saunders (Philadelphia), is issued quarterly. Each issue focuses on a different topic, such as the emergency treatment of the injured athlete (January 1989) and patellofemoral problems (April 1989). A brief synopsis is provided for each paper as well as a profile of the contributor. There is a subject index for the whole volume at the end of each volume.

The bimonthly *American Journal of Sports Medicine*, the official publication of the American Orthopedic Society for Sports Medicine (Columbus, Georgia), contains a variety of research papers chosen by its editorial board. Each paper is accompanied by an abstract, and bibliographic references. The 'Announcements' section lists upcoming conferences, courses and seminars.

The official journal of the American College of Sports Medicine, the bimonthly *Medicine and Science in Sports and Exercise* is published by Williams & Wilkins (Maryland). Subject content is clinical studies, basic sciences/regulatory physiology, and applied sciences. There is a special 'communications' section, containing short papers on methods, and a 'technical note' section. Each paper is abstracted, and has extensive references.

The American College of Sports Medicine also sponsors the annual *Exercise and Sport Sciences Reviews* (published by Williams & Wilkins), which concentrates on current research involving exercise science (behavioral, biochemical, biomechanical, clinical, physiological and rehabilitation aspects). Selected papers are heavily referenced and there is a subject index.

The monthly, peer-reviewed *Physician and Sportsmedicine*, published by McGraw-Hill, presents information on the medical aspects of sports, exercise, and fitness of use to both the lay person and the practitioner. Articles are accompanied by an abstract and references, and many include colour photographs. A 'News Brief' section provides a one- to two-page topic, and a section entitled, 'Bridging the Gap' contains a practical applications section. The quarterly supplement focuses on topics in physiology, anthropometry and related areas. Papers are abstracted and contain references.

The International Journal of Sport Biomechanics is published quarterly by Human Kinetics Publishers, Illinois. Papers are selected by an editorial board and focus on original research involving the biomechanical analysis of specific sport techniques.

MULTI-DISCIPLINARY COVERAGE

Perceptual and Motor Skills, published bi-monthly by Behavior Engineering Associates, Missoula, Montana, is interdisciplinary and international in coverage. The authorship of the papers is geographically and occupationally distributed. A wide range of fields are covered: anthropology, physical education, physical therapy, orthopaedics, time and motion study, and sports psychology. Each issue carries over 50 articles, some of which are one-page reports of preliminary experimental findings which may not be finalized for some years.

The multi-disciplinary *Adapted Physical Activity Quarterly* (Human Kinetics Publishers) is a scholarly journal focusing on topics related to physical activity for special populations. In addition to the submitted papers which are accompanied by an abstract and references, issues often include other sections: 'Editorial', 'Research Reports', 'Applied Investigations', 'Case Study Reports', a 'Books & Media' review section, and a digest of abstracts of recently published research from around the world.

The official research journal of the Canadian Association of Sport Sciences, the quarterly *Canadian Journal of Sport Sciences* (published by University of Toronto Press), contains editorials, original papers selected by its editorial board, lectures, abstracts of outstanding papers, book reviews, letters to the editor, and invited papers. Papers are often accompanied by bilingual (English/French) abstracts.

The Research Quarterly for Exercise and Sport is published quarterly by the American Alliance for Health, Physical Education, and Dance, Reston, Virginia, and contains research-level articles on topics related to the art and science of human movement. Papers are abstracted, and include a biography of the author. 'Research Notes', 'Book Reviews' and a 'Dialogue' section are included in each issue.

SPORTS Science Periodical on Research and Technology in Sport is published eight times a year by the Coaching Association of Canada. Each issue usually consists of one paper, approximately eight pages long. The range of topics includes sport psychology, social psychology, administration, physical training, exercise physiology, biomechanics, strength, strategy and sports medicine, A 'Testing' section is also included. Each topic is colour coded and has a special code which allows an individual to file the papers by subject. This periodical is published in French under the title, *SPORT: Documents de Recherche et de Technologie*.

Fitness/exercise

American Fitness is the official publication of the Aerobics and Fitness Association of America, located in Sherman Oaks, California. This glossy, illustrated, bi-monthly magazine contains practical fitness information with sections on nutrition and beauty in addition to fitness-related advertisements.

The magazine, *Fitness Industry*, is a commercial publication produced by Industry Publishers Inc., Miami, Florida. Published eight times a year, it is a useful source for new technologies for rehabilitation, as well as industry news. The advertisements are useful for keeping up with trends in new equipment.

The Canadian newsletter, *Fitness Report*, published by F.S. Productions in Collingwood, Ontario, is a valuable source of news and trends in Canadian fitness, and is useful for its lists of upcoming conferences, workshops, resources and other ideas. Contact addresses are always provided for the convenience of the reader.

The glossy, *IDEA Today For the Fitness Professional*, continues the magazine, *Dance Exercise Today*, and is published by the Association for Fitness Professionals, San Diego, California. Issued ten times a year, it contains practical information on such topics as nutrition, strength development, aerobics and industry trends.

Leisure/recreation/physical education

Most of the major North American serials on leisure, recreation, or physical education are produced by national associations. The exceptions are: *Leisure Sciences*, published by Taylor and Francis (New York), *Loisir et Société/Society and Leisure*, published by Presses de l'Université du Québec, and *Journal of Leisurability*, published by Leisurability Publications, Concord, Ontario.

Articles for *Leisure Sciences* are authored primarily by North American academics, and are research oriented. A 'Book Review' section has returned to the journal, and the 'Upcoming Research Meetings and Conferences' continues to alert readers to international events. Particularly useful is an index of all articles appearing from 1977 to 1988, found in *Leisure Sciences*, **10**(4), 1988.

While *Loisir et Société/Society and Leisure* is also oriented toward academic research in the field of leisure, the journal is definitely international in scope. Despite a Quebec bias, it has an international advisory board. Articles are in French or English and each has an abstract in French, English and Spanish. Issues revolve around particular themes or topics, and are usually guest-edited. 'Research Notes' and 'Book Reviews' are produced in French or English, depending on the language preferred by the author.

Journal of Leisurability is a quarterly journal concerned with leisure, disability, community, advocacy and integration. Issues are thematic and although the journal is small, the articles reflect an effort to consider not only the research side of an issue, but the practitioner's and public's view as well.

The *Journal of Leisure Research* is published by the National Recreation and Park Association (Alexandria, Virginia), in co-operation with Ohio State University. The journal is devoted primarily to original investigations that contribute new knowledge and understanding to the fields of leisure studies. Authorship is predominantly from the USA and from academic institutes.

World Leisure and Recreation is the least 'academic' of the North American serials dealing with leisure listed here. It is published by the World Leisure and Recreation Association (the headquarters of which are at Sharbot Lake, Ontario), and is distributed to members of the Association. The articles are authored by people who are involved in leisure or recreation in many occupations, worldwide. The journal contents tend to be short, informative articles without bibliographies. The format of the journal is more 'popular' than the aforementioned leisure journals, and the articles are intended for a wider audience. A 'Calendar of Events' column is a useful feature to check for international conferences, seminars, etc.

Parks and Recreation is the official publication of the National Recreation and Park Association (Alexandria, Virginia). The popular magazine format has practical articles of interest to those working in the field. Most of the feature articles are written by non-academics who work in many areas of the park and recreation industry. The regular features of this monthly journal, such as: 'From the Field', 'Washington Scene', NRPA Law Review', 'Product Roundup', 'New Products', and an advertising index, while very useful to the North American audience, may be of minimal interest to an international readership.

Similar to *Parks and Recreation* is *Recreation Canada*, which is the official publication of the Canadian Parks/Recreation Association (Ottawa). Although *Recreation Canada* has considerably fewer advertisements than its American counterpart, and is less 'commercial' in presentation, the articles are generally non-research oriented when compared to the articles in a journal such as *Leisure Sciences*. Articles appear in English or French, along with a summary in the language not used for the article. Like *Parks and Recreation*, the intended audience for *Recreation Canada* is broad, and practically oriented.

Also published by the National Recreation and Park Association, is the *Therapeutic Recreation Journal* which is the official journal of the National Therapeutic Recreation Society (NTRS), a branch of NRPA. It has a North American bias and research papers cover a wide variety of topics, from autism to activity choices of disabled persons.

Covering the administrative aspects of park, recreation and leisure services is the *Journal of Park and Recreation Administration*, the official publication of the American Academy for Park and Recreation Administration. The journal 'provides a forum for the analysis of management and organization of the delivery of park, recreation, and leisure services'. Each issue contains six to eight research articles and one or two resource reviews.

Also endeavouring to reach practitioners as well as academics is the Canadian journal, *Journal of Applied Recreation Research* (formerly *Recreation Research Review*). Published quarterly by the Ontario Research Council on Leisure, the papers tend to profile the work and interests of the Council and the University of Waterloo Press, and are predominantly authored by researchers in Ontario. Topics cover a wide range of material – from papers dealing with issues specific to sites in Ontario, to articles which would be of interest to any recreation or leisure researcher worldwide.

Covering the combined areas of physical education, recreation and dance are *CAHPER Journal*, published by the Canadian Association for Health, Physical Education and Recreation (Gloucester, Ontario), and its American counterpart, the *Journal of Physical Education, Recreation, and Dance* (*JOPERD*) published by the American Alliance for Health, Physical Education, Recreation, and Dance. Both journals adopt a magazine format, including pictures and visual effects to enhance appearance, and advertising. *JOPERD* has a regular 'Feature' section of eight to ten articles on a particular topic (e.g. Assessing Physical Fitness), along with an 'Articles' section covering a variety of topics. A 'Departments' section covering letters, news, issues, research works, teaching tips, legal issues, new products and books/reviews is a regular offering and would be primarily useful to teachers. *CAHPER Journal*, in comparison, has fewer articles (each appearing in English and French), and few regular departments. A 'Special Interest' section covers book reviews and any other short items of interest to the physical education professional.

Quest is another journal covering physical education, but the emphasis is on issues critical to physical education in higher education (editorial policy is verso of contents page), and the readership includes academics and administrators, as well as teachers. The journal is published by Human Kinetics Publishers for the National Association for Physical Education in Higher Education. Articles are written and reviewed by academic researchers at American universities. Special issues on particular topics (e.g. Youth Fitness) appear occasionally, as do book reviews, announcements, or review essays.

Also published by Human Kinetics Publishers, is the quarterly *Journal of Teaching in Physical Education*, which focuses on the aspects of teaching and teacher education in physical education.

Other

Champion is an illustrated bilingual magazine published quarterly by the Canadian Athlete Information Bureau (AIB), Gloucester, Ontario. In addition to the biographical articles on leading Canadian elite athletes, issues often contain articles on topics such as fair play, doping, and the commercialization of sport.

The Olympian is an illustrated magazine published 10 times a year by the United States Olympic Committee. Like *Champion*, this magazine contains biographical articles on leading American elite athletes as well as occasional articles on sport-related topics.

Directories

Directories, which are national in scope are usually complemented by those offering more regional information, and they can be produced by national sport/recreation bodies, professional organizations, or commercial enterprises.

The *Sports Directory/Répertoire Récréation* published annually by the Sports Federation of Canada, lists the addresses of contact individuals for key Canadian sport/recreation groups, multi-national games associations, and related educational and specialized support agencies. Addresses for sport-relevant government departments (federal and provincial) are included, as are those for selected professional teams (baseball, Canadian football, ice hockey, soccer). Background information on several Canadian sport awards and brief descriptions of the activities and mandates of organizations, such as the Canadian Olympic Association, the Coaching Association of Canada, and PARTICIPaction are provided. The *Sport directory* is complemented by the *Canadian fitness sourcebook: organizations & resource materials* (1988), which is published by Fitness Canada, and provides directory information for 58 Canadian fitness-related organizations, 86 Canadian suppliers of fitness resource materials, and includes listings for 307 resource items.

Commercially produced by Sportsguide, and edited by R. A. Lipsey, the *Sports Market Place* is a major source of American information. Published annually, with a regular updating service, this comprehensive reference work includes not only addresses to the major sport/recreation organizations in the USA, but also information on the broadcasting industry, sport promotion/marketing firms, companies producing athletic equipment, and market data/directory/information services. There is selective coverage of Canadian organizations and publications.

The *United States Olympic Committee Fact Book* (annual) is a small, but useful directory. It contains a description of the USOC organization, its special programs and Olympic training centres, as well as addresses and contacts for U.S. sports organizations (specific sport and multi-sport) affiliated with the USOC.

Although somewhat dated, *The big book of halls of fame in the United States and Canada* (1977), compiled and edited by P. Soderberg, H. Washington and the Jacques Cattell Press, is a valuable lead to sport-related halls of fame in North America. More than just a directory, this reference work also provides, for some sections, short biographical sketches of some of the inductees into selected halls of fame.

There are specific directories for university and college sport. In Canada, the Canadian Inter-University Athletic Union (CIAU) publishes an annual *Directory* listing its member universities, their addresses, male/female enrolment information, and the names and telephone numbers of athletic department staff and coaches. In the USA, there are a number of directories which provide similar information. Among these is the National Collegiate Athletic Association's annual *NCAA directory*, which lists its member associations with addresses and telephone information, as well as contact names for individuals such as the presidents, directors of athletics, and faculty representatives. The men's and women's editions of *The 1988–1989 national directory of college athletics* are published by the National Association of Collegiate Directors of Athletics (NACDA), and provide address information for U.S. and Canadian college/university sport programmes, and for the specific junior and senior college conferences. The annual *Blue Book of Senior College and Junior & Community College Athletics*, containing the same type of information, includes a win/loss record for each institution and excludes advertising. The National Intramural-Recreation Sports Association publishes its own annual directory with a focus on recreational programs at both American and Canadian institutions.

Published in North America by the World Leisure and Recreation Association, and edited by Max d'Amours, the *International directory of academic institutions in leisure and related fields* (1986) covers programmes offered by major institutes in Africa, Asia, Central America and the Caribbean, South America, Europe, North America and Oceania. For each country listed under these divisions, a brief overview of the educational system is presented, followed by descriptions of the leisure and recreation programs offered. Almost half of the *Directory* is devoted to North American institutions.

The *Acadirectory: a Canadian sourcebook for physical education, kinesiology and human kinetics* (1986) by Yuhasz, Taylor and Haggerty, and the *Physical education gold book 1987–1989: a directory of physical educators in higher education* (1987) are useful in tracking down university faculty for sport research. The former is a very basic listing of faculty according to Canadian university affiliation as well as by primary areas of teaching interest and research. The *Gold book* focuses on American institutions and is not comprehensive. The first part lists four-year, followed by two-year, institutions and provides brief information about the programmes they offer. A listing of physical education faculty with addresses and major areas of interest follows.

Both the *Chronicle sports guide: intercollegiate athletics and scholarships* (1987), and *The directory of athletic scholarships* (1987), by Alan Green, provide useful directory information on the availability of sport-related scholarships in American colleges and universities. Both tools indicate funding availability for men and/or women. The Green directory also includes a section on the Ins and Outs of the Recruiting Process which provides advice to the scholarship/funding seeker.

In addition to the information found in the annual *Sports Market Place*, there are other sources of directory information for the sporting goods industry. Among these is the annual *Jim Rennie's desk reference directory/Guide de l'Acheteur 1989*, published by Jim Rennie's Sports Letter, which provides a listing of 325 key sporting goods suppliers in Canada. Special issues of specific American sporting goods magazines, such as the February issue of *Athletic Business*, are also good reliable information sources. The *1989 Buyers Guide* from Athletic Business includes a product index, addresses for manufacturers of athletic equipment and of sport/recreation facility components, and a directory of architects, builders, and consultants.

Amusement Business publishes a unique annual guide to sporting facilities in North America. The *AudArena stadium 1990 international guide* contains a directory to auditoriums, stadiums, exhibit halls, sports facilities, concert halls and convention sites in both the USA and Canada. There is also limited coverage of international facilities. In addition to address information, each entry indicates the owner of the facility, the seating capacity, and the availability of special features.

The above works are a small selection of the many sources of sport-related directory information in North America. A more complete listing can be developed by searching the SPORT database, by checking sport-related bibliographies, as well as by directly contacting the individual organizations listed in the aforementioned works.

Encyclopaedias and dictionaries

The *New encyclopedia of sports* (1977) by R. Hickok, provides over 500 pages on North American competitive sports. Each sport has a separate entry which presents its history, a summary of the rules, a list of results and records, and quite often, a biographical section. Historical essays on particular topics, such as amateurism, or Black athletes, and short entries on specialized subjects, such as the field events of track and field are also included. The directory of sports associations, organizations and leagues provided in this work is dated.

The encyclopedia of sports (1975) by F.G. Menke, is yet more extensive providing the history of nearly 80 sports and the records of events for them, as well as the life stories of thousands of men and women athletes.

Worthy of mention because of its format, the 20 volume set, entitled, *The Lincoln Library of sports champions* (1989) is designed with young readers in mind. Athletes from 43 sports have been chosen but baseball, basketball, football, and track and field predominate. The many photographs, and up-to-date information make this an attractive set.

Another set, a four-volume series, entitled *Encyclopedia of physical education, fitness and sports* (1977–1985), has been published by various publishers, all under the auspices of the American Alliance for Health, Physical Education, Recreation, and Dance. Covering the topics of philosophy, programmes, history, training, environment, nutrition, fitness, sports, dance, and human performance, each of the four volumes has its own editors, while the series as a whole is edited by Thomas K. Cureton.

The *Sport rules encyclopedia* (1990), edited by J.R. White is a comprehensive and valuable source of rules for 50 sports from archery to wrestling. The layout of facilities, court or playing fields are also included for each sport as well as the address of the American governing body. Appendix A lists the addresses of organizations concerned with sports for the handicapped, and Appendix B lists additional sources of sport rules in the USA.

While the *Biographical dictionary of American sports* (1987–1989) by Porter, and *Webster's sports dictionary* (1976) use the term 'dictionary' in their titles, their formats are definitely encyclopedia-like. Porter's work comprises four large companion volumes covering *Baseball* (1987), *Football* (1987), *Outdoor sports* (1988), and *Basketball and other indoor sports* (1989). These comprehensive volumes provide brief biographies of over 2000 players, coaches, administrators and officials, most from the twentieth century. *Webster's sports dictionary* (1976) offers over 500 pages of sport terms, and also has a pictorial section of referee signals for football, basketball and hockey, and a section on the how-to of scorekeeping for baseball and bowling.

Examining injuries and illnesses that may occur in physical activities and sports of all kinds, is the *Encyclopedic dictionary of sports medicine* (1986) by Tver and Hunt. Arranged alphabetically, each injury or illness and related symptoms is explained in detail with some illustrations.

Specific to Canada's sports heritage, is *Who's who in Canadian sport* (1985) by Bob Ferguson. Listed alphabetically, 2800 athletes and sports figures, both amateur and professional, living and dead, and representing virtually every sport are presented. As a finding aid, personalities are also listed by sport. A listing of Halls of Fame inductees and Games winners is also included.

Not only is there *Who's who*, but also a *What's what in sports: the visual glossary of the sports world* (1984) by R. Bragonier Jr. and D. Fisher. This volume provides definitions, highlighted by many illustrations, to sport-related terminology and is arranged alphabetically by sport.

Several North American dictionaries cover the language of sports. These are *The language of sport* (1982) by T. Considine, *Sports lingo: a dictionary of the language of sports* (1979) by H. Frommer, and *Sports talk: a dictionary of sports metaphors* (1989) by Palmatier and Ray. While the Considine book covers nine sports in detail (baseball, basketball, bowling, boxing, football, golf, ice hockey, soccer, tennis) and primarily from an American viewpoint, the Frommer book covers 40 sports, offering but one definition for each term. The Palmatier volume offers a unique approach to sport terminology by covering sports metaphors in American usage. The origin of each metaphor is given, along with an explanation of its meaning.

Rather than providing definitions to sport terms, the *Lexicon of terms related to the sports of the XV Olympic Winter Games/Lexique de terms reliés aux disciplines sportives inscrites aux XVes Jeux Olympiques d'hiver* (1987) by Gelinas-Suprenant and Burgers, and the *Multilingual lexicon for universiade sports* (1983) by Busch, Bergman, Figueroa and Holden provide sport-related terms in several languages. The Gelinas-Suprenant and Burgers lexicon deals with the terminology of sports of the Olympic Winter Games, and is arranged alphabetically by English term, with French and German equivalents given in parallel columns. There is no index from the French or German term to the English term, indicating that the volume has been prepared for English-speaking users. This is not the case with the Busch *et al.* book, which not only covers the English, French, Spanish, German and Russian languages, but also provides language-specific indexes to allow the individual to search by specific term. The *Multilingual lexicon for universiade sports* is primarily intended to assist athletes, coaches and translators in communication about the 10 sports of the World University Games.

Bibliographies

The most comprehensive bibliography for sport published in North America is the 13-volume *Sport bibliography*, edited by the staff of the Sport Information Resource Centre (SIRC). The bibliography, a subset of the SPORT database, lists sport and physical activity references to periodical articles, books, theses, microforms, conference proceedings and other research published in the years 1974 to 1984 with a substantial but less comprehensive coverage prior to 1974. Although no longer published, the series can be updated by searching the SPORT database.

Another important general guide to the literature of sport and physical education is the annotated bibliography, *Sports and physical education: a guide to the reference resources*, compiled by B. Gratch, B. Chan and J. Lingenfelter (1983). Although dated in some ways, this work provides a scan of English-language reference sources (monographs and serials) published in the USA and/or Canada. Reference works for 29 individual sports are provided and a second section is devoted to general reference works for sport and physical education. A third section provides a description of print indexes, databases and information centres.

Several publishers periodically produce bibliographies dealing with sport-related topics. For example, Vance Bibliographies have produced concise, basic bibliographies on selected topics such as: *The Olympic Games of 1932 and 1984: the planning and administration of the Los Angeles Games* (1985), by G. Dunning, and *Swimming centers: a selected bibliography* (1986) by S.S. Richardson. In some of the Vance Bibliographies, references are accompanied by a brief annotation. ABBE Publishers Association of Washington, D.C., have also published a number of bibliographies on sport-related topics. These are often very basic indexes to selected periodical literature, and as such are not as useful to the serious researcher as other sources are. Garland Publishing Inc. have also produced several specific bibliographies. Examples of titles to date include: *Sociology of sport: an annotated bibliography* (1988) by P. Redekop, *The Olympics: a bibliography* (1984) by B. Mallon, *Weight training in sport: a reference guide* (1985) by D.D. Macchia, and *Horsemanship: a bibliography of printed material from the sixteenth century to 1974* (1985) by E.B. Wells. There seems to be no standard format for these works. Each of the Garland bibliographies has its own author and is organized in a different manner. The merits of each must be judged on an individual basis.

There are a wide variety of specific subject bibliographies published in North America, ranging from sport violence and sport law, to sport medicine. There are also bibliographies focusing on the sport literature on women, black athletes and the disabled.

Statistical material

Government

CANADA

In Canada, the federal government department responsible for publishing statistical material is Statistics Canada (Ottawa). Sport and leisure statistics are minimal and difficult to pinpoint without the help of the index in the *Statistics Canada catalogue 1987–1988* (1988). Subject terms in the index include 'sporting goods industry', 'sports industry', 'leisure and personal services' and 'recreation'. Figures are given for Canada as a whole, and breakdowns by province. *Perspectives Canada III* (1980) contains information on participation in leisure time activities and expenditures by federal and provincial governments on culture and recreation; *1986 Manufacturing industries of Canada: national and provincial areas* (1989) gives various statistics on sporting goods and toy industries, and sporting goods manufacturers; *1986 Other manufacturing industries – sporting goods industry* (1989) presents 1986 census figures for the number of establishments, number of workers, person-hours paid, wages, costs of running the industry (fuel, materials, value of shipments, inventories, etc.); *Canada Year Book* provides very general statistics on federal government expenditures for recreation and culture, along with expenditures for other functions; and *Leisure and personal services 1984–86* (1989) gives the most detailed and current statistics on leisure and personal service industries for Canada and the provinces. Included, are statistics on commercial spectator sports, professional sports clubs, horse-race tracks, sports and recreation clubs and services, golf courses, curling clubs, skiing facilities, boat rentals and marinas, other sports and recreation clubs and other amusement and recreational services.

While Statistics Canada does not go far enough in its coverage of sport and leisure information, and the statistics are outdated by the time they are published, it is one of the few statistical information resources available in Canada.

USA

A USA equivalent to the *Statistics Canada catalogue 1987–1988* is not available. However, the *Statistical abstract of the United States 1989* (1989) packs an enormous quantity of information into its one volume. The index lists 17 sub-headings under the term recreation, including consumer and government expenditures, participation rates, park information, etc. In addition, there are four main headings dealing with various aspects of sport. As expected, the statistics are in tables and charts, and at the bottom of each, the source is given, should the user wish to track down more detailed information than is given in the table.

Other sources of statistical information

Statistical information for sport- and fitness-related topics can be found in a variety of forms and sources. For individual sports, data is recorded and analyzed for such particulars as team win/loss records and individual player performance. Retailing and market trend data is often available from individual companies in the sporting goods industry, such as Sports Market Data (Collingwood, Ontario), or from national professional organizations, such as the National Sporting Goods Association (Mt. Prospect, Illinois). Two of the major types of statistical information on sport- and fitness-related topics are in the areas of physical activity and sport participation levels, and injury occurrence.

PARTICIPATION STATISTICS

In Canada, a major source of statistical data on sport participation is the Canadian Fitness and Lifestyle Research Institute, Ottawa. In 1981, this organization implemented the Canada Fitness Survey, which examined not only the fitness levels of Canadians, but also their preferences in physical activity. This 1981 Survey generated a variety of reports which covered the physical activity levels and interests of youth, women, activity-limited and disabled adults, as well as the aged. Its successor, the Campbell's Survey on Well-being in Canada was conducted in 1988 and examined the exercise habits of Canadians, as well as other aspects of lifestyle. Published in 1990, *The well-being of Canadians: highlights of the 1988 Campbell's Survey* not only presents the 1988 data but is a longitudinal follow-up to the 1981 survey. There is a seperate French-language edition.

In the USA, there are a number of sources for this kind of statistical information. The National Sporting Goods Association (NSGA) produces and sells an annual detailed study based on a sampling of 10 000 U.S. households. Twenty-six sports are covered, and the 1988 Series I includes participation data by size of metro area, as well as by composition of the household. American Sports Data, Inc. (Hartsdale, New York) also publishes its own study of U.S. sport participation, based on a sample size of 17 000 adults and children, and monitoring 58 sports activities. Both of these studies provide detailed participation data useful to the sporting goods and related industries.

INJURY STATISTICS

Statistical information on the frequency of sport- or fitness-related injuries can be difficult to track down at times. Some organizations, such as the National Ski Areas Association, and the Red Cross, may keep such statistics relevant to their own field of interest. In Canada, the Régie de la Sécurité dans les Sports, a provincial government agency in Trois-Rivières, Québec, gathers injury-related data for different sports and publishes specific French-language reports relating to injury prevention and sport safety. In the USA, there are a number of organizations which gather sport injury data. A major collector and distributor of such data is the National Injury Information Clearinghouse, an agency of the U.S. Consumer Product Safety Commission (CPSC) in Washington, D.C. Operating the National Electronic Injury Surveillance System (NEISS), this clearinghouse collects from selected hospital emergency rooms throughout the USA, data relating to injuries and illnesses associated with consumer products. Other sources of sport-related injury data include organizations such as: the Athletic Health Care System (AHCS) at the University of Washington, which maintains data on athletic injuries from 20 different high schools; the Big Ten Injury Surveillance Survey (University of Iowa Hospitals), which produces an annual report surveying injuries in selected men's, as well as women's sports; and the Interscholastic Athletic Injury Surveillance System (Mooresville, Indiana), which provides a computerized registry of injury data pertaining to high school athletes (football, basketball, gymnastics and volleyball). The January 1990 issue of *Physician and Sportsmedicine,* **17**(1), pp.157, 160 and 165–167, provides a listing, with descriptions of 17 groups gathering this type of statistical data. This is an annual feature.

Bibliography

AudArena stadium international guide (1989). Nashville, Tennessee: Amusement Business.
The big book of halls of fame in the United States and Canada (1977). New York: R.R. Bowker and Company.
The blue book of senior college and of junior & community college athletics (1988). Akron, Ohio: Rohrich Corporation.

Bragonier, R. Jr. and Fisher, D. (1984). *What's what in sports: the visual glossary of the sports world.* Maplewood, New Jersey: Hammond Inc.

Busch, R.L., Bergman, H.J., Figueroa, P. and Holden, K.T. (1983). *Multilingual lexicon for universiade sports.* Edmonton, Alberta: University of Alberta Press.

1989 Buyers guide. The industry's bible (1989). Madison, Wisconsin: Athletic Business Publications.

Canada year book 1988 (1987). Ottawa, Ontario: Statistics Canada.

Canadian fitness sourcebook: organizations & resource materials (1988). Ottawa, Ontario: Fitness Canada, Skills Program.

Chronicle sports guide: intercollegiate athletics and scholarships (1987). Moravia, New York: Chronicle Guidance Publications.

Considine, T. (1982). *The language of sport.* New York: Facts on File, Inc.

D'Amours, M. (ed.) (1986). *International directory of academic institutions in leisure, recreation and related fields.* Sharbot Lake, Ontario: World Leisure and Recreation Association.

Directory/annuaire 1989–1990 (1989). Gloucester, Ontario: Canadian Interuniversity Athletic Union.

Draayer, I., Chiasson, G., Replansky, L. and Wheeler, L. (eds.) (1981) *Sport bibliography.* Ottawa, Ontario: Sport Information Resource Centre.

Dunning, G. (1985). *The Olympic Games of 1932 and 1984: the planning and administration of the Los Angeles Games.* Monticello, Illinois: Vance Bibliographies.

Ferguson, B. (1985). *Who's who in Canadian sport.* Toronto, Ontario: Summerhill Press Limited.

Frommer, H. (1979). *Sports lingo: a dictionary of the language of sports.* New York: Atheneum.

Gelinas-Suprenant, H. and Burgers, H. (1987). *Lexicon of terms related to the sports of the XV Olympic Winter Games/Lexique de terms reliés aux disciplines sportives inscrites aux XVes Jeux Olympiques d'hiver.* Calgary, Alberta: XV Olympic Winter Games Organizing Committee.

Gratch, B., Chan, B. and Lingenfelter, J. (1983). *Sports and physical education: a guide to the reference sources.* Westport, Connecticut: Greenwood Press.

Green, A. (1987). *The directory of athletic scholarships.* New York: Facts on File Publications.

Hickok, R. (1977). *New encyclopedia of sports.* New York: McGraw-Hill Book Company.

Jim Rennie's desk reference directory/Guide de l'acheteur 1989 (1989). Collingwood, Ontario: Jim Rennie's Sports Letter.

Leisure and Personal Services 1984–1986 (1989). Ottawa, Ontario: Statistics Canada.

The Lincoln Library of sports champions, 5th edn. (1989). Columbus, Ohio: Frontier Press Company.

Lipsey, R.A. (ed.) (1988). *Sports market place 1988*. Princeton, New Jersey: Sportsguide.

Macchia, D.D. (1985). *Weight training in sports: a reference guide.* New York: Garland Publishing.

Mallon, B. (1984). *The Olympics: a bibliography.* New York: Garland Publishing.

1986 manufacturing industries of Canada: national and provincial areas (1989). Ottawa, Ontario: Statistics Canada, Industry Division.

Menke, F.G. (1975). *The encyclopedia of sports*, 5th rev. edn. Revisions by S. Treat. South Brunswick and New York: A.S. Barnes and Company.

NCAA Directory (1989). Shawnee Mission, Kansas: National Collegiate Athletic Association.

The 1988–1989 National directory of college athletics (women's edition) covering senior and junior college intercollegiate athletics (1988). Amarillo, Texas: Ray Franks Publishing.

The 1988–1989 National directory of college athletics (men's edition) covering all senior and junior colleges (1988). Amarillo, Texas: Ray Franks Publishing.

1986 Other manufacturing industries – sporting goods industry (1989). Ottawa, Ontario: Statistics Canada, Industry Division.

Palmatier, R.A. and Ray, H.L. (1989) *Sports talk: a dictionary of sports metaphors.* New York: Greenwood Press.

Perspectives Canada III (1980) Ottawa, Ontario: Statistics Canada.

Physical education gold book 1987–1989: a directory of physical educators in higher education (1987). Champaign, Illinois: Human Kinetics Publishers.

Porter, D.L. (ed.) (1987). *Biographical dictionary of American sports – baseball.* New York: Greenwood Press.

Porter, D.L. (ed.) (1989). *Biographical dictionary of American sports – basketball and other indoor sports.* New York: Greenwood Press.

Porter, D.L. (ed.) (1987). *Biographical dictionary of American sports – football.* New York: Greenwood Press.

Porter, D.L. (ed.) (1988). *Biographical dictionary of American sports – outdoor sports.* New York: Greenwood Press.

Redekop, P. (1988). *Sociology of sport: an annotated bibliography.* New York: Garland Publishing.

Richardson, S.S. (1986). *Swimming pools: a bibliography.* Monticello, Illinois: Vance Bibliographies.

Sports directory/Répertoire récréation (1989). Gloucester, Ontario: Sports Federation of Canada.

Statistics Canada catalogue 1987–1988 (1988). Ottawa, Ontario: Statistics Canada.

Stephens, T. and Craig, C.L. (1990). *The well-being of Canadians: highlights of the 1988 Campbell's survey.* Ottawa, Ontario: Canadian Fitness and Lifestyle Research Institute.

Thesaurus of psychological index terms, 5th edn. (1988). Washington, D.C.: American Psychological Association.

U.S. Department of Commerce and U.S. Bureau of the Census (1989). *Statistical abstract of the United States 1989.* Washington, D.C.: U.S. Government Printing Office.

United States Olympic Committee '88 fact book (1988). Boulder, Colorado: United States Olympic Committee.

Webster's sports dictionary (1976). Springfield, Massachusetts: G. & C. Merriam Company, Publishers.

Wells, E.B. (1985). *Horsemanship: a bibliography of printed material from the sixteenth century to 1974.* New York: Garland Publishing.

Wheeler, L., Belanger, S., Chiasson, G., Rogers, M. and Stark, R. (eds.) (1983) *Sport bibliography. Update 1983.* Ottawa, Ontario: Sport Information Resource Centre.

Wheeler, L., Chiasson, G., Nadeau, H., Rogers, M. and Stark, R. (eds.) (1987) *Sport bibliography: the international sport bibliographical system*, Volume 11. Champaign, Illinois: Human Kinetics Publishers.

Wheeler, L., Chiasson, G., Nadeau, H., Rogers, M. and Stark, R. (eds.) (1986) *Sport bibliography: the international sport bibliographical system*, Volume 12. Champaign, Illinois: Human Kinetics Publishers.

Wheeler, L., Chiasson, G., Nadeau, H., Rogers, M. and Stark, R. (eds.) (1986) *Sport bibliography: the international sport bibliographical system*, Volume 13. Champaign, Illinois: Human Kinetics Publishers.

White, Jess R. (1990). *The sports rules encyclopedia.* Champaign, Illinois: Leisure Press.

Yuhasz, M.S., Taylor, A.W. and Haggerty, T.R. (1986). *Acadirectory: a Canadian sourcebook for physical education, kinesiology and human kinetics.* London, Ontario: Sports Dynamics.

CHAPTER SIXTEEN

Australian sport

N. CLARKE

Introduction

For Australians sport is, according to Dunstan (1981) a national obsession. It is something which has the power to attract over 100 000 spectators to the Melbourne Cricket Ground to watch cricket in summer or Australian Rules football in the winter. Sport is that something in Australian culture which can send people to the streets in celebration of a yachting victory and cause the Prime Minister to declare a national holiday in recognition of that victory, as it did with the Australian Americas Cup victory in 1983. It is sport which can virtually bring all parts of Australia to a standstill on the first Tuesday of November every year for the running of a horse race, the Melbourne Cup.

Australians have a sporting obsession but they are not just spectators of sport. They are also participants and according to the *Australian Sports Directory* (Australian Sports Commission, 1990) some 9 million Australians out of a population of 16.5 million are registered sports participants of one or more sports, although many more engage in sports activities without registering formally with a club or organization.

There are in Australia a number of information sources for sport and leisure, both primary and secondary. However because of Australia's geography and its political structure and because of the way sport is generally organized at the local, state and federal level, there has, in the past, been little co-ordination of resources for sport information. It is not possible therefore to identify one place or one source for sport information.

In Australia, sport is organized into three broad areas: government (local, regional, state and federal), the sports club system and the business sector. Each of these generates its own brand of sport information.

Australia's first sporting club was established in 1814 and this marked the commencement of the administrative structure for sports and the volunteer effort in sports administration which continues today. State governing bodies for a number of sports were formed in the 1850s and these were followed by several national organizations. Today these number in excess of 100 and they are listed in the publication *The Australian Sports Directory* (Australian Sports Commission, 1990).

In addition to organizations representing individual sports a number of umbrella sporting organizations have developed, some of which have long histories. These organizations act as liaison groups between government and individual sporting organizations in particular areas of interest. These include the Australian Olympic Federation, founded in 1920, the Commonwealth Games Association established in 1929 and the Confederation of Australian Sport formed in 1976. Other organizations include the Australian Coaching Council, the Australian Council for Health, Physical Education and Recreation (ACHPER), the Australian Sports Medicine Federation, Australian Universities Sports Association, the Australian Society of Sports Administrators and the Australian Society for Sports History.

Government assistance to sport in Australia has increased significantly in the 1970s and 1980s with the establishment of Commonwealth and State departments with specific responsibility for sport and recreation. In addition to this, the establishment of the Australian Institute of Sport, the Australian Sports Commission and State Sports Institutes has further increased the commitment to sport by governments at the Commonwealth and State levels. At the same time there has been a significant increase in the volume of publications on sport and leisure produced by the government sector.

Major sports collections in Australia

There are a number of libraries which are excellent sources of sport information. These have recently become more widely known following the implementation of union catalogue systems for books and periodicals and shared cataloguing systems. For example, the Australian Bibliographic Network run by the National Library of Australia, was established in 1981 and now has 800 participating libraries.

Sport information in Australia is available from the State Library in each State. Some of these, for example, the State Library of New South Wales has extensive historical collections of sport information, as a result of the fact that it was founded long before national collecting agencies like the National Library of Australia or the National Sport Information Centre.

The National Library of Australia, established in 1968 as the legal deposit library for Australia, has a large collection of Australian sporting monographs, periodicals, films, photographs and newspaper clipping files on athletes. It also houses collections of private papers of some prominent Australian sporting personalities (e.g. Sir Hubert Opperman) and of organizations such as the Australian Olympic Federation. The oral history programme of the National Library also includes recordings of prominent Australian sportsmen and women and the music and sound recording section also contains material on sport. In 1980 the National Library produced a guide entitled *Materials and services on sport provided by the National Library of Australia*, which although now outdated does provide some idea of the material collected by the National Library. The National Film and Sound Archive in Canberra also has a significant collection of material on Australian sport dating from 1915.

Other libraries which collect Australian sporting information include a number of tertiary institution libraries which have courses related to sport and physical education, the libraries of State Government Departments responsible for sport and recreation, and the Federal Department of the Arts, Sport, the Environment, Tourism and Territories in Canberra. A number of other special libraries include state sports institutes and the library of the Melbourne Cricket Club. All such libraries are listed in the publication *Guide to sports collections in Australia* (Australian Sports Commission, 1989). Some Australian sporting organizations have collections of information relating to their sport, for example *Tennis Australia*. However, these collections tend not to be well documented and access is often restricted. A number of private collections of sporting information are held in Australia, particularly in cricket, but once again these are not often easily accessible and may only be located with the assistance of the Australian Society for Sports History or a sporting organization.

The National Sport Information Centre of the Australian Sports Commission (formerly the Information Centre of the Australian Institute of Sport) based in Canberra developed in the 1980s and has a role to document all Australian sporting information. It houses a large collection of material in book, periodical and audio-visual format. The Centre also has a comprehensive collection of newspaper clipping material, athlete profiles, slide and photographic material of current sporting personalities and events, and theses and dissertations on Australian sport. Whilst the Centre is not strong in its collection of material prior to 1980, it has the resources to locate historical material and its collection policies will ensure that it develops into the major collection of sport information in Australia. The Centre is open to the public and assists with personal, telephone and postal enquiries on all aspects of sport and actively promotes its services.

Major reference sources on Australian sport

The identification of reference sources for Australian sport and leisure is not an easy task. Firstly, because sport and leisure covers such a multiplicity of activities, the full range of these activities is rarely listed in one reference source. Secondly, many sport-specific publications contain information which means they could be equally relevant to the reference or lending collections of a library. This is particularly so with books in a field like cricket which may contain a narrative section and a large amount of statistical information. Another problem in identifying reference sources is that for some activities there are several reference sources while for others it is difficult to identify any reference source. For the purpose of this chapter, only the major reference sources for Australian sport have been identified — those which deal with terminology, rules, addresses, records/statistics and biographical information for sport in general. Reference information for specific sports is best sought from sport-specific reference tools. For example, *Who's who in international tennis* (Emery, 1983) lists biographical information on Australian tennis players, the *Complete book of VFL records* (Rodgers, 1987) lists records in Australian Rules football, the *Complete book of Australian golf* (Smith, 1988) lists records and personalities in golf. Journals such as *Athletics Australia News* list records and results. The annual reports of Australian sporting organizations are also useful reference tools for financial, historical and statistical information about particular Australian sports.

Material relevant to specific sports can be located with the assistance of the indexing and abstracting services described below, and through major bibliographical tools such as *Australian Books in Print*, the *Australian National Bibliography*, which is published on a monthly basis and lists books and pamphlets published in Australia, by Australians or about Australia and online systems such as the Australian Bibliographic Network, the Australian library community's online shared cataloguing system administered by the National Library of Australia.

Standard reference tools include the *Encyclopedia of Australian sport* (Andrews, 1979) and the *Encyclopedia of Australian sports* (Shepherd, 1980), although now out of date the latter does contain useful biographical information. There is currently a need in Australia for an updated encyclopaedia of sport, particularly one which provides biographical information on a variety of sportsmen and sportswomen, rather than just Olympians, as publications such as *Aussie gold* (Howell and Howell, 1988) have done in the past. The book *AMPOL Australian sporting records* (Blanch, 1988) is frequently updated. It is arranged by sport and contains a potted history of each sport together with a large amount of information on sporting records and achievements. *Miller's Guide*, published annually provides statistical information on sporting records in a number of sports, although a large part of it is dedicated to horse-racing results. The *Winfield book of Australian sporting records* (Shepherd, 1981) and *200 years of Australian sport* (Heads and Lester, 1988), are also useful general reference tools. The recent publication the *Australian sports chronicle* (Abelson and O'Connor, 1989) provides useful information on records, results and forthcoming sporting events. It covers all sports and is regularly updated. The *Australian Sport Source Directory* (1990) lists a wide range of sporting organisations including those at State level. The *Australian Sports Directory* and the *Australian Recreation Directory* are extremely useful publications which give the names and addresses of a wide variety of governmental and non-governmental organizations responsible for sport and recreation in Australia. The *Australian Sports Directory* also lists forthcoming domestic and international sporting events and includes a statistical breakdown of the number of registered participants within each particular sport. The company, Event Salesbank also compiles listings of forthcoming sporting events and maintains a database of these with contact addresses. The *Directory of Australian associations* (Einhorn, 1985–) with regular updates, gives the names and addresses of some sporting organizations and their State affiliates. However, for most State sporting body addresses, it is necessary to use listings published by government agencies responsible for sport in each State, or the State telephone directories.

The major general reference tools on Australian sport are listed in the publication *Information resources on Australian sport* produced by the National Sport Information Centre which is continuously updated. The publication also contains details of the major annual reports and journals on Australian sport, the major general monographs on Australian sport, significant journal articles and relevant audio-visual material (all listed with particular library holdings indicated) together with a list of major sports libraries in Australia.

Indexing, abstracting and online services

Prior to 1982 Australia had no specific indexing or abstracting service for sport and recreation although some material was indexed in the general indexing service Australian Public Affairs Information Service (APAIS) begun by the National Library of Australia in 1978. *APAIS* is a subject index to Australian periodicals, newspapers and conference proceedings which fall within the broad disciplines of the social sciences and humanities and focuses particularly on issues and subjects of current interest in the public arena. Some general sporting and recreation material is included in this monthly service which is available through the OZLINE network of the National Library of Australia, and as a hard copy and microfiche.

In 1983 the *Australian Leisure Index* which indexed current Australian sport, recreation and tourism information and the *Australian leisure bibliography* (Dow, 1983), a retrospective listing of the holdings of Australian monographs on sport recreation and tourism in Australian libraries were produced by the Australian Clearing House for Publications in Recreation, Sport and Tourism (ACHPIRST) based at the Library of Footscray Institute of Technology. The *Australian Leisure Index* was produced as an annual index between 1982 and 1988 when publication ceased. Subsequently the National Sport Information Centre of the Australian Sports Commission has produced the annual *Australian Sport Index* which comprehensively indexes all Australian periodicals, monographs, theses, reports, conference papers, government reports and audio-visual material relating to sport in Australia. This index is produced as a by-product of the submission of data to the international SPORT database and therefore includes abstracts for material designated as Level A according to the guidelines set down by the Canadian Sport Information Resource Centre. This index is arranged under broad subject categories and contains a list of Australian sporting periodicals indexed. Chapters 1 and 15 contain more information on the SPORT database.

Footscray Institute of Technology Library has continued to index Australian tourism information and produces the annual publication *Australian Tourism Index*. However, this index also covers a number of aspects of sport. These include sporting events and tourism attractions such as the Olympic Games, sport as a tourist activity (e.g. winter sports, golf) and some physical recreations (e.g. bicycling and camping). Australian recreation information is not currently indexed in any systematic manner.

With the production of the *Australian Leisure Index* in 1982, ACHPIRST developed an online database entitled LEISURELINE. This database has been running on the Australis network in Australia since 1983; however its usefulness for sport information has decreased since 1988 when ACHPIRST stopped indexing Australian sporting information and the National Sport Information Centre began submitting Australian data to the SPORT database. The LEISURELINE database is useful for information on Australian sport from 1982 to 1988 but the more recent data are to be found on the SPORT database.

In 1990, the National Library of Australia and the National Sport Information Centre mounted an Australian sport database entitled AUSPORT on the National Library's online network OZLINE. This database covers all material indexed by the National Sport Information Centre since 1988, using data derived from that submitted to the SPORT database. Also in 1990, a CD-ROM entitled AUSTROM was produced by Informit. This includes all the data from the LEISURELINE database on sport, recreation and tourism from 1982 to 1988, the information from the AUSPORT database on Australian sports since 1988, the Australian Public Affairs Information Service (APAIS) database, *Australian Education Index* and several other files of data relating to the social sciences in Australia.

The *Australian Medical Index* online database AMI, which is available through the Australian Medline network, indexes Australian medical information and contains some material relevant to sport. However this database is scanned by the National Sport Information Centre for relevant material to index for the SPORT database.

The *Australian Education Index* begun in 1957 as a hard-copy index and its subsequent online database begun in 1978 contains some references to information on sport and physical education in the educational environment including theses. Once again this material is now largely covered by the *Australian Sport Index*. The *Australian Education Index* online database is available through the Ausinet online system and the CD-ROM AUSTROM.

As stated previously the Australian Bibliographic Network (ABN) is the country's major database for the location of monographic material on Australian sport and leisure. This database also contains information on Australian audio-visual material, conference papers, reports and periodical holdings. It has recently implemented an automated inter-library loan module to facilitate the supply of materials between Australian libraries.

Non-bibliographic databases for sport information

Full-text, statistical and directory databases for public access in the area of sport and leisure are not well developed in Australia, although this situation is changing. Several full-text newspaper databases are available which are described in the section on primary sources, below. However, these generally only include feature articles on sport and do not include results information. Teletex services which include daily sporting results and summaries of major sporting stories are available through the Australian television network on a large number of city and country television stations at no cost to the user.

Australia has a 'user pays' teletex service, 'Discovery' managed by Telesoft (previously managed by Telecom and called 'Viatel') which has some very limited sporting information available at present. It has the *Australian Associated Press file* available which contains some unedited sporting news stories and results and a football and horse-racing betting system. This system has great potential for development in a country where information has to reach a widely dispersed population, but it has yet to be fully exploited.

A full-text database NICAN: the National Information Communication Awareness Network, has been established to provide directory information on sport and recreation programs, contacts and activities for disabled people in Australia and is accessible through the National Library of Australia's online system OZLINE.

In Victoria, a project is currently being undertaken to develop a comprehensive database on Victorian sport. This database would include information on sporting organizations, participation rates and information on sponsorship. Similar systems are being examined at the Australian Sports Commission for sport as a whole. However, these databases appear at present to be quite some way from the stage of providing public online access to the data.

Journals on Australian sport

Journal publishing in sport in Australia has a long and varied history with a great many publications having been produced both for the commercial and non-commercial market. In Australia, general sporting periodicals have come and gone and currently there is no general sporting journal for Australia such as the USA's *Sports Illustrated*. In the past, general sporting journals covering a number of sports like *Amateur Sports Weekly, Australian Sportsfan, Sport Magazine, Australian Amateur, Your Sport* and *Sports World Australia*, have surfaced but have died after relatively short runs.

On the other hand, a number of journals from major organizations in sport have been produced continuously over a number of years. These include: the *ACHPER National Journal* produced by the Australian Council for Health, Physical Education and Recreation, a major journal for the physical education profession, *Sports Coach* from the Australian Coaching Council and aimed at accredited coaches; the *Australian Journal of Science and Medicine in Sports* from the Australian Sports Medicine Federation; *Sport Report* produced by the Confederation of

Australian Sport; and the *Australian Olympian* from the Australian Olympic Federation.

More recently, journals aimed at special-interest groups have developed. These include: *Sporting Traditions*, the journal of the Australian Society for Sports History; *Australian Parks and Recreation*, the quarterly journal of the Royal Australian Institute of Parks and Recreation; *Sportsnetwork*, the journal of the Australian Society of Sports Administrators Inc.; *Aqualink*, the journal for the Institute of Swimming and Recreation Centre Management of Australia; and *Sports and Leisure Retailer* for the retail trade in sport. In the area of sports science, medicine, and physical fitness the major journals are: *Australian Journal of Science and Medicine in Sport; Excel*, produced by the Australian Institute of Sport; *Sport Health*, a publication of the Australian Sports Medicine Federation aimed at sports trainers; *Australian Fitness and Training, The International Health Reader* and *Network News*, aimed more at fitness leaders.

A large number of sport-specific journals are produced and these are listed together with general sporting journals in the publication *Australian sporting periodicals*, produced by the National Sport Information Centre. Some sport-specific journals such as *Australian Runner, International Swimmer, Modern Athlete and Coach*, and *Tennis, Australia, Asia, the Pacific*, have had lengthy publishing histories whilst others and particularly those produced by sporting organizations on a voluntary basis have had more erratic histories. Recently there have been a number of more professionally-produced sport-specific journals (for example *Australian Basketballer* and *Australian Rowing*). It remains to be seen how long these publications can exist in a country where there does not appear to be a large market for sport-specific journals, because of television and detailed newspaper coverage of sport.

Australian sporting journals are listed in the publication *Australian sporting periodicals*. They are also listed on the Australian Bibliographic Network which acts as a union list of serials for Australia and in the publication *Australian serials in print*.

Locations for periodicals in Australian libraries can be obtained through the Australian Bibliographic Network although not all sport libraries are contributors to ABN. The publication *Physical education, health and recreation serials in Australian libraries: a union list*, prepared and updated by Victoria College, Rusden Campus, covers the holdings of the major sport libraries in Australia many of whom do not contribute to the national union catalogue. This is an extremely useful tool to use in conjunction with ABN.

Audio-visual material on Australian sport

Recent years have seen an increase in the availability of commercially available audio-visual material relating to Australian sport, particularly in videotape and audio-cassette format. Videotapes like *Green and gold greats* which looks at the achievements of Australian sporting personalities and a number of other sport-specific tapes have been produced. The National Sport Information Centre indexes all of this material together with international videotapes on sport for the SPORT database. *A guide to commercially available videotapes* is produced which lists videotapes according to subject; it also includes details of suppliers and major libraries holding film and video loan collections.

The National Library of Australia Film Lending Collection contains a large volume of Australian films and videotapes including sport and leisure. These holdings have now been added to the Australian Bibliographic Network, as have the audio-visual holdings of a number of large tertiary institutions. However, there still remains a large amount of material held in individual libraries which has to be approached individually to locate material.

The Australian Broadcasting Commission has an extensive archive which contains a great deal of sporting information but access to this collection may be difficult for an individual. The National Film and Sound Archive as mentioned previously, has a large amount of material relating to sport and leisure. However this material is not always indexed in detail and may be time consuming to locate.

Theses and dissertations on Australian sport

In the absence of a consolidated listing of all Australian theses and dissertations, the National Sport Information Centre has undertaken a project to identify and collect as many Australian theses and dissertations on sport and its related disciplines as possible. The National Sport Information Centre has a fairly comprehensive collection of theses and dissertations from the University of Western Australia and the University of Queensland, who are the major higher degree-granting institutions in sport and physical education. Other institutions are being encouraged to submit their theses and dissertations for indexing.

Once identified these are indexed for the SPORT database. This makes them accessible through SPORT, SPORT DISCUS, the Australian AUSPORT database, AUSTROM and the *Australian Sport Index*. In future it is planned to produce a hard-copy listing of Australian theses and dissertations on sport and related subjects.

For the location of higher-degree theses relating to sport, an additional source is the *Union list of higher degree theses in Australian libraries* produced by the University of Tasmania Library since 1958, with annual cumulations. The Australian Council for Educational Research also produces the listing, *Theses in education and educational psychology accepted for degrees at Australian universities* which lists some sports theses particularly in the area of physical education.

Primary sources of sport information

Primary sources are an important source of information in sport. As stated, newspapers are not generally comprehensively indexed in Australia. However, major articles are indexed for the SPORT database by the National Sport Information Centre. A few newspapers do offer an indexing service. *The Sydney Morning Herald* newspaper has a full-text online database available through Ausinet. This includes all items published in the newspaper since 1986, including sport. *The Brisbane Courier Mail* also has a full-text database including sports feature articles which is available on a subscription direct dial-up basis. Presscom Australia has full text of the editorial content including sport of South Australian, Victorian and Tasmanian newspapers owned by News Ltd. and this is available online.

The Australian and State Archives are important sources of primary documents and do have material related to sport. Other institutions such as the National Library of Australia and State Libraries have the papers of sporting personalities and sporting organizations, such as the Australian Olympic Federation. However for the historical records of many sporting organizations, it is necessary to go to the organization itself, as archives management has not been seen as a priority in Australian sport.

Records of government involvement in sport are contained in *Parliamentary papers* and *Hansards* of both the Federal and State governments of Australia. Currently, projects are underway to automate these records to provide greater public access.

As in all areas of endeavour — and sport is no exception — personal contacts are used a great deal as information sources. There are several name directories in Australian sport which are useful in making personal contacts. The *Australian Sports Directory* lists the names, addresses and telephone numbers of Australia's national sporting organizations together with those of significant other governmental and non-governmental agencies involved in sport. The *Australian sports science directory* (Draper, 1989) lists the names and addresses of 273 sports scientists throughout Australia.

Registers of sportswomen in Tasmania, Victoria, New South Wales,

Western Australia, South Australia and the Australian Capital Territory have been compiled by the Women's Sport Promotion Unit of the Australian Sports Commission in co-operation with State government departments. In the case of Queensland this was undertaken in co-operation with the Australian Council of Health, Physical Education and Recreation, Queensland Branch. These registers list sportswomen, their achievements and contact details.

Sport information in Australia is a developing field and its importance is becoming more widely recognized in a country where sport is becoming increasingly 'professional'. The documentation of Australia's information sources on sport and leisure has really only begun in the last decade; however with an increasing number of professional information providers being employed in sport, the developments in technology and the increasing need for sport information, more and more sources will appear and these will be documented in a systematic manner in the future, particularly through the efforts of organizations such as the National Sport Information Centre which sees as its primary role the documentation of Australian sporting information.

References

Abelson, P.W. and O'Connor, B. (1989–). *Australian Sports Chronicle.* Australian Professional Publications.
ACHPER National Journal (1983–). Australian Council for Health, Physical Education and Recreation.
Amateur Sports Weekly (1928–). Amateur Publications.
Andrews M. (1979). *Encyclopedia of Australian sports.* Golden Press.
Aqualink (1988-). Market Link Publications.
Athletics Australia News (1989–). Athletics Australia.
Australian Amateur (1951–). Amateur Publications.
Australian Basketballer (1983–). Magnum Opus.
Australian Books in Print (1970–). Thorpe.
Australian Education Index (1958–). Australian Council for Educational Research.
Australian Fitness and Training (1987–). Australian Workout Publications.
Australian Journal of Science and Medicine in Sport (1984–). ACHPER and Australian Sports Medicine Federation.
Australian Leisure Index (1982–1988). ACHPIRST.
Australian National Bibliography (1961–). National Library of Australia.
Australian Olympian (1982–). Australian Olympic Federation.

Australian Parks and Recreation (1964–). Royal Australian Institute of Parks and Recreation.

Australian Public Affairs Information Service (1978–). National Library of Australia.

Australian Recreation Directory (1985–). Australian Government Publishing Service.

Australian Rowing (1984–). Australian Rowing Council.

Australian Runner (1980–). Australian Runner.

Australian Serials in Print (1981–). Thorpe.

Australian Sport Index (1988–). National Sport Information Centre, Australian Sports Commission.

Australian Sport Source Directory (1990/91–). Step Ahead Promotions.

Australian Sporting Periodicals (1989–). National Sport Information Centre, Australian Sports Commission.

Australian Sports Directory (1985–). Australian Sports Commission.

Australian Sportsfan (1972–). Percival Publishing.

Australian Tourism Index (1986–). Footscray Institute of Technology Library.

Blanch, J. (ed.) (1988). *AMPOL Australian sporting records*, 8th edn. Transworld.

Dow, D. (1983). *Australian leisure bibliography*. ACHPIRST.

Draper, J (1989). *Australian sports science directory*. National Sports Research Program, Australian Sports Commission.

Dunstan, K. (1981). *Sports*. Sun.

Einhorn, J. (ed.) (1985–). *Directory of Australian associations*. Information Australia.

Emery, D. (ed.) (1983). *Who's who in international tennis*. Sphere.

Excel (1986–) Australian Institute of Sport.

Green and gold greats. Videotape (2 vols.) (1986). Boroku.

Guide to commercially available videotapes (1989). National Sport Information Centre, Australian Sports Commission.

Guide to sports collections in Australia (1989). National Sport Information Centre, Australian Sports Commission.

Heads, I. and Lester, G. (1988). *200 years of Australian sport, a glorious obsession*. Lester-Townsend.

Howell, M.L. and Howell, R. (1988). *Aussie gold: the story of Australia at the Olympic Games*. Brooks Waterloo.

Information resources on Australian sport (1989). National Sport Information Centre, Australian Sports Commission.

International Health Reader (1989-). Centre for Health Promotion and Research Pty Ltd.

International Swimmer (1964–89). Speedo Knitting Mills Pty Ltd.

Materials and services on sport provided by the National Library of Australia Microform (1980). National Library of Australia.

Miller's Guide (1875–). Herald and Weekly Times.

Modern Athlete and Coach (1963-). Australian Track and Field Coaches Association.

Network News (1988-). Network Australia.

Rodgers, S. (1987). *The complete book of VFL records*. Rodgers.

Shepherd, J. (1980). *Encyclopedia of Australian sport*. Rigby.

Shepherd, J. (1981). *Winfield book of Australian sporting records*. Rigby.

Slattery, K. (ed.) (1988). *Physical education, health and recreation serials in Australian libraries: a union list*, 4th edn. Victoria College Library Rusden Campus.

Smith, T. (1988). *The complete book of Australian golf*. Australian Broadcasting Commission.

Sport Health (1983–). Australian Sports Medicine Federation.

Sport Magazine (1954–63). Sport Magazine.

Sport Report (1981). Confederation of Australian Sport.

Sporting Traditions (1984–). Australian Society for Sports History.

Sports Coach (1977–). Australian Coaching Council.

Sport and Leisure Retailer (1990–). Yaffa Publishing.

Sportsnetwork (1986–). Australian Society of Sports Administrators.

Tennis Australia, Asia, the Pacific (1976–). Tennis Publications.

Theses in education and educational psychology accepted for degrees at Australian universities (1953). Australian Council for Educational Research.

Union list of higher degree theses in Australian libraries (1958). University of Tasmania, Library.

Your sport (1985–86). Sportsworld Australia.

Appendix I

International organizations

Association for the Advancement of Applied Sport Psychology (AAASP) is a relatively new organization. It is divided into three sections — performance intervention, health, and social psychology. The official journal is the *Journal of Applied Sport Psychology*.

Association Internationale des Écoles Supérieures d'Éducation Physique (AIESEP). This organization, based in Belgium, was founded in 1962 to provide research facilities for physical education. It co-operates with other international bodies.

Council of Europe. The Committee for the Development of Sport (CDDS) is the committee responsible for sport and has set up a number of projects.

European Non-Governmental Sports Organizations (ENGSO). An informal association which meets twice yearly, supplemented by working parties. It considers all aspects of European development and its impact on sport.

European Sports Conference (ESC) established in 1971, the biannual ESC has traditionally been the only organization where sports administrators from all over Europe meet to discuss current problems and philosophies in sport. There are thirty member states. It has three working groups which cover anti-doping, scientific research and co-operation and women and sport.

The Fédération Internationale d'Éducation Physique (FIEP) encourages the development of activities concerned with movement in education, sport, and the outdoors in all countries and to foster and contribute to international co-operation. It was founded in 1923 and has published the *FIEP Bulletin* for many years.

General Association of International Sports Federations (GAISF) was founded in 1967 to act as a forum for discussing matters of mutual interest in sport, particularly the Olympic Games, and to distribute information. 56 full members cover all the major sports. They hold an annual three-day congress.

International Association for Sports Information (IASI) had its first meeting in Rome, in 1966. Its aim is to stimulate and disseminate information sources for sport and leisure. It publishes *Sport Information Bulletin.*

International Association for the History of Physical Education and Sport was founded in Zurich in 1973 to further the study, teaching and research, of history of physical education and sport to improve communication between scholars and institutions. It publishes the *HISPA Bulletin.*

International Association of Physical Education and Sport for Girls and Women (IAPESGW). The Association was formed in Paris in 1953 to bring together women from many countries working in the field of sport and physical education.

International Council for Health, Physical Education and Recreation (ICHPER) was established in Rome in 1958 to assist WCOTP (World Confederation of Organizations of the Teaching Profession) by encouraging developing programmes in health, physical education and recreation throughout the world. ICHPER publishes a journal.

International Council of Sport Science and Physical Education (ICSS-PE). Established in 1958, it is an umbrella organization for promoting sports science. It enjoys Consultative A status with Unesco and is a 'Recognized Organization' of the IOC. Members are drawn from the national and international organizations in the field of sports science, physical education and sport. It has a number of committees for specific topics.

International Olympic Committee (IOC), was founded in 1894 to encourage the organization and development of sport and sports competition, to inspire through the Olympic ideal, and to ensure the regular celebration of the Olympic Games. It disseminates its ideas through the *Olympic Review* and the *Olympic Message.*

International Society of Sport Psychology (ISSP), was founded in 1965 in Rome to promote research in sports psychology. The Society also promotes international seminars and publishes the *International Journal of Sport Psychology.*

International Society for Comparative Physical Education and Sport (ISCPES) first met in Israel in 1978. Its aim is to promote research and to provide assistance to those wishing to develop programmes in comparative physical education and sport throughout the world.

International Working Group for the Construction of Sports and Leisure Facilities (IAKS), has, since 1965, disseminated information gained on the planning, construction equipping and maintenance of sports and leisure facilities. The Group publish a journal *Sportstattenbau + baderanlagen.*

The Philosophic Society for the Study of Sport aims to foster interchange among scholars interested in the better understanding of sport. It publishes the *Journal of the Philosophy of Sport* annually.

The Sport Literature Association publishes, *Aethlon* and organizes seminars and conferences.

Supreme Council for Sport in Africa was established in 1966 to promote sport in Africa by co-ordinating sporting activities among its members and organizing training programmes.

World Leisure and Recreation Association (WCRA) was formed in the USA in 1956 to improve individual and community life through the constructive use of leisure and recreation. It circulates a bulletin and other publications targeted at certain groups.

Appendix II

Acronym list

AAASP	Association for the Advancement of Applied Sport Psychology
AAHPERD	American Alliance for Health, Physical Education, Recreation, and Dance
ACC	Australian Coaching Council
ACHPER	Australian Council for Health, Physical Education and Recreation
ACHPIRST	Australian Clearing House for Publications in Recreation, Sport and Tourism
ACSM	American College of Sports Medicine
AEFA	Amicale des Entraîneurs Français d'Athletisme
AFAA	Aerobics and Fitness Association of America
AFTA	Aerobics Fitness Teachers Association
AIB	Athletic Information Bureau
AIESEP	International Association for Physical Education in Higher Education
ALATIR	Latin American Leisure and Recreation Association
APAIS	Australian Public Affairs Information Service
APPEL	Association of Polytechnic Physical Education Lecturers
ASA	American Sociological Association
ASME	American Society of Mechanical Engineers
ASSET	Association of Exercise Teachers
ASSH	Australian Society of Sports History
AVO	Aanvullend Voorzieningen Onderzoek

BAALPE	British Association of Advisers and Lecturers in Physical Education
BASM	British Association of Sport and Medicine
BASS	British Association of Sports Sciences
BBC	British Broadcasting Corporation
BISC	British Institute of Sports Coaches
BISp	Bundesinstitut für Sportwissenschaft
BPS	British Psychological Society
BSA	British Sociological Association
BSSH	British Society of Sports History
BTA	British Tourist Association
BTEC	Business and Technical Education Council
CAB	Commonwealth Agricultural Bureaux
CAHPER	Canadian Association for Health, Physical Education and Recreation
CCCS	Centre for Contemporary Cultural Studies
CCPR	Central Council of Physical Recreation
CDDS	Committee for the Development of Sport
CIPFA	Chartered Institute of Public Finance and Accountancy
CONI	Comitato Olimpico Nazionale Italiano
CPRA	Canadian Parks and Recreation Association
CRRAG	Countryside Recreation Research Advisory Group
CSO	Central Statistical Office
CSSS	Centre for the Study of Sport in Society
DES	Department of Education and Science
DHfK	Deutsche Hochschule für Körperkultur
DoE	Department of the Environment
DS-SI	Committee of Experts on Sports Information
DS-SR	Committee of Experts on Sports Research
ELRA	European Leisure and Recreation Association
ERIC	Education Resources Information Centre
ESB	European Society of Biomechanics
ESRC	Economic and Social Research Council
FEPSAC	European Sport Psychology Foundation
FIEP	International Federation of Physical Education
HEA	Health Education Authority
HISPA	International Association for the History of Sport
HMSO	Her Majesty's Stationery Office

IAPESGW	International Association of Physical Education and Sport for Girls and Women
IASI	International Association for Sports Information
IBRM	Institute of Baths and Recreation Management
ICHPER	International Council for Health, Physical Education and Recreation
ICSP	International Committee on Sport Pedagogy
ICSS	International Committee for Sociology of Sport
ICSSPE	International Council of Sport Science and Physical Education
IDEA	International Dance-Exercise Association
IFF	Institut für Freizeitwirtschaft
ILAM	Institute of Leisure and Amenity Management
ILEA	Inner London Education Authority
INSEP	Institut National du Sport et de l'Éducation Physique
ILO	International Labour Office
IOC	International Olympic Committee
ISB	International Society of Biomechanics
ISCPES	International Society for Comparative Physical Education and Sport
ISSP	International Society of Sport Psychology
JANET	Joint Academic Network
KFA	Keep Fit Association
LGMB	Local Government Management Board
LSA	Leisure Studies Association
MCC	Marylebone Cricket Club
NACOB	North American Congress on Biomechanics
NAPEHE	National Association for Physical Education in Higher Education
NASSH	North American Society for Sport History
NASPEM	North American Society of Pediatric Exercise Medicine
NASSS	North American Society for the Sociology of Sport
NCF	National Coaching Foundation
NCVQ	National Council for Vocational Qualifications
NGB	National Governing Body
NIH	Norges Idrettshogskoles Biblioteket
NIIC	Northern Ireland Institute of Coaching
NOC	National Olympic Committee
NRPA	National Recreation and Parks Association

NSGA	National Sporting Goods Association
ODPHP	Office of Disease Prevention and Health Promotion
OECD	Organization for Economic Co-operation and Development
OPCS	Office of Population, Censuses and Surveys
PEA	Physical Education Association of Great Britain and Northern Ireland
RSA	Royal Society of Arts
SCOTVEC	Scottish Vocational Education Council
SEAC	Schools Examination and Assessment Council
SIRC	Sport Information Resource Centre
SIRLS	Specialized Information Retrieval and Library Services
SPRIG	Sport and Recreation Information Group
Unesco	United Nations Educational, Scientific, & Cultural Organization
USOC	United States Olympic Committee
WLRA	World Leisure and Recreation Association
YMCA	Young Men's Christian Association

Index